TEMPLE OF THE HOLY SPIRIT

TEMPLE OF THE HOLY SPIRIT

*sickness and death
of the Christian
in the liturgy*

*the twenty-first Liturgical
Conference Saint-Serge*

translated by Matthew J. O'Connell

PUEBLO PUBLISHING COMPANY • NEW YORK

Design: Br. Aelred-Seton Shanley

Originally published in French as *La maladie et la mort du Chrétien dans la liturgie* © 1975 Edizioni Liturgiche, Rome.

English translation © 1983 Pueblo Publishing Company, Inc. 1860 Broadway, New York, New York 10023. All rights reserved

Printed in the United States of America.

ISBN: 0-916134-64-4

CONTENTS

PREFACE

In the life of the Churches, the various liturgies have expressed and developed the specific meaning that bodily illness should have for a Christian who wishes to be conformed in an existential way to Christ in his suffering and death on the cross. When we attend to this aspect of the liturgies, we realize how much the Churches are trying to accomplish—in faith, hope, and charity—with regard to the "holy but still to be sanctified" members of individual Christians.

In my opinion, this thought lurks in the background of all the papers read at the Twenty-first Week of Liturgical Studies held at the Saint-Serge Institute of Orthodox Theology in Paris, July 1–4, 1974, on the subject: "Sickness and Death of the Christian in the Liturgy."

The publication of almost all these papers (two were not submitted to the editor) is intended to demonstrate several points: (1) the liveliness of the presentations given at the Twenty-first Liturgical Week; (2) the competence of the various lecturers; (3) the variety of nuances and accents with which each liturgy develops the theme of the Christian's sickness and death; (4) the genius with which the various Churches interpret Christ's attitude in dealing with the sick; (5) the many liturgical actions with which the

Churches have in a concrete way attended to the body of the Christian, which is "the temple of the Holy Spirit" (1 Cor 3:16, 6:19; 2 Cor 6:16, etc.); and (6) the new vision that Christ and the Church have of death as being the culmination of one form of existence because it is also the beginning of another new life.

The "Acts of Saint-Serge 1974" thus not only provide an examination of the liturgical celebrations that prepare Christians for death (visiting of the sick, viaticum, etc.) and an analysis of the prayers for the dead. They also make clear the basic outlook of the liturgies with regard to sickness, namely, that sickness is not simply an unfortunate incident in the course of earthly existence but is rather an event that transcends the physical and biological order and is to be viewed in the light of the suffering of Christ. For Christ turns suffering and sickness into a phase in the process of salvation and transforms them into an act of love. Sickness and suffering are a "visible sign" of spiritual weakness. In order to rescue human beings from this weakness, the Word became flesh and assumed human nature along with all its weaknesses except sin (Heb 4:15).

In addition, some liturgies for the anointing of the sick celebrate the restoration of the sick person's solidarity with the world and other human beings. Moreover, almost all the concrete expressions of the liturgy show an integration of finitude, which is embodied in death and temporality, into an affirmation of the eschatological world. These are aspects of liturgical theology that are found in most of the liturgies of East and West.

A meeting like that of 1974 shows how liturgical celebrations are inspired by pastoral and liturgical intentions that are extremely important for the cohesion of ecclesial life. Among these intentions are the following: (1) that sickness should be seen as a characteristic mode of existence that the Christian is to regard as redeemed and liberated, and therefore as finalized and brought into ontological accord with an interior conformity to Christ; (2) that the various Churches should become conscious of the need of concern for the sick; and (3) that there should be an awareness that the liturgy of death is quasi-sacramental by reason of the sacraments with which it surrounds the dying person, and also by reason of the fact that a Christian does not undergo death passively, but rather celebrates an event that his baptism has already given him the right to accomplish, namely, to die with Christ in order then to rise with this same Lord (cf. Rom 6:4–10).

There is a question that may be asked legitimately in regard to the Twenty-first Saint-Serge Week: Did the papers given treat all aspects of the theme that was the object of the week? The answer, of course, is no. A negative answer is required especially since a careful reading of the papers included here[1] shows a certain contrast between the more ancient witnesses and those that are later in time. The older witnesses, which are more firmly rooted in scripture and an authentic Christian sense, are richer and more infused with Christian hope. Perpetual light, refreshment, paradise, rest, heavenly Jerusalem, bosom of Abraham: such are the figures and symbols that these sources use in an effort to communicate the content of a faith that is lived in a prayerful way. The other, more recent sources show a composite tonality; there is a strong sense of gloom, of fear and trembling. In any case, the special character—sometimes joyous, sometimes penitential, sometimes mixed (but in a Christian way), sometimes rich in paschal feeling—of the liturgy of death makes clear to us how the liturgy exercises its function of anticipating the eschaton within our present life. And since "Sister Death" places the final seal on the whole sacramental economy and brings it to its connatural *pleroma*, or fulfillment, it also leads that economy to its flowering in the eschatological reality to which it points.

Our intention, then, in publishing these papers is to render a further service by making it possible for readers to understand and assimilate what the various Churches have to offer one another in their liturgies. This is the best gift the Churches can bestow on one another by way of the ecumenical liturgical enrichment that is the first, though not the only step in the attainment of unity "in truth" (cf. Jn 14:6).

Achille M. Triacca, S.D.B.
Rome, Easter 1975

Constantin ANDRONIKOF

The Dormition
as Type
of Christian Death

"Let us sing for the feast of the departure (exodus), let us raise the light-filled funeral chant! For the Mother of God is making ready now to pass from earth to the highest places and present herself for the divine glory of eternal life" (lucernarium, Vespers of the Vigil).

This feast "is the last of the mysteries having to do with the Word" (litia). Like the first of these mysteries, the Annunciation, this final mystery involves Mary, the Mother of God (the liturgy will bring out the connection between these two events). Now we human beings are often called in the hymns "her new generation, her family, her inheritance." Mary is regarded as a model for her posterity. For this reason "the last of the mysteries" is likewise a revelation concerning the final state of human beings, the ending of Christian life in the world, and the coming of our future life. From the anthropological standpoint and with regard both to human nature and to human destiny, Mary is the New Eve, just as her Son is the New Adam; she too is "the mother of all the living." As we shall see, the same is true from the soteriological standpoint.

Mary is the Church in microcosm; at the same time she is the ikon of the Church that is "vaster than the heavens." In this sense, she is the apotheosis of the human person, because she is the archetype of theanthropic perfection both in life and in death. Her death is the glorious prefiguration of the resurrection of her fellow human beings.[1]

"Today heaven opens . . . and earth, blessing the source of life, is adorned with splendor" (litia). "The universe is filled with grace . . . the world is vibrant with life" (Lauds). The deeper meaning is doubtless this: the Dormition of the Virgin is the gateway to the kingdom. It shows in an overwhelming way the real finality of death, namely, the victory of life, and resurrection in imitation of Christ. It shows the removal of "the sting of sin," and marks the completion of salvation. "The tomb becomes a ladder leading up to heaven" (Vespers).

The Assumption is the final step in the entire economy of salvation, short of the Parousia. It is true, of course, that the Mother of God takes this step in a privileged way which is not granted to everyone. She is immediately translated beyond the last judgment. She does not undergo the painful process which mortals undergo in the next life, nor does she wait on the threshold of the kingdom until the world completes its destined course. I shall be referring presently to the basic differences between the rest of us and her whose spirit God received directly, almost immediately after her death (I say "almost" because she too experienced a mysterious delay due to her burial). Despite this her Dormition is nonetheless an exemplar, just as is each act in the life and death of her Son. Here is the most striking example of this exemplarity: just as the Transfiguration shows us what human beings will be in eternal life, so the Dormition prefigures the passage of the saints through death. In this sense the Assumption is a transfiguration of death. Just as the Transfiguration of Christ took place before his passion, so the Assumption takes place before the Judgment and, as it were, independently of it. It is clear, moreover, that both of these feasts are apocalyptic and eschatological. By that very fact, and even when full regard is had for their paradoxical character, they are essentially typical.

The exemplarity in both cases does not hold only for the spirit; it applies to the body as well. Neither the Transfiguration nor the Assumption[2] is a disincarnate feast; neither is a feast of incorporeal ideas. "Jesus . . . who by God's mercy was born of your womb, himself brought you, soul and body, from earth to heaven" (fifth

ANDRONIKOF

Ode of the canon, Vigil). "You have been the dwelling place of the divinity in its entirety, and therefore the divinity brought you in your entirety from earth to heaven" (ibid.).

The hymns several times mention the body of the Virgin being touched and venerated by the apostles who are gathered around her. This emphasis makes it clear that the flesh is transfigured and that while it is attacked by death, this is only in order that it too may then be transfigured in the presence of God. The Assumption affects not only the soul or spirit but the whole of the human entity.

We must attend here once again to the difference between the Dormition of the Virgin and the usual death of human beings. The difference is an unfathomably vast one, and the hymns for the feast (as well as all the prayers addressed to the Mother of God) emphasize it. These texts never make a comparison between Mary and simple mortals, but the description they give of the person of Mary and of her Assumption make clear enough what separates us from her.

First, as I have already indicated, the mystery of the virginity that is preserved despite conception is paralleled with the mystery of Mary's incorruptibility in her Dormition. "God, King of all, grants you what is beyond the powers of nature: in childbirth he keeps you a virgin; in the tomb he keeps your body uncorruptible" (Matins, canon of Cosmas, sixth Ode). This dogmatic statement is developed in the subsequent troparion: "Being the temple of life, you received eternal life, for you replaced death with life."

This definition contains various elements; let me call your attention to what is directly relevant to my subject here. On the one hand, the Virgin Mother transmits a life unaffected by sin. On the other, by virtue of her absolute purity she wins a victory over death which we may describe as a personal victory. Her very life makes any judgment after death unnecessary; judgment has already been passed. The glorification and deification which are the goals of Christian life are given to Mary as soon as her earthly life is complete.

Is there any need to emphasize the first of these two points? By the power of the Holy Spirit, the life which the Virgin conceived was an utterly perfect one: that of the Son of God whom the liturgy describes as "the only one without sin" and "the only Holy One." In this sense the Virgin is the Immaculate Conception. Man and woman, on the contrary, have, ever since the fall, engendered life that is vitiated by death. Moreover, the original sin which human beings cannot avoid consists in transmitting death, according to a constant tradition in Byzantine theology. Thus we find David bewailing long ago the fact that he had been conceived in sin. But the Mother of God escapes this hellish cycle, for by preserving virginity, which according to the Fathers is the symbol of all the virtues and of theanthropic perfection, even though she remains subject to the law of original sin, the Mother of God preserves the image of God unbesmirched and whole. As a result, when death comes upon her in its time, it does not affect the integrity of her created nature; in other words, death does not cause the separation of Mary's soul from her body. Her being remains whole and undivided, and her body remains incorruptible "by nature," in keeping with the likeness of God and the nature of the first Eve. Mary can therefore enter the kingdom as an integral being, with her body, independently of the consummation of time and before the judgment which ratifies this consummation. As a result, the Church does not have to pray for "the repose of her soul," whereas such prayer provides a dominant motif in her prayer for the dead.

St. Paul tells us that "while we are at home in the body we are away from the Lord" (2 Cor 5:6). But, as he points out, what we want and aspire to is that "what is mortal may be swallowed up by life" (2 Cor 5:4).

For "God did not make death"; on the contrary, "he created all things that they might exist" (Wis 1:13–14). More precisely and specifically, "God created man for incorruption, and made him in the image of his own eternity. . . . and immortality brings one near to God" (Wis 2:23; 6:19). Can there be the least doubt as to doctrine? The Council of Carthage, as early as 418, anathematized anyone "who asserts that Adam was created mortal." In addition, the Creed settles the question, if indeed there ever was any question. And Mary bears witness by her life and her death to this natural order of creation.

The most important point for us is that Mary's destiny represents not an exception but the rule. Hers is the destiny God wills for each of us. No one has stated this more magnificently than St. Paul: "Just as we have borne the image of the man of dust, we shall also bear the image of the man of heaven. . . . For this perishable nature must put on the imperishable, and this mortal nature must put on immortality" (1 Cor 15:49, 53).

Certain conditions must of course be satisfied: for each person the cross and death proper to him or her. And did not the Mother of God fulfill these conditions to the utmost by her love and by the suffering she endured for her Son, probably from the time when she accepted the message of the Annunciation? "We are . . . heirs of God and fellow heirs with Christ, provided [because, in the French Ecumenical Translation of the Bible] we suffer with him in order that we may also be glorified with him" (Rom 8:17); "If we have died

ANDRONIKOF

with him, we shall also live with him; if we endure, we shall also reign with him" (2 Tm 2:11–12). This teaching is confirmed in 1 Peter 4:13. Here again it is sufficiently clear that the Virgin is a type of us—an ideal type, indeed, but not an unreal one. We are, in the words of the liturgy, her "posterity." And while "it does not yet appear what we shall be" (1 Jn 3:2), the Transfiguration of Christ and the Assumption of his mother make known our destiny through a prophetic action. In this sense, even after making all the necessary qualifications, we are justified in saying that Mary's death is a type of our death.

Even though the canon sings of "the divine procession" of Mary's body (canon of Cosmas, first ode) or of the fact that "Jesus himself brought you from earth to heaven with your soul and your body" (fifth ode), and even though these statements do not apply to us nor do we make any claim to be holy like the Theotokos, nonetheless the Dormition continues to be in many respects the model for our own death, the eschatological dimension of which the Dormition embodies. In short, the Dormition is a prefiguration of the resurrection.

At no moment of her life, whether on earth or on high, does the Mother of God cease to be the microcosm of the Church to which I referred earlier. She is par excellence the ikon of the Church, of the heavenly Jerusalem, and of the world in which God dwells, of the catholic and universal cosmos, or in short, of the entire theanthropic order. And she is this ikon no less when she holds Christ in her arms than when her Son and Lord receives her among his disciples in heaven. The Assumption is an image of the Church no less than are the Ascension and Pentecost.

Of course—let me say it once again—the lot of human beings after death is not this kind of immediate glorification. They must pass through the Judgment which determines whether or not they are worthy of glorification. Nor do their bodies immediately enter the kingdom, since they have decomposed and need to be raised up. But I have already given a partial response to this objection. The Dormition is symbolic and prophetic. To it I may add the witness of a number of personages in the Old and New Testament who give us a glimpse of an immediate passage into the kingdom, or at least into an unmediated proximity to God, without waiting for the Last Judgment (unless we say that God in his omnipotence anticipated the judgment for these individuals). Thus there are Moses and Elijah, who are present on Mount Tabor; the mysterious Enoch; the thief at Jesus' right hand, on whom the judge immediately pronounces sentence: "Today you will be with me in Paradise"; perhaps also Stephen, who sees "the heavens opened, and the Son of man standing at the right hand of God." These examples help make it easier for us to grasp the typical character of Mary's assumption. "Just as prior to the birth of the Virgin every human birth either led to the incarnation of the Messiah or delayed that historical moment, so every death after the death of the Mother of God hastens or delays the time when 'the dwelling of God . . . with men' descends from heaven (Rv 21:2–3)."[3]

The liturgy has some important things to say about the Virgin's Dormition as a type. "Taking your most pure soul in his hands, [God] placed it in Paradise. There the tree of life stands; those mortals who had eaten of it acquired their immortality through you" (ikos). That is really the point here: the Dormition shows the ideal way of gaining access to eternal life. The woman has overcome the serpent; the ultimate weapon of the implacable enemy no longer has any power. The Assumption is the final victory which a human creature wins over death, and it is won by carrying out completely the will of God which that creature has freely accepted and made her own. The Assumption is a return to the Garden of Eden, to the shade of the tree of life. The fearsome cherubim lower their flaming swords and sing hymns of joy: "Come, let us celebrate the universal Dormition of the Mother of God, for the angels are eulogizing her coming . . . and are calling us too, the dwellers on earth, to share the joy" (Lesser Vespers). A very large number of hymns give expression to this universal jubilation.

Universal—but not completely so. The liturgy does not forget the other area of the universe that belongs to the everlasting enemy, the area governed by incorporeal spirits who serve not the King but the Prince of this world. Since the Dormition of the Mother of God is the triumph of life and "gives life to the world," it also, and by that very fact, means the defeat of the forces of death, that is, of sin. "May the evil spirits in the air stand aside; may the master of the world himself depart and fall into shame . . . as he sees the Mother of God being taken up" (Vigil, fourth ode of the canon). This is the only allusion made in the liturgical texts to the mighty exorcism wrought by the Assumption, but this is not a reason for minimizing its importance. Exorcism is one of the most paradoxical but also most astonishing effects of death. Here again the Dormition provides us with a key to this mystery.

We are dealing here with the deepest meaning of death. The ultimate purpose of the enemy is corruption to the point of utter destruction. The purpose of creation and all of God's action is life to the point of eternal duration. As a result of original sin, corruption is part of the very life process, and in the end it is triumphant: the soul is separated from the body. But Christ himself freely accepted this process for himself, and he was raised from the dead. The power of his resurrection is also imparted to other human beings. They do not escape the law of their nature as perverted by the fall: they are imprisoned in a temporal duration whose length is inescapably determined, and when they reach the end of that duration they die. The enemy thus triumphs and accomplishes his purpose, but in that very same moment he fails. The event which, according to his calculations, will topple the human person into the nothingness of evil proves to be in fact the threshold as it were of a new—*novissima*—process that is no longer located within time and over which the devil has no power.

This is why the Church and her liturgy speak of death as a "way out, exodus, passage, transition," and why Eastern Christians speak of the dead as "the sleeping" or "in a state of sleep." As the very incarnation of the Church, the Mother of God has this kind of death in its perfection. But the fact of her uniqueness does not lessen her status as example or type. Does not God himself call us to share completely in the divine holiness? "Your nature has made its own the honors of victory, since it gave birth to God; for you are conformed to your creator and your Son; you obey the laws of nature in a supernatural way. Having deceased in accordance with these laws, you rise up with your Son to eternal life" (canon of Cosmas, first ode). Do not the prayers of the Church and the hope of every human being say of all death what John Damascene cries out in speaking to the Mother of God? "Your death is a passage to eternal and incomparable life: from a life in time to a life that is truly divine and does not pass away" (fourth ode). Is not the ultimate meaning of the funeral office the same as that of the paschal liturgy? While Christ is in absolute terms the author of this meaning, the Mother of God is the most perfect example of its human and historical fulfillment. "In you the limitations of death have been overcome . . . as life prevails over death. You were a virgin after having given birth; you live after having died" (hirmos of the ninth ode). This final exclamation ought to be verified, by analogy, in everyone who has died.

In addition to being an incomparable example, the Dormition has other consequences for the death of Christians or, more accurately, for their entire life both here below and in the next world, since death is only a partial end to the life that precedes the Judgment. The hymns make this point several times: "By ascending to your Son in the heavenly dwellings you save your inheritance" (ninth ode). I have already referred to this notion of Christians as Mary's "inheritance." The successive (or simultaneous) meanings of the Dormition now emerge clearly from the liturgical texts: fulfillment of the resurrection in virtue of the pasch or passage of Christ: "Having rejected (death), the Lord has led you into heaven" (canon, first ode); exorcism and fall of the "master of the world"; immediate accession of the Mother of God to another lofty function which she will exercise in sovereign fashion, namely, the function of Orant: "From earth you have become present to him who was born of you . . . and you pray ceaselessly that evil may be warded off from those who in faith celebrate the office of your passing" (Matins, kathism). Having reached the ultimate goal of human life, namely, entrance into the kingdom, and this even before the Second Coming and the Last Judgment, the Mother of God is able to work powerfully for the salvation of the human race which she now represents in heaven, after having previously been the supreme flower and adornment of that race while she was on earth.

The ascension of the God-Man had been, among other things, the mysterious entrance of the human race into the kingdom in the person of the incarnate Word. The Assumption of the Virgin is as it were a splendid application of that archetypal entrance to the entire human race, in the person of her who had formed the body of Christ. This is what I referred to earlier as the realization or fulfillment of the theanthropy. In the Mother of God this fulfillment is an accomplished fact. For other human beings it is a reality that is revealed to their minds and a reality that is proposed to them as a goal of their action, with the Assumption making it clear that the goal is not only a promised ideal but also something that can be brought to pass, something that is not only a prophetic good news but also a dynamic eschatological goal to which a practical way is now open.

The integral fulfillment of the theanthropy by the Mother of God in her Assumption is the fulfillment of the reign of God, both interior and exterior; in other words, the kingdom of God which is in us in the form of God's image as preserved by the Spirit, the Giver of life, is linked to the kingdom which is the heavenly Jerusalem, via the passage or Assumption of Mary. This fulfillment is not yet the apocatastasis (restoration), the universal palingenesis (rebirth), because history is not yet finished and this world has not yet passed away, as we know it will. On the other hand, an example has now been given to us, not only by God but by a woman, of the essential goal of Christian life. And it is the Church's divinely inspired hope that she will be able to say with perfect truth at the death of each of her members that, as in the case of Mary's Dormition, "the tomb

ANDRONIKOF

and corruption have not prevailed" (kontakion). "The tomb becomes a ladder to heaven" (Great Vespers, lucernarium). By analogy with the holy tomb of Mary, the grave of each dead person is a gate by which the Church enters heaven.

It is natural that the joy of which the Church sings, and which is caused by the fact that through her "coming to dwell in the tomb" the Mother of God "has shown us paradise" (canon, eighth ode), should be accompanied by an important and equally joyous assurance, namely, that as advocate and mediatrix par excellence of the human race, the Virgin acts on behalf of human beings living and dead. The many relevant qualifications which the liturgy (especially the Akathistos) attributes to Mary show the constancy of this view on the part of the Church.

I have adequately pointed out the differences between the Dormition and the usual kind of death, and I need not return to the point in dealing with this matter of Mary's prayer and intercession. But I cannot fail to remind the reader that here again the Mother of God is the prime example of a large number of other human beings. I am referring to all those whom, on the basis of their earthly lives, the Church has deliberately chosen to describe officially as saints, although they do not of course cease thereby to be her members, any more than Mary ceases to be a member of the Church whose head Christ has always been and will forever be, since he is the archetype of each and every person. All these members pray for one another during their lives on earth, and we believe that these prayers do not cease in their life beyond the grave. But in addressing the Mother of God, the prayer "Pray for us!" is supplemented by the words "I beseech you!" Yet even this supreme form of communication with the sacred is not reserved exclusively to the Mother of God, since the members of the Church use the same formulas in addressing those from among them whom they recognize as now being saints. Only to the Mother of God, however, do Christians say "Save us!" or, in the words of the troparion for the Dormition, "By your prayers you redeem our souls from death."

It is noteworthy that the shift from the intransitive form "Pray for us!" to the transitive form "I beseech you" can traditionally occur only after the physical passage of the saint to the next life. For it is only after the transition of death that the supreme mystery of the human person can be fulfilled, namely, deification. Human beings pray, of course, only to God or to a deified person, one wholly filled with divine grace. Here again Mary is the model, as we indicate in calling her "full of grace." This title is an ontological description which expresses the very nature or *ousia* of the Mother of God, just as are so many other attributions which, while poetic, are nonetheless of a substantial (and, more accurately, *homoousian*) character.[4]

The Assumption of the Virgin, then, presents us with the very type of deification. This is why we can say, in particular, in the words of an apostichon for the feast: "Receive me *noetically*, O couch of the Virgin, surrounded by the choir of apostles," precisely because "the ark of the Lord . . . has been transferred to the heavenly temple by way of the tomb," as John Damascene puts it in a homily on the Dormition and again in his hymns for the feast. This is why we are justified in singing this stichology from Vespers: "Today let us sing the hymn of David to Christ our God, for through her who is of the seed of David we have been divinized."

All this would have to be further developed, because it is essential to a grasp of the deepest meaning of death as a mysteriously necessary condition for the deification that is the goal of the entire economy. For us, too, death is "the last of the mysteries." But I do not have much time at my disposal here, and there are other themes calling for attention. Let me simply sketch them quickly and without following any particular order.

The polyeleos, for example, sees in the Dormition a symbol of the marriage of the soul to the Spouse. It sings, therefore, of the joy of the mothers, daughters, and brides of Christ. Mary's "presentation before the kingdom on high" marks the union of the Church with Christ, a union in which St. Paul saw "a great mystery" (Eph 5:32). Nor is this to be thought of in spiritualist terms. Even though Mary's nuptial entrance into the kingdom precedes the Judgment, it is nonetheless the model for the coming of the Church-Bride into the kingdom with the human persons, in their psychosomatic integrity, who make her up. Need I remind the reader of the emphasis which the hymns of the feast place on the already incorruptible body of the Mother of God? Recall, for example, the idiomelos of Byzantios after Psalm 51: "When preparation was being made for the presentation of your most pure body . . . ," or the first ode of Cosmas: "May the orders of immaterial spirits accompany the procession of your body to Zion!" This is why an apostichon of the Vigil can say: "Let the entire being of those born of earth rejoice! For the Virgin, the daughter of Adam, is entering heaven."

Another theme, which applies to all the dead and which the funeral office—whether of monks, clergy, or laity—emphasizes, is that every dormition, every passage through death, every burial and the prayers accompanying these, marks a high point in liturgical action, in every sense of the term. An office for ' 'ead person and, a fortiori, the office of the Assumption, is a catholic and universal liturgy. As they gather around a dead person, the living are communicating, through this mystery, with one another, with their near and dear ones in the next world, with the immaterial beings who are God's witnesses and agents, and with God himself whom this ecclesial group invokes after the manner of the apostles when gathered around the body of Mary, and after the manner of the "angels who form a choir in union with the apostles as they contemplate with awe her who is transported from life to life" (litia). Like the Dormition, every funeral office is an ikon of the Church in which joy gains the upper hand over sorrow, because the Pasch is at work.

I shall say nothing here about the mysterious delays which, according to the tradition, accompanied the death of Mary (thus Damascene says in his *Homilies* that Mary was "transported to the heights after three days"); the liturgy makes no reference to these delays, although we should note that according to the liturgical books "this feast is celebrated for nine days." Two other themes, however, are suggested more or less clearly by the offices of the Assumption: the voluntary, free aspect of death, and the state of the dead beyond the grave. These are vast and difficult matters, and I can only try to mention one or two aspects of them here.

On the first question there is a suggestive text which reads: "The most precious ark is *preparing* now to pass from earth to heaven and present itself to the divine light that lives eternally. . . . She who is mistress of all beings *intends* tomorrow to commit her soul into the hands of her Son as she presents herself in the eternal dwelling" (Vigil, lucernarium). It seems then that just as at the Annunciation the Virgin had agreed to give her flesh to the Word by the power of the Spirit who is Giver of life, so at her Dormition she consents to pass into the other world. According to a solid tradition of the Church, death comes not by chance but at a moment which God's will determines in the light of the works or intentions of man; in other words, it comes when man has shown his mettle for good or for ill; when the earthly time allotted to him is exhausted. This means that his freedom and love have had adequate opportunity to prove themselves. The liturgy and all the manifestations of the Church's life maintain on this point a silence that is surely prudent but that is also surprising and even distressing; I say this with all due respect to the theologians.

The problem has nonetheless been raised, or, more accurately, two problems with regard to death force themselves upon our consciousness and cannot fail to cause anxiety. The first is this: Does man participate in the decision which cuts short his present existence and hurls him from time into eternity? The second is this: Is man's state beyond the grave one of motionless, fixed hibernation, as one kind of western theology would have it, with some basis in the Old Testament? Or does he enjoy a life even before Judgment, life marked by the dynamic development which is part of the very definition of life?

Let me take the first of these two problems. We saw a moment ago that the Dormition suggests some kind of volitional activity on the part of the Mother of God. John Damascene, author of a canon from which I have quoted, assigns to the Virgin these words which likewise indicate volitional activity: "I hasten to return to you who descend me, annihilating all distance." In other words, death or the passage from time to eternity consists in overcoming the separation between the world here below and the world on high and entering into direct contact with the divine. St. Paul speaks of this, and so do a large number of hymns on the Dormition. If life consists essentially in being in communion with God, even to the point of making oneself his dwelling place, then death enters life as a positive action which makes possible the inauguration of true life "in the most high places."

We must therefore qualify the Christian definition of death. Death can no longer be looked upon solely as a dissolution of the human entity (in the narrow sense indicated in, for example, Phil 1:23); that is, as the inevitable separation of soul and body that would entail a paralysis of the resultant entity, which is reduced to the state of an inert precipitate. That kind of death is real; it occurs where there is "mortal" sin, that is, where the person is not absolved. This is death marked by a rejection of the *homoousios* or consubstantiality with God, by rejection of theanthropy, that is, by the sin against the Spirit. At this moment the dissolution is irremediable and signifies damnation.

It is immediately obvious, however, that the Dormition of Mary is not that kind of death. Nor is that the kind of life beyond the grave that St. Paul envisions when he says *"desiderium habens dissolvi; tēn epithumian echōs eis to analusai"* (literally: desiring to be dissolved) (Phil 1:23), and adds "and to be with Christ." Nor is this the kind of rest and everlasting remembrance which the Church asks God to bestow on her deceased members. On the contrary, the death of Mary is a liberation and an entrance into "the dwelling of God, the new Jerusalem, which is adorned for her Spouse," in the kind of fulfillment promised in the Apocalypse (Rv 21:2–3). For the rest of us, this entrance will take place only once we have been judged, if indeed we are judged worthy; the Dormition of the Mother of God is nonetheless the exemplar.

ANDRONIKOF

The Dormition of Mary also demonstrates the lifegiving effect in time and eternity of her fulfillment of God's will which she freely accepted from the Annunciation to the Assumption. Unfortunately, the liturgy does not bring out this point. But it does at least mention several times the act which consists of embarking upon the passage from this life to the other and which begins with expiration or the surrendering of the spirit. Listen to the exapostilarion: "My Son and my God, receive my spirit." The language expresses clearly the dynamic aspect of dying, which scripture notes on several occasions. The God-Man himself says: "Father, into thy hands I commit my spirit!" (Lk 23:46). And Stephen cries out: "Lord Jesus, receive my spirit" (Acts 7:79).

Death is indeed an ontological expiration: the human organism is rent, and a constitutive, essential element of the being is withdrawn; thus death effects a transition which could not be wholly involuntary. But, as the Dormition shows, this act is only a prelude, condition, and means to a definitive reconstitution, a palingenesis, in eternal life. In the case of the Mother of God, the restoration of wholeness is almost instantaneous. For this reason her death is indeed an assumption (the only title of the feast in the Byzantine Liturgy is "Dormition," but the hymns speak often enough of her "entrance," her "presentation," her "procession," for the fact of her assumption to be beyond doubt). In ordinary deaths the Judgment must come before the resurrection. Of what happens in the meantime, however—insofar as we can still speak of "time"—we know absolutely nothing. Since the offices of the Dormition breathe not a word about it, neither shall I.

One thing is clear, however, and we must assert it, especially on the basis of the liturgy. That to which eternal life is promised and that which in the case of the Virgin (we must add the case of the saints as well) enters into eternal life is by no means just a part of the human person. It is the entire person, according to the dogmatic statement in the Creed. Nowhere is there question of the immortality of the soul; there is not even mention of immortality in general, which may seem surprising. Mary does present her soul or her spirit, which her Son receives into the eternal dwellings into which her body also enters. But nowhere in the liturgical texts nor anywhere in scripture is it said that the soul (whatever be the meaning of this word) has some power of immortality within itself.

As far as I am aware, immortality in the proper sense comes up only twice in the New Testament: in 1 Corinthians 15:53, which I cited earlier and which proclaims that "this mortal nature must put on immortality" ("nature" means the entire being; v. 54 repeats the assertion), and in 1 Timothy 6:16, where the Lord Jesus Christ is said to be the only possessor of immortality. I think that we must imitate the liturgical texts and not confuse immortality with eternal life. Immortality is a negative idea, and one that loses much of its interest when we consider that death exists and that there are even two deaths (Book of Revelations), the second probably being that definitive dissolution of which I spoke above.[5] Eternal life, on the other hand, is an entirely positive idea and reality, and it is this that is promised to the holy person, this that the Virgin enters, and this that is the object of the Church's faith as expressed in her Creed.

Let me say a word, finally, on the second of the two problems I mentioned above: the problem of activity in the next life, insofar as our liturgical texts have anything to say about such activity. As far as the Mother of God is concerned, there can be no doubt, for her activity is all-embracing. She prays for the salvation of the world. The same can be said, with the necessary qualifications, of certain of the dead, those at least who are already saints. What of the others, those of whom we do not normally speak? Some fruitful suggestions may be found in Serge Boulgakov's book *L'Epouse et l'Agneau* and in the manuscript of his *La Sophiologie de la mort*, to both of which I refer the scholar.[6] In the few minutes left to me I shall simply offer Boulgakov's views, in succinct form, for your consideration.

Death is not an annihilation, but a *dormition*, that is, a temporary cessation of the soul's action on the body. It is in this sense that we may speak of the *ousopchie*, "those who are asleep," as the Eastern liturgy calls the dead. But, argues Boulgakov;

". . . the spirit lives beyond the grave by reason of its immortality, and freedom is its innate characteristic. It can therefore decide its own state in a creative way. It is wrong and even contradictory to imagine that the spirit remains motionless and that it is in a kind of swoon. Quite the contrary, since new sources of knowledge, inaccessible to it in its earthly garment, are available now for the life of the spirit."

We may suppose that because it breaks the connections of the soul with the body, death is in fact:

". . . a great initiation, a revelation of the spiritual world. . . . If the person had remained forever imprisoned in the 'garments of skin' of his own body, he would not have become a person in the fullest way possible. He is created, after all, to be a citizen of both worlds: of heaven as well as of earth. . . . God's love and wisdom have found the means of completing the person's being by placing him in direct contact with the spiritual world. This contact is brought about

ANDRONIKOF

through an event which is catastrophic in human life: the event of death."

Now there seems to be no doubt that in passing through death the person has several experiences that affect him at a fundamental level. First, "he sees his past life as a whole. This whole is already the object of a judgment: the judgment of 'conscience,' the judgment we pass on ourselves before the face of the God who knows us." Second, there is established among the dead a communication not subject to limitations of space or time. Furthermore, the dead undoubtedly acquire a clear and profound knowledge of the living or at least of those who were close to them and whose behavior they were able to influence while they were on earth. Finally, direct dialogue with God becomes possible (parable of the rich man and Lazarus).

We are therefore justified in thinking that the dead undergo a moral development from the standpoint of repentance and of an awareness of the value their past life had, and that this development quite naturally brings in its train a growth of heart and spirit (to which the prayer of the rich man to God for his relatives bears witness), barring a hardening of the heart which it would be difficult to admit at this "stage." The Church, moreover, constantly affirms that the possibilities of prayer, far from being abolished by the passage into the next world, are really and powerfully increased: the dead saints pray for us, and the prayers of the Church for the dead influence their lot.

All this bears witness to the spiritual dynamism at work in life beyond the grave; the exemplar of this activity is Mary, the Mediatrix par excellence, who has received even the power to save. In other words, those living on earth act upon those living beyond the grave, and vice versa. The liturgy of the "living" is completed and enriched by the liturgy of the "dead" (Rv 5–7; 14; 15). Thus between history and eternity there is a vast "communion of saints" in which the Mother of God is the crowning figure.

The decisive argument for the acquisition of knowledge of the truth by the deceased is evidently the Triduum of Christ. It is not improper to think of there being an analogous triduum of the Mother of God. This idea is put forward, though not developed, in the tradition of St. John Damascene (*Homily on the Dormition:* "The ark of the Lord is transferred to the heavenly temple by way of the tomb after three days"). On the other hand, it seems quite inconceivable that the action of the Holy Spirit should cease completely during the passage of a human being, in whom the image of God remains inalienably. Finally, the boundaries of the

New Testament Church are not determined by the definition of the baptized Christian nor by the framework of earthly life. Besides, we who are alive "shall not precede those who have fallen asleep" (1 Thes 4:15).

To these brief remarks may perhaps be added this thought of Father Serge Boulgakov, whose words shall form my conclusion:

"If we on earth have received hints regarding the 'times and seasons' that are drawing near and in terms of which we are called upon to act within history, why should we think that the souls of the dead or at least of the elect would be deprived of such knowledge and such provision . . . and of activity during this time of waiting? . . . If they have been allowed to take part, in the way proper to them, in the life and history of the world, much more are they allowed to take part, through love, thought and activity, in the worldwide prayer for the resurrection, in which heaven, earth and hell are conjoined." [7]

For the moment, I will say what we sing on August 15: "Let us pray to her! O sovereign Lady, do not forget your family as we celebrate in faith your holy Dormition" (litia).

Bernard BOTTE

The Earliest Formulas
of Prayer
for the Dead

The revelation of Jesus Christ has put death in a new light. "I am the resurrection and the life," Jesus says to Martha; "he who believes in me, though he die, yet shall he live" (Jn 11:25–26). It is understandable, then, that Paul should tell his converts not to "grieve as others do who have no hope." (1 Thes 4:13).

And yet, even though the hope of resurrection can allay the anxiety of men in the face of death, it does not completely draw aside the veil of mystery. Human beings have always found themselves full of questions regarding the mystery of what lies beyond this life. Their misgivings have found expression in funeral rites, legends, and the dreams of the poets. At the very beginning of Western literature, we find two accounts of descents among the dead coming from the pen of "Homer." Christian revelation contains nothing comparable, but there is no way of keeping human beings from dreaming. The Church has never even considered muzzling the poets, but it has been careful not to make their dreams her own. St.

Patrick's legendary vision of purgatory became part of medieval literature, while at the dawn of the Renaissance the great poet Dante developed his genial poetic visions. But the Church has always maintained a reserve toward these, and her prayer has never been contaminated by elements alien to authentic revelation. We can readily prove the truth of this claim by examining the earliest prayers for the dead.

A distinction has to be made in dealing with prayer for the dead in Christian antiquity. The dead themselves were divided into the martyrs, who ended their lives in a glorious struggle, and ordinary Christians, whose lot was the one common to all human beings. The martyrs soon became the object of a cult. Their suffering was in fact a glorious victory for which they were rewarded. There was no doubt whatever about their lot after death. I shall leave aside here the problem of the veneration paid to the martyrs, and shall discuss only the Church's prayer for the other dead, who shared the common lot.

When a Christian has breathed his last, the Church continues to pray for him. But there has been a preparation for such prayer. The usual fate of human beings is that they approach death gradually. They pass through old age and sickness, and the Church supports them in this struggle. The Roman Ritual has always had a section devoted to the pastoral care of the sick. This care takes the form, initially, of visits to the sick; for these visits the Ritual provides a series of readings from the Gospel and of prayers to be said in the presence of the sick person. If the person's illness worsens, recourse is had to a special sacrament: the anointing of the sick.

Of all the sacraments this one has undergone the greatest distortions in the course of Western tradition. It has even been turned into the sacrament of the dying and, as such, could only be administered at the last moment. But such a view of this sacrament is contrary to the entire tradition. To prevent abuse of the sacrament, the Latin Church has required that the person's illness be a serious one which can lead to death, but it has not required that the danger of death be immediate. The purpose of the sacrament is to strengthen Christians in their illness and even, if possible, to lead them back to health. The real sacrament of immediate preparation for death is viaticum, that is, the eucharist. It is an ancient Christian tradition that as they begin their final journey Christians should take with them, as provision for the journey, the viaticum, the bread of life which is a pledge of immortality and resurrection: "He who eats my flesh and drinks my blood has eternal life, and I will raise him up at the last day" (Jn 6:54). Finally, when the sick enter into their agony, there are special prayers to help them in this final struggle.

Once they have breathed their last, the prayers for the dead form a natural continuation of the prayers that preceded. The dead have not left the Church, but have passed from the earthly Church to the Church of heaven. In our Roman Ritual the prayer *Subvenite* ("Saints of God") follows immediately upon death: "Saints of God, come to his (her) aid! Come to meet him (her), angels of the Lord! ℟. Receive his (her) soul and present him (her) to God the Most High." (*The Rites* 1:628).

Prayer for the dead has undergone extensive development, and there can be no question of my attempting to sketch its history here.[1] My aim is a more limited one: to call attention to some of the formulas which in my judgment go back to the earliest stratum of the tradition. These prayers have in common that they develop symbolical themes which are inspired for the most part by the biblical tradition but which sometimes have parallels in the pagan religions. The reader will also note that these themes are rarely treated in isolation and that a single prayer will often bring together several of them. This fact will justify my manner of exposition, which will be based on the following themes: paradise, rest, light, peace, refreshment, the bosom of Abraham, the first resurrection, and the heavenly Jerusalem.

PARADISE

Anyone who has been present at a funeral celebrated according to the Roman Rite will have heard the antiphon *In paradisum* that is sung when, after the absolution, the coffin is removed for the journey to the cemetery: "May the angels lead you into paradise; may the martyrs come to welcome you and take you to the holy city, the new and eternal Jerusalem" (*The Rites* 1:679).

In the monastic rite this antiphon is repeated between the verses of Psalm 114 (113): "When Israel went forth from Egypt," which celebrates the entrance of God's people into the promised land. It is natural to think in this context of Jesus' promise to the Good Thief: "Today you will be with me in Paradise" (Lk 23:43). "Paradise" is for the Jew the symbol of that perfect happiness which human beings, created in the image of God, enjoyed in the "garden of delights" (cf. Gn 2:8), and from which they were exiled because of sin.

So at least the antiphon was understood until 1922. In that year a Belgian Jesuit, P. Van Sull, published an article in which he proposed a new interpretation: the *paradisus* is simply the cemetery, the garden surrounding the church.[2] There is a certain confirmation in the fact that the word "parvis" is simply a deformation of *paradisus*. But as far as I know no one has ever adopted this interpretation. Is it likely that Christians would summon the angels for such a very brief journey (the garden began, after all, at the church door)? In addition, it would be necessary to assume that the antiphon was composed at a period when it was common practice to bury people right around the church, that is, in the Middle Ages. In fact, however, the antiphon seems to belong to a much older tradition. Van Sull's article nevertheless proved useful since it provided Dom Bernard Capelle with a reason for a detailed study of the history of this antiphon.[3]

The task was not an easy one. The antiphonary, or liturgical book containing the antiphons, is the latest of all the liturgical books. The old sacramentaries usually do not give the antiphons. It so happens that Ms. *Rheinau 30*, a Gelasian sacramentary of the eighth century, cites the first two words *In paradisum*, but we have no idea how the text read from that point on. Another document of the same period, the funeral ritual given in the Supplement (by Alcuin or Benedict of Aniane) for the Gregorian Sacramentary, makes absolutely no reference to the antiphon. Only later on does the *In paradisum* show up almost everywhere. In all likelihood it was not originally a part of the Roman or the Romano-Germanic liturgy, but originated elsewhere. Fortunately, Dom Capelle discovered the most archaic form of the text in the Milanese Rite. This Rite has a series of psalms to be recited during the preparation of the body of the deceased, and in this series the antiphon *In Paradisum* is assigned to Psalm 72,[3a] in the following form: "In paradisum *deducant* te angeli et *cum gloria suscipiant* te martyres," "May the angels lead you into paradise and the martyrs receive you into glory."

As everyone knows, the composers of antiphons always endeavored to use words from the psalm. Here the connection of the antiphon with verse 24 is clear: "In voluntate tua *deduxisti* me and *cum gloria suscepisti* me," "You led me to do your will and you received me into glory."

The two successive verbs *deducere* and *suscipere* in both texts might be accidental, but the presence of the words *cum gloria* removes any doubt. This is surely the original form that explains all the others. It is undeniably archaic in character. Why this special mention of the martyrs unless the antiphon goes back to a period when the only saints receiving a special cultus were the martyrs? Mention of the martyrs is inseparable from mention of the glory they won by their victory over suffering. This link between martyr and glory would be weakened later on. Once the antiphon crosses the Alps, becomes part of the Romano-Germanic Liturgy, and is disconnected from Psalm 72, the words *cum gloria* are removed. In some witnesses these words are replaced by the hackneyed reading *cum gaudio* (with joy *or* into joy). Other witnesses have the reading found in our present-day text: "in tuo adventu suscipiant te martyres," "May the martyrs receive you at your coming" (literal translation of the Latin text).

Finally, a third member was added to the text. The primitive text had two parts joined by the conjunction *et* (and). The conjunction was taken out, and a third section was added: "et deducant te in civitatem sanctam Jerusalem," "and lead you into the holy city, Jerusalem." As a result, the whole antiphon reads somewhat haltingly. "Heavenly Jerusalem" is another image of happiness in the next world, and I shall come back to it later on, but it does not harmonize well with the image of paradise. It is impossible to think of the heavenly Jerusalem as built in the middle of paradise, or of paradise as located within the precincts of Jerusalem. There is thus a certain lack of coherence between the two images. The Fathers indeed asked themselves where paradise might be located, and some of them situated it in the third heaven. But the Church does not give such speculations any place in her prayer; she limits herself strictly to the data of the Bible.

ETERNAL REST

This is a well-known theme. In the Roman Rite it is introduced into the entrance song of the funeral Mass and repeated in the Gradual (old Missal) and the communion song and in Vespers: "Give them eternal rest, O Lord, and may perpetual light shine on them for ever." From the literary standpoint, the source of this antiphon is the Fourth Book of Esdras, the Greek original of which is lost but of which an ancient Latin version has been preserved:

"Expectate pastorem vestrum,
requiem aeternitatis dabit vobis,
quoniam in proximo est ille,
qui in fine saeculi adveniet.
Parati estote ad praemia regni,
quia *lux perpetua lucebit vobis,*
per aeternitatem temporis" (4 Esd 2:34–35).[4]

Rest or repose is doubtless a very natural image, since death resembles sleep. In telling the disciples that Lazarus is dead, Jesus says that he sleeps (Jn 11:11), and St. Paul speaks of those "who have fallen asleep in Christ" (1 Cor 15:18). But in addition to its natural meaning, the image had a religious aspect for a Jew. Genesis speaks to us of God resting: he created the world in six days, and on the seventh "he rested . . . from all his work which he had done" (Gn 2:2). This rest serves as a norm, for on the seventh day man must imitate God's resting. Psalm 94 refers to a promise by God that he will give his people a share in his rest; it is a promise from which rebels are excluded: "I swore . . . that they should not enter my rest" (v. 11). The author of the Letter to the Hebrews tries by subtle exegesis to show that God's promise to his people has not yet been kept: Joshua did not bring the people of God into the Lord's rest when he led them into the promised land; Christ Jesus alone will lead believers into the rest of God (Heb 4:1–11).

For a Christian, then, eternal rest carries a new connotation, being the fulfillment of a promise which God carries out through Christ. Let me refer finally to the Apocalypse: " 'Blessed are the dead who die in the Lord henceforth.' 'Blessed indeed,' says the Spirit, 'that they may rest from their labors!' " (Rv 14:13).

LIGHT

Eternal rest is directly connected in our prayer, as it is in 4 Esdras, with unending light. This too is a natural kind of symbolism. Light is everywhere a symbol of joy and happiness and is even a vital element in these. The last cry of those whom a tragic fate removes from life is a farewell to the light: *Chaire moi, philon phaos*, "Farewell, dear light!" (Euripides, *Iphigenia in Aulis*, 1509). But light is also a symbol of hope. Almost everywhere in the pagan world we see evidence of hope in a light beyond the tomb. Franz Cumont devoted a large volume to *Lux perpetua* as found in the pagan world; one of his disciples added the material on Christianity.[5] We are in the presence here of one of human nature's deepest longings.

The Church could not remain indifferent to this longing; moreover, her own tradition inclined her to take it into account. The God of Israel is a God of light. When Moses came down from the mountain after his conversation with Yahweh, his face was so radiant that the Hebrews could not look at him (Ex 34:29–35). This is certainly the meaning of the original text. St. Jerome, however, following Aquila's text, introduced a learned misinterpretation. He claimed that the verb used in the Hebrew text was from the root *qrn* and that this root is the same as that of the Latin word *cornu* (horn). He therefore translated the text as saying that Moses' head was surmounted by horns (*cornuta*). As a result the patriarch is shown in iconography as bearing a pair of horns.

The psalms speak to us of the light that radiates from the face of God: "Lift up the light of thy countenance upon us, O Lord" (Ps 4:7; cf. Ps 88:16). And Israel's great hope is that it will see a new light: "The people who have walked in darkness have seen a great light; on those who dwell in the land of the shadow of death a light has risen" (Is 9:2). "Arise, be illumined, Jerusalem, for your light has come, and the glory of the Lord has risen over you. For while darkness covers the earth and blackness the peoples, over you the Lord will rise, and his glory will be seen in you. The nations shall walk in your light, and kings in the brightness of your rising" (Is 60:1–3). "No longer will you have the sun to give you light in the day, nor shall the brightness of the moon illumine you; but the Lord himself will be your everlasting light, and your God will be your brightness. Your sun will not set again and your moon will not wane, but the Lord will be your everlasting light" (Is 60:19–20).

We find the same ideas in the New Testament. "God is light and in him is no darkness at all" (1 Jn 1:5). St. Paul says that God "dwells in unapproachable light" (1 Tm 6:16), and St. Peter tells us that God has called us "out of darkness into his marvelous light" (1 Pt 2:9). The Word of God, too, is light, or "Light from Light," as the Creed will say. "I am the light of the world," Jesus says; "he who follows me will not walk in darkness, but will have the light of life" (Jn 8:12). In its description of the heavenly Jerusalem, the Apocalypse takes over the images used by Isaiah: "And the city has no need of sun or moon to shine upon it, for the glory of God is its light, and its lamp is the Lamb" (Rv 21:23). "And night shall be no more; they need no light of lamp or sun, for the Lord God will be their light" (Rv 23:5). It is therefore no cause for surprise that the Church should have taken over the image of eternal light as an expression of her hope of the world to come, while giving the image its biblical meaning: the eternal light is God himself.

The image is to be found in the Canon of the Roman Mass (Roman Canon). The prayer for the deceased, after listing their names, continues: "Lord, grant, we pray, to these and to all who rest in Christ a place of refreshment, light and peace." As I observed earlier, the themes intermingle and reinforce one another. Here light is mentioned between refreshment and peace: *locum refrigerii, lucis et pacis.* The same connection of light with refreshment is found in the Byzantine prayer "God of spirits," to which I shall return later on.

PEACE

I shall not dwell at any length on the theme of peace. It is well known that in the Semitic world the word "peace" sums up the human longing for happiness; the Hebrew *shalom* is matched by the Arabic *salam.* Christianity came into existence in the Semitic world and it has retained the ancient salutation. In his instructions to the disciples as he sends them to do missionary work Jesus bids them say: "Peace be to this house!" (Lk 10:5), and when he appears to them after the resurrection his greeting to them is: "Peace be with you" (Jn 20:19, 21, 26).

The Earliest Formulas of Prayer for the Dead

On the other hand, "peace" has a special meaning for Christians: "Peace I leave with you; my peace I give to you; not as the world gives do I give to you" (Jn 14:27). The peace which Christ brings to us is not related solely to earthly things. He brings us, before all else, peace with God, and he does so by taking on himself the sin of the world through his sacrifice.

REFRESHMENT

Like the theme of light, this one is also found outside of Christianity. The term has elicited a vast literature.[6] Attempts have been made to determine its origin, with special attention being paid to the cult of Osiris. I do not think that such studies have been of much help to an understanding of the Christian *refrigerium*. The primitive symbolism is easily grasped. It is no less natural than the symbolism of light, and it reflects an experience that is readily to be had in any climate in which a pitiless sun withers the vegetation and turns the land into a burning desert. Under such conditions the word *refrigerium* suggests a green oasis around a water hole, where the exhausted traveler can refresh himself and recoup his strength.

The question that is raised, however, by the Christian *refrigerium* is whether the primitive image has been preserved in it or whether, on the contrary, the terms *refrigerium* and *refrigerare* have undergone a semantic development. Two facts must be mentioned. The first is that these terms are used in connection with the funeral banquets which were current in paganism and which were continued by the Christians of the first few centuries. St. Ambrose had done away with them at Milan, but they were still being celebrated at Hippo in St. Augustine's time. We may therefore ask whether *refrigerium* had not acquired the meaning of the Italian *rinfresco*, which refers to something quite other than pure water. The second fact is that in Christian Latinity the meaning of the word has broadened. In Wisdom 2:1 (Vg.), for example, which reads: "Non est refrigerium in fine hominis," "There is no *refrigerium* when man comes to his end," the Greek word translated by *refrigerium* is not *anapsyxis* or *anapsychē* ("relaxation, relief"), which would be the equivalent of *refrigerium*, but *iasis*, "remedy." And in Wisdom 4:7 (Vg.), which reads: "in refrigerio erit," "he will be in *refrigerium*," the Latin word translates the Greek *anapausis*, "rest, repose." In these passages there has been a shift from the concrete meaning of *refrigerium* to the psychological result of the concrete action. This shift of meaning obviously depends on the context.

The Greek verb *katapsychein*, Latin *refrigerare*, is used in the parable of Lazarus and the wicked rich man. The latter asks Abraham to send Lazarus to him with a drop of water that will cool and refresh his tongue (Lk 16:24). Here we have the concrete meaning of the word. But what about the Commemoration of the Dead in the Roman Canon? After listing names the prayer continues: "Ipsis, Domine, et omnibus in Christ quiescentibus, locum, refrigerii, lucis et pacis ut indulgeas deprecamur." Should we translate this as "Grant . . . a place of refreshment, light and peace" or as "Grant . . . a place of consolation, light and peace"? We may well hesitate. But I think it preferable to retain here the concrete meaning of the word, since the point of it is not to define the state of the dead person but to describe the place where he will dwell.

In the Roman Rite, the *refrigerium* theme will not be further developed later on in the liturgical creations of the fifth and sixth centuries. It is, however, one that recurs frequently in the Spanish Rite.[7] The most explicit formulation of it is in the *Liber ordinum* of the Visigothic Church: "Sitientem velut terram servi tui animam celesti perfusione refrigera . . . in loco viridi, Domine, ibi eum conloca, super aquam refectionis educa animam eius ad vitam," "Lord, refresh the soul of your servant with a heavenly shower as you would the parched earth; set him in a verdant place, near invigorating water lead his soul to life."[8] The "verdant place near invigorating water" is an image taken directly from Psalm 22:2.[9] We find it again in the East in the prayers of the Coptic Liturgy of St. Cyril and in the Euchologion of Serapion.

One of the most interesting Eastern witnesses to the *refrigerium* theme is the prayer *Ho Theos tōn pneumatōn*, "God of spirits." It has been preserved for us in the two oldest euchologia: ms. *Barberini 336* and the euchologion of Uspenski (Leningrad, *Bibl. publ. gr. 226*). But it is also known from an even older document, the Nessana Papyrus,[10] which may date from around 600. It is also used in a whole series of inscriptions from Nubia. It is perhaps the oldest of all prayers for the dead and has been the object of a recent study by V. Bruni.[11] After the invocation of God and before the plea for forgiveness, the prayer reads: "Give rest to the soul of your servant in a place of light, in a place of refreshment (*anapsyxeōs*), from which pain, distress and wailing have departed."

This may be compared with a prayer in the Coptic Liturgy of St. Cyril in which, after reading the diptychs, the priest makes this petition: "Lead them into a verdant place near waters of rest (*meton, anapauseōs*), in the paradise of delights whence pain, distress and wailing have departed, and in the light of your saints."[12]

THE BOSOM OF ABRAHAM

The image of the bosom of Abraham, like that of refreshment, comes from the parable of Lazarus and the wicked rich man, where we read that after his death Lazarus is carried to the bosom of Abraham (Lk 16:22–23). The expression does not occur in the Old Testament, but we find the beginnings of the theme in 4 Maccabees 13:17: "When we die in this way, Abraham, Isaac and Jacob will receive us, and all the fathers will praise us." Abraham is the father of believers, for he was the first recipient of the promises. St. Paul is not alone in asserting this; Jesus himself says it: "Your father Abraham rejoiced that he was to see my day; he saw it and was glad" (Jn 8:56). It is not surprising, then, that Abraham should be chosen to symbolize the joy of the elect.

In addition, the statement is also made in the New Testament that "many will come from east and west and sit at table with Abraham, Isaac, and Jacob in the kingdom of heaven" (Mt 8:11). The term used here for "sit" is *anaklithēsontai*, Latin *recumbent*, which suggests "sit at table." The same holds for Luke's expression in the parable of Lazarus; it recurs in the account of the Last Supper with reference to the place which the beloved disciple occupies next to the Master: *en tō kolpō tou Iēsou*, "in (on) the bosom of Jesus" (Jn 13:23). The banquet, however, is one of the images which the gospels use to signify the kingdom or reign of God. Consequently the prayers in which we find the theme of the bosom of Abraham are really asking that the dead person may have a place at the messianic banquet which God has prepared for his elect. This is one of the oldest themes of prayers for the dead and is to be found in both East and West.[13]

The oldest witness to it in the East is the prayer in the *Apostolic Constitutions* (VIII, 41, 2). There God is asked to transfer the dead person "to the land of the devout people who rest in the bosom of Abraham, Isaac and Jacob, with all those who in every age have pleased him and done his will."[14]

The theme reappears in the Euchologion of Serapion: "Grant rest to his soul and spirit in verdant places, in the dwellings of rest, with Abraham, Isaac and Jacob, and all the saints."[15]

The formula occurs frequently in other Eastern Liturgies, especially in the Coptic Liturgy of St. Cyril: "Mercifully grant rest to all their souls, in the bosom of our holy fathers Abraham, Isaac and Jacob."[16]

Pseudo-Dionysius, whose writings reflect the liturgical practices of Antioch at the end of the fifth century or the beginning of the sixth, was familiar with a prayer of this kind: "The prayer asks (God) . . . to locate him in light and in the land of the living, in the bosom of Abraham, Isaac and Jacob."[17]

In the Byzantine Rite, the manuscripts (papyri, euchologia) which contain the prayer "God of spirits" omit the Abraham theme, but most of the inscription-bearing steles of Nubia that contain this prayer do insert, before mention of the place of light and refreshment, the words: *en kolpois Abraam and Isaak and Iakōb,* "in [the] bosoms of Abraham, Isaac and Jacob."[18] In the present-day Byzantine Liturgy the prayer "God of spirits" makes no mention of Abraham, but mention is found in the three other prayers assigned for the funeral of a priest.[19]

The theme of the bosom of Abraham is not absent from the Roman Liturgy. In the verse of the response *Subvenite* we sing: "May the angels lead you to the bosom of Abraham" (literal translation of the Latin text).

The theme is used with notable frequency in the ancient liturgies of Spain and Gaul, where it is joined to that of the first resurrection, of which I shall speak in a moment. Some years back I collected a number of formulas of this kind.[20] The prayers differ fairly widely in their composition, but a comparison shows nonetheless that all derive from a primitive formula, of which the following is an approximate reconstruction: "In sinu Abrahae collocati, partem in prima resurrectione habeant," "May they be gathered in the bosom of Abraham and share in the first resurrection." In some of the texts the mention of Abraham is expanded to include all three patriarchs, as in the East.

THE FIRST RESURRECTION

The theme is taken from the Apocalypse (20:6). It is common knowledge that in this book of scripture the eschatological perspective embraces two stages. Prior to the definitive stage in which God will create "a new heaven and a new earth" (Rv 21:1), there is an intermediate stage which separates the present world from the end of time. This phase is to last a thousand years and will be introduced by the first resurrection, in which only the just will share. The thousand-year period will be one of paradisal happiness that is depicted in rather realistic terms. The various groups called "millenarists" have taken all this quite literally; they were never regarded as heretics, but in practice this interpretation was soon rejected everywhere, especially after St. Augustine.

The purpose of the Apocalypse is to strengthen the early Christians during persecution. This thousand-year period has therefore been interpreted as a symbol of the peace of the Church that made possible the spread of the gospel message. But this Augustinian interpretation evidently does not fit our prayer. The prayer is for the deceased, and the resurrection to which reference is made can only be a real bodily resurrection. We are thus confronted with a difficult problem. On the one hand, it is impossible to assign the redaction of the prayer to a late period when the Augustinian interpretation had already prevailed. And in fact St. Ambrose already uses the formula: "Ideo eum rogemus ut in prima resurrectione partem habeamus," "This is why we pray to have a share in the first resurrection."[21] But on the other hand St. Ambrose does not seem ever to have professed millenarianism. It seems, then, that he did not himself invent the formula, but simply used a prayer already well known in his day, without ever asking himself any questions about it.

It is more than likely that the formula originated in a millenarist milieu and that people in general continued to use it in a broad sense as referring simply to the resurrection of the just. The two parts of the prayer complement each other: the first asks that the dead may join the first believers at the banquet in the kingdom of God ("May they be gathered in the bosom of Abraham"); the second draws the conclusion from such a communion, namely, that the dead have a right to share with them in the resurrection ("and share in the first resurrection").

THE HEAVENLY JERUSALEM

We have already met this theme in the West in connection with the antiphon *In paradisum*, where it was added to the primitive text: "et deducant te in civitatem sanctam Jerusalem," "and take you to the holy city Jerusalem."

The East was also familiar with the prayer, but did not depend for it on the Apocalypse, which was never read in the Eastern liturgies. One formula occurs with special frequency in these liturgies: *apedra odunē kai lupē kai stenagmos,* "pain and distress and wailing have departed." The words are from Isaiah 35:10 and 51:11 (in the LXX), who is speaking here of Zion. The citation occurs in the prayer of the *Apostolic Constitutions* and the prayer in Pseudo-Dionysius, in the Coptic Liturgy of St. Cyril, and in the prayer "God of spirits" of the Byzantine liturgy.

I am not justified, of course, in drawing any sweeping conclusions from the few formulas I have analyzed. But several points may be made. The first concerns what we might call the context: the fact that under normal circumstances there has been a preparation for Christian death. The Church has given the individual her support throughout his last illness. At the final moment she has given him the bread of life, which is a pledge of immortality and resurrection. The earthly Church has done all that she is capable of doing. From this point on it is the Church in heaven that must care for the soul of the deceased person; therefore the earthly Church calls upon the angels, martyrs, and saints. She asks that God fulfill the promises he

BOTTE

has made to those who believe. She does this in simple language that is inspired by scripture.

All the formulas we have looked at express the Christian hope in a symbolic manner. They ask that the deceased person enter into the rest of God, not in the promised land into which Joshua led the earthly Israel, but in the kingdom of God to which Jesus Christ gives us access. There the believer will find the perfect happiness for which man had been created but of which he had been deprived by sin.

Beyond the darkness of the grave the believer will find the everlasting light of which human beings have always dreamed. But this light is not to be seen in any dream, because the light now is God himself. The imperfect knowledge given by faith, "in a mirror simply" is to be replaced by a more perfect knowledge: "face to face" (1 Cor 13:12), "we shall see him as he is" (1 Jn 3:2). Such knowledge is beyond our power to imagine: "What no eye has seen, nor ear heard, nor the heart of man conceived, what God has prepared for those who love him" (1 Cor 2:9).

After enduring sufferings the believer will join Lazarus, the poor men, and all of the just at the banquet in the kingdom of God, there to await the glorious resurrection.

All these images of hope are still part of our liturgy. It may even be said that they constitute its substance. At this point I must ask a question I feel quite unable to answer, thus replacing my "conclusion" with a question mark. How did it happen that our liturgy of the dead, at least in the West, became increasingly somber in tone, to the point at times of lugubriousness?

Room must of course be made in the funeral liturgy for the pain and sorrow which human beings feel. Christians feel no less than other people the pain of separation. But that has always been the case. The first Christians suffered just as much as we do from the loss of a father, a mother, or a child. The intensity of sorrow is not to be measured by the length or opaqueness of the widow's veil. It is to be regretted that the Church allowed her sanctuaries to be invaded by the black tapestries, spangled with silver tears, which depended for their size on the bank account of the deceased or his heirs. Fortunately, in our part of the world I believe the question of classes of burials has been given answers more in keeping with the spirit of the gospel.

But there is something more serious involved. An abundance of tapestries was, after all, a purely external element of the funeral celebration. There were also changes, however, that affected the spirit of the celebration. Texts came into use which expatiated on the fear of judgment. The most remarkable of these texts in the West was the *Dies irae*. This sequence is too well known for me to have to reprint it here. But it should be noted that the *Dies irae* is not properly a prayer for the dead, but rather a meditation on the Last Judgment as seen from an individual's standpoint. As a literary and musical composition the value of the sequence is beyond dispute. If it is not a masterpiece it is at least extraordinarily well done, and it is this quality that explains its success and the deep impression it makes. But its very quality and its length combined to cast a shadow of terror over the entire liturgy; the result was a mood in sharp contrast with the serenity of the ancient prayers.

The reader may object that the apocalypses familiarized Christians with visions of horror. In the synoptic gospels, Jesus himself foretold the calamities that would precede the coming of the kingdom. Yes— but the purpose of these visions is never to frighten. On the contrary, they are meant to be reassuring. The conclusion of the discourse in Luke is: "Raise your heads, because your redemption is drawing near" (21:28). There is more than a nuance of difference between the *Maranatha*, "Come, Lord!" of the first Christians and the *Dies irae, dies illa*.

The *Dies irae* brings us to the twelfth and thirteenth centuries and is evidently an end result rather than a point of departure. There are other details that point to same overall change of mood. There is, for example, the response that used to be part of the absolution, or final commendation, after the funeral mass: "Libera me, Domine, de morte aeterna in die illa tremenda," "Lord, rescue me from eternal death on that dreadful day." The very multiplication of absolutions pointed in the same direction. For the funeral of a bishop, the Pontifical provided five successive absolutions. Why not ten or a dozen?

Let me get back to the question I raised. At a certain point a change of attitude took place in Christian piety. There was a tendency to see things the wrong side up: to emphasize the negative rather than the positive. Being saved meant, first and foremost, escaping a terrible and pitiless judgment rather than entering peacefully into the joy of the Lord. At what moment did the change take place? What factors played a role in the change? For example, did the fears felt at the advent of the year 1000 play a role? As I said above, I have no answer to these questions. A valid answer would require a study on a vast scale, for which I have neither the time nor the competence, inasmuch as the study would have to embrace not only the liturgy, but theology, spirituality, and preaching, to say nothing of literature and iconography. In short, the need would be for a history of Christian attitudes to death. Nor, in my opinion, could so vast a work be done by any single individual.

But partial studies might well be undertaken, for example, on how death is seen in the preaching of the Fathers or the Middle Ages.

I am thus ending this essay with a question. But I admit that I have no scruple about this, because questions have their value and we are perhaps wrong in not ending more often with a question mark. We deal with complicated and sensitive problems, and we tend to simplify them. This is especially true in periods when a reform spirit is abroad. It is better to be modest and not claim to know everything.

Above all, we must not think we have exhausted the riches of tradition. For twenty years now the Saint-Serge Institute has been taking the initiative and asking Christians of different rites and confessions to study their liturgical traditions as objectively as possible, in the interests not of controversy but of uncovering beneath the variety of forms the essential elements common to all. The experiment has already borne fruit, but it must continue. This book with its wealth of material shows that there are still unexplored areas. May it mark a new stage in the work Saint-Serge has undertaken for the gathering of Christians: *Ut sint unum.*

Edouard COTHENET

Healing as a Sign
of the Kingdom,
and the Anointing of the Sick

How far we have come from the Congress held by the Centre de Pastorale Liturgique at Vanves in 1948! At the end of a fruitful session in which Dom Bernard Botte's liturgical studies proved so enlightening, the Congress expressed a wish that the term "Extreme Unction" might be replaced by the more traditional "Anointing of the Sick."[1] The Second Vatican Council was eventually to respond to that wish:

" 'Extreme Unction,' which may also and more fittingly be called 'Anointing of the Sick,' is not a sacrament for those only who are at the point of death. Hence, as soon as anyone of the faithful begins to be in danger of death from sickness or old age, the fitting time for him to receive this sacrament has certainly arrived."[2]

While the history of the liturgical rites has played an important part in this change of fortune in Catholic theology, we may not overlook the role played by exegesis as well. It would of course be wearisome for me to list the works published between 1948 and Vatican II. It will be more worthwhile to signal the reasons for a renewed interpretation of Chapter 5 of the letter of James. At the level of the New Testament as a whole, I may mention current interest in the significance of miraculous healings in the gospels; the apologetic aim which was the principal concern of conservative exegetes has been succeeded by a search for the meaning of the narratives. This has yielded a more fruitful approach to the significance of the anointing of the sick. In addition, exegetes today are more sensitive to the literary genre of the letter of James and are therefore concerned to explain the text in terms of the practices and beliefs of the Jewish-Christian milieu in which the letter was composed. These points indicate the approach I shall follow in my effort to situate the anointing of the sick as a sign of the kingdom.[3]

HEALING AS A SIGN OF THE KINGDOM

Old Testament

It can be said that by and large sickness and healing play a much more important part in the New Testament than they do in the Old. Admittedly, Father A.-M. Dubarle has shown us in his paper at this session that sickness, like famine and war, was one of the trials or punishments which human beings in the Old Testament had to accept with resignation from the hand of God. Many of the psalms seem to be entreaties of sick people who put their trust in Yahweh, the God of the living and the only one who can bring them back from the gates of Sheol. Every healing in serious illness was therefore seen as a direct intervention of God on behalf of one of his faithful followers.[4] At the same time, however, the Old Testament reports only a few instances of miraculous cures; for example, those of Naaman in 2 Kings 5 and of Hezekiah in Isaiah 38:5.

Period of Jesus

The Israelites of the early period did not hesitate to attribute to Yahweh everything that happened in the world, whether good or evil (Is 45:7). After the exile, however, faith in providence became more reflective, and distinctions began to be made. Both the prologue of the book of Job and the Chronicler (1 Chr 21:1) make Satan responsible for sickness and temptation. At the same period, popular belief assigned an increasingly extensive role to the "impure spirits" who scoured the land looking for victims to torment.

In illustration of this change of outlook let me compare the story of the punishment and healing of Pharaoh in Genesis 12:7 with the same story in the Genesis *Apocryphon,* which was discovered in Cave

I at Qumran. In the Yahwist story, Pharaoh is afflicted with great plagues because he has taken Sarai into his harem when Abraham passed her off as his sister. When told the real facts, Pharaoh not unreasonably complains bitterly to the unscrupulous patriarch. The author of the *Apocryphon*, however, adopts the more edifying perspective of the Elohist (Gn 20:7) and emphasizes the intercessory role of Abraham; the scene depicted by this writer is one of exorcism. Pharaoh asks Abraham: " 'But now pray for me and for my household that this evil spirit may be rebuked (to depart) from me.' So I prayed for that . . . I laid my hands upon his head. The plague was removed from him and the evil [spirit] was rebuked (to depart) [from him], and he was cured." (XX, 27–30).[5]

Flavius Josephus has the story of a strange exorcism performed by a Jew named Eleazar in the presence of the Emperor Vespasian:

"This fellow placed under the demoniac's nose a signet ring, containing in its seal a root prescribed by Solomon; the odor of it drew the demon out through the man's nostrils. The possessed man immediately collapsed, and our fellow pronounced an exorcism in which he mentioned Solomon and the spells he had composed, and forbade the demon to return into his victim."[6]

We may also note that due to an overly juridical understanding of the doctrine of retribution, the Pharisees made the connection between sickness and sin a hard and fast thing. This mentality shows through in the story of the man born blind. Thus the disciples ask Jesus: "Rabbi, who sinned, this man or his parents, that he was born blind?" (Jn 9:2). Even stronger is the statement made by the Pharisees to the man miraculously healed: "You were born in utter sin, and would you teach us?" (Jn 9:34).

The Healings of Jesus[7]

Such is the backdrop against which are to be seen the proclamations of Jesus and his actions, which are inseparable from his words. "The time is fulfilled, and the kingdom of God is at hand; repent, and believe in the gospel" (Mk 1:15).

In thus announcing the fulfillment of time, Jesus bases himself on the prophecies. Typical in this respect is his preaching at Nazareth, which takes a reading from Isaiah as its starting point:

"The Spirit of the Lord is upon me,
because he has anointed me to preach good news to the poor.
He has sent me to proclaim release to the captives
and recovery of sight to the blind,
to set at liberty those who are oppressed,
to proclaim the acceptable year of the Lord" (Lk 4:18–19).

We must not too quickly interpret this text in purely spiritual terms and strip it of what Péguy would call its carnal or fleshly content. Liberation (aphesis) does involve the forgiveness of sins, but it cannot simply be isolated from all the concrete elements referred to in the proclamation of the great Jubilee.[8] God, the author of life and the source of light, establishes his reign by raising up the supreme prophet. By means of his message and his deeds, the latter restores sight to those plunged in the darkness of death, and freedom to those who experience the chains of slavery in body and soul.

The chief reason why moderns find it so difficult to believe in miracles is the scientific mentality, which cannot conceive the possibility of a derogation from the laws of nature. But another factor that needs to be taken into account is an excessive dichotomy between body and soul, between temporal salvation and eternal salvation. If we want to grasp the meaning of the miracle, we must get beyond this restrictive viewpoint and realize that Christ is addressing the concrete human being with his weakness and limitations and is opening him up to the freedom of the children of God. Consequently, during this privileged time of his presence in the world, a time which is one of nuptial joy (Mk 2:19), Christ gives believers a sign of what the creator intends the world to be like when it reaches its state of ultimate completion.[9]

St. Matthew the Evangelist, in particular, has sought to draw up a list of "the deeds of the Christ" (Mt 11:2); he locates this list between the Sermon on the Mount and the missionary discourse to the Twelve.[10] The order in which the miracles are grouped is heavy with meaning. The first cure is of a leper (Mt 8:1–4). This means that the action which follows upon the proclamation of the Beatitudes is a gesture at once of healing and purification, restoration to society and witness: "I will; be clean. . . . Offer the gift that Moses commanded, for a proof to the people" (Mt 8:3–4).

The second sign is given to a foreigner, the centurion of Capernaum, whose faith fills Jesus with admiration: "Truly, I say to you, not even in Israel have I found such faith" (Mt 8:10). As I shall indicate later on, the healing of Peter's mother-in-law seems to suggest the spiritual resurrection of the Christian who is called in baptism to serve his Master.[11] It is at this point that the evangelist accounts for the miracles of Jesus with a citation from Isaiah: "He took our infirmities (*tas astheneias*) and bore our diseases (*tas nosous*)" (Mt 8:17, citing Is 53:4). The text of Isaiah is different from that found in the Septuagint and seems to be a translation made especially for this occasion.[12] Even before Jesus begins to unveil the mystery of his death (Mt 16:21, par) by referring to the poems of the

Servant, Matthew shows Christ to us as the compassionate Savior who shares the suffering of human beings. In the face of a harsh and proud world he proclaims the beautitude of the merciful (Mt 5:7) and is himself profoundly moved by pity at the sight of the suffering he encounters.[13] Such is the first phase in the mystery of redemption that will reach its culmination when Jesus takes our sins upon himself.

Is further evidence needed of the connection between healing and the coming reign of God? I remind you of the mission of the Baptist's delegates: "Are you he who is to come, or shall we look for another?" (Mt 11:3).[14] The Precursor is evidently bewildered by the manner in which Jesus is working: when will he decide to swing the ax and winnow the grain (Mt 3:10–12)? In his answer Jesus urges his hearers to read the "signs of the times": "The blind receive their sight and the lame walk, lepers are cleansed and the deaf hear, and the dead are raised up, and the poor have good news preached to them" (Mt 11:5–6).

The succession is significant; each term calls for attention in its turn. The fact that the sick are healed is not enough for a sign of God's reign; the fact that the gospel is proclaimed does not mean that the reign has already come. But that those whom infirmity kept from access to the sanctuary should be rendered mobile and become part of God's people again and that the message should be heard by the lowly—this is a manifestation of the great renewal that is to effect a transformation of hearts. There is nothing automatic here, nothing inevitable, for the gospel is a call. The inhabitants of Chorazin and Bethsaida are insensible of the dynamism present in the signs, and they draw down a harsh curse on themselves (Mt 11:21).

Sending the Disciples as Missionaries

The mission of the Twelve has an important place in the Galilean ministry. The apostles are not only to preach the good news of God's reign; they are also to produce signs of it: "Preach . . . saying, 'The kingdom of heaven is at hand.' Heal the sick, raise the dead, cleanse lepers, cast out demons. You received without pay, give without pay" (Mt 10:8).

Whereas Matthew devotes his whole attention to the missionary discourse, Mark has more of a narrative interest and describes what the apostles did on their mission: "They cast out many demons, and anointed with oil many that were sick, and healed them" (Mk 6:12).

Anointing of the Sick. For a long time now commentators have asked themselves whether Mark 6:12 offers evidence with regard to the institution by Jesus of the sacrament of the sick. Victor of Antioch (ca. 450),[15] the first commentator on Mark, thought that it did, and so in the sixteenth century did Maldonatus, the best exegete of his time. But, as C. Ruch observes:

". . . the theologians have pointed out that the anointings were administered to Jews and that the apostles were not ordained to the priesthood until the Last Supper. Consequently, there could be no question in this passage of a sacrament in the strict sense. To get around the objection Maldonatus was forced to say that that the rules regarding the minister and subject of Extreme Unction were set aside here."[16]

This kind of argumentation brings a smile to our lips today. But even if they could not justify their point of view with a scientific argument, Victor of Antioch and Maldonatus nonetheless started with a valid intuition. The gospel narratives are based both on the memory of the life of Jesus and on the religious experience of the early community. The excesses of the form-critical method, which has laid such a heavy emphasis on the role of the community as to make it the creator of many sayings and stories, should not make us reject the value of the method itself, which starts with the life of the early Church and works back to the tradition about Jesus. The mission in Galilee is the prototype of later apostolic missions; the actions of the Twelve anticipate those which they will perform after Easter by the power of the Spirit.[17] The author of the ending of Mark's gospel intended to emphasize the correspondence between the post-Easter mission and the pre-Easter mission: "And these signs will accompany those who believe: in my name they will cast out demons; they will speak in new tongues . . . they will lay their hands on the sick, and they will recover" (Mk 16:17–18).

Theological reflection on the "matter" of the sacrament of the sick would certainly profit by connecting these two texts (i.e., Mk 6:13 and Mk 16:18) and determining the complementary meanings of the two actions, with the anointing referring more to healing and the imposition of hands more to authority exercised in the name of the *Kyrios*.

The importance which the stories of healing have in the four gospels already suggests a conclusion of a pastoral kind. The Church should feel responsible in a special way for the world of the sick and should be most attentive to their sufferings both physical and moral. At a time when social and political problems are attracting so much attention, this point needs to be made strongly. Of course, the action of the Church cannot be limited to consoling words and strengthening gestures; it must aim at a "liberation" which restores the sick person to his place in the world. Surely the humanization of hospitals is a more evangelical task than ever today! Allow one who often visits sick foreigners to deplore the fact that the extraordinary technical progress made in medicine is only too often accompanied by forgetfulness of the sick person as a human being!

THE ACTION OF THE LORD IN THE ANOINTING OF THE SICK ACCORDING TO JAMES 5:13–16

In the New Testament letters, only one passage speaks explicitly of a pastoral visiting of the sick; it is the passage in James 5. I shall here follow the version in the French *Traduction Oecuménique de la Bible* (TOB), despite necessary reservations on one important point.

"Is anyone among you sick? Let him call for the elders of the Church, and let them pray after having bestowed on him an anointing with oil in the name of the Lord. The prayer of faith will save the sick person; the Lord will raise him up, and if he has sins to his discredit, these will be forgiven him. Therefore confess your sins to one another, in order that you may be healed."

Because there are no parallel passages, the interpretation of this text poses difficult problems. It is advisable, therefore, to begin by determining the literary genre of the text, and to follow this with a detailed study of all the words. I shall ask, finally, what contemporary studies on Jewish Christianity can offer by way of help in determining the meaning and significance of the rite.

Literary Genre

This letter, attributed to James, the first bishop of Jerusalem, has nothing epistolary about it except its address (1:1).[18] From one end to the other it is a moral exhortation; the tone frequently reminds us of the wisdom literature, while at other times the prophetic spirit moves in it (2:1–13; 4:13–17). The letter fits into a long parenetic tradition and draws its inspiration from the wisdom sayings of the Old Testament and the words of Christ. Like other wisdom writers, the author makes no effort to establish connections among his observations and pieces of advice. The only thing a commentator can do is to show the presence in the letter of a number of small units, each of which is to be explained as a separate entity. Writing in polished Greek, James makes use of the literary procedures common in the moral philosophy of his day; I mean the procedures of the diatribe (*diatribē* = "conversation"). He likes to take his listener aside as it were, to ask questions, to imagine various situations or objections.

Despite the general fragmentation of the thought in the letter, 5:13–18 seems to me to form a real unity that should be treated as such in a commentary on it. This, however, is not the view of an exegete as qualified as Franz Mussner, who gives vv. 13–15 the title "Instructions for various concrete situations," and vv. 16–18 the title "Confession of sins and intercession."[19]

The TOB and J. Cantinat rightly put vv. 13–18 together under a single title: "Pray!" (TOB) or "Pray in every situation" (J. Cantinat). For in fact the verb *proseuchesthai* ("to pray") and words derived from the same root[20] recur like a leitmotiv in each verse of the section. Also to be noted is the device of inclusion, which is characteristic of Jewish homilies: let him pray (*proseuchesthō*, 13a)— Elijah prayed (*proeuxato*, 18).

Verse 13, which begins the section, belongs to what has been called "the literary genre of totality,"[21] in which a pair of expressions (bind-loose, enter-leave, descend-ascend) is used to represent all the situations occurring between the two extremes. From the "moral" standpoint, suffering and joy represent two extremes. In both cases prayer is appropriate: the prayer of petition in hours of darkness, hymns of exultation on days of gladness. It is from the standpoint of the necessity of prayer in every situation that James will approach the case of the sick.

The determination of the literary genre of James enables us to get rid of a false problem. Theologians who have thought it necessary to connect each sacrament with a specific scriptural word of institution have in the past often presented James 5:14–15 as the text which promulgates the anointing of the sick.[22] But James is in fact far too much of a traditionalist to promulgate anything whatsoever! He is simply recommending a practice already well established in the communities to which he is writing.[23]

Explanation of the Text

In the same elliptical form for expressing a possibility that has already been used in v. 13, v. 14 envisages the case of someone who is sick (*asthenei*). The verb used here has a quite general meaning: we find it applied to Lazarus (Jn 11:4) who is in danger of death, but also to the infirm; thus in a synagogue on the sabbath, Jesus heals a poor old woman who is afflicted with "a spirit of infirmity (*astheneia*)" (Lk 13:11). The other verb here applied to the sick person—*kamnein* in v. 15—emphasizes the suffering of one who is ill. From the fact that the man calls the elders of the Church to his bedside, it follows that he is confined to his room. Nothing more specific can be said about the seriousness of the sickness or infirmity.

COTHENET

Let Him Call for the Elders of the Church. This is the only reference in the Letter of James to the presence of elders (*tous presbyterous tēs ekklēsias*) in the community. Is the reference simply to older men who have some kind of directive role, as in the synagogues, or are we to think here of the "presbyters" whose functions are detailed in the pastoral letter, 1 Peter (5:1–4), and the letters of St. Ignatius of Antioch?[24]

The presbyteral organization of the Church certainly owes a good deal to the model provided by the Jewish communities. But there is also one essential difference between them. The Law of Moses provided only for a priestly hierarchy. Unlike the priests, who had a direct divine mandate, the office of those in charge of the synagogues was a matter only of customary law. These men had their authority from the community which appointed them. The liturgical distinction between the two groups was very clear, since even in the synagogue priests alone could bless the people with the formula given in Numbers 6:24–27. But we see the elders of whom James speaks acting in the name of the *Kyrios,* and therefore as his agents. They therefore have a special rank and, according to the information provided in the pastoral letters, have been appointed by a rite of imposition of hands. By mentioning their activity with the sick, James 5 provides an important landmark for the history of ministries in the primitive Church. In order to emphasize the authority with which "the elders of the Church" are invested, I shall refer to them henceforth as "presbyters."

Prayer of the Presbyters. The first thing the presbyters are to do when they visit the sick person is to pray. Whatever be the intrinsic importance of the rite that is described, it is presented first of all as a prayer service.

At this point I must depart from the TOB translation: "Let them pray after having bestowed on him an anointing with oil." The prepositional phrase *ep'auton* ("on him, over him") belongs directly with the verb "let them pray."[25] The construction is admittedly surprising, but the interpretation given in TOB is philologically impossible, since the verb "to anoint" (*aleiphein*) is always transitive in the New Testament.[26] Intercessory prayer is usually followed either by the preposition *peri* or the preposition *hyper.*[27] On the other hand, the use here of *epi* is not arbitrary, for, as R. Béraudy points out, the presbyters are standing while the sick person is lying in bed; the presbyters are therefore praying "over" him.[28] But this commonsense observation does not account for the use of the accusative case with the preposition. For this we must refer to uses of *epi* with the accusative that manifests authority, as, for example, to establish someone as judge *over* another (Lk 12:14) or to reign *over* (Lk 1:33). The presbyters are not offering just any prayer, but are acting in accordance with their office and with the authority of the *Kyrios*. More concretely, this turn of phrase suggests a laying on of hands, as Origen realized[29] and as the oldest Ambrosian ritual prescribed.[30]

Anointing with Oil. The use of an aorist participle (*aleipsantes*) does not by itself prove that the anointing precedes the prayer; the verb conveys rather the noncontinuous, nonrepetitive character of the action which is here linked to the prayer of the presbyters. Without going into the various meanings attached to anointing in Jewish-Christian circles, let me remind the reader that oil belonged among the medications used in antiquity. Everyone will recall the action of the Good Samaritan in pouring oil and wine into the wounds of the injured man (Lk 10:34). One of the points to which the rabbis turned their attention was the determination of cases in which one could anoint with oil and wine on the sabbath. Thus according to the Palestinian Talmud, the action was permissible provided the materials had been prepared the day before.[31] Too bad if the need for them arose unexpectedly!

In the Name of the Kyrios. With the formula "in the name of" (*en tō onomati*) we are still in the same Semitic environment. How are we to determine the precise meaning of the phrase? In a now classic book,[32] W. Heitmüller started with exorcisms, in which a name plays a key role. Recall Flavius Josephus' description of an exorcism, which I have already cited: Eleazar calls upon the name of Solomon as he forbids the demon to torment his victim any longer. The gospel tells us that impure spirits were subject to to the disciples "in the name of Jesus" (Lk 10:17). It does not follow, however, that exorcisms were the sole starting point for the spread of the formula.

A more detailed study should distinguish between the use of the dative case (*en tō onomati*, corresponding to the Hebrew *beshem*) and the use of the accusative case (*eis to onoma*, corresponding to the Hebrew *leshem*). The dative is more suggestive of authority and power, of an agent acting with the authority of his principal (e.g., Mt 21:9, 23:39); thus in a baptismal context "to baptize in the name of Jesus Christ" means "to baptize by the authority, with the power of Jesus Christ."[33] The expression *eis to onoma*, on the other hand, looks rather to the belonging-to which the rite effects: the baptized person belongs to him in whose name he has been baptized (Acts 8:16; 19:5; 1 Cor 1:13, 15; etc.). We must realize that all these usages reflect the importance attributed in Christian preaching to the prophetic promise which St. Peter recalls on Pentecost: "Whoever calls on the name of the Lord shall be saved" (Joel 3:5, cited in Acts 2:21). For Christians, the name thus invoked is the name of Jesus *Kyrios;* so much so, that from now on "the Name" (without further qualification) means Christ.[34]

The area in which we find ourselves here is thus far from being one of superstition or magic. The Name does not operate by itself like a physical force; it acts insofar as it is invoked and confessed. In keeping with the overall theme of vv. 13–18, the rite of anointing is accomplished in an atmosphere of intense prayer and, we may add in view of v. 16, of prayer for one another. This is why the anointing of a comatose person raises a serious problem.[35]

The Prayer of Faith Will Save the Sick Person. The expression "prayer of faith" (*euchē tēs pisteōs*) occurs only here in the New Testament. Judging by James 1:6, the reference is to prayer offered with complete trust, without the least doubt, and inspired by the faith that moves mountains.

In expressing the effect of such prayer, James does not use the ordinary verbs for healing (*therapeuein, iasthai*),[36] but has recourse to a term with strong religious connotations: *sōzein* (save). In the New Testament world, it was used to describe the interventions of divine healers; the hellenistic kings bestowed on themselves the title of "savior" (*sōtēr*).[37] In the Old Testament, "saving" is an attribute of Yahweh, ever since the foundational experience of Israel, namely, the exodus from Egypt. The salvation of the individual who prays takes place within the framework of a covenant that benefits the chosen people. Consequently, when Christ tells a sick man: "Go, your faith has saved you," he is not granting simply an individual healing, but is giving a sign of the kingdom.

This point emerges clearly from the story of the woman with a flow of blood (Mk 5:24–34, par), in which the formula just cited occurs in a most typical way.[38] The woman is not just any sick person, but one who is afflicted with a serious uncleanness. A Pharisee could only have been enraged at the boldness of a woman who would thus render him unclean without his realizing it. However, Jesus leads the woman from a state of still quite imperfect faith (v. 28) to a state of explicit faith which she confesses in the presence of all (v. 33). It is at this point that he says the decisive words: "Daughter, your faith has made you well; go in peace, and be healed of your disease" (v. 34). Jesus is here declaring a complete restoration: "Enter into the state of fulfillment and grace that is the peace which God wills for his people in the hour of salvation." He will end his conversation with the repentant sinful woman in the same way: "Your faith has saved you; go in peace" (Lk 7:50).

Ought we therefore to ask, as some commentators do, whether James is here using the verb *sōzein* in the physical sense of healing or in the eschatological sense of spiritual salvation? In other passages of the letter (1:21; 2:14; 4:12; 5:20), *sōzein* does indeed signify definitive salvation, but in the present passage the parallelism with *egeirein* and *iasthai* ("raise up" and "heal", in vv. 15 and 16) shows that the meaning "to heal" is not forgotten. Verse 15 refers explicitly to the forgiveness of sins, a point also taken up in verse 16. Evidently, then, the text is open to both levels of meaning; this is something which a theological synthesis on the anointing of the sick should not forget.

The Lord Will Raise Him Up. The action of the presbyters who act in the name of the Lord is matched by a personal intervention of the risen *Kyrios:* he will raise up the sick person. The verb used here for "raise," *egeirein,* has rich connotations since it is one of the key terms for the resurrection in the primitive kerygma.[39] It is also to be noted that the verb recurs with unusual persistence in the gospel stories of healing. It occurs, for example, in the story of Peter's mother-in-law: Jesus "came and took her by the hand and lifted her up (*ēgeiren*), and the fever left her, and she served them" (Mk 1:31). The verb keeps cropping up in an almost stereotyped way in many other stories: the epileptic boy whom Jesus takes by the hand (Mk 9:27), the paralytic who is forgiven and healed (Mt 9:5, 7), the little daughter of Jairus (Mt 9:25), and so on. As X. Léon-Dufour says: "These are gestures which, because reported by a word, *egeirein,* which is a technical term for the resurrection of Jesus, suggests to our minds a further reality of a different order: the spiritual resurrection of the Christian. The word and action can be called symbolic, because they participate in the reality they express."[40]

And if He Has Sins, These Will Be Forgiven Him. Despite popular beliefs which St. Paul himself to some extent accepts (1 Cor 11:30), James is careful not to assert a necessary connection between sickness and sin. Verse 15b is introduced by a word indicating a possible situation (*kan*) and allows for the case in which the sick person has serious sins on his conscience. In the Jewish manner with its avoidance of a direct reference to God's action, James uses an impersonal passive construction, "it will be forgiven him" (*aphethēsetai*). We are reminded of Jesus speaking to the paralytic at Capernaum: "Which is easier, to say, 'Your sins are forgiven,' or to say, 'Rise and walk'?" (Mt 9:5, par). We may ask, with J.-C. Didier,

COTHENET

whether theologians have done full justice to James' text on the forgiveness of sins[41]; we must not, however, overlook the fact that there is a connection between the verse on anointing and the subsequent verse on the mutual confession of sins.

Therefore Confess Your Sins to One Another. Now, at first sight there is in fact no connection between the scene of the anointing at the sick person's bedside and the exhortation of v. 16, which has to do with the entire community. Verses 14–15 are concerned with the college of presbyters and the individual sick person; v. 16, on the other hand, is addressed to the community, no distinction being made between presbyters and simple faithful, and it emphasizes a reciprocity of relations (the reciprocal pronoun occurs twice). It is understandable, therefore, that F. Mussner and J. Cantinat should interpret v. 16 as a separate entity and connect it with a penitential rite which can be explained in the light of a brief reference in 1 John 5:16.[42] The confession in question is not merely a declaration of a general kind: "We have sinned against you, Lord." According to the *Didache* 14, 1–2,[43] it includes an avowal of sins against the neighbor and against mutual reconciliation, a phenomenon quite conceivable in small communities in which each member is aware of the estrangements within families and the disputes among neighbors!

Despite the differences already indicated between the two situations (i.e., in vv. 14–15 and v. 16), James introduces v. 16 with the conjunction *oun* (therefore) and thus establishes a link of some kind between the counsel given to the sick individual (vv. 14–15) and the exhortation addressed to the whole community (v. 16). "*Therefore* confess your sins to one another." I believe that the Jewish background can help us discover the connection of ideas here. Among the works of mercy recommended in Judaism, the visiting of the sick has a place of honor. Among the other pieces of evidence cited in Strack-Billerbeck, I mention the following tradition from the Babylonian Talmud: "When a person is sick and on the point of dying, he is told: 'Make your confession!' For all those on the point of dying have done so."[44]

This practice is justified by means of a parable that closely resembles one found in the gospel (Mt 5:25–26 = Lk 12:57–59): "He who makes his way to the tribunal to be judged will be saved if he finds some important intercessors (*peraqletin*); otherwise, he will not be saved. And what are man's intercessors? Repentance and good works."

This text is followed by a citation from Job 33:23–24 which speaks of an angel who acts as mediator (*peraqlit*, according to the Targum) and intervenes on behalf of the repentant sinner. I must leave the dating of these traditions to specialists. However, we do have one point of reference: in the New Testament period, a man condemned to death was to confess his sin at the moment of execution so that he might have a share in the life of the world to come. He was supposed to say: "May my death be an atonement (*kappārā*) for all my sins."[45]

Conclusion

If my observations on the unity of vv. 13–18 are justified, I am in a position to summarize in a more precise way the steps which St. James recommends in the case of a sick Christian. It is up to the sick person to take the initiative and summon the presbyters of the community; the latter act in a collegial manner[46] in calling upon the *Kyrios* as they lay their hands on the sick person and anoint him with oil. The sick person should take an active part in the rite through his own prayer (v. 13a); he is indirectly (v. 16) urged to confess any sins that are opposed to good relations in the community. The community itself finally should feel itself to be affected by the sickness or health of its members: "Therefore confess your sins to one another and pray for one another, in order that you may be healed (*iathēte*). The prayer of a just man is very effective." The atmosphere in this passage is the same as that found in the Jewish-Christian communities of the *Didache:* "In the assembly confess your sins and do not go to prayer with a bad conscience. . . . Anyone who is at odds with his neighbor is not to join you (on the Lord's Day) unless he has been reconciled, lest your sacrifice be profaned" (4, 14; 14,2).

This close likeness bids us, does it not, to look more closely at the links between the text of James and the milieu from which it came?

THE JEWISH-CHRISTIAN BACKGROUND

The Oil of Faith

In 1967 Father Emmanuele Testa, already well-known for his studies of Jewish-Christian symbolism, published a little book that attracted a certain amount of attention: *The Oil of Faith. The Anointing of the Sick on a First-Century Lamella.*[47] This lamella (thin sheet) of silver, discovered in the Judean desert, is inscribed with seventeen lines of Hebrew characters and strange signs.

"Oil of faith": this, it is claimed, is the meaning of the first line. Lines 2–4 are said to describe the action of the demon, *Qur'el*, who is the cause of the patient's sickness. Lines 5–7 deal with the ritual to be performed: "Examine him in the Name"—by which we are to understand: the Name of Jesus. After two wavy lines, the essential statement: "God lightened the trial."

COTHENET

Though Father B. Bagatti accepted this interpretation,[48] J. T. Milik categorically rejected it[49]: in his view the amulet dates from only the fifth century and the text is a magician's spell. Without attempting a detailed examination, which would be beyond my competence, I shall simply point out a major difficulty which was raised by J. Starcky in an irenic report on the Testa-Milik controversy[50]: the *mem* of the first line is written as a final *mem*. It is therefore not possible to read *shemen* (oil); the reading must instead be *shem* (name).

Although his results are open to question, Father Testa's brochure is valuable in that it calls our attention to the rites and beliefs of the Jewish Christians of Palestine. For too long, historians forgot that Palestinian Jewish Christians continued to exist after the second Jewish War (132–135); as a result, there was a wide gap between the period of the Church's origins in Palestine and the Constantinian period. But as a matter of fact, faith in Christ did not disappear, even if it expressed itself in forms alien to us. Even the rabbinical writings attest to the presence of Christians. Here is one story having to do with a healer:

"The grandson of Rabbi Joshua ben Levi (ca. 250) had swallowed something. A man came and whispered in his ear in the name (*bsmyh*) of Jesus Pandera, and he was cured. When the Christian had come out, Rabbi Joshua asked him: 'What did you say over him?' The man replied: 'A saying of a certain Someone.' Then the rabbi said to him: 'It would have been better for him to die rather than to have heard this saying.' "[51]

The story says a good deal about the inviolable barriers the rabbis wanted to see between their community and that of the *Minim* (= "heretics," Christians). But the fame of healers broke down the barriers, and even the family of a rabbi did not hesitate to disobey the prohibition when the life of a child was at stake! As far as ritual is concerned, only the invocation of the Name is mentioned, as in Peter's healing of the lame man at the Beautiful Gate (Acts 3). Of the Jewish Christians who had the charism of healing the best known was James the Just, whose tomb B. Bagatti thinks he has identified at Saknin, a village in Galilee.[52] In this context we might also recall the exorcisms mentioned by Justin—a Palestinian born at Nablus—in his *Dialogue with Trypho* (30, 3).

Anointing with oil, imposition of hands, invocation of the Name (of Jesus): these are so many manifestations of this faith in the active presence of the *Kyrios*. In order to explain the text of James, must we agree with R. Béraudy that faith in a proximate parousia plays a role?[53] But the letter of James is exhortatory in style and mentions the return of the *Kyrios* (5:8, 9) only as part of an exhortation to patience and perseverance: "Behold, we call those happy who were steadfast. You have heard of the steadfastness of Job . . ." (5:11). I do not see that an understanding of the rite requires us to distinguish between two periods: the one in which people still believed the parousia to be imminent, and another in which they accepted the fact of a long history still ahead!

The Oil of Life

B. Reicke has made an interesting suggestion in his commentary on James: "Here the oil is apparently regarded as a kind of life elixir, in accordance with the Jewish idea that the precious fruit of the olive tree possessed life and spirit." This interpretation is developed more fully in an essay (in French) entitled "The Anointing of the Sick According to St. James."[54] In this essay the author gives a short presentation of apocryphal, Jewish, and Christian texts and concludes: "This is the background of James' exhortation regarding anointing with oil, oil being the symbol of the power of life in paradise or of the primeval state."

This thesis is of considerable interest because it connects up with all the speculations in Judaism on the return to paradise[55] as well as with a theme that is basic in Christian mysticism.[56] But a more careful judgment on the proofs offered is needed.

Generally speaking, if we want to establish the meaning of a religious rite, we must take as our starting point those current usages that are closest to it and in which the symbolism has its roots more or less in the natural world. In the Mediterranean world, oil plays an essential role as food, as a means of beautification, and as a source of light. In Mesopotamia the oil is from the palm tree; the earliest representations of the Tree of Life show it as a palm tree, not an olive tree. The Ethiopic Book of Enoch (24, 4) is still faithful to this ancient imagery.

I refer the reader to my article on anointing[57] for the various uses of oil and the meanings attached to them. In our present context the only relevant uses are the medicinal use and the use of perfumed oil for beautification. As a food that gives strength (olive oil is the father of muscle, according to an Arabic proverb) and a soothing ointment, oil is marvelously suited for use in a ritual of healing. In addition, when a dead person is being prepared for burial, the use of perfumed oils is a necessity in Eastern countries where decomposition of the body sets in very quickly.

At the time when faith in the resurrection of the dead was becoming widespread, perfumed oil must have been connected with the oil of paradise which will restore life to the elect at the

Judgment. It is along this line that I interpret the texts cited by B. Reicke. Take, for example, the *Apocalypse of Moses*, a Jewish-Christian text that surely depends on a Jewish source from the first century of the Christian era. When Adam falls seriously ill, Seth, accompanied by Eve, goes to paradise to ask for the oil of the tree of life. Michael the archangel says to Seth:

"Seth, man of God, weary not thyself with prayers and entreaties concerning the tree which floweth with oil to anoint thy father Adam. For it shall not be thine now, but in the end of the times. Then shall all flesh be raised up from Adam till that great day—all that shall be of the holy people. Then shall the delights of paradise be given to them."[58]

So concerned is the author of this document with the fate of Adam that he even tells us of the funeral, in paradise itself, of the first created human being[59] and of his son Abel (chap. 41). How can we fail to think, on reading this, of the earliest *Transitus Mariae*, which depict the angels carrying the body of Mary to the foot of the tree of life?[60] Here her body is preserved incorrupt until the day of the general resurrection.

The anointing of the dead was kept up for a long time in the Eastern Church. Pseudo-Dionysius seeks to justify it by a clever comparison with baptismal anointing:

"In discussing baptism I explained how the initiate was first anointed with oil after stripping off his garments. The same is done at the end [of life], and rightly so. Just as those preparing for a struggle are anointed, and then anointed again after having returned from the struggle and washed away their sweat, so here: the person facing the struggle is anointed in the beginning; then the same person, having ceased from the struggle, is anointed again when all struggle is past."[61]

The comparison of a struggle had deep roots in the Greek world, and consequently Pseudo-Dionysius' erudite explanation cannot be regarded as giving the original meaning of the rite. Shall we look for this meaning in the direction which Irenaeus suggests when discussing a practice of the Marcosians?

"In order to redeem the faithful who were ready to leave this life they poured oil mixed with water on their heads and at the same time uttered the invocations mentioned earlier. This they did in order that the dead might not be seized and held by the principalities and higher powers and in order that the interior man in them might ascend higher by invisible paths."[62]

The interpretation of this rite is a matter of dispute. The ancient writers took it to be a kind of anointing of the dying, but nowadays it is interpreted as a baptismal initiation.[63] The gnostic formulation, however, suggests a connection with certain Jewish-Christian ideas, those of the "cosmic ladder" or "ladder of the seven heavens" which the soul must ascend after death in order to reach the heavenly dwelling place.[64]

CONCLUSION

The distinction I am proposing between rite of healing and funeral rite cannot always be maintained; the overlappings of each with the other are numerous, as are overlappings with the baptismal anointing and its very complex set of meanings.[65]

I trust, however, that I have shown the rite envisaged by James to be a rite of healing that is described against the background of the miracles worked by Jesus. This reference to Jesus deserves to be emphasized, because elsewhere in his letter James makes extensive use of the sayings of Christ[66] but mentions no concrete incident of his life.[67] In the present text the vocabulary is too characteristic of the gospel scenes of healing for the allusion to be in doubt; the prayer of faith and the verbs "save" and "lift up" (sōzein and egeirein), together with the mention of the "Name of the Kyrios," also occur in the passages connected with the mission of the disciples (e.g., Lk 10:17). One miracle in particular can be seen in the background of James' exhortation, that of the paralytic who was forgiven and healed (Mt 9:1–8, par.). Matthew's conclusion is especially significant: "When the crowds saw it, they were afraid, and they glorified God, who had given such authority to men." The plural ("crowds") is deliberate,[68] for in his narrative the evangelist wants to bring out the continuity of the saving activity of Christ in his Church. James gives us a specific instance of this divine intervention: through the ministry of the presbyters and the trustful prayer of all, the Lord will raise up the sick Christian and, if the person has sinned, will forgive him.

The theologian who wants to locate the anointing the sick within the overall sacramental economy and within the concrete conditions of a health ministry has a sensitive task of reinterpretation before him. He cannot offer the oil of faith as a supermedication! Is he therefore to deny it all influence on health? To do this would be to cut himself off from the scriptural sources and the practice of the Church for many centuries. As a matter of fact, the passage in James 5 provides an excellent point of departure for reflection on the matter, provided we keep in mind the inclusive meaning of "life" in the Bible. It refers to life not as a purely biological entity but as a gift of God and an openness to communion with him; it refers to the life whose meaning and dignity are revealed to us by the risen Christ who is "the resurrection and the life" (Jn 11:25).

In contrast with those theologians who have interpreted "Extreme Unction" as the sacrament of the passage to glory, and to those others who have laid a too one-sided emphasis on healing as an effect, B. Sesboüé has properly brought out the twofold orientation of the sacrament. Ordered as it is to healing in the comprehensive sense of this word, it can reveal to the person the meaning of health as a gift of God. "Having been restored to physical health, the healed sick person achieves a new understanding of his existence in the light of the mystery of Christ." On the other hand, when death is drawing near, the anointing becomes "a call to eschatological healing." "Its purpose is not to spare the Christian the experience of death. . . . The anointing will give the sick person the strength to die in Christ so as to be able to rise with him."[69]

The instruction given by James is overly concise and needs to be completed by the texts of Paul on the paschal mystery and on the Christian's identification with his dead and risen Lord. It is appropriate, therefore, to cite the very characteristic passage in which Paul reveals to us the secret of his own life as one of striving to reach the glorified Christ by the way of his suffering: "I have suffered the loss of all things . . . that I may know him and the power of his resurrection, and may share his sufferings, becoming like him in his death, that if possible I may attain the resurrection from the dead" (Phil 3:8, 10–11).

André-Marie DUBARLE

Sickness and Death
in the Old Testament

In this essay, I shall be focusing on the practices of the people of God in the old covenant insofar as these provide a precedent for our Christian practices, whether we think of ourselves as studying the forms of the past or as looking for renewal through the Bible. I shall be examining the beliefs and especially the activities by which the community, including the individual concerned, foresaw, anticipated, and struggled against sickness and death, and then those beliefs and activities by which the survivors responded to death, expressed their sorrow at it, and then rounded out the process with burial.

I shall thus be leaving aside certain questions which are important in themselves but which cannot be discussed in such a short space: (1) Where do suffering and sickness come from? Where does death come from? What part do they play in the divine plan? (2) What is the lot of the dead? How did the idea of a resurrection or a happy survival arise?

Neither shall I take the time to summarize the medical knowledge which the Israelites possessed as indicated by occasional references in the Bible[1] or to present an anthology of more or less magical practices or of naive or superstitious popular views on sickness or death.[2] Our interest here today is in learning what God said to a group of human beings whose mind-set was in certain respects less developed than ours, and in determining what profit we can derive from this message when account is taken of our more scientific approach to things and our more fully explicated faith. We have a more accurate knowledge of the complex of natural causes that control sickness and death, and we do not immediately assign these to religious causes or superhuman agents. This does not dispense us, however, from the need of taking a personal position on these inescapable facts of life.

In my survey I shall make use of all the books which the Catholic Church holds to be inspired, including those which were known in antiquity as the *antilegomena* or "disputed" books, as "deuterocanonical" by sixteenth-century Catholics, and as "apocryphal" or "intertestamental" by Protestants, and which in the Eastern Orthodox Churches have a rather indeterminate status as far as actual use is concerned, while more or less explicit doubts are expressed at times. The omission of these would be a less than honest fiction on my part and a kind of tour de force that is difficult to carry out. In addition, these books have influenced the Christian liturgies.

BEHAVIOR IN TIME OF SICKNESS

The psalms contain many prayers that can suitably be used by the sick.[3] The ones most clearly meant for them are Psalms 38, 41, and 88. These show the sufferer turning to God, asking forgiveness of his sins, asking God's help against his malevolent neighbors, and hoping for the healing that will confound his enemies. Sickness is an occasion for interior purification and a more fervent trust in God.

Ben Sira preaches the same lesson in a set of counsels which he gives his disciple for the time of sickness (Sir 38:1–15). But there is something relatively new that strikes our attention in this passage: the place assigned to the doctor in the hoped-for healing. The Hebrew text is even more emphatic here than the Greek translation: it says "the doctor's art comes from God," instead of (in the Greek) "healing comes from the Most High." The Hebrew also says that "they [the doctors] will pray to the Lord that he should grant them success in diagnosis," and not simply (with the Greek) that he would grant them "the grace to relieve" (Sir 38:2 and 14H). This approach opens the door, in principle, to progress in medical science.

DUBARLE

But Ben Sira realizes that doctors cannot go on indefinitely healing those who depend on their skills. When a person's end comes, he must make a will disposing of his goods (Sir 33:23). The wise man is thinking here chiefly of the material possessions the seriously ill person will leave behind him. But prior to Ben Sira, the biblical accounts are interested in the advice, the special commands, the predictions about the future which a dying father may hand on to his children at the moment of leaving them.

Abraham takes steps to ensure the marriage of his son, and to this end he sends his chief servant to look for a wife in Abraham's own country of origin (Gn 24:6–8). He gives preference to his last-born son, a practice that will later be forbidden by the Law (Gn 25:5–6; Dt 21:15). Isaac in his turn blesses the one he thinks is his eldest son but who in fact is the younger son supplanting his brother. The word spoken cannot be recalled; it guarantees the preeminence of Jacob, even though he has used trickery to get ahead of his elder brother (Gn 27).

Jacob deliberately favors the second of the sons of Joseph (Gn 48:8–20). His eyes have grown dim, but he has the clairvoyance of the prophets with regard to the future and he predicts the future lot of the various tribes (Gn 49). He gives orders for his own burial, as Joseph will likewise do later on (Gn 47:29–31; 49:29–31; 50:25). We already find in these early stories the desire to be united with the ancestors in the same burying place.

Moses makes the most solemn testament to be found in the Old Testament; this is in keeping with the greatness of the covenant of which he had been the mediator. He makes Joshua the commander in the wars of conquest and entrusts to the Levites the Law, which they will have to read to the assembly every seven years (Dt 31). He commends to the memory of all the canticle telling of the unmerited mercies of Yahweh, the infidelities of the chosen people, and the ultimate forgiveness of the offended deity (Dt 32). Finally, he reveals the destiny of each tribe (Dt 33). Moses is thus the prophet who has no equal (Dt 34:10).

Joshua, the successor of Moses, and Samuel, the last of the Judges and the unwilling inaugurator of the monarchy, at their deaths exhort the people to be faithful to the God who freed Israel from Egypt (Jos 23–24; 1 Sm 12).

David has some final pieces of advice for Solomon, whom he has appointed his successor (1 Kgs 2:1–9). According to the later Book of Chronicles, David also sets down the rules for liturgical worship and instructs Solomon to build the temple for which he, David, has accumulated the various precious metals (1 Chr 23–29).

There is no further mention of a last will and testament until the time of Mattathias, who began Jewish resistance to pagan hellenization in the time of Antiochus Epiphanes. Before dying, Mattathias divides responsibilities among his sons and exhorts them to do battle for the Law. On this occasion he reminds them of the exemplary men of the past (1 Mc 2:49–68). Alcimus, the usurping high priest, however, is stricken with paralysis and unable to speak and give final orders before dying (1 Mc 9:55).

The edifying story of Tobit shows the unfortunate blind man giving his son advice about virtuous behavior as well as specific recommendations about his future course of action (Tb 4:1–21). After being healed and reaching a very great age, this devout man receives prophetic insight so that he may tell his descendants what to do before the fall of Nineveh (Tb 14:3–11).

The examples I have been giving already show a tendency that will become even more marked subsequently: the tendency to attribute to an important personage of the past a testament that has permanent value. By means of a fiction which in the beginning could hardly have deceived the reader, authority was given to moral teachings or to prophecies which would be profitable to the people generally. The *Testaments of the Twelve Patriarchs* is the best-known example of this literature. There are good reasons for thinking that the second letter of Peter in the New Testament belongs to this literary genre.[4] The supposed author of the letter foretells his coming death and voices his concern for the lot of his correspondents after he himself has departed from this world (2 Pt 1:12–15). The solidarity between members of the same community lasts beyond death: the dead and the survivors are called to the same kingdom and can count on one another.

SICKNESS AND ITS CURE

The Bible does not oppose life and death in such a way that each strictly excludes the other. We need to think of them rather as two realities which vary in inverse proportion: when the one increases, the other decreases.[5]

There are, of course, many passages in which the words for death indicate simply the physical decease, the cessation of organic life that issues in the process of decomposition. Jacob sat on his bed as he gave his sons their final instructions; when he had finished speaking, "he drew up his feet into the bed, and breathed his last" (Gn 49:33). But around this fundamental experience in which life and death appear as two successive periods of temporal duration, all kinds of positive and negative values came to be grouped. Life and death are then no longer two lines that touch only at one point,

DUBARLE

namely, the moment of decease; they are two circles that are contrary in value but that are nonetheless capable of overlapping more or less completely in the same individual. In this context attention is attracted no longer to the exercise of biological activities but to the things that give existence its value.

When using the words of life and death in this second manner, the biblical writers contrast life, that is, normal, happy existence, with an unhappy fate, the premature death which a person can cause for himself by unwise and unjust behavior. Although the writers are aware that on occasion even the just and innocent person may fall victim to unexpected misfortune, they devote their attention to what seems to be the most frequent occurrence, but also the most intelligible, inasmuch as it brings out best the fact of a connection between actions and their result.

In the Law (e.g., Dt 30:15–20) and in Proverbs, life and death are the objects of a choice which is offered to those concerned and the effects of which are set forth in advance: with life go happiness and the blessing of God; with death go unhappiness and a curse (Dt 30:15–20). The things that give value to human existence: material prosperity, the affection of one's fellows, considerateness, justice, prudence, and the reverence for God that leads to a trusting familiarity with him—these belong to life. Poverty, on the contrary, along with hostility from neighbors, injustice, folly, and the forgetfulness or contempt of God belong to death.

In this perspective all serious dangers, and therefore especially sickness, interrupting as they do in a more or less decisive way the enjoyment of these blessings, represent the approach of death and give an advance experience of death's bitterness. The person who is subjected to suffering, the paralysis of his activity, the ebbing of his strength, and abandonment by his friends, and who is already confined to his bed, can already see himself lying in his grave, in that pit which common parlance more or less confuses with Sheol, the underground dwelling place of the departed.

The Old Testament texts never envisage a complete destruction, a total annihilation, of the dead. The soul or shade descends into Sheol, a place of darkness and oblivion, and subsists there not in a true life but in a kind of inactive state of numbness, a stupor vaguely stirred by half-wakenings on certain great occasions. In this gloomy gathering place God seems to have abandoned his creatures (Ps 88:5). Praise of God is no longer possible for those good servants who had found their joy in attending the temple and had been sure of a mutual attachment between God and themselves (Ps 6:5; 30:9; 88:5–12; 115:17; Is 38:18).

The sick person thus sees himself at the gates of Sheol or on the way to them, if indeed he is not already the companion of the ancient shades (Ps 28:1; 88:3–4; 107:18; 143:7). The danger of death from a sudden attack by enemies or from drowning can give rise to the same cries of distress (Ps 18:5–6; 116:3; Jon 2:3–7). It is not always easy to distinguish between literal language and language that is metaphorical or hyperbolical and due to intense emotion.

The sick person or the one in danger of death turns to God for protection. He asks unceasingly not to go down into the pit or into Sheol. When he is cured or rescued, he thanks God for having been brought back from death; Yahweh has brought him up out of Sheol (Ps 30:3; 49:15; 86:13; 103:4; Sir 51:5–6; Is 38:17).

Healing, then, is from God. Some texts introduce healing into a striking parallelism that expresses God's providential control of human life in its entirety: "I kill and I make alive; I wound and I heal" (Dt 32:39). "The Lord kills and brings to life; he brings down to Sheol and raises up" (1 Sm 2:6; cf. Tb 13:2; Wis 16:13). These two-membered formulas that juxtapose two contraries are commonplace in the biblical writers. They appeal to all sorts of areas of life in order to express the fact that God's power is limited by nothing and extends to all existing things.

When we read of the descent into Sheol and the ascent up out of its depths, we may have the impression that this is a hyperbole which by its excess has lost almost all meaning. But this would be failing to recognize a hidden power of suggestion that goes much beyond the realm of clear ideas that are consciously accepted after reflection. The prophet Ezekiel describes an impressive scene in which the bones scattered over a plain assemble to form skeletons, the skeletons become covered with flesh, and the reconstituted bodies are then animated with the breath of life and rise to their feet. This is simply an image of that restoration of the nation, which during the exile might have been regarded as an illusory hope. But Yahweh speaks and makes a firm promise: "You shall know that I am the Lord, when I open your graves, and raise you from your graves, O my people" (Ez 37:13). The imagery of the psalms and the emotional picture painted by a visionary were remotely preparing hearts to accept belief in the resurrection. In the healing of sick persons whom all had abandoned and in the reestablishment of the community of believers at Jerusalem after their return from deportation, the important thing was not the concrete incident with its limited empirical dimensions, but the gift of God's goodness and power which they had enjoyed in an extreme situation. This experience, which was of the religious order, justified a still greater hope. Human beings had, as it were, touched the very reality of Yahweh and could depend on him to escape death.

DUBARLE

In this way the Old Testament serves as prelude to the text in James 5:15 with its ambiguous tonality. The term *egeirein*, "to awaken, to lift or raise up," here refers directly to the healing and restoration of the sick person, but it can also be understood as connoting the resurrection, since the New Testament uses it in both senses. Bodily healing is an image and promise of the resurrection for James 5:15, just as it had represented for the psalmists a return from the dwelling place of the dead.

THE DUTIES OF THE LIVING TO THE DEAD

Israel was aware that the living have duties to the dead. Friends and relatives have an obligation to mourn[6] and to see to the burial of the dead person; his heir must avenge any injuries done to his father and keep alive the memory of the departed (Sir 30:4–6; 1 Kgs 2:5–9).

Mourning is shown by torn garments, fasting, neglect of dress, and songs of lament. It usually lasts for seven days but in special circumstances may be continued for as long as thirty days.

The corpse is placed in a tomb which will keep alive the memory of the dead person; usually this is a family tomb. The children of the patriarchs carried out this duty: Isaac and Israel for Abraham (Gn 25:9), Jacob and Esau for Isaac, Joseph and his brothers for Jacob (Gn 50:2–14). Contact with a corpse entails a ritual uncleanness; therefore priests and the high priest are more or less completely excused from the obligation of burying their relatives (Lv 21:1–3, 11). But this uncleanness does not keep the burying of the dead from being an act of kindness and charity to the deceased, comparable to alms given to the living. The Book of Tobit is an illustration of this belief (Tb 1:17; 2:7; 12:12–13). Ben Sira expresses the same truth in a didactic way (Sir 38:16).

The fate of the dead person is not independent of his being buried. Such at least was the belief of the Babylonians, as known to us from the epic of Gilgamesh. The hero goes down among the dead, questions his friend Enkidu who had died earlier, and learns from his mouth the sad fate of certain categories among the deceased: "If a man's body is left abandoned on the plain, his spirit has no rest in the lower world. One whose spirit has no one to pay it a cultus eats what is left in the pot and the scrapings of dishes that are thrown out into the street."[7]

Such ideas are not as clearly expressed in the Old Testament. Job longs for Sheol as a place in which all are completely equal (Jb 3:18–19). But a few poetic texts suggest the acceptance of a difference of condition in the kingdom of the dead, depending on whether the person had received an honorable burial, such as was accorded to heroes and denied to criminals (Is 14:9–21; Ezk 32:18–32). There is a confused idea that the lot of the dead person (whoever he might be) is conditioned by the attitude of the living toward him. This notion had been inherited from distant pagan ancestors and continued to exist in the recesses of men's minds without having as yet been explicated in a way that would make it completely compatible with faith in Yahweh, the God of the covenant. It emerges in a roundabout way in certain passages from which allusions to the gods of the lower world have already been removed.

If we keep this ancestral notion in mind, we can better understand the concern about burial that crops up clearly and frequently, whether in survivors or in a man who has no posterity but desires to have his memory live on (2 Sm 18:18; Sir 40:19).

Although no reason for the conviction is given, the burning of even an enemy's bones and their reduction to lime is regarded as an act of savage cruelty for which God will demand vengeance (Am 2:1), just as he will for the enslavement of prisoners (Am 1:6, 9) or the slaying of pregnant women (Am 1:13). The Philistines cut off the heads of Saul and his sons after these have fallen in battle and expose them in the temple of their god Dagon at Ashdod (1 Chr 10:10); they fasten the bodies to the walls of Beth-shan, near the battlefield (1 Sm 31:10). But the inhabitants of Jabesh in Gilead, a city which Saul had once liberated in his first exploit (1 Sm 11:1–11), remove the corpses during the night and give them proper burial in Jabesh (1 Sm 31:13). David thanks the people of Jabesh for this work of mercy (2 Sm 2:5–7); David himself will later transfer the bones to the family tomb of Kish, father of Saul, in the land of Benjamin (2 Sm 21:12–14).

The great massacres accompanying coups d'etat and the assassinations of kings who had become unpopular meant that bodies were abandoned to the animals: to dogs within the towns, to birds of prey in the countryside. Such was the lot of Jeroboam, Baasha, Jehoram of Israel, and their families (1 Kgs 14:11; 16:4; 21:24; 2 Kgs 9:36). Only one son of Jeroboam is buried in a regular grave because in him alone is found something good and pleasing to Yahweh (1 Kgs 14:13; cf. Is 57:12). The tyrannical Jehoiakim will have the burial of an ass, whose decaying carcass is left to the dogs at the city gate (Jer 22:19; cf. 16:4). Rizpah wants to spare her sons so cruel a fate and therefore she keeps guard over their bodies after their execution (2 Sm 21:10).

Violation of a tomb is a serious wrong against the person who rests therein. Worshipers of the stars are supremely punished by having their bones taken from their tombs and spread out on the ground in the sight of the stars which they had served during their lifetime, as if they were now being forced to continue forever this wicked and foolish cult (Jer 8:1–2). A proud and blaspheming king is in the end dragged from his tomb and thrown out among the rocks (Is 14:19). But people refuse to commit such an outrage against a dead person whose memory is respected. Thus King Josiah, who had desecrated the altar at Bethel by burning anonymous bones on it (2 Kgs 23:16, 20), gives orders that no one disturb the tomb of the prophet from Judah who had predicted this desecration (2 Kgs 23:17). It is noteworthy that this gesture of clemency is made in favor of a prophet who had indeed carried out the general mission he had received from God, but had disobeyed one particular command by accepting hospitality at table and had been slain by a lion in punishment for his disobedience (1 Kgs 13:20–32). This shows that a distinction of degrees was made among serious sins and that an individual failing in a life marked by fidelity did not merit a rigorous judgment.

On the other hand, the living still have ties of solidarity with the dead, and they have an obligation to repair and punish the injustices committed by a dead person, in order that the disorder caused by these injustices may not finally harm the survivors.

One example of this is David's behavior in regard to Saul. A famine, probably due to a drought (cf. 2 Sm 21:10), is attributed by a divine oracle to the murders committed by Saul among the population of Gibeon, a little village north of Jerusalem, despite the protection guaranteed them by an ancient oath of peace (Jos 9:3–27). Blood must be avenged by blood (Gn 9:5). David therefore hands over seven descendants of Saul to the Gibeonites, who execute them before Yahweh, that is, in front of his sanctuary. As a result God once more shows his favor to the land (2 Sm 21:1–14).

On this occasion David gathers up the bones of Saul and Jonathan, which had previously been buried at Jabesh in Gilead, and places these, along with the bones of the hanged men and of all their kin, in the family tomb in the land of Benjamin (2 Sm 21:12–14). In his conduct David combines justice and mercy, for he is convinced that the dead are not utterly cut off from the living and that relations with the dead must be characterized by both equity and kindness.

PRAYER FOR THE DEAD

If in our approach to the relatively recent passage in 2 Maccabees 12:43–46, we keep in mind these antecedents and their testimony to the value set on burial, we will find the sacrifice for the dead to be much less of a novelty than it seems to be at first glance.[8]

Some guerrillas taking part in the holy war under the command of Judas Maccabeus have fallen in a battle on the coastal plain. After the sabbath a party goes out to collect the bodies of Jewish soldiers in order to lay them in the tombs of their ancestors (2 Mc 12:39). In the process they find under the tunics of the dead men idolatrous objects previously carried off from the pagan city of Jamnia. The presence of these objects did not necessarily mean that the dead men practiced a polytheistic worship, but at least they had wrongly appropriated objects which could only stir horror and had indulged a lust for unclean wealth that was condemned by the Law (Dt 7:25–26; cf. 1 Chr 14:12). These men who had died on the field of honor were thus in an ambiguous position: on the one hand, they had given their lives in the fulfillment of sacred duty, the defense of their native land and their Law, and thus had "fallen asleep in godliness"; on the other hand, they had transgressed a precept of the Law. They were thus comparable to the prophet who had come to Bethel to curse the altar there, in accordance with a commission received from God, but who had disobeyed his instructions by accepting hospitality. This was the prophet whom Josiah later expressly ordered should be left at peace in his tomb.

Judas Maccabeus believes that a splendid reward awaits these faithful patriots, but also that there is an obstacle to their enjoying that reward at the resurrection. He therefore has a sacrifice offered for sins (2 Mc 12:43). The order violated by the infraction of the Law must be restored, just as David had restored it in the case of Saul, who had unjustly caused the death of the Gibeonites out of zeal indeed for Israel, but also in violation of a solemn oath (2 Sm 21:1–3). The sacrifice is offered to God, since he is the one offended in the case of the soldiers who stole the pagan idols. Just as after the execution of Saul's descendants David has secured the repose of the entire family by bringing together the bones of all in the ancestral tomb (2 Sm 21:12–14), so Judas hopes that after the expiatory sacrifice the guilty soldiers will enjoy the future resurrection.

Many exegetes, especially Jewish scholars,[9] think that this passage on sacrifice on behalf of the dead gives an anachronistic interpretation of Judas' action. In their view the practice of expiation on behalf of the dead did not exist at the period to which it is assigned here but came into existence in Diaspora Judaism. It is the narrator—either Jason of Cyrene himself, or the abbreviator responsible for the final version—who attributes to Judas a mentality he did not have. The sacrifice was in fact meant to preserve the survivors from the consequences of the sin committed by the dead soldiers, just as the execution of Saul's descendants had been meant to win the cessation of the famine caused by the now long past murders which the king had committed.

Whatever the thinking of Judas himself may have been, the very explicit approval given by the narrator to the expiatory sacrifice on behalf of the dead did not win unanimous approval from his readers. Marginal glosses, later introduced into the text itself, bear witness in the one instance to a complete disagreement ("it is superfluous and foolish to pray for the dead") and in the other to a fervent agreement ("a holy and pious thought"). A careful comparison of the various recensions of the Greek text, the tenor of the old Latin version, and the variant construction in a different Latin version that is incorporated into the Vulgate, shows that two contradictory reflections, both of which break the flow of the text, have been more or less skillfully linked to the general context. One of these glosses reflected the thinking of the Sadducees, who did not accept the resurrection, the other the thinking of the Pharisees, who did believe in it. But even if we suppress these two glosses, the narrator still praises (though in a less enthusiastic style) the initiative taken by Judas and the thinking that inspired it.

CONCLUSION

I have heard Dom Botte express the view, on this very spot, that the liturgy is a counterbalance and almost an antidote to an excessively conceptual theology. Allow me to alter these terms slightly and speak instead of a counterpoint, thus emphasizing the hidden harmony rather than the seeming opposition.

The liturgy and, more broadly, the traditional rites may contain values which a more rational theory has not yet fully grasped or is no longer able to express. Under the old covenant, burial customs or stereotyped formulas in hymns (such formulas as "bring down to Sheol and bring up again") gave rise to an unexpressed conviction that everything did not end with death; that the living remained in communion with the dead; that God could raise up those now sleeping in the tomb.

When faith in the resurrection developed, when the almost invisible bud had opened and shown what it contained, then the ancestral practices acquired a new extension. People became concerned to restore the order upset by the sins of the dead, not only in order that the latter might enjoy rest in their dismal bed or that the repercussions of their sins might no longer affect the living, but also that the dead might reach the resurrection promised to the just. Prayer for the dead gathers up in itself, and transfigures, the heritage of a distant past, a heritage never completely rejected, despite some partial reservations (Lv 19:27–28; Dt 14:1; 26:14). When the Christians of Corinth had themselves baptized in place of the dead, they were continuing or bringing back a tradition the traces of which can be seen throughout the entire Old Testament (1 Cor 15:29). They were bearing unconscious witness to the reality of the resurrection which some among them were denying.

DUBARLE

Alexis KNIAZEFF

The Death of a Priest According to the Slavic Trebnik

The present liturgical practice of the Slavic Churches of the Byzantine Rite, and that of the Russian Orthodox Church in particular, has four distinct funeral offices: for laypersons, for monks, for children under 7 years, and for priests. The service for the funeral of a priest is the longest of the four, as well as the one with the fullest content from a theological standpoint. The reason for this is that in the office for the funeral of a priest the Trebnik has brought together and expressed, sometimes with great literary artistry, its ideas not only on the death of priests but also on death in general. The subject of my study will be this office for the funeral of a priest. I shall analyze its liturgical structure and the religious content of the various units that make it up; some of these units are to be found in the various offices of the dead, but many others appear only in this particular office. I shall then turn to the doctrinal content of this very lengthy liturgical function, which certain Churches of the Byzantine Rite, among them the Russian Orthodox

Church, now celebrate when a priest dies and the community commits his body to the earth.

I

In using the phrase "doctrinal content," I wish to remind the reader that this office is a relatively recent creation. Only in the fourteenth century did the Byzantine liturgy introduce a funeral rite that is special to priests. Prior to that period the Byzantine liturgical documents had no such office, just as they had no special funeral rite for laypersons, monks, or small children. They had only one funeral service that was used for all categories of deceased persons that in many respects was very like our present funeral office for monks. Apart from this common service there were prayers geared to each category of deceased persons: monks, laypersons, priests, bishops, small children. These texts would be inserted into the common office, thus relating it to the particular category of person whose funeral was being celebrated.

A specific funeral service for laypersons appeared in the Church of Constantinople in the fourteenth century. Funeral services for priests and for children under 7 years are found only from the fifteenth century on.[1] The situation was the same in the Russian Church: in the beginning there was only one office, the one for monks, which also served as a common office for all the deceased; a special rite for priests appeared among the Russians only in the fifteenth century and one for small children only in the sixteenth.[2] It was the same in the Church of Georgia, but the rise of special funeral rites for various categories of the deceased is a much more recent phenomenon there: until the seventeenth century, Georgian liturgical documents showed only one office, which was entitled: "Office to be celebrated at the funeral of a deceased person," and the four distinct offices we know today appeared only at the end of the seventeenth century.[3]

I shall not go into detail regarding the historical development of the office, but shall be satisfied to refer the reader to the authoritative work of V. Bruni.[4] Here I shall say only that in my opinion the funeral office for priests was first composed at Constantinople during the patriarchate of Philotheus. This patriarch, who held the see of Constantinople from 1354 to 1355 and then again from 1362 to 1376, and who canonized Gregory Palamas, is known to be the author not only of theological and exegetical works but of liturgical works as well.[5] Moreover, in the time of Philotheus, Byzantium, now close to its end, experienced a final renewal that manifested itself in the areas of spirituality, thought, and the arts, and in the area of liturgical creation.

KNIAZEFF

As far as the Russian Church is concerned, it is possible to say with certainty that the adoption of a special office for the funerals of priests was connected with the liturgical activity of Metropolitan Cyprian. Cyprian occupied the primatial see of Russia from 1380 to 1406 and was canonized by the Russian Church in 1472. He was a disciple, friend, and protégé of Philotheus, who ordained him a bishop, and he contributed greatly to the shift of the Russian Church from the Typikon of Constantinople to that of Jerusalem. He also contributed greatly to the revision of the Russian liturgical books and personally emended certain akolouthias (offices) of the Sluzebnik and the Trebnik by harmonizing them with Greek and Eastern practice, for one of his special concerns was precisely to bring the Russian books into agreement with those received from the East, and to bring the various rites into conformity with the prescriptions of the Typikon of Jerusalem.[6]

Let me say simply that once the special office for priests had appeared, it went through several redactions or variants both at Constantinople and in Russia. It also contained some rites that no longer exist today. Thus a Greek redaction of the fifteenth century provides for a deceased priest the ceremony of *enthronion*, which has survived only in the rite for the funerals of Eastern patriarchs. Another Greek redaction of the fifteenth century prescribes an akolouthia which comprises the reading of the Hexapsalm,[7] the singing of troparia, antiphons, and stichera from St. John Damascene, the singing of Psalm 118 (kathism 117), and the chanting of the ikoi, with fourteen gospel pericopes (twelve of them from the passion narratives) being scattered throughout. The same redaction then prescribes the celebration of the eucharist, during which there is a fifteenth reading from the gospel; finally, to the singing of the great canon of St. Andrew of Crete, the body is carried in procession to the grave where a sixteenth passage from the gospel is read.

Another Greek redaction, this one of the sixteenth century, provides a celebration which, like the redaction just described, seems bent on imitating the structure of the Office of the Sacred Passion, that is, the orthros for Great Friday. For in this Greek redaction, we find the orthros with the singing of the entire psalter, kathism 177, some antiphons, stichera of St. John Damascene for the eight modes, and a reading of eight epistles and eight gospels. After the eighth gospel reading the deceased is given the final kiss; then at the grave there is a ninth reading from the gospel, this one on the resurrection of Lazarus.[8]

In the Russian Church, too, the service went through several redactions prior to the office as we now have it. These differed from the Greek redactions only in the number of kathisms, stichera, and troparia. The only important difference is one of ritual action: into the hands of the deceased was put a prayer which asked for absolution from his sins and listed a vast number of names of angels whose intercession was sought. The office we use today appeared in the Trebnik of Peter Mogila, Metropolitan of Kiev (seventeenth century) and has not varied since then.

In the present-day Trebnik, the title of the rite is "Funeral Office for a Deceased Priest." According to this title and according to current practice, this office is sung only when the deceased had been a diocesan priest; priest-monks, higoumenoi, and archimandrites are buried in conformity with the funeral rite for monks. Russian practice, however, probably because of the imposing solemnity that is one of the striking traits of the office for the funeral of a priest, has retained this office for the burial of bishops as well, even though in the Russian Church the latter are all monks.

The Trebnik of Peter Mogila also prescribes this office for the funerals of deacons, but the Holy Synod of the Russian Church has not followed him and on several occasions has expressly excluded deacons from among those for whom this office is to be celebrated. Deacons are to be buried with the rite proper to laypersons.[9] The Synod has justified its position by referring to the content of the office for priests' funerals, since in several places, especially in the stichera of Lauds, this office presents the person for whom it is being sung as a sacrificer and celebrant of the sacred mysteries; such language evidently is not appropriate for deacons. Nowadays, however, it is possible to celebrate this office for the funeral of a deacon, if the dead man had requested it and if the bishop of the diocese authorizes it.[10]

A special problem arises in the case of priests who have lapsed or who have been put under interdict or been suspended for disciplinary reasons: Which rite should be used for their burial? In this connection the Holy Synod has developed an extensive legislation which is expounded in detail in Boulgakov's great manual[11] and which contains in essence the following prescriptions. If the deceased had been put under an interdict or incurred a temporary suspension and if he repented of his sin but then died before the required time of punishment was complete, he can be buried according to the rite for priests; if he had been reduced to the lay state without incurring an excommunication, he is to be buried as a layperson; if he was about to be tried for a sin entailing a possible reduction to the lay state, he is to be buried as a layman, even if his death occurred before sentence has been pronounced by the ecclesiastical authority competent to try and judge his case.

Now then, what is the order followed in the funeral of a priest according to the present Trebnik? What are the various components of the office to be sung on this occasion?

II

The present Slavo-Russian office takes the form of a double Byzantine pannychis[12] and ends as an orthros for days with no feast. The text of the office is preceded by rubrics which give instructions on preparing for burial the body of a priest who has just died. Three priests take the body from the bed and extend it on the ground on a blanket of some kind. Whereas the body of a deceased layperson is washed, that of a priest is to be anointed with a simple oil. After the anointing the body is clad in ordinary clothes, new ones if possible, since the deceased is called to put on incorruptibility (1 Cor 15:53). Then all the priestly vestments are put on the body, to indicate that the man must appear before God as a priest and, as such, render an account of the mission entrusted to him. The body is then placed on a funeral couch; in the dead man's hands a book of the gospels is placed and, in Russia, a crucifix as well. If the man had been a bishop, the clothing of the body is accompanied by the singing of the verses used in the vesting of a bishop for the celebration of the eucharistic liturgy. When the clothing of the deceased bishop is completed, the *dikirotrikira* (candlestick with five candles) is placed in one of his hands, and with the other he is made to give a final blessing. Instead of the usual *eis polla etē despota* (May you have many years, your Lordship), those present then sing: "Eternal remembrance!"

The face of the dead man, be he priest or bishop, is then covered with the aer, that is, the large liturgical cloth used for covering both the discus and the paten at the end of the proskomide. This veil is not to be removed again; the dead man remains with face covered during the entire funeral service, and he is buried with the veil in place. According to a pious custom of which the rubrics say nothing, a band is placed around the dead man's head (as it is around the head of everyone who dies) which bears a little image of the Savior with his Mother and the Precursor at his side. The band also has the words of the Trisagion written on it: "Holy God, Holy Strong One, Holy Immortal One." Popular devotion sees this band as symbolizing the fact that the dead man belongs to Jesus Christ.

After this the funeral vigil begins, during which various pannychides are sung beside the body, these consisting chiefly in an uninterrupted reading of the gospel.[13] St. Symeon of Thessalonika sees in this reading an appeal for divine mercy on the deceased person, for, he says, "what other sacrifice is better suited for calling down divine mercy on the deceased than that which is the object of the gospel message?"[14]

On the day of the funeral, the body is taken out to the singing of a litia. This litia is the same for all the deceased. It includes the Trisagion, the Lord's Prayer, and the following troparia: "In your place of rest, O Lord," "With the spirits of the departed just," and "You are the God who went down into the abode of the dead," followed by their theotokion, "Virgin who alone is pure and spotless." The litia also includes a diaconal ectenie, followed by the prayer, "God of spirits and of all flesh," an ancient prayer that can be found in Goar and that makes its first appearance in the sixth century.[15]

After the litia the body is carried to the Church, to the singing not of the Trisagion (as in the case of laypersons) but of the hirmoi of the great canon of St. Andrew of Crete. The rubrics prescribe that the body is to be brought into the narthex of the church (*en tō nartheki tou naos*) and that the holy gospel is to be placed on it. Does this rubric imply that the office is to be celebrated in the narthex? In his *Manual*, Nikolsky says that the rubric means only that the procession stops in the narthex, where the book of the gospels is to be placed again in the dead man's hands, as it had been when he was clothed for burial.[16] The funeral office, then, is to be sung in the church proper. It is almost always preceded by the celebration of the eucharist.

As I said above, this office begins with a kind of double pannychis. The first is represented by Psalm 117 ("Blessed are they whose way is blameless"), which is divided into three stanzas. The verses of the first and third stanzas are accompanied by the singing of the Alleluia, those of the second stanza by "Have mercy on your servant." After the first and second stanzas, the ectenie and the prayer "God of spirits" are repeated. After the third, this ectenie and prayer are preceded by the singing of the usual troparia for the dead, along with the verse "Blessed are you, O Lord, teach me your precepts." They are followed by the troparion "Grant rest, O Lord" and its theotokion "You who sprang from the Virgin as a light for the world," which is also to be found in the funeral office for the laity.

The second pannychis has a more complicated structure. It is composed of psalms, antiphons, troparia, kathisms, and prayers. The whole is interspersed with five groups of readings, each containing an epistle and a gospel. Here is the order of the whole.

1. Each epistle is preceded by a prokimenon and followed by the singing of the Alleluia with verses from the psalms.

2. Before the second epistle there is a kathism and a psalm.

3. The first epistle is also preceded by troparia and gradual antiphons.

4. Before the third epistle there are again antiphons, a psalm, a troparion, and a kathism.

5. Before the fourth epistle, in addition to the prokimenon there are antiphons, a psalm, and troparia.

6. Before the fifth epistle there is the singing of the beatitudes with troparia, and after the fifth gospel Psalm 50 is read. In other words: (a) antiphons are sung: in the sixth mode before the first epistle, in the second mode before the third epistle, and in the third mode before the fourth epistle; (b) Psalm 22 is read before the second epistle, Psalm 23 before the third, and Psalm 83 before the fourth (the verses of these psalms are accompanied by the Alleluia); Psalm 50 is read after the fifth gospel.

7. After the first, second, and fourth gospel readings a prayer is said. The prayer differs each time and is not the usual "God of spirits."

8. Here are the five groups of readings: (a) 1 Thessalonians 4:13–17 and John 5:24–30; (b) Romans 5:12–21 and John 6:17–24; (c) 1 Corinthians 15:1–11 and John 6:35–39; (d) 1 Corinthians 15:20–28 and John 6:40–47; (e) Romans 14:6–9 and John 6:48–54.

The entire collection of antiphons, troparia, psalms, kathisms, and prayers is divided in a seemingly arbitrary way by these five groups of readings. This would indicate that they were inserted at a later date. After Psalm 50 the office takes on the structure of an ordinary Byzantine orthros, that is, the one sung for memorials that are not of a festive character.

Psalm 50 is in fact followed by the canon. Odes 1, 4, 5, 7, 8, and 9 are sung according to the hirmoi of the canon in the orthros for Great Saturday, while the hirmoi for odes 3 and 6 are taken from the canon in the sixth mode that is usually sung for the deceased. The sixth ode is followed by the kontakion for all offices of the deceased: "With your saints grant rest, O Christ." But in the funeral office for priests, this kontakion is accompanied by twenty-four ikoi, just as in the days when the kontakion had not yet been supplanted by the canon. This is the only place in the present Byzantine liturgy where the kontakion still retains its ancient form.

After the third, sixth, and ninth odes of the canon, the ectenie for the deceased and the prayer "God of spirits" are repeated. Then comes the exapostillarion, which is sung with verses from Psalm 102. The office continues with the psalms of Lauds, Psalms 148, 149, and 108, which come at this point in every Byzantine orthros.

Between the verses of the last of these three psalms the stichera for Lauds are intercalated; they are sung in the sixth mode. There are three stichera, followed by a theotokion and "Glory to the Father. . . . Now. . . ." The great doxology which follows is read and not sung, as it is especially every day of Passion Week, with the exception of Great Saturday. The doxology ends with the prayer "Make us worthy, Lord, to remain without sin this day"; this too is a regular prayer in a nonfestive orthros. The ectenie and the prayer "God of spirits" are then said again. After this, still as in the manner of the orthros, comes the singing of the stichera with aposticha.

The verses sung with these stichera are taken from Psalms 22, 119, 120, 121, 122, and 83, some of which have been sung during the antiphonal part (second pannychis). As for the stichera themselves, their place is taken by the idiomela in the eight modes by St. John Damascene. Whereas in other funeral offices there is only one idiomelon for each mode, in the office for priests we find for each mode a group of two and sometimes three idiomela, which end at the "Glory to the Father" with a theotokion in the same mode. These eight sets of idiomela are followed by a ninth group of stichera; this group includes three stichera in the eighth mode, one in the sixth at the "Glory to the Father," and a theotokion in the same mode at "Now. . . ."

Just as at the orthros, after the aposticha there is a recital of the Trisagion and Our Father, which are preceded by a proclamation of the verse "It is good to confess the Lord. . . ." The troparia are sung, "Lord, give your servant repose with the just," with at the "Glory to the Father" another, "Lord, in our place of rest," and at the "Now and for ever" the theotokion, "Mother of ineffable Light, we praise you with angelic songs and devoutly honor you." Then for the last time in the part of the office that is celebrated in the church, the ectenie for the dead and the prayer "God of spirits" are repeated. Then the congregation passes before the coffin for the ritual of farewell while the stichera are sung that accompany this rite in every funeral service, "Come and give deceased a final kiss." The office ends like all funeral offices with the prayer of absolution, the dismissal, and the singing of "Eternal remembrance."

The body is then carried in procession to the cemetery, while the hirmoi of the great canon of St. Andrew of Crete are sung. Generally, the procession circles a church, either the one in which the funeral office was celebrated, or the one near the cemetery. The manner of interment is the same as for the laity: a litia is sung, the body is lowered into the hole, the ashes from the censer are emptied into the grave, and the first shovelsfull of earth are thrown. Only the funeral rite for monks has kept the ancient custom of pouring oil on the body of the deceased before it is covered with earth.

Such is the makeup and structure of this grandiose celebration, the office for the funeral of a priest according to the Trebnik. By way of summary, I shall outline this office as a seven-part entity:

1. *Psalm 118*, divided into three stanzas and followed by the usual troparia for the dead; each stanza is followed by an ectenie and the prayer "God of spirits" (first pannychis).

2. The *antiphonal section* (second pannychis):

VERSES	PSALMS	READINGS
antiphons (3 special prayers)	22	1 Thes 4:13–17; Jn 5:24–30
troparia	23	
kathisms	83	Rom 5:12–21; Jn 5:17–24
Beatitudes	50	1 Cor 15:1–11; Jn 6:35–39
		1 Cor 15:20–28; Jn 6:40–47
		Rom 14:6–9; Jn 6:48–54

3. *Canon* with ectenie and prayer "God of spirits" at the third and sixth odes and after the ninth ode. After the sixth ode, *kontakion* for the deceased, followed by twenty-four strophes or ikoi. After the ninth ode an *exapostillarion*.

4. *Lauds*, with Psalms 148, 149, 108 and *stichera*; the *doxology*, "Make us worthy, Lord," ectenie, and prayer "God of spirits."

5. The *aposticha*: idiomela of St. John Damascene, stichera in the eighth mode, "Glory," and theotokion in the sixth mode.

6. *End of the office inside the church:* "It is good to confess," Trisagion, Lord's Prayer, troparia, ectenie, prayer "God of spirits," farewell to the deceased, singing of stichera, dismissal, "Eternal remembrance," absolution.

7. Procession, hirmoi of St. Andrew of Crete, interment.

Each of these seven parts, which are placed within the framework of the orthros, is composed in its turn of quite varied elements, some scriptural, others hymnographic. The office is therefore a very full one and lasts almost three hours, not including the time for the eucharistic liturgy that usually precedes it. It was evidently composed with the idea that it would be celebrated by a large body of clergy. And in fact it is almost always led by one or more bishops, who are surrounded by a large number of priests and deacons who have gathered to honor the deceased and conduct him to his final dwelling.

What is the theological content of this lengthy office? I shall
analyze the religious witness given by its various components,
beginning with the scriptural.

III

The biblical inspiration of an office finds expression in the choice
of readings during it as well as of the scriptural texts that are to be
proclaimed, sung, or chanted. It also finds expression in the
scriptural themes used in the hymnographic part of the office. In my
theological analysis of the funeral rite for priests, I shall examine
these themes along with the hymns, but shall limit myself here to
an analysis of the biblical texts included by the authors of the office.

The office has no Old Testament readings. It has, however, taken
many psalms from the Old Testament: either entire psalms or verses
that serve as prokimena to introduce the readings or as versicles to
introduce certain hymnographic texts. Some of these biblical texts
are also found in other offices for the dead, but some occur only in
the office for priests. I turn first to the verses from the psalms.

Some of these verses are also found in other funeral offices. Here
are the texts, which speak of the happiness of the elect, and the
blessedness of the just, but also sometimes contain a prayer of
petition[17]: Psalm 64: "Happy those whom you have chosen and
have taken, Lord; their memory abides from age to age" (v. 4);
Psalm 24: "Their souls shall dwell in happiness, their posterity shall
possess the earth" (vv. 13 and 1); Psalm 27: "I cry to you, O Lord;
be not deaf to my call" (v. 1).

These verses are sung during the antiphonal part, either as
prokimena to the epistles or at the Alleluia between the epistles and
the gospels. We should also note the prokimenon that is sung before
the first epistle and that is found in all funeral offices. It is not a
textual citation from a psalm, but rather a composition using the
language and imagery of the psalms. Here is a translation of it:
"Blessed is the way you follow today, O soul, for the Lord has
prepared a place of rest for you. Turn, my soul, to your rest, for the
Lord has prepared happiness for you."[18]

This composition helps us grasp the manner and meaning of the
use of psalm texts in the office for the deceased. These texts contain
images which serve as a kind of language enabling the authors of
the Trebnik to depict life beyond the grave and express what faith
permits the follower of Christ to expect after death. The repose and
happiness of the just, of which the Old Testament speaks, is a
distant prefiguration of the blessedness of the just in the kingdom of
Christ, a kingdom which already manifests its power here below as
well as in death. The prayer of petition contained in Psalm 27:1 can

KNIAZEFF

be understood, in the office of the dead, as expressing the anxiety which even a believer sometimes feels at the thought of death; after all, Christ himself experienced this anxiety during this agony in Gethsemane. Generally speaking, however, the psalmic images used by the authors of the office show that these authors had a reassuring vision of the death of a Christian and especially of a priest.

This impression is confirmed and deepened if we move on to the psalm verses proper to the funeral office of a priest. Between the fourth epistle and the fourth gospel, Psalm 111:1–2 is sung at the Alleluia: "Happy the man who fears the Lord and greatly loves his commandments; his posterity on earth will be mighty." These two verses are appropriate because they evoke the future happiness of the Christian who fears God and also voice the hope that the labors of the zealous priest will be blessed with fruit after his death. The image of a posterity can be applied by the praying Church to the spiritual heritage of the dead man; the grace of the Holy Spirit will keep this alive among the people despite the departure of one whom death has withdrawn from the number of the living. The same Christian hope in the face of death finds expression in the verses chosen to be sung with the idiomela of St. John Damascene. Here are the verses:

For the stichera of mode 1: Psalm 22:1, "The Lord is my shepherd. . . ."

For the stichera of mode 2: Psalm 119:1, "I cry to the Lord when I am in distress. . . . Lord, rescue my soul from lying lips."

For the stichera of mode 3: Psalm 120:1, "I lift my eyes to the hills whence help comes to me"; v. 8: "He will keep you at your going and your coming, now and for ever."

For the stichera of mode 4: Psalm 121:1, "I rejoiced when they said to me: Let us go to the house of the Lord."

For the stichera of mode 5: Psalm 121:2, "We are here, our steps have halted in your precincts, O Lord."

For the stichera of mode 6: Psalm 122:1, "I have raised my eyes to you who abide in heaven."

For the stichera of mode 7: Psalm 83:1, "How desirable are your dwellings, O Lord of hosts."

For the stichera of mode 8: Psalm 83:2, "My soul sighs and languishes for your courts, O Lord."

The reader will observe that for the idiomela in modes 2 to 6, the verses are from Psalms 119 to 122, which are part of the group (Pss 119–133) known in the Psalter as "Songs of ascent" and which are pilgrimage songs. The choice of these psalms and of the verses from them show that the intention of the authors of the office is to remind the Christian and especially the faithful priest that the passage from life to death is an ascent to the Jerusalem on high, a journey to the truest of courts. On this journey the deceased is under the protection of him who sends genuine aid and who in particular can defend the soul against those with lying lips, that is, the demons.

For the stichera in modes 7 and 8, verses from Psalm 83 have been chosen; this too is a psalm of pilgrimage to Jerusalem. The images from it enable the authors of the office to say that the place where the soul of the deceased is called to dwell from now on is the true and desirable dwelling place: the presence of the Lord. Verse 1 of Psalm 22, chosen to be sung with the idiomela in mode 2, enables the authors of the office to say why this new dwelling is so desirable: the dead man, though he had been a pastor (shepherd) here on earth, was also and will continue to be under the protection of the Good Shepherd, the true Shepherd, and will therefore lack nothing.

Let me turn now from psalm verses that have been removed from their context, to an examination of the whole psalms which are used in the funeral office of priests. Here a distinction must be made: some psalms are in the office because they are part of the orthros, which provides the structure for this office. Others are found in all funeral offices and therefore are a characteristic part of every office for the dead. Finally, still others are, in the present liturgy, peculiar to the office for priests.

Psalms 148, 149, and 108, then, are in the funeral office simply because they are the psalms for Lauds and as such are an integral part of the orthros on nonfestive days and because this orthros provides the model for the funeral office of priests, at least after the antiphonal part of the latter. Psalm 50, which ends this part, has been kept for two reasons: in every orthros it precedes the singing of the canon, and it is also found in all funeral offices. In a funeral office it serves to remind us that every Christian is called to examine his conscience before death and that all prayer for the deceased is necessarily penitential prayer. The psalm can be thought of as recited by the deceased person for himself and by the community that prays with and for the deceased.[19]

The funeral office for a priest, like the other funeral offices, also uses Psalm 117: "Blessed they whose way is spotless," a psalm which forms the eighteenth kathism, that is, the eighteenth of the twenty liturgical sections into which the Byzantine psalter is divided. The psalm is also part of the parastasis, a special orthros in memory of the dead, which is sung especially on the Saturday before

Carnival Sunday[20] and the Saturday before Pentecost Sunday. It is also in the orthros for Great Saturday, where the singing of its verses is accompanied by the troparia glorifying the death and burial of Christ, proclaiming his descent to Sheol, and announcing his resurrection as imminent. This psalm has been traditional in funeral offices since before the fourteenth century.[21]

The psalm glorifies the divine law and those who obey its precepts, bearing witness by their love of the law and its precepts to their love for God himself. In the orthros of Great Saturday, it must be related to Christ who came to fulfill the Law and bore witness to his love for the Father by obeying him unto death, even a death on a cross (Phil 2:5–10). As used in Christian funerals, this psalm, which is accompanied by the Alleluia and "Have mercy on your servant," can be interpreted as a eulogy for a faithful Christian and in particular a Christian who is entering the church for the last time in order there to take leave of the earthly community that has gathered to help him with its prayers as he enters a new existence where he will await the resurrection. In this context, then, Psalm 117 provides an image of the baptized person, who is called upon to be like Christ in his obedience to the Father's will. The psalm also recalls the ideal of holiness that every Christian should have and that will serve as the norm in deciding his lot throughout eternity.

The psalms which in the present-day Byzantine funeral liturgy are found only in the office for priests are grouped in the antiphonal part of this office. I have described this part as a second pannychis because, like the first part (which is made up of Psalm 118), it follows the structure of the traditional Constantinopolitan pannychis, which is a set of psalms, hymns, readings, and prayers. The psalms in the antiphonal part of this office have therefore evidently been chosen as giving expression through their images to a theology of death in general and a theology of the death of a priest in particular.

If we leave aside Psalm 50, which I have already discussed, the psalms of this second pannychis are three: Psalms 22, 23, and 83. I indicated earlier that Psalms 22 and 83 also provide verses to be sung with some of the idiomela in the aposticha. Psalm 22 is the Good Shepherd psalm: "The Lord is my shepherd, I shall want for nothing; he makes me lie down in fields of green grass, to waters of rest he leads me. . . ." It is from this psalm that the liturgy borrows most of the images which depict the place of the just after death as a place of rest, refreshment, and delight.

Psalm 23 is a liturgy for entry into the sanctuary: "The Lord's is the earth and its fullness, the world and those who dwell in it. . . . Who shall ascend the mountain of the Lord and dwell in his holy place? The one with innocent hands and pure heart. . . . Who is the king of glory? The Lord of hosts is the king of glory."[22] This psalm, then, reminds us that in the case of a Christian and especially of a priest, the passage from life to death can be interpreted as his entry into the heavenly sanctuary. As for Psalm 83, of which I spoke earlier and which begins with the words: "How desirable are your dwellings, O Lord," this is a song for pilgrimage to Jerusalem. In the context of the present office, it repeats and develops the theme of ascent to the heavenly sanctuary, which has been enunciated in Psalm 23.

The opening words of Psalm 23: "The Lord's is the earth and its fullness," can be understood in the context of a Christian funeral as words that solemnize the return to earth of one who had originally been taken from it.[23] However, the three psalms, in the context of the funeral of a priest, serve to recall that the dead man had himself been a shepherd, that he too used to enter the temple of the Lord and ascend to the sanctuary, and that for these reasons the Church is entitled to ask the Good Shepherd to admit him to a place of rest and refreshment and allow him to go on glorifying God, but now in the true sanctuary, the sanctuary of heaven. In any case, the three psalms reinforce the image of the next life that has already emerged from the psalm verses sung as prokimena or with the stichera: the image of life after death as a desirable place, a dwelling for which the soul of every Christian and especially the soul of a priest must long. Let me note here that the funeral office for a priest, and in fact all the funeral offices in the Trebnik, avoid using psalms which speak of the Old Testament Sheol and describe man's dwelling after death as a pit, a land of oblivion, a place from which all hope has been banished.[24]

The New Testament readings specify still further the vision of the glory which Christ's death and resurrection makes possible for believers after death. As we saw earlier, the office has five epistles and five gospels, all grouped together in the antiphonal part. The first epistle is 1 Thessalonians 4:13–17, where St. Paul instructs Christians on the fate of the deceased and offers them reassurance, so that they will not be saddened as the pagans are. He proclaims the resurrection of the dead but also speaks of a mysterious taking up of Christians into the clouds at the second coming of Christ. The second epistle, Romans 5:12–21, draws a parallel between the first man and Christ and contrasts the fateful deed of the first Adam with the superabundant reparation made by the last Adam (vv. 15–19); the latter is now head of a new race, and in and through him God restores his creation.

The third epistle is 1 Corinthians 15:1–11, where St. Paul speaks of the resurrection of Christ as the foundation for Christian faith in the resurrection of the dead, and lists the various witnesses from whom he knows of the appearances of the risen Jesus. In 1 Corinthians 15:20–28, which is the fourth epistle, St. Paul presents Christ as the first fruits of all who have fallen asleep, and proclaims that the last enemy, death, will likewise be conquered; after that the Son will hand over the kingdom to the Father, and God will be all in all. The fifth epistle is Romans 14:6–9. Here, on the basis of the vision of hope that is opened up to us by the resurrection of Christ and his victory over death, a kind of practical conclusion is drawn about the way Christians should regard their mortal state on this earth: "If we live, we live to the Lord, and if we die, we die to the Lord; so then, whether we live or whether we die, we are the Lord's. For to this end Christ died and lived again, that he might be Lord both of the dead and of the living" (vv. 8–9).[25]

The gospel readings are also explicit on the subject of Christian hope with regard to death and resurrection. All the readings are taken from chapters 5 and 6 of the gospel of St. John. The first pericope to be read is John 5:24–30. Here Jesus says that those who believe in the Father as he calls them through his Son have a share in the divine life and that the eschatological judgment will not touch them; then, while making resurrection in its essence (participation in divine life) a reality here and now, he also retains the perspective of resurrection as attaining its full form on the last day. The second gospel is John 5:17–24. Here Jesus says: "My Father is working still, and I am working." He locates his own activity on the same level as the Father's and within the Father's unceasing activity as he brings the world to its consummation. Christ is implicitly presenting his own work as a work of new creation. He also says that the works of his public life will be surpassed by those connected with the paschal event, namely, judgment and the gift of eternal life that is climaxed by the resurrection of the dead (vv. 20–24).

In the third gospel reading, John 6:35–39, Jesus says that he is the bread of life because he bestows true life, and that to believe in him is therefore to share in true life. But while emphasizing a present sharing of heavenly blessings, Jesus continues to maintain firmly (in vv. 38–39) a properly eschatological perspective and, more particularly, the expectation of the resurrection of the dead. John 6:40–47, which is the fourth gospel pericope, continues to develop the themes of the bread of life and eternal life. It adds a further detail: it is the Father who by his action directs the disciples to the one in whom resurrection from the dead and the fullness of revelation are to be had (vv. 43–44). Finally, the fifth gospel, John 6:48–54, speaks expressly of the sacrament of the eucharist. It also reminds us that the Son of Man comes from heaven and returns there and that those who cleave to him through faith and through participation in the sacrament of his flesh and blood will share in the Son of Man's heavenly life. The principle proclaimed here is that the eucharist is the leaven of resurrection for believers.

The message of the gospel pericopes, then, is the same as that of the epistles: the resurrection of the dead and eternal life. But while the epistles stress more the foundation, namely, the resurrection of Christ himself, the gospels remind us that eternal life is already at work in the faithful because of their faith and their sharing in the eucharist. There is thus a bond between Christ and the believer and especially between Christ and his priest who presides over the celebration of the sacrament of the flesh and blood of the Word made man. It is entirely fitting in an office of Christian burial and especially of the burial of a man whose mission was to proclaim the gospel and celebrate the eucharist, that emphasis should be put on the New Testament message regarding the union which redemption and the sacraments establish between Christ and those who believe in him. Even death cannot destroy this union, which is a pledge of glorious resurrection for all who fall asleep in Christ.

Such is the biblically inspired religious content of this office. How does it find expression in the various components of the office?

IV

First of all, how is the biblical message of victory over death translated into prayers? The office contains four prayers. The first is repeated over and over; the other three are not repeated at all.

The first prayer occurs in the other funeral offices beside the one for priests, as well as in all the akolouthias for the deceased.[26] It begins with the words: "God of spirits and of all flesh." It is found in the common funeral rite for all the dead which dates from before the fourteenth century; Father Bruni recently showed that the prayer was already in use in the sixth century.[27] It asks for the soul of the deceased the forgiveness of sins and rest in a place of light, refreshment, and peace; it is addressed to Christ as conqueror of death and destroyer of the devil's power. It appeals to the fact that all men are sinners ("No human being is without sin") and contrasts man in his fallen state with Christ who alone is without sin. It invokes the goodness of Christ and his love for human beings and ends with a euphonesis that emphasizes the bond established by Christ's resurrection between the Son of God and the deceased: "For you, Christ our God, are the resurrection, the life, and the repose of your deceased servant. We give you glory. . . ." This prayer is thus of interest not only for its antiquity but also for its theological witness. It makes clear that Christ's victory over death has changed the condition of the dead in the next life, and it expressly connects the resurrection of the Savior with the possibility for the living to pray efficaciously for the dead.

The other three prayers occur in the antiphonal part of the office, being said after the first, second, and third gospels respectively.[28] The first is addressed to God the Father and invokes him as author of the created world and providential organizer of it: "Master, Lord our God, who alone possess immortality, you live in inaccessible light; you slay and bring back to life; you lead down into the abode of the dead and back from it again. By your wisdom you created man and then cause him to return to the earth." The prayer then asks rest for the deceased: "Receive the soul of your servant and grant it rest in the bosom of Abraham, Isaac and Jacob. Give him the crown of your justice, the inheritance of the saved for the glory of your elect." It then gives the reason why the praying community believes itself justified in making this request for the deceased: ". . . in order that in your holy dwellings he may receive a rich reward for the goods he did on earth for your name's sake." This prayer thus uses the traditional imagery for life after death. It does not appeal to the resurrection of Christ as the basis for its request, nor does it contain a petition for the forgiveness of the dead man's sins. Rather it voices the hope that he will be welcomed into the repose of the Lord and receive the crown of justice as a reward for the deeds he did on earth for the glory of God.

The prayer said after the second gospel is a prayer of thanksgiving. It begins with the words: "We give you thanks, Lord our God, who alone possess immortal life. Your glory is unfathomable, your love for human beings ineffable, your lordship immutable." The prayer is found in manuscripts of the sixteenth century,[29] and it used to be added to the common office of the deceased when this was celebrated for a priest. It ends with the same euphonesis as the prayer "God of spirits."

Like the ordinary prayer for the dead, this one is addressed to Jesus Christ, who is the life, resurrection, and repose of his deceased servants. It mentions the fact that with absolute impartiality the Lord has set a limit to every human life, and it calls upon him to grant rest in the bosom of Abraham, Isaac, and Jacob to one whom it describes as a fellow celebrant of those who are gathered here and of those others who have died with the hope of resurrection to eternal life. Then it continues:

The Death of a Priest

"Just as here below you made him a priest of your Church, so make him a priest in your heavenly sanctuary, and since you bestowed a spiritual dignity on him here among his fellow human beings, receive him without condemnation into the glory of the angels. You yourself glorified him here on earth: grant now that his departure from this life may be an entrance into the dwelling place of your saints."

This prayer thus repeats the theme, which has been emphasized earlier and given expression with the help of texts from scripture, of the dead priest's call to glorify God in the heavenly sanctuary. It sees this call as a manifestation of divine mercy, for it was this mercy that made a celebrant here on earth of the man now being buried, and it is from this mercy that we ask for him the grace of being able to continue his ministry in heaven.

The third prayer, which is said after the third gospel, is likewise one of the prayers which, before the fourteenth century, used to be introduced into the common funeral rite for all the deceased when this was sung at the funeral of a priest.[30] It too ends with the same euphonesis as the prayer "God of spirits," namely: "for you, Christ our God, are the resurrection, the life, and the repose of your deceased servant, N. We give you glory. . . ." It too, then, is addressed to the Second Person of the Blessed Trinity. It is shorter than the others, and I give it here in its entirety:

"Lord of hosts, consoler of those who mourn, defender of those who are prostrated, console in your goodness those who are captives of their sorrow for the deceased. Heal all the pain in their hearts. Grant rest in the bosom of Abraham to your servant, N. the priest, who has fallen asleep in hope of the resurrection to eternal life. For you are the resurrection, the life, and the repose. . . ."

This prayer, which asks not only repose for the dead man's soul but also consolation for those who are afflicted by his departure, is the last in the group of prayers proper to the funeral office of a priest.[31] While not losing sight of the resurrection of all the dead, these prayers lay greater emphasis on the lot of the deceased in the next life. They express hope that this lot will be a happy one. The hope in turn is based on Christ's victory over Sheol, on God's mercy, on the good deeds done by the deceased during his earthly life in the service of God, and on the fact that here below the grace of priesthood had established a union with spiritual realities, that is, realities of heavenly origin.

But as in every Byzantine office, so in the funeral office for a priest the hymnographic component is by far the most dominant one. What religious testimony does the latter offer?

V

The number of hymnographic texts in the office we are studying
is an especially large one. Moreover, the hymnography belongs to
very diverse hymnographic genres and categories. There are
troparia, stichera, antiphons, kathisms, and compositions in the
genres of canon and kontakion. At the same time, however, a good
number of these texts are also found in other funeral offices. This is
true of the following compositions:

1. The *troparia of the litia,* namely, "With the spirits of the just,"
"In your place of rest, O Lord," and "You are the God who went
down into the place of the dead." These troparia assert that
happiness in the next life has become possible thanks to Christ's
descent into Sheol for the purpose of breaking the chains of those
imprisoned there. The theotokion that ends these troparia ("Virgin,
who alone are pure and spotless") attests that the Mother of God is
able to pray for the dead just as she prays for the living. This theme
is implicit in all the theotokia of the office.

2. The *troparia following Psalm 118* and the singing of which is
accompanied by repetition of the verse "Blessed are you, Lord; teach
me your precepts." The troparia are: "The choir of saints has
discovered the fountain of life," "You who have borne witness to
the divine Lamb," "You who have followed the narrow way," and
"I am the image of your ineffable glory even though I carry the
wounds of my sins." These troparia are remarkable for their
theology of man and death. They recall the creation of man in
God's image, the fall of man which is the cause of death, man's
restoration in Christ, and man's heavenly calling. They speak also of
the happiness of the saints who shine as stars in heaven. They
emphasize the power of the martyrs to pray for deceased Christians,
a theme developed by the Oktoechos in the offices of Saturday.
Finally, they ask the Holy Trinity to save from the eternal fire both
the deceased person for whom prayers are being offered and those
who are gathered to pray for him.

3. Certain *kathisms,* as, for example, "Grant rest with the just";
these repeat themes emphasized in the troparia and in the various
prayers of the office.

4. The *kontakion:* "With the saints grant rest, O Christ, to the soul
of your servant, in that world where there is no sickness or sadness
but only unending life."

This kontakion, with the ikos that follows it, is already found in
the common office for the dead as celebrated in the fourteenth
century.[32] Here is a translation of the ikos: "You alone are immortal
who created and made man. We are earthly, having been made of
earth, and we must return to the earth as ordained by him who

formed me and said: 'Earth you are and to earth you shall return.' We shall all return to it, for we are human, we who raise the funeral lament: Alleluia, Alleluia, Alleluia."

While the funeral offices for the laity, for monks, and for small children contain only the kontakion and the ikos, in the funeral office for priests these two compositions are followed by twenty-four further strophes containing a poetic meditation on death. I shall return below to the religious content of these strophes.

5. The *first sticheron in each of the eight modes* in the important set of idiomela that come from St. John Damascene. I shall speak of these again when I present the theological content of the whole set.

6. The *farewell stichera to the deceased,* twelve in all, followed by a thirteenth at "Glory to . . ." and by a theotokion at "Now and for ever. . . ." Here is a translation of the first of these hymnographic texts:

"Come, brothers and sisters, let us embrace the deceased with a final kiss, while thanking God. He [whom we embrace] has left those near and dear and is hastening to the grave. No longer does he remember the vanities [of this world] nor the flesh with its throng of passions. Where now are his relatives and friends? Behold, we are leaving. Let us pray the Lord to grant him rest."

The remaining stichera take up the same themes and develop them with almost cruel realism as they confront us with the brutal fact of death and all that it entails: separation, decomposition of the human body, awareness of the transitoriness of all that men value here on earth, the soul's confusion as it leaves the body and enters a new world and a hitherto unexperienced kind of existence. The sticheron at the "Glory" presents a gripping of the person's last hour, the sorrow of his people, and his entry into a world in which greatness, power, strength, and wealth are valueless and the only things that count are the fruits of faith, hope, and charity, and the prayers of the brethren.

VI

In addition to these classical hymnic texts which are found in all the funeral offices currently used in the Churches of the Byzantine Rite, there is an abundance of other texts which are proper to the rite for priests. This literature, too, contains various hymnographic types. There are:

1. *Antiphons, troparia,* and *kathisms* peculiar to the antiphonal part of the office. The *antiphons,* which are called "gradual antiphons," contain penitential prayers addressed to the divine Word: "I raise my eyes to you, O Word; fill me with your rich blessings so that I

may live through you. Have mercy, O Word, on us who are laid low, and make of us instruments for a good purpose."

The second antiphon seems to be a prayer said in the name of the deceased who asks that the soul which has just left the body may be protected against demons: "Let their teeth not bite into my soul, O Word, as though it were a fledgling. Woe is me! How shall I escape the enemy, for I am a sinner?"

At the end of each group of antiphons there are hymns to the Holy Spirit at the "Glory" and the "Now and for ever." As in the Oktoechos, these hymns speak of the renovative action of the third person of the holy trinity: "The Holy Spirit has power to effect everything relating to salvation. If he breathes into someone, as he is said to do, he immediately raises his person from the earthly sphere, elevates him to heaven, transforms him completely, and establishes him in the heights." "Through the Holy Spirit comes the deification of all, the gift of understanding, peace and blessing. For in his action he is the equal of the Father and the Son."[33]

The *troparia* speak of man's mortal condition: a human being is but dust; death brings him rest; his life passes like a dream, like a sparrow taking flight, like a ship that leaves no mark behind it on the sea (first troparion, second mode). But we are dealing here in particular with a deceased priest. The man is considered to have in fact lived a life worthy of a priest in faith, hope, charity, and humility. For him, then, the living ask repose in a place brilliant with light and beauty (second troparion, second mode). Some troparia are also addressed by the dead man to his brothers and sisters on earth: "Beloved brothers and sisters, do not forget me when you sing to the Lord but remember that I am your brother. . . ."

Like the other hymnic texts of the office, the troparia also repeat and develop the theme of the suddenness of death and the pain caused by the separation which death inflicts.

The *kathisms*, whose presence, like that of the antiphons and the gospel readings, calls to mind the office of the Passion, likewise take up the themes of death's suddenness, the brutal nature of the separation (first kathism, second mode), and the fallen condition of man, who is born in sin (second kathism, fifth mode). They ask for the deceased that he have rest and the intercession of the Mother of God and the saints.

2. The *troparia sung with the Beatitudes:* by analogy with the other funeral offices but also in keeping with the model, that is, the office of the Passion (since the troparia with Beatitudes are here included in the antiphonal part which I have been calling a second pannychis), the funeral office for priests provides for the singing of

the Beatitudes together with troparia that are intercalated between the verses of the gospel text.

The troparia here are not the same as those in the other offices. On the other hand, they do not focus to any great extent on the death specifically of a priest. As in the other offices, the troparia develop the theme of the prayer of the good thief on the cross. They also recall the fall of Adam, man's mortal condition, the mystery of the creation of man, who is both earth and divine breath, and the mystery of salvation by which man is restored to his original integrity. They also describe the condition of the body of the deceased which lies in its coffin disfigured by corruption. But they also emphasize the point that death brings rest to man. Thus they depict the dead man as saying: "Human beings, why so greatly afflicted on my account, why this vain agitation? . . . Death brings rest to all. Listen to Job as he says: 'Death is man's rest.' O God, grant rest with your saints to him whom you have taken."

The theotokion that concludes the Beatitudes recalls the mystery of the incarnation, using the terms in the dogmatic formula of the Council of Chalcedon.

3. The *canon:* the only thing peculiar to it is the fact that the first, fourth, fifth, seventh, eighth, and ninth odes are sung according to the hirmoi of the canon for Great Saturday, "Through the sea wave." The third and sixth odes are sung according to the hirmoi of the usual canon for the deceased. In its content the canon focuses on death in general rather than on the death of a priest in particular. Thus odes 1 to 6 pray for the forgiveness of the deceased man's sins and make no reference to his priesthood; they ask that he be given rest with the elect and a share in the delights of paradise. Odes 7 and 8 describe Gehenna and contrast it with the land of happiness in which the gentle dwell. Ode 8 also describes the parousia. Ode 9 reminds us that the passion of Christ has freed human beings from affliction, but then it returns to the theme of the final judgment and stresses the need of appearing at that judgment with works done in charity, since these alone can help a human being before the fearful judgment seat of Christ by assuring him of the fraternal prayer of those around him when he was on earth. The ode ends with a description of the glory of the world to come.

4. The *twenty-four strophes or ikoi that follow the kontakion:* this is the most unusual component of the office, making the latter the only one in the present Byzantine Liturgy to have a kontakion in its original full form. Some attribute these twenty-four strophes to Romanus Melodus (Cyprien Kern in his unpublished course on the Trebnik). The Slavic Trebnik, as published by the monastery of Grottaferrata in 1945, attributes the composition to Anastasius the

Monk. Is the reference to the Anastasius who was a friend of
Maximus the Confessor and shared his exile in 653, as did another
Anastasius, known as Apocrisiarius, who was author of two letters
printed in the Greek Patrology of Migne (PG 90:133–36)? What is
the evidence that makes such an attribution possible? No answer is
offered to these questions.

Let me point out only that the composition is not alphabetical, a
fact which suggests that it is of Syrian rather than Greek origin. In
any case, it is a powerful work of great literary beauty and develops
with careful artistry the theme of man's anxiety in the face of death.
Death (there is no special focusing on the death of a priest) is here
represented as something inevitable which every human being
experiences and which confronts him with a new manner of
existence that is utterly beyond the ken of those who are still in the
present life. What, then (the author asks), will be the state of the
human person when he leaves behind his present life, his
possessions, his friends and relatives? Will he recognize those who
have gone before him into that new world? Will he be able to pray
with them and sing Alleluia? Is he sure of finding mercy in the next
life? Who will serve as his guide in that unknown country?

The author is aware that after death a human being cannot rely
on power or money or any of the other things that rendered earthly
life pleasant for him. Was he generous enough here below to the
outcasts of fortune, so that they might come to his aid in turn, in
the world to come? He sees with misgivings that death strikes
persons of every age, carrying off little children as well as old men
and women, youngsters as well as adults. The feeling of anxiety
deepens as the strophes succeed one another, but at the end
Christian hope suddenly bursts forth. The ikos at the "Glory to the
Father" ends thus: "We are fired with hope only when we hear that
yonder is the eternal light, yonder the source of our life, an eternal
heritage, a paradise that brings joy to every holy soul. Let us
therefore gather in Christ so that we may all cry Alleluia to God."

The theotokion that comes at "Now and for ever . . ." is
addressed to her who bore the inaccessible Light. It asks her to pray
unceasingly for the departed so that his sins may be forgiven on the
day of judgment.

5. The *exapostillarion,* which comes immediately after the canon,
is full of hope and consolation in the face of death. Here is what the
deceased man is depicted as saying (no indication is given of
whether the deceased is a priest or a layperson): "I have found rest,
I have been given a mighty deliverance, for I have passed from
corruption to incorruptibility and I have been transformed into a
living being. Glory to you, Lord!"

This hymn is repeated three times with the verses of Psalm 102. These verses emphasize the transience of earthly life and contrasts this with the permanence of the blessings to which divine mercy gives man access: "Man's days are like grass . . ."; "A wind passes over him and he is no more . . ."; "The truth of the Lord remains for ever. . . ."

The theotokion, which comes next, does not refer to the theme of death, but confesses the Mother of Christ as Mother of the Savior.

6. The *stichera of Lauds*. Together with the antiphons, these are the only component peculiar to this office that expressly speaks of the deceased as a priest. This statement applies especially to the third sticheron of this group. It is said there that the deceased was set apart by the priesthood; that the man being buried had been a priest, a sacrificer; that he had been called to offer the divine mysteries. The sticheron also says that it is by God's order that the man has left the things of earth and has gone to Christ, who is asked now to welcome him as a priest and grant him repose with the just.

The first two stichera of the group remind us that the death of the man being buried occurred at the command of God. They also remind us that we are all equal in the face of death: higoumenoi, scribes, doctors, bishops, or, in short, all who have been given the grace of priesthood in its very varied forms. Like the antiphons earlier, the stichera depict the distress of the soul of the deceased who, like a defenseless fledgling, asks God to accept him. Then the stichera hark back to another theme of the antiphons: in death the priest has been deified thanks to the life-giving mystery of Christ.

7. The *idiomela of St. John Damascene*. These were composed for all eight modes and are much more numerous here than in the other funeral offices, each mode being here represented not by a single sticheron but by two or three and by a theotokion. The idiomela repeat and develop all the themes dealing with death, most of which are to be found in the other hymnographic parts of the office. They speak of man's painful state during his life on earth: his life is short (mode 2); any joy felt during it is mingled with sadness (mode 1); everything here below is smoke, mist, and ashes (mode 4); and death makes us aware that we are nothing. The idiomela also recall the greatness of man as the creator intended him to be: a sharer in both the visible and invisible worlds; his body taken from the earth but his spirit breathed into him by God himself; placed by God over all earthly creatures and solely responsible for his own present condition of wretchedness; he has allowed himself to be led astray and to the food that leads to life he prefers the bitter food that leads to death (mode 7).

But according to the idiomela, death also has a comforting side, since it brings man repose, rescues him from the ills he suffers on earth, and can introduce him to the joy of contemplating the light that radiates from the face of Christ and of discovering his beauty (mode 1). These hymnic texts also stress the need of faith in Christ as Light from Light, true God, the one who came to save the human race (mode 5). Since Christ's coming, death has turned into a sleep; this change was already clear in connection with the resurrection of Lazarus (mode 1). The idiomela also speak once more of prayer for the deceased; such prayer has power to rescue the deceased from the fire, especially if it manifests the true love that never loses its vitality (mode 2).

It must be acknowledged, however, that despite these various motifs from Christian anthropology, the theology of salvation, and the theology of prayer, the dominant theme of these idiomela is the description of man's anxiety in the face of the death as the most important event in his existence. The anxiety arises because death comes suddenly and, without warning, snatches away someone from our midst (mode 2); it initiates a hitherto unknown kind of existence (mode 3); decomposition attacks the body, and no one can escape it, be he king or beggar (mode 5). The idiomela express surprise at this destruction of beauty that was created in the image and likeness of God, but at this point they remind us that divine mysteries are precisely divine in nature and they implicitly bid the Christian to submit humbly to God's decree (mode 8).

This important set of idiomela from the pen of St. John Damascene is followed by another small group of stichera. The group contains three stichera in the eighth mode, one in the sixth mode at "Glory to the Father," and a theotokion in the same mode at "Now and for ever." The theotokion asks that prayers for the deceased be offered not only to the Mother of Christ but also to St. John the Precursor, the prophets, the apostles, holy bishops, holy monks, the just, and all the saints. The stichera in the eighth mode present a picture of the parousia and the last judgment that emphasizes the torments awaiting those who have lived in lust and in the other sins. They also ask that he who became man for the salvation of human beings not condemn his deceased servant. The sticheron in the sixth mode repeats almost all the themes that have found expression in the hymnographic part of the office, and it further accentuates the *Dies irae* atmosphere:

"Come and contemplate this strange and terrible vision that is accessible to the minds of all, and cease to talk nonsense about beings that have but a short time to live. The image that is visible now is destroyed. Today the soul parts from the body and enters the world of eternity. It sets out on a road it never traveled before, a road leading to the judge who pays no heed to the outward face of human beings and who sits amid the angelic orders. Brothers and sisters, it is a fearful tribunal before which we must appear stripped of everything. Some will be given eternal life, others will know shame. Therefore let us pray to the eternal king: 'When you judge the hidden reality of man, have mercy on your servant whom you have just called back to yourself, O Lord who are friend to human beings!' "

VII

Such, then are the chief characteristics of the office whose theological content I am analyzing. In the form which it has in the present Trebnik, the funeral office for priests says rather little about the death of the priest as such. As the analysis makes clear, the death of a priest seems rather to provide the authors of the Trebnik with an opportunity for meditating on death in general.

It is possible to say that taken as a whole the office has two approaches to death. On the one hand, it represents death as having been conquered by Christ. This is the vision that emerges especially from the biblical message in the office. The hymnic texts pick it up and speak of death as leading not only to a glorious resurrection but also to a next world that is no longer Sheol but a place of rest, refreshment, and light, a place in which grace continues its work. This vision enables the Church to pray for the dead and to ask that Christ forgive their sins. The next world is also presented—thanks again to Christ's victory over death—as the place where the deceased will meet the angels and the glorified saints who, along with the Mother of God, add their prayers to those of the living for the person being buried. The office goes so far as to imply that in that new world, the deceased may be called even now to live in the presence of the glorified Christ; at least it speaks of a life lived in the light that streams from his face. All these comforting themes play an important role in the office. But it must be acknowledged that they do not play as extensive a role here as they do in the funeral office for monks.

But there is another vision of death in this office, a vision that emphasizes what I have been describing as the tragic aspect of death. This aspect appears in the greater part of the hymnic texts of this office. It can even be said that it is especially emphasized here as compared with the part it plays in the other funeral offices of the Trebnik. The office comes back a number of times to the fallen condition of the human being and to the moment of separation of soul from body; it expresses surprise at the destruction of beauty that had been created in the image and likeness of God (the idiomela). It also stresses the pain caused to the survivors by separation from their deceased and by the decomposition of the body in the grave; it frequently depicts the parousia, the last judgment, and eternal punishment.

This vision, distant alike from that given in the New Testament and that familiar to Christian antiquity, is not specific to the Byzantine and Byzantine-Slavic liturgies. It is also found in other liturgies and especially in the Roman Liturgy after the Middle Ages. It is nonetheless surprising to find so much emphasis on this vision in the liturgy that features such a magnificent cry of triumph as is found in Matins for Easter with its canon from St. John Damascene and that contains the catechetical sermon on the resurrection which is attributed to St. John Chrysostom.

In any case, the question arises: given this twofold vision of death, how does the office locate the death of the priest in the few hymnic texts that speak explicitly of it? Here again the total vision is both comforting and frightening. It conveys reassurance to the extent that some stichera, antiphons, and troparia show the priest as a man chosen, as a man who has been given a dignity that leads to deification; this calling and this office give the deceased a kind of claim to be allowed to glorify God in the heavenly sanctuary and to contemplate the light that shines from the face of Christ. But the claim is not an unconditional one, since at the same time prayers are offered for the forgiveness of the dead man's sins. The vision of a priest's death ceases to be a reassuring one because the office stresses the heavy responsibility a priest incurs if he carries out his task poorly. It is easy to understand that the office should underscore the strict account a man must render who has been graced with the priesthood. Nonetheless we may ask why it is that such emphasis should be laid, in the funeral of a priest, on the wretched side of man's mortal condition.

In order to answer this question let us ask first what the role of a priest is in the Church, according to this office. At first sight the office sees him as above all a liturgical figure. This appears especially in the stichera of Lauds, which depict the deceased as a sacrificer, a man who offers the divine mysteries. The tenth ikos suggests that the priest who has died has reason to fear condemnation for having been a poor man of prayer (the dead man is speaking): "Why, O man, do you distress yourself inopportunely? An hour strikes and all things pass away. There is no repentance in hell, nor any forgiveness of sins there. The worm that does not sleep lives there. There the land is murky and filled with darkness to which I must be condemned, because often I did not exert myself to say the psalm. Alleluia."

Other texts, especially the antiphons, present the priest as one who is supposed to have lived in faith, hope, and love; this implies, of course, that he had given an example of such virtues. The seventeenth ikos even implies that a heavy judgment awaits the deceased if, though a man of prayer, he had been attached during his earthly life to material goods and had failed to do good to the poor:

"Those inclined to attachments to material things will not find liberation yonder. Yonder there are terrible accusers, and mouths shall be opened yonder. When, O man, will you see around you yonder, and who then must come to your aid? You will receive help if in your earthly life you did good and brought help to the poor, while singing: Alleluia!"

But the image which the authors of the office have of the priest's role and of the ideal he must follow would be incomplete if I did not attend in my analysis to the teaching that seems to flow from the very structure which the authors thought the office should have. What peculiarities, then, does this structure manifest?

The few details which I gave earlier regarding the historical development of this office and its various redactions seem to show that an effort was made to turn the funeral office for priests into a kind of replica of the offices for the last two days of Holy Week. The same can be said of the office as we now have it. The antiphonal part with its gradual antiphons, kathisms, troparia, theotokia, ectenies, and Beatitudes—with five groups of readings interspersed—as well as the stichera at Lauds with the recited and not sung doxology, and the stichera at the aposticha—all this recalls the office of the Holy Passion. Psalm 117, the hirmoi for the canon "Through the sea wave," and the fact of the casket being carried in procession around the church—these items recall Great Saturday. Everything seems to show that the intention is to have the burial of a priest recall the Church's liturgical celebration of the death of Christ. This would imply that the death of a priest and especially his life should be modeled upon the death and life of Christ.

As a matter of fact, the parallel between the priesthood of Christ and that of the deceased priest is shown fully. Both are priests according to the order of Melchisedek, and the mortal priest derives his priesthood from that of Christ. The priest presides over the eucharistic assembly as Christ presided over the Supper. But Christ is also the Good Shepherd who gives his life for his sheep, as his death shows. The resemblance between the funeral office for priests and the offices of Holy Week can therefore be taken as implying that the Church's priest is likewise a good shepherd who is ready for the same sacrifice that his Master made and who, if he is not ready, will be seriously guilty. The funeral office is thus both a prayer and an exhortation: a prayer for the deceased pastor in case he had not fulfilled the obligations of a good shepherd, and an exhortation to surviving pastors, reminding them that their ministry calls for a total sacrifice of themselves.

If this sacrifice does not always mean that the pastor dies for those God has entrusted to him, it means at least that he is obliged to carry their cross. His own cross is inseparable from that of his flock. But one part of every man's cross is death. Every human being must pass through death, and must do it as a believer in Jesus Christ. And we know very well that one essential task of a pastor of souls—a task he finds among his most difficult—is to prepare the faithful for death, to help the dying die as Christians, and to help those who survive for a while likewise to die a Christian death and, meanwhile, to accept in a Christian spirit the departures of their dear ones. In the light of these considerations, the office I am studying here seems to be a lengthy pastoral reflection on the great theme of death.

If this is indeed its meaning, then we can accept the twofold approach to death that we find in it. Death has indeed been overcome by Christ and really does lead to a glorious resurrection and eternal life. This is what faith tells a Christian who believes in the salvation Christ has brought to us. Nonetheless death continues to be an existential fact in the world that awaits the second coming of Christ. It remains an event that brings anguish to every human being, an event that causes pastoral concerns and even problems for the Church. The two aspects of death are not mutually exclusive. The gap between the two approaches or attitudes to death is meant to be crossed by the experience of faith. But one means of acquiring this experience, as the example of Job or Daniel (Dn 9:1–19) shows, is to challenge oneself in prayer. That is what the Byzantine-Slavic Church seems to be doing in this funeral office for its priests.

For completeness' sake, let me remind the reader that like this office, all the other funeral offices in the present Trebnik manifest the same two ways of looking at death and the same two attitudes toward it. As I mentioned earlier, all these offices developed out of a common office for all the deceased, an office that was still being celebrated in the fourteenth century. I mentioned, too, that that original office is still rather faithfully reflected in the present funeral office for monks. This last-named office, more than all the others, emphasizes the consoling, even luminous aspect of death. It is easy to understand why this is so: the office for monks, inasmuch as it continues the original common office, is the oldest of all the present offices.

The other offices developed from the original common office, but under the influence of the same concerns as shaped the funeral office for priests. But it is in the last-named that the tragic aspect of death has been expressed most fully and forcefully. The pastors who worked on the composition of this office did so with the deaths of their colleagues in the priesthood before their eyes. Quite naturally, then, they were more keenly aware of the manner in which they in turn ought some day to die and of what would be demanded of them when they appeared before the only true Shepherd and true Priest.

These pastors therefore confessed their faith in the resurrection of Christ and in his victory over death and over all that death entails. But we must remind ourselves that the same John Chrysostom who is the presumed author of the paschal catechesis also wrote a treatise on the priesthood. As a great pastor of souls, he wrote of the serious tasks and responsibilities laid on those who receive the sacrament of orders. The funeral office for priests according to the Trebnik is the echo in the Byzantine Liturgy both of Chrysostom's triumphant Easter sermon and of his no less sublime treatise with its emphasis on the seriousness of the priesthood.

Pierre KOVALEVSKY

Funeral Rites in the Easter Season and Prayers for the Dead from Easter to Ascension

Within the general theme chosen for the Twenty-First Saint-Serge Conference, "Sickness and Death of the Christian according to the Liturgy," a place has been made for discussing a problem which at first sight is the contrary of sickness and death. I am referring to paschal joy.

Yet there are two reasons for this juxtaposition: the transformation of affliction and grief into jubilation is real and most characteristic of liturgical life in the East. It is very perceptible or, let me say, more externalized during Easter Week, but it is no less present during the entire period from Quasimodo Sunday (Second Sunday of Easter) to the Vigil of the Ascension. But the point must be made here that throughout the year funeral services are celebrated in white vestments and not in black.

On the other hand, there are two important reasons that determine the liturgical transformation in the funeral rites: the desire not to sing songs of sadness and repentance during this season of universal joy, and the desire to associate the Church triumphant, made up of those who died in the hope of the resurrection, with the joy of the Church suffering here below.

Since during Easter week all services, including the liturgy of St. John Chrysostom, are changed in important ways, the funeral rite too, as one of the sacramentals of the Orthodox Church that is richest in theological texts, must manifest the spirit of paschal jubilation.

It is to be noted that both the Easter cycle and the funeral cycle, if not composed by St. John Damascene, have at least acquired a definitive poetic form thanks to this great writer of hymns.

In the texts which I shall be citing, the theme of the union of the dead and the living is constantly repeated, while the descent of Christ among the dead before the resurrection and his saving of the just of the Old Testament will be a link between the two parts of the Church in their celebration of the feast of feasts.

I shall study two of the funeral rites, while leaving aside the second, which is the subject of a study by Father Alexis Kniazeff, and the fifth, that of children, which has been presented by Father Alexander Nélidow, as well as the two "abridged" rites—the pannychis and the litia—which are celebrated nowadays in a number of the autocephalous Orthodox Churches. I shall then compare the two rites in question with the same rites as completely transformed in the Easter season, in order to make clear to you how Easter sets its marks on the entire liturgical life, including services for the dead.

The four rites are those for the laity, for priests, for bishops, and for monks. Since bishops in the East are not only prelates but monks as well, some combination of rites was needed, but as we shall see, this is done only in a partial way.

First we shall discuss, in broad outline, the rites as celebrated outside the Easter season.

BURIAL OF LAYPERSONS

The service for the dead is in three stages: once the dead person has been clothed for burial and laid on a table or bed, a pannychis is celebrated. This is an abridged office of Matins, without the reading of the epistle, the gospel, and the beatitudes, while the canon comprises only a few chants. This short service will be repeated over the corpse until the body is placed in a coffin. At this point the priest blesses the coffin, and it is then carried out to the accompaniment of the chant: "Holy God, Holy Strong One, Holy Immortal One, have mercy on us."

The second part of the office begins when the body reaches the church. It is here that the principal part of the service takes place; in structure it is a combination of Matins and Orthros.

After the usual beginning, Psalm 90 (often omitted) is read, and then the singing of Psalm 119 in three (much shortened) parts is begun. The three parts are separated from one another by short litanies and by a prayer that will be repeated several times and is part of every office of the dead:

"God of spirits and of all flesh, you have overcome death and conquered the devil and have given life to the world. Grant rest to the soul of your deceased servant, in a place of light, a delightful place of refreshment and repose, from which all sickness, affliction and grief are banished. Forgive him all the sins he may have committed by word, deed or thought, for you, our God, are good and you love human beings. No human being is without sin, for you alone are free of sin. Your truth is eternal truth, and your word is truth, for you, Christ our God, are the resurrection, the life, and the repose of your deceased servant. We give you glory, together with your eternal Father and your good and life-giving Spirit, now and for ever and through all the ages. Amen."

This is one of the oldest of all prayers for the dead, and has recently been studied by Father V. Bruni.

Next come the troparia, each preceded by the invocation: "Blessed are you, Lord; teach me your judgments."

"The choir of saints has found the fountain of life and the gate to paradise. May I too find the way of repentance. I am the lost sheep. Call me, Lord, and save me.

"Holy martyrs, who proclaimed the divine Lamb and were sacrificed like lambs, and who reached the everlasting life that is ever young, pray earnestly for the forgiveness of our sins.

"During life you followed the narrow and difficult way; you carried your cross like a yoke and followed Me in faith. Come now and enjoy the heavenly honors and crowns I have prepared for you.

"I am the image of your indescribable glory, even though I bear the wounds of my sins. Have pity on your creature, purify me in your mercy, and grant me the homeland I desire by making me a new inhabitant of paradise.

"You once created me from nothing and honored me with your divine likeness, but because I transgressed your commandments you made me return to the earth from which I had been taken. Restore me to your likeness and give me back my former beauty.

"My God, grant rest to your servant and place him in paradise, where the choirs of the saints now are and where the just shine like stars. Grant rest to this dead person by forgiving him his sins.

"Glory to the Father and to the Son and to the Holy Spirit. Let us offer fitting praise to the threefold Light of the one Godhead by proclaiming: 'Holy are you, eternal Father and your coeternal Son and your divine Holy Spirit.' Enlighten us who serve you in faith, and save us from the everlasting fire.

"Now and for ever and through all the ages: rejoice, you who have given birth to God in the flesh for the salvation of all and through whom the human race has recovered salvation. Through you we regain paradise, O pure and blessed Mother of God."

These troparia, attributed to St. John Damascene, are a prayer for a dead person, an appeal uttered by the soul of this person, and a proclamation of faith in eternal salvation. The dead person seeks to recover the divine image in the likeness of which man was created, but which was then obscured by sin.

After the reading of Psalm 51, the singing of the canon is begun; this is a very important part of the office of the dead. The canon is a set of nine chants with interspersed troparia and the Magnificat. It is part of Matins. It shall give only some characteristic extracts from this canon, which is attributed to St. Theophanes Graptos, in order to show that it could not form part of the office during the Easter season. Theophanes, bishop of Nicea, along with his brother St. Theodore, was a defender of holy images. He was persecuted on this account and had an insulting inscription incised on his forehead (whence the name Graptos, "written" or "inscribed"). He composed 145 "canons" and died about 850.

While the canon for the dead may be the poetical work of Theophanes, it contains much older elements in its many mentions of the martyrs as intercessors. During the early centuries of Christianity, liturgical offices were often celebrated at the tombs of martyrs, and the cult of the latter took precedence over the commemoration of the other saints to such an extent that right down to our own time the troparion (hymn) for All Saints mentions only the martyrs.

The troparia are introduced by the invocation: "Grant rest to your servant."

Here are some texts from this canon. They show that, on the one hand, the purpose of the canon is to glorify the martyrs, who are the most representative members of the Church triumphant and therefore the intercessors best qualified to speak for the dead, and that, on the other hand, it is a supplication to the Lord for the forgiveness of sins. These two themes could not form part of offices proper to the Easter season.

"In the heavenly dwellings the heroic martyrs plead with you, O Christ, to grant eternal blessings to this person whom you have summoned back from earth.

"You created me to dwell in paradise and cultivate it, but you expelled me from it because I did not observe your commandment. Grant rest to the soul of your servant.

"May the martyrs, who suffered for you, the Creator of life, and have been given crowns of victory, bring eternal deliverance to those who have died.

"Welcome him who sings your divine power and whom you have received at his coming forth from this world. Make him a child of the light and purify him of the darkness caused by sin, for you are merciful.

"Nailed to the cross, you brought to yourself the choirs of the martyrs who imitated you in your suffering. We pray you, grant rest to him who has died."

After the sixth chant of the "canon" come the kontakion and the ikos, hymns that are part of every office for the dead, even of the most abridged forms of this office, such as the litia.

"Grant rest with your saints, O Christ, to the soul of your servant, in that place where there is neither sickness nor affliction nor mourning, but only everlasting life.

"You alone are immortal who created and formed man. We who are earthly were formed of the earth and shall return to it as you ordained. For you who created me said to me: 'Dust you are and to dust you will return,' and indeed all we human beings shall return to dust as the funeral hymn is sung. Alleluia."

The canon is followed by eight chants, executed according to the eight modes and composed by St. John Damascene, who is also author of the eight Sunday offices, which follow the same modes.

After the reading of the beatitudes, with intercalated strophes, the deacon or cantor proclaims the Gradual: "Blessed is the way you set out on today, O soul, because a place of rest has been prepared for you." There follows the reading from the first letter to the Thessalonians (4:13–18) and from the gospel of St. John (5:24–30). The office ends with a litany and hymns of farewell, during which all present bow before the coffin and kiss the cross or holy image placed on it. Finally "Eternal remembrance" is sung.

The departure from the church is accompanied by the same chant that accompanied the entrance: "Holy God, Holy Strong One, Holy

Immortal One." The priest blesses the grave in the cemetery. In addition to these three ceremonies, a paper crown bearing a holy image is placed on the brow of the dead person, and the absolution is read, the text of it being then placed in the hand of the dead person. This is ordinarily done in the mortuary, since the coffin is usually closed when the time comes for the departure from the home. In prerevolutionary Russia the coffin remained open in the church throughout the office; people kissed the brow of the dead person, and the priest read the absolution at the end of the office.

BURIAL OF A LAYPERSON DURING EASTER WEEK

The ritual contains an introduction which explains why the office of the dead must be changed during this period. These changes are, in fact, so extensive that I should rather point out what is left of the ordinary rite! Here is the introduction to the five rites:

"It must be realized that if a person dies on Easter or on a day during Easter week, before Thomas Sunday, little of the chanting which is ordinarily part of the office is retained. This is out of respect for the greatness and dignity of the resplendent feast of the Resurrection, which is a feast of joy and not of lamentation. As we shall all rise in Christ, in the hope of resurrection and eternal life, through this same resurrection of Christ the dead pass from the afflictions of this world to joy and happiness, and the Church proclaims this in the hymns of resurrection. Some of the chants and litanies and some prayers proper to the dead tell us that the dead person died repentant. If his sins kept him from doing good, he is set free by the prayers of the Church."

It used to be a firm belief of the Russian people that anyone whom God called to himself during Easter week went to paradise without being judged.

In the East generally and especially in Russia, Easter joy used to be one of the most striking characteristics of the life of the people. Easter is not only the feast of feasts; it is truly a feast of reconciliation as well, when all the things that divide human beings are forgotten. In the offices of Easter, the troparion "Christ is risen from the dead; by his death he has conquered death and given life to those in the grave," is repeated over and over. People give each other the kiss of peace with the words: "Christ is risen—He is truly risen." It is impossible therefore that chants marked by sadness or repentance should be mixed in with these expressions of universal joy.

The funeral office too—whether for laypersons or for priests and bishops or even for monks—is filled with this same paschal joy and

KOVALEVSKY

with this faith in the resurrection that has become a real certitude of the soul.

The office for Easter Matins, which provides the fabric of the burial office during Easter week, acquired its definitive form thanks to St. John Damascene (d. 754), but the liturgical celebration of the feast goes back to the first Christian centuries. We possess today a whole series of books dealing with the question and in particular with the oldest Easter text that has survived, the third-century *Homily on the Pasch* by Melito of Sardis.[1]

The hymns of Easter have for their subject not only the resurrection, but Christ's descent into the lower world. The oldest ikons of the feast make no attempt to depict a mystery which no one saw and which took place in darkness; instead they show the Savior leading the just of the Old Testament by the hand through the shattered gates of the lower world.[2]

OFFICE OF BURIAL DURING EASTER WEEK

As the corpse is taken from the home, the troparion "Christ is risen" is sung, with its strophes: "May God arise and his enemies be scattered. May those who hate him flee before his face"; "May they vanish away like smoke, and as wax melts near the fire, so will sinners perish far from the face of God but the just will have joy"; "This the day that the Lord has made. On this day let us rejoice and be glad." Then comes a litany and the prayer "God of spirits."

In the church the service once again begins with the troparion and strophes, as does every office during Easter week. Next comes the Easter Canon of St. John Damascene, which replaces the canon of St. Theophanes Graptos. Here are some extracts from it:

"It is the day of the resurrection. Peoples, let us be filled with joy. It is the Pasch of the Lord. We who sing this triumphal hymn have been changed by Christ our God from death to life, from earth to heaven.

"May the heavens rejoice and the earth be glad. May the world both visible and invisible celebrate the feast, for Christ, our eternal joy, is risen.

"Now everything—heaven, earth and lower world—is filled with light. May every creature celebrate the resurrection of Christ, who is our strength.

"Those who had been held in the chains of the lower world bore witness to your immense mercy, O Christ, as they hastened with joyous steps to the light and applauded the everlasting Pasch.

"You descended into the lowest depths of the earth and broke the eternal bolts that held the captives in, O Christ, when you rose from the tomb.

"This day is splendid and holy, and unique in all the weeks. It is the king and lord of days, the feast of feasts, the solemnity of solemnities, on which we bless Christ through all the ages.

"Be filled with light, O new Jerusalem, be filled with light, for the glory of the Lord has risen over you. Exult and adorn yourself, O Zion. And you, Mother of God: rejoice at the resurrection of your Son!"

Even the reading from the New Testament is different, for the gospel of Matthew is read (28:16–20).

The very beautiful troparia for the dead, during which the incensing is done, are replaced by the troparia for Sundays. This is regrettable, because the former contain thoughts of great spiritual beauty. Here is the text of the troparia for Sundays:

"Blessed are you, Lord; teach me your judgment. The angelic host was astonished to see you counted among the dead as you destroyed the power of death, awakened Adam, and freed all those in the lower world.

"Why, O disciples, do you mingle tears with the myrrh? The angel who shone with light at the tomb said to the women: 'See the tomb for yourselves and understand that the Savior is risen.'

"Early in the morning the women bringing myrrh ran weeping to your tomb, but the angel showed himself to them and said: 'The time for mourning is over; weep not, but tell the apostles of the resurrection.'

"The women bringing myrrh ran weeping to your tomb, O Savior, but they heard the angel saying to them: 'Why do you count the living among the dead? As God he is risen from the tomb.'

·"Let us adore the Father, the Son, and the Holy Spirit, the Holy Trinity that is one in substance, as we proclaim with the seraphim: 'Holy, holy, holy is the Lord.'

"By giving birth to him who is the source of life, you freed Adam from sin, and you replaced Eve's sorrow with joy. He who took flesh of you as God and man has sent sinners to you."

The office ends with the Easter hymns "May God arise and his enemies be scattered . . . ," and the farewells to the departed. The hymns which remain unchanged are "With the saints give rest . . ." and "Eternal remembrance."

OFFICE FOR THE BURIAL OF PRIESTS AND BISHOPS AND
ITS ADAPTATION TO THE NORMS FOR EASTER

Father Alexis Kniazeff has given us a study of the office for the burial of priests. This office is one of the longest celebrated in the

Orthodox Churches. In addition to readings and complementary hymns, it contains ten New Testament passages instead of two. The ten are: (1) 1 Thes 4:13–17 and Jn 5:24–30; (2) Rom 5:12–21 and Jn 5:17–24; (3) 1 Cor 10:1–11 and Jn 6:35–39; (4) 1 Cor 15:20–28 and Jn 6:40–47; (5) Rom 14:6–9 and Jn 6:48–54. The hirmoi, composed by the nun Cassia, are from the canon for Holy Saturday, but the troparia of that canon (which were composed by St. Mark, bishop of Idraea, and St. Comus, bishop of Maioum) are replaced by those for the dead, authored by St. John Damascene.

Between the sixth and seventh hymns of the canon, twenty-four prayers are intercalated which are improperly called ikoi and were written by the monk Anastasius. Each ends with a sung alleluia.

While the coffin is being transferred and during the procession around the church, the hirmoi of the Great Canon of St. Andrew of Crete are sung. During Easter week this service is completely transformed, as are all the other services for the dead.

The office for the burial of bishops is in practice the same as that for priests, but it is more solemn. There used to be a special rite, but it was suppressed by Peter the Great in his Church reform of 1721. In his *Regulations in Matters Spiritual* (which was the work of Theophanes Prokopovitch), the emperor wanted to take away from the clergy anything that could give them power over the people, and to humble them and turn them into civil servants charged with the care of souls. Only quite recently, in 1963, did Archbishop Modestos of the Russian Patriarchate compose a special rite for bishops that was accepted by the other Russian bishops.

During Easter week the rite for the burial of bishops undergoes the same changes as the rite for laypersons. We have two interesting texts which show in some detail how this transformed ceremony was conducted. The first text was by Metropolitan Philaretos of Moscow and was composed on the occasion of the death of Bishop Cyril, archbishop of Padolia, whose funeral was celebrated on Easter Monday, March 31, 1841.

The second text is very recent and was composed by Archpriest Alexander Tchékan, on the basis of earlier texts, for the funeral of Bishop Methodios, coadjutor of the Russian Orthodox Archbishop for Western Europe (jurisdiction of the Patriarchate of Constantinople), which took place in the Cathedral of St. Alexander Nevsky in Paris (12 rue Daru) on Easter Wednesday, April 17, 1974.

Since the texts for the burial of bishops are less well known, I think it useful to give some bibliography. I should mention first and foremost the works of Professor Nicholas Krasnoseltzev, who in 1881–1882 studied the Slavonic manuscripts of the eleventh to the fourteenth centuries as preserved in the Vatican Library and at

Mount Athos. A. A. Dmitrievsky drew heavily on these studies for his work, *History of the Divine Offices in the Orthodox Church* (1889). A second stage was marked by the study of the manuscripts from the monastery of Solovki by the White Sea in the far north of Russia. These manuscripts had been deposited in the library of the Theological Academy at Kazan. While the rite for the burial of bishops acquired its definitive form only in the seventeenth century, we find special prayers for bishops in the Barberini Euchologion, which dates from the seventh to ninth centuries. In Russia a special rite was in use from the sixteenth century on, and in 1623 the text, composed by the Bulgarian monk Eremius, was printed at Moscow, but suppressed in 1639 by order of Patriarch Ioasaph. From the time of Peter the Great on, only the texts for the burial of priests were used for the burial of bishops as well, until Bishop Manuel Lemechevsky offered a text which he had worked on from 1950 to 1960. This text was accepted by the Patriarchate on December 13, 1963. It contains a larger number of passages from the gospels and epistles.

The most complete study of the entire question is that of A. A. Dmitrievsky, which deals with the rites of Holy Week and of Easter (2 vols.; St. Petersburg, 1888, 1895).

The two rituals for bishops, that of 1841 and that of 1974, are almost identical. The principle that all prayers and hymns expressing sorrow or mourning should be replaced by others expressing Easter joy is observed here, as in the rite for the burial of laypersons during Easter week.

BURIAL OF MONKS

There is a special rite for the burial of monks, and it too changes during Easter week.

The rite of burial for monks is much shorter than the rite for priests or even the rite for laypersons, and it contains prayers and hymns which make references to monastic asceticism and the life of monks. The Easter rite has the same hymns as the other funeral rites of this same period.

The burial of deacons had long been a problem for Church authorities. The general rule required that the rite for laypeople should be followed. On the other hand, the deacon plays an important role in the Church's liturgical life: he ministers at the altar; he is the intermediary between the people and the celebrant; he is the direct assistant of the priest. It was therefore quite natural for his burial to be assimilated more to that of priests than to that of laypersons.

No definitive and universally binding decision was made on this problem, and a rather strange practice was established in Russia which was based not on liturgical norms but on the wishes of the deacon's family. If his relatives asked for burial according to the rite for priests this was allowed, although those prayers were of course omitted that had to do specifically with the priesthood and priestly functions. The Great Ritual of Metropolitan Peter Mogila (seventeenth century) grants deacons the honor of a funeral according to the rite for priests, but before the revolution of 1917 the permission of the Ordinary had to be asked on each occasion.

The rite of burial for monks is used for all of the regular clergy, whether the individual be a monk, a hieromonk (i.e., a priest-monk), a higoumenos (prior) or an archimandrite (abbot of a large monastery).

BURIALS DURING THE PERIOD FROM ST. THOMAS SUNDAY
TO THE VIGIL OF THE ASCENSION

Changes in the ritual for burials taking place between St. Thomas Sunday (second Sunday of Easter), known in the Orthodox Church as Anti-Easter or Renewal Sunday (because it focuses on the apostle's distrust and lack of faith in the resurrection and on his subsequent conversion), and the day known as the "end of Easter," that is, the Vigil of the Ascension, are common to all funeral services. At the beginning of the rite the Easter troparion is sung, and certain prayers are replaced by texts corresponding to the feast being celebrated. There is, however, one day that is specially devoted to the commemoration of the dead, when all of the dead are associated with the great joy of the feast of feasts.

On Tuesday (or in some parts of the world on Monday) of St. Thomas Week, the Orthodox go to the cemeteries in order to sing the Easter troparion over the graves of their relatives and to place on them an egg painted red, thus associating the dead with the joy experienced by the living. This day is known as *Radonitsa*, "Day of joy."

The Orthodox custom of exchanging eggs painted red at Easter is very ancient and is connected with the legend which claims that St. Mary Magdalene visited Rome and gave Emperor Tiberius an egg painted red as a symbol of the life that is hidden in a grave and of the blood shed on the cross.

To summarize what I have been saying: I may conclude that the feast of Easter has an extremely important influence on the world of the liturgical life and that it completely alters most services, inasmuch as these now express joy and jubilation rather than sadness and repentance. On the other hand, the texts of the Easter offices emphasize the unity which exists between the Church triumphant and the Church still struggling on earth, and associate the two Churches in one and the same celebration.

I shall end by citing the words which Pastor Marc Boegner, President of the Protestant Federation of France, spoke at the first ecumenical meeting held at the Romanian Church in Paris, in the presence of Catholics, Anglicans, and Reformed. Taking the pulpit at the end of Vespers that day he said: "Despite everything that separates us from the Orthodox in our manner of worship, we admire the way in which they celebrate and proclaim the resurrection of the Lord."

Peter MEINHOLD

Healing
and Sanctification
in Luther's Theology

Adolf Köberle, well-known Evangelical theologian, deserves our gratitude for repeatedly renewing the dialogue between medical science and theology. In his recent book, *Heilung und Hilfe. Christliche Wahrheitserkenntnis in der Begenung mit Naturwissenschaft, Medizin und Psychotherapie* (Healing and Help. The Christian Understanding of Truth in Encounter with Natural Science, Medicine and Psychotherapy, Darmstadt, 1968), he makes the following remarks:

"Thank God, the Christian Church in its various confessions has never become so spiritually impoverished as to lose that noble blessing which is healing through faith. Admittedly it is not possible to speak of a broad river of faith-healing running through the centuries of Church history. But it is indeed possible to speak of an ever-flowing spring. At times it may have gone underground, so that people thought it would never reappear, but then suddenly there it was again, refreshing and vital.

"The 'great saints' of the Catholic Church, such as Benedict of Nursia, Bernard of Clairvaux and Francis of Assisi were all miracle-workers. The startsy, those individuals who have played such an important role in Russian piety, are not only pastors who help the people in their struggles; they have also been able in many instances to relieve of sickness those who come to them for help. As far as the Evangelical Church of the Lutheran and Reformed confessions is concerned, we may recall the Blumhardts, father and son, at Bad Boll, Samuel Zeller and his assistant Dorothea Trudel at Männerheim am Zürichsee, Fräulein von Seckendorff at Villa Cannstatt, the evangelists Johannes Seitz and Elias Schrenk, Father Stanger at Möttlingen, and Frau Minna Popken. In fact the number of men and women who attempted such healings through faith and whose prayers were answered is much greater than any statistics can tell us. Down through the generations countless Christian pastors, official and unofficial, have experienced the wonderful effects of the name of Jesus, and this in distresses not only of heart but even of body."[1]

As we reflect on these remarks of Köberle, the question arises whether Protestant theology has registered and given theological expression to the phenomenon here described of faith-healing, that is, bodily healing through intercessory prayer and the power of faith. But as soon as we formulate the question in this way, it is immediately clear that no answer is forthcoming, indeed that the very question usually receives no attention from theologians.[2] This is all the more surprising because at the very beginnings of Reformed theology, in the writings of Luther, the idea of healing through faith crops up repeatedly and from a variety of viewpoints. What Luther has to say on the subject provides a good many suggestions for a theological discussion of the theme. These are not simply of historical interest, as bringing to light an unknown side of Luther's theology; they are also of value in modern theological reflection on healing through faith. I am limiting myself in this paper to Luther's statements, but I believe that it would also be possible and fruitful to trace the development of his thought in the Lutheran theology of subsequent centuries.

The miraculous healings reported in the gospels were one occasion for Luther to reflect on the relation between health and sickness and on the fact of healing through faith. Most of what he has to say in this connection is to be found in his sermons; this very context gives it a practical value. On the other hand, his reflection on prayer, and the fact that in the Old Testament, too, sickness and its healing through faith and prayer play an important role, compelled Luther to go into this matter of faith-healing more thoroughly. Then too, the need of coming to grips with the sacrament of extreme unction called upon him to reflect on the basis for this action and on the justification for such a sacrament and, once he had rejected its sacramental character, to provide a new meaning for the action and to replace it with another ecclesial rite. Finally, the emphasis on the bodily effects of the Supper forced Luther to reflect especially on the connection between healing and sanctification and to elucidate the somatic and the intellectual-spiritual meaning of the connection. As everyone knows, Luther himself put into practice or would have others put into practice the practical consequences of theological positions.

In this essay, then, I shall be approaching Luther's views on healing through faith and prayer from four different angles.

I

In a sermon of 1518 Luther preached on the story of the healing of the man born blind as told in John's gospel.[3] In this early sermon he is still wholly under the influence of Augustine, to whose treatment of this gospel passage he refers at the beginning of his own explanation. Now Luther does repeat Augustine, but at the same time he is so responsive to the latter's thinking that as he presents the Augustinian views he at the same time interprets them; as a result, there is an imperceptible shift from the repetition of Augustinian ideas to Luther's own interpretation of them.

Luther remarks that in dealing with this pericope Augustine distinguishes between the words and the works of Christ. The "works" include the actions or activity of Christ; therefore, his meeting with the man born blind and his ultimate healing of the man. The words of Christ accompany his works and are to be understood as exegesis and interpretation of them. The words point beyond the particular event and bring to light a content that is of universal application. The story of the healing of the man born blind, to whom the Lord restores sight, is accompanied by words that point to the blindness in every human being. In an imperceptible transition, "blindness" is now understood in a spiritual sense, for the words Christ uses in the process of healing the blind man signify "every man born of Adam. For we are all blind and our light and our illumination comes solely from Christ, our good and faithful God."[4]

This reinterpretation of the healing event and of the blindness involved, so as to derive a spiritual and universal meaning which applies to every human being by his or her very nature, is not to be dismissed as simply exegetical whimsy on Luther's part. As a matter of fact, Luther evidently was aware of the danger of such a dismissal, for he goes on to say—and bases himself on Augustine—that the distinction between work and word in Christ is one made by an enlightened mind, that is, by reason operating in the service of faith. Only such a believing mind can discover the real meaning hidden in the works of Christ. Only thus is the listener or reader carried beyond a purely external grasp of the action of Christ, that is, the healing of a blind man. There were, after all, many people who saw the healing take place, but did not grasp its deeper meaning.[5] The reason for this purely external view of the event is, according to the Luther, a non-understanding, or rejection, of the word of Christ. On the contrary, if a person were to take Christ's word as a manifestation of the meaning of Christ's work and thus were to recognize its real significance, he would doubtless thereby establish a personal connection with this healing event which takes place outside of himself. Only this kind of reception of the word brings a penetration through external appearances to true reality, and a realization of how closely interwoven appearance and reality are in our world. Only faith is able to distinguish the two.

According to Luther, then, we attain to a right understanding of the healing of the man born blind only when we do not stop at the miracle as such but, under the influence of the word, recognize the connection between the event and ourselves, namely, that we are "far more blind" than the man whom Christ healed.

"And that's the right understanding of it; and so it is to this day, that the number of them [blind people] is great even among those who shine before the world in their great power, culture, wisdom, piety, holiness, chastity, purity, and so on. But it is certain that always it has been so ordained that with a powerful man there is found an outcast, with the wise a fool, with the pious an impious, with the holy an unholy, with the healthy a sick man, with the handsome an ugly man, and so on."[6]

There is thus an indissoluble coexistence of health and sickness, and a corresponding view of the world which, on the one hand, remains dependent on outward appearances, to the extent that it cannot separate out the two entities, but on the other hand is not incapable of judgment amid this pile-up of oppositions and thus has power to unravel the confusion in a proper way. Thus the blindness of one individual must serve to reveal this interweaving of opposites to the believer and enable him to reach a new understanding of himself.

MEINHOLD

The ultimate reason for this constant coexistence of opposites is to be found in God's decision to reveal himself through the opposition. But in revealing himself, God always casts down human presumption and humbles all the supposedly wise and clever. Man must therefore turn his gaze completely away from himself and fasten his gaze solely on God: "And it is not without cause that God in his unspeakable wisdom should so desire to cast down the rule of the proud and the wise."[7]

Furthermore, God has given each man in his neighbor a mirror in which he can see himself and thus come to self-knowledge. The neighbor is like a God-given mirror in which a person can contemplate himself and thus learn about himself. The self-knowledge to be gained consists in this, that the individual is to pay no heed to any gifts God has given him or the grace bestowed on him, so that he may learn from his neighbor his own weakness and sin:

"So let every man, if he has received a blessing or gift from God, learn to divest himself of it, shun it, give it up, in order that he may not look to himself, but rather note how his neighbor looks and how his neighbor is reflected in himself. Then he will surely say, 'Ah, there God has hung a mirror before my eyes, and a book in which I am to learn to know myself. Ah, God, now I see clearly that what my brother is outwardly, I am inwardly.' Thus he learns to know himself and not to exalt himself. So it is ordained and nobody can evade it."[8]

In this way the sickness of the man born blind and ultimately every human sickness becomes a demonstration, a way in which a person comes to recognize his own sickness, which is not something external but is hidden within him in the form of sin. "The blind man was a sign of the blindness that lay hidden in our hearts."[9]

As Luther explains in connection with the man born blind, sickness serves to keep those individuals from presumption who recognize the *forma Dei* in themselves, that is, are conscious of the gifts and graces God has bestowed on them. Those thus graced will humble themselves and look upon themselves as the least of all human beings in the world. Human blindness, after all, consists in not having an eye for the hidden holiness of God. "He who does not see and know God's hidden holiness is blind. And therefore this man in the Gospel is only a figure of that other blindness which is in the soul."[10]

Luther's point in all this is that sickness, as seen in the case of the man born blind, can open the eyes of a human being to the true realities of life and even lead him to a real reversal of all human values. The person begins by seeing himself in an entirely new way. He realizes that the very members of his body really do not belong to him but are God's instruments, the means God uses for doing his own work, insofar as he himself rules all their movements. But if God abandons a person, only then do the person's members become instruments which man, in his blindness, uses as if they were actually his own. Then he thinks he sees, but in truth he is blind.

With these thoughts Luther links up the teaching of Genesis, according to which the devil leads man astray precisely by promising that his eyes will be opened and he will acquire the knowledge of good and evil. But in fact, as a result of the devil's misleading, man's eyes are now closed, whereas previously they had been open:

"You see what he [the devil] is doing; he is trying to lead them to the form of God, so he says, 'Your eyes will be opened,' that is, they will become blind. Before their eyes were closed, but after the Fall they were opened. The consequence of this, as Origen, the wise and acute schoolmaster, teaches, is that man has two kinds of eyes, his own eyes and God's eyes. But the fact is that both kinds of eyes, our inward eyes and outward eyes, are God's. Indeed, all our members and everything that is in us are instruments of God and nothing is ours if they are ruled by God. But they are ours when God forsakes us."[11]

Now Luther's view is that this deception of man—namely, the idea that he dispose of his bodily members in an utterly independent way—also leads him astray into a completely erroneous judgment on the world. As a result, worldly charm and beauty lead a person to think more highly of a young girl or young man than of an old woman or an old man. But the supposed beauty of the world is the "mousetrap" that deceives all our senses, and our attraction to it is only a sign of our entirely false evaluation of everything in this world. Christ came in order to heal human beings of this blindness and restore an awareness of reality and the true humanity that lies hidden behind external appearances.

"That's why we would rather see what is fine and pretty and well formed rather than what is gold or silver, rather a young Jill or a young Jack than an old woman or an old Jack. And this is the mousetrap that dupes our minds, as is written of Adam in the book of Genesis. So our eyes have been opened, which really means that we have become totally blind, so that, as was said a moment ago, we consider the sham to be good and what is poor and misshapen to be evil. . . . But Christ came to teach these eyes to see and to take away the blindness, in order that we should not make this distinction between young and old, beautiful and ugly, and so on. Rather all are equal, wise man or simpleton, sage or fool, man or woman; it is enough that he is a man with our flesh and blood, a body common to all."[12]

This new attitude to sickness entails a new appreciation of the divine activity as well. According to Luther this action takes place in or through human beings. God never looks at the outward form when he acts in the corporeal nature of man; he gives children to an ugly woman as well as to a pretty one, and vice versa. But ultimately this action of God is directed to turning the human person away from himself; to this end God gives the person what does not please him. This reversal of values is something Christ himself "practiced," beginning with the incarnation; it is also made evident in the fact that human beings are subject to old age and sickness, that is, to what does not please them. "Paul says, 'Thus is the call of God, that it receives the sick and the fools, in order that he may confound and shame the wise.' So because Christ does this and considers that [to be] evil which we consider good and vice versa, he takes away that which we delight in and gives everything that vexes us. This Christ practiced and proved."[13] Thus sickness too is from God, who gives it in order that men may regain a true vision of the realities of life. On the other hand, sickness is also meant to test and purify man.

"Therefore those who are farther along should pay little regard to these things and lift their eyes higher; for Christ will bring to their very door something better than they can find anywhere in the world. For he will send them reverses, tribulation, anxiety, care, grief, poverty, ill will, and so on. He will send you sickness. . . . And so it comes about that we think we see clearly and yet are totally blind, so that we call evil what Christ calls good."[14]

This appraisal of sickness by Luther must thus be seen against the background of his spiritual interpretation of reality. According to this interpretation, the divine life and divine being are the only true reality while the "realities" of the world are only deceitful appearances which human beings in their spiritual blindness mistake for ultimate realities. In Luther's view, it is the function of an enlightened and truly healed mind to grasp the difference and provide a correct evaluation of things. When a person does this he becomes a kind of "monstrance" in which God dwells in his reality and presence. The soul of man then truly becomes an inner sanctuary in which God is carried and preserved. As a result, the whole person will be "healthy" when he has experienced this divine healing, whereas he must be called "blind" and "sick" as long as God has not given him this healing. "All the goldsmiths together cannot make a vessel to enclose this relic. It requires a spiritual, living, eternal monstrance. For this sacred relic is a living thing like the soul of man. Therefore, it is the inward relic we must seek, not the outward."[15]

Only through this divine action that heals the entire person because it penetrates through him from within can human beings be preserved from the illusions affecting our present life. The exegesis of the passage about the man born blind thus leads Luther to a new evaluation of sickness and blindness, healing and recovery of health that must be seen against the background of his general spiritual interpretation of the world. Luther judges all of the reality which we supposedly encounter in this world to be in fact deception and illusion, while he locates the highest and most perfect reality solely in the being and action of God. Since the human person does not by his nature experience this reversal of values his eyes must be opened to it. This opening of the eyes is a work reserved to Christ, who takes from man his supposed power to see and know, and gives him new eyes with which to see both reality in general and true humanness in particular, this latter having nothing to do with outward appearances.

Luther never lost this vision of sickness and health, but gave expression to it over and over again. It led him to a new interpretation of life and reality that is fundamental to his theology; it led him, above all, to a new appreciation of his own being and his own sickness. As evidence I cite the last note which Luther wrote down as death was drawing near: "We are beggars, and that is the truth of the matter."[16] In these few words Luther also makes it clear that a human being must humbly think little of himself and recognize how completely he is dependent on the grace of God.

II

It was not only reflection on the miracles of healing and meditation on the illnesses depicted in the gospels that led Luther to think about the healing and sanctification of man. His criticism of the Catholic sacrament of extreme unction also gave him an occasion for reflecting on the meaning of this action, which is one of the seven sacraments of the Catholic Church and is meant to provide a closing ecclesial action for a Christian life that began in baptism. As everyone knows, Luther discusses the sacrament of anointing in detail in his *The Babylonian Captivity of the Church* (1520),[17] in which he discusses the seven sacraments of the Catholic Church and proposes his criteria for the special nature of a sacrament.

Since Catholics have always based the sacrament of last anointing, or extreme unction, on James 5:13ff.,[18] Luther in his criticism of the sacrament was forced to examine the validity of this appeal. The critical sense with which he was beginning to approach the New Testament was awakened here. The connection of this sacrament with the well-known passage in James is highly dubious. To begin with, it is an open question whether the letter was written by the apostle James or whether it came from the pen of some other individual who possessed the apostolic spirit. But (Luther argues), even if the letter was from James, no apostle can claim the power to institute a sacrament; this is a power which Christ alone possesses.[19]

After these considerations of principle, Luther turns to a detailed discussion of the legitimacy or illegitimacy of such a sacrament of extreme unction. How is it possible to speak here of a "final" and "once only" anointing when, as the wording of the passage makes clear, the apostle is speaking of a "general" anointing and not one restricted to the dying? The words of the letter of James are being completely misunderstood when they are made to justify a "last" anointing and a sacrament. But even the sacrament itself contains a contradiction, since the prayers which accompany the action say nothing of death and departure but rather speak of the "improvement" and "healing" of the sick.[20]

According to Luther, the result of this misunderstanding of the words of James' letter has been a distorted attitude on the part of human beings. For when a sick person experiences recovery and restoration after receiving extreme unction, people attribute this not to the sacrament but to "nature" or "medicine."[21] As Luther sees it, this represents the influence of that false judgment on reality which he had so sharply condemned earlier in his sermon on the story of the healing of the man born blind. In this context Luther makes the perceptive remark that even the letter of James or the apostle himself contradicts himself according to the Catholic interpretation of the passage.

"For if it is extreme unction, it does not heal, but gives way to the disease; but if it heals, it cannot be extreme unction. Thus, by the interpretation of these masters, James is shown to have contradicted himself, and to have instituted a sacrament in order not to institute one; for they must have an extreme unction just to make untrue what the apostle intends, namely, the healing of the sick by it."[22]

After his criticism of the theological argument usually given since Peter Lombard for a sacrament of last anointing, Luther then develops the positive meaning of this ecclesial action by a careful exegesis of the words in the letter of James. In his interpretation, the letter is speaking of the healing of the sick through the faith-filled prayer of the elders of the community. It is as representatives of the community that these men visit the sick. Luther offers a critical reflection on these "elders." It is his view that the "elders" of whom James speaks do not possess a properly priestly office but act as representatives of the living faith of the community; it is for this reason that they are called "elders" in the sense of "more experienced" or "tested" men. Luther adds the observation that at one time the Churches were not led by ordained ministers and priests but by "elders," men who, without being ordained and consecrated, were chosen as representatives of the community by reason of their age and spiritual experience. These individuals visited the sick, performed a work of mercy, and healed them through the prayer of faith.[23]

The anointing was simply an action that accompanied the prayer. Here again Luther makes some critical observations on the use of anointing in the early Church. He connects Mark 6:13ff. with James 5:14ff. The passage in Mark has to do with the sending of the Twelve by Jesus and says that they went forth, preached repentance, drove out many evil spirits, and anointed many sick people with oil and healed them. Luther is of the opinion that even by the time of James, this primitive Christian practice had undergone a certain distortion. He also refers to Mark 16:15–18, where we are told that the risen Lord himself gave the disciples authority to preach the gospel to all creatures and that those who would believe and be baptized would be saved. Then, says the gospel, the risen Jesus also spoke of the signs that would accompany believers and be evidence of the strength of their faith: They would drive out devils in the name of Jesus, speak in new tongues, tread on serpents unharmed, and not die of any deadly poison they might drink. And finally: "They will lay their hands on the sick, and they will recover."

According to Luther, the imposition of hands by the elders is the original practice, whereas the anointing is a "counsel" of the apostle James. Anyone who wished to do it was free to do so, but in any case it was a counsel based on the situation of the community as described by Mark.[24] Luther adds the further critical remark that in his opinion even this "counseled" anointing was not given to all the sick, since sickness and death are part of the Church's glory. Only they received the "last anointing" (in Luther's interpretation) who did not have sufficient patience and could hardly endure their sickness because their faith was coarse and too superficial. Christ himself left such people in their weakness and then filled them with his power so that the miraculous power of faith might become clear through them.[25] The imposition of hands and prayer, then, are the decisive factors in the anointing.

Luther developed these points in further reflection on the meaning of this ecclesial action. He observes that we must deal cautiously and carefully with this tradition that comes from James, for it is certain that James connects the promise of healing and forgiveness not with the anointing as such but with the prayer of faith.[26] But, says Luther, the "faith" here cannot be the faith of the priest who administers the anointing, but must rather be the faith of the recipient, since the latter alone can be the recipient of the divine promise. Luther therefore asks a critical question: In the present-day practice of the sacrament of the dying where do we find faith or even the prayer of faith? "But where is the prayer of faith in our present use of extreme unction? Who prays over the sick one in such faith as not to doubt that he will recover? Such a prayer of faith James here describes, of which he said at the beginning of his epistle: 'But let him ask in faith, with no doubting.' And Christ says of it: 'Whatever you ask in prayer, believe that you will receive it, and you will.'"[27] Luther's opinion, then, is that even today the prayer of faith and the healing it effects are possible at all times, but that in fact faith today is largely neglected, with the result that people do not attain the goal connected with the apostolic promise of healing, but rather experience the very opposite.[28]

In concluding, Luther sums up his position: the anointing is simply a "sacramental" action in the same sense as the blessing of water or salt, but is in no way necessary for the sick. It is the community's duty to visit the sick, and to do this through those members who best represent its faith, namely, the elders, who are also capable of healing nature and sickness.

"For we cannot deny that any creature whatsoever may be consecrated by the Word and by prayer, as the apostle Paul teaches us [1 Tm 4:4–5]. We do not deny, therefore, that forgiveness and peace are granted through extreme unction; not because it is a sacrament divinely instituted, but because he who receives it believes that these blessings are granted to him."[29]

The faith of the minister may err, but the faith of the recipient need not. The power of faith is manifested even in a mistaken use of the sacrament, provided the recipient accepts the word connected with it and directs his faith to this word.

Even today, then, the anointing may be accepted and retained as a rite of the ancient Church, but in no sense as a sacrament. Later, in 1528, in a personal confession of faith that accompanies one of his writings against Zwingli on the Lord's Supper, Luther remarks:

"If anointing were practiced in accordance with the gospel, Mark 6[:13] and James 5[:14], I would let it pass. But to make a sacrament out of it is nonsense. Just as, in place of vigils and masses for the dead, one might well deliver a sermon on death and eternal life, and also pray during the obsequies and meditate upon our own end, as it seems was the practice of the ancients, so it would also be good to visit the sick, pray and admonish, and if anyone wished in addition to anoint him with oil, he should be free to do so in the name of God."[30]

The important thing, therefore, is the visiting of the sick, with the prayer of faith playing the chief role in it. Everything else is "an ordinance of human devotion, not a commandment of God."[31] For this reason, as Luther says to Elector Joachim II of Brandenburg in a letter of December 1539, a Reformed church-order should not include the custom of anointing and of bringing this "sacrament" to the sick, lest this become a new occasion for misinterpreting the anointing as a real sacrament.[32] As in the ancient Church, so in the Churches of today customs need not be everywhere the same. A principle of plurality operates within the unity of the Church, as Luther experienced in the healing of the jewel-case maker of Wittenberg, as he tells it himself in 1545.[33]

Let me say by way of summary that according to Luther's critique of the sacrament of extreme unction, the visiting of the sick and the prayer of faith are essential elements in the life of the Christian community. The spiritualistic interpretation of sickness which Luther had given two years prior to his writing of *The Babylonian Captivity of the Church* is not yet entirely set aside, but it does recede into the background in favor of this new approach which lays all the emphasis on the visiting of the sick and on prayer by the representatives of the community.

III

In a later sermon on the healing of the paralytic in Matthew 9:1ff. Luther reflected further on the power of prayer to effect healing through a faith that can heal even nature itself. He continues to regard the faith both of the paralytic himself and of those who carried him into Christ's presence as the decisive factor in bringing them to him. Luther also stresses the point that this faith is presupposed by the healing Christ effects here. The important thing, then, is that in this miracle there is a healing not only of the body but of the soul as well, and that the latter healing is even a greater work than the healing of the body. The forgiveness of sins must precede the healing of the body; the latter results from the healing of the soul. While the man desires the healing of his limbs, God forgives his sins, and a consequence of this forgiveness is the bodily healing. For Luther, then, the miracle of bodily healing is not the most important thing, but the faith with which the man approaches the Lord and with which others bring him. "Christ saw their faith and healed the man. It follows that Christ looks only to faith and to nothing else. God therefore does not heal the man in body alone; no, he makes him healthy and blest in soul as well."[34]

This pericope also makes it clear to Luther that not only the faith of the paralytic himself but also the "alien faith" of the man's carriers is to be regarded as a presupposition of the miracle. The sick man's porters, too, looked to Christ alone for all help, and this, for Luther, is the important thing. For this reason "alien faith" is always a sign of love, such as the porters give here by bringing the sick man to the Lord. In the final analysis the "alien faith" was a help not so much for the sick man as for God or Christ, in accomplishing the work of healing the paralytic. "You see that the faith of others, in the person of the porters, helped the paralytic; there is a good deal that might be said on this subject. . . . We see this faith of others, in this case, in the men who carried the paralytic; they helped their neighbor with their faith. This faith did not help themselves; rather through their faith they helped God."[35]

When Luther discusses the healing of the paralytic in this sermon on Matthew 9:1ff. from the year 1522, he is no longer interested in the spiritual character of the sickness, as he had been in the sermon of four years earlier. The spiritual approach has been replaced with a more intellectual and psychological one; or, it might be said, the latter developed out of the former. Luther now describes Christ as a "most learned physician," who unerringly diagnoses the sickness of the afflicted and oppressed conscience. Above all, Luther attributes to him insight into the psychological effects on the person of fear, intimidation, and pessimism with regard to any help. Christ knows that these attitudes of soul have their basis in the sins of these same human beings. Therefore Christ, as "perfect physician," gives forgiveness of sin priority over bodily healing, inasmuch as sickness of body is but a consequence of sickness of soul.

"Thus before he acts [as perfect physician] and heals the sickness of [bodily] paralysis, he removes what would be called the causes of this sickness, namely, sin. He is telling us that it is easy to heal the sickness of the body once the sickness of the soul has been healed, since this is the cause of the bodily sickness. For this reason he first gives health to the spirit [= mind and heart] and raises it up. The raising up of the spirit means that the body is already more than half healed."[36]

This view of the priority of the psychic and mental over the bodily is not further developed by Luther in terms of the possibilities of psychosomatic healing. Nonetheless his approach does provide theological reflection with a starting point for a conception of healing that uses the psychic as a basis and systematically works to uncover and eliminate sin by awakening an awareness of forgiveness and to make a corresponding psychic analysis of sickness itself.

The bases for this conception are certainly present in Luther's thinking on psychotherapy, as is clear from his further treatment of the blind man. Luther describes a man who lives without power to hear and see as a "deformed body," as a "lump" or "stump," that is capable only of a life restricted to tasting and feeling and is unable to grasp and penetrate with the mind the objects apprehended in these limited ways. While Luther speaks elsewhere of the unconsciousness that marks all life—"the foolish live but do not realize it"[37]—he emphasizes here the consciousness of a life that grasps its own being and action. As compared with such a conscious individual, a blind man, who is able to perceive the world about him only in an imperfect way, is only an "image" of true man. He is truly a being that is unknown to itself, a nothing that in a sense does not exist at all or at least leads only a quasi-existence.[38]

As thus viewed, the healing of a blind man, such as Jesus effected, will inevitably appear in a new light. It is not simply a restoration of sight, but is in a true sense a new creation of the entire person; it is in fact a new creation of the new man from nothing, a creation that is on a par with the creation of Adam and Eve or the creation of each individual person from human seed. Luther remarks that

". . . after receiving his health that blind man undoubtedly thought he had previously not existed in the world [i.e., as a self-conscious person] but was only beginning at this moment truly to be and become [i.e., beginning his truly human development], because he could remember nothing from his earlier life, just as Adam could only think that he had not previously existed. For this reason the miracle so freely bestowed is truly magnificent."[39]

Luther's distinction between a sickness of the soul and a sickness of the body is intelligible only in terms of a conception of man as embodied spirit. The result is a new understanding of the person and a holistic conception of the human being, as well as a correlation of "health" and "sickness" and the idea that consciousness of life is a constitutive element of personhood.

It is worth noting that precisely in connection with the idea of man as a spiritual and corporeal unity, Luther emphasizes the "alien faith" or "faith of others" (*fides aliena*) which must lead us to the prayer of faith not solely for ourselves but for others as well.[40] This emphasis on prayer and intercession for others makes it clear that the existence of the new man cannot be conceived as independent of the community of which he is a part and which sustains him, but on the contrary, is rendered possible and is supported only by this community, even though the ultimate ground of this new existence is divine creation from nothing. As Luther repeatedly emphasizes, the intercessory prayer of the community "obliges" and in a sense "forces" God to perform the requested miracle, inasmuch as he does not withdraw from his creatures and leave them to themselves. Luther repeatedly emphasizes this great power of prayer.

In a late work, *Comfort for Women Who Have Had a Miscarriage* (1542), Luther goes into the problem of intercessory prayer as something that distinguishes a Christian from an atheist, a Muslim, or a follower of some primitive religion, inasmuch as he prays for others and others in turn pray for him. But intercessory prayer does not mean in this context a passing heartfelt sigh; it means rather urgent and continuous prayer, prayer that repeatedly rises without formulas from the heart: such prayer is "a great, unbearable cry in God's ears. God must listen."[41]

Luther is, of course, quite clear on the distinction between hearing a prayer (or listening to it) and answering it (fulfilling the desire voiced). The prayer of the heart, this constant and urgent beseeching of God, is heard indeed, but the answer is not always what the one praying has in mind. Think of how God deals with stillborn children or with children who die right after birth and before baptism. We hope and believe that God will act to give salvation and blessedness, where there can be no personal faith on the part of the child but only intercession from others.

"For this reason one ought not straightaway condemn such infants for whom and concerning whom believers and Christians have devoted their longing and yearning and praying. Nor ought one to consider them the same as others for whom no faith, prayer, or yearning are expressed on the part of Christians and believers. God intends that his promise and our prayer or yearning which is grounded in that promise should not be disdained or rejected, but be highly valued and esteemed. I have said it before and preached it often enough: God accomplishes much through the faith and longing of another, even a stranger, even though there is still no personal faith. But this is given through the channel of another's intercession, as in the gospel Christ raised the widow's son at Naim because of the prayers of his mother apart from the faith of the son. And he freed the little daughter of the Canaanite woman from the demon through the faith of the mother apart from the daughter's faith. The same was true of the king's son, John 4[:46–54], and of the paralytic and many others of whom we need not say anything here."[42]

As far as the Old Testament is concerned, the granting of a child to Rebecca as a result of Isaac's urgent prayer serves Luther as an example of the power of the faith of another and of the effects of intercessory prayer. This and the other examples already mentioned are, as it were, a commentary on and illustration of the words in James 5:16, with which Luther had to come to grips in his criticism of the sacrament of extreme unction and which led him to a new emphasis in the practice of this ecclesial rite: an emphasis on prayer for the sick. "The prayer of the just has great power when it is serious."[43] Luther's conclusion is that God wants us to pray to him in all needs, even those of the body.

IV

In connection with this conception of man as embodied spirit, I shall by way of conclusion say something about Luther's views on the bodily effects of the Lord's Supper. These views stand in conscious contrast with a reduction of the eucharist and its effects to the spiritual and the interior.

In connection with the well-known Marburg Colloquy with Zwingli, Luther was quite able to accept the view that the Supper is a "spiritual food" and "very necessary for everyone."[44] At the same time, however, he was convinced that Christ is "essentially" and "personally" present in the Supper; in other words, he is present in spirit and body, with his divinity and his humanity.[45] In saying this he is not simply making a statement about the full meaning of the bread and the body of Christ, the wine and the blood of Christ. He is also saying that the Supper is both a spiritual and a bodily food. This is important in the question of the effects of the Supper. In keeping with his holistic view of the eucharist, Luther maintains in complete opposition to Zwingli that the Supper has its effects not only on the spirit but also on the body.

Luther is here following a line of thought found in Eastern theology as he thinks of our bodies being glorified by the body and blood of Christ. The "flesh of Christ" or "flesh of God," as Luther very realistically describes the bread of the Supper in keeping with his holistic conception, has its effects on the whole person, including the body, for it permeates the entire person, makes him spiritual, sanctifies him, and creates in him a resurrection body.[46] Christ's flesh, which we eat in the Supper, is "pure spirit, pure holiness, utter purity"; it is a "deathless spiritual flesh" which the worthy and the unworthy, the believing and the unbelieving alike receive. But only the worthy and the believing eat it in the right way, that is, spiritually, while for the others it brings only "poison and death," since they are nothing but "flesh-eaters."[47] The Supper works on our bodies in such a way as to renew them in their very nature, turning them into resurrection bodies; the gift of the eucharist turns the person who receives it aright into a truly spiritual person.[48] "The poor bag of worms that is our body" becomes a "holy, living man," who is already present though hidden in faith and hope, in order to be fully manifested on the last day.[49]

It must be noted that into these considerations on the bodily effects of the Supper, Luther introduces "faith" and "hope" and the concept of hiddenness, thus relieving his thinking of any lack of differentiation. He did not subsequently develop these ideas, which are opposed to a pure intellectualization and spiritualization of the Supper. In fact, they have already disappeared in the Large Catechism. Luther did, however, hold fast to the incarnational character of the eucharist and the holistic conception of man, although neither emerges so clearly as in the discussion of the nature of the Supper. The Supper, by reason of its inherent structure, must touch both areas of the human person, that is, spirit and body, because both of these together are required for the "whole man." The "sanctification" of man that is effected by the Supper is therefore at the same time the "healing" of man, in the sense of a renewal, a re-creation of the entire person.

Now that we are at the end of these considerations, we find we have covered a great deal of ground. What significance do the views of Luther presented here have for the present day, and in particular for a special field of pastoral care in which the concurrence and collaboration of doctor and pastor are desirable and necessary? As a response to this question, let me summarize the results of my exposition in the following several points.

1. Luther's thinking of the various subjects treated shows a keen sense of reality. This manifests itself even where his spiritual

interpretation of sickness seems to carry him farthest from a realistic view of the latter. This interpretation of sickness in terms of its spiritual and psychic bases is precisely a perspective that is or should be fully intelligible to us today. It is based, on the one hand, on a holistic conception of man and, on the other, on the idea that psychic processes can find bodily expression. Such a view of sickness, therefore, makes possible the development of a psychotherapy. Above all, however, it presents the pastoral worker with the task of adopting a holistic view of the sick person and seeing pastoral work as a contribution to a healing process in which he is especially qualified to engage by reason of the kerygma which is entrusted to him and the calling which has been given to him.

2. The approach to sickness as "sign," which Luther developed in his early sermon on the man born blind, can be of service today in helping individuals adopt a specific attitude in their dealings with the sick. If we look upon sickness as a "sign," we will necessarily emphasize its social aspect as well. The sick person can never be considered in isolation, that is, as unrelated to the environing society. Since social conditions have often contributed to his illness, either at the physical or at the spiritual level, all the members of society must be challenged to face their own responsibility for the sick person and must be called to service, concern, and a cooperative attitude. Society's responsibility for the sick must also find expression in creating and supporting such health institutions as sanatoria, old-age homes, and hospitals, and this in as open and healthy a location as possible. Such an approach is the only correct response to the sign-nature of sickness, for only then is sickness no longer regarded as solely the fate, deserved or undeserved, of the individual.

3. Even more than society generally, the Christian community and the Church must realize the special duty imposed on them by such an interpretation of sickness. Greater attention must be given to pastoral care of the sick by training future pastors for this work. Only such ministers must be accepted for this work as have the needed human and charismatic qualifications. Among the human qualifications is an intensive study of many areas of modern medicine and psychology; this study must be undertaken with the understanding that man is always a unity of body and soul.

4. The intercession for the sick which Luther so greatly emphasizes has largely disappeared in our communities, and one is tempted to apply to the Evangelical Churches of our day the sharp criticism Luther leveled at the sacrament of extreme unction, namely, that no one believed any longer in the power of the prayers for healing that accompanied the rite. It is precisely in intercessory

prayer that the Church exercises a unique power of caring for the sick in ways other than the ministry of visitation exercised by the community. A serious involvement in intercessory prayer would open up to the Church a vast field that has become in good measure closed to it because many of its members now seek healing and help in secular ways and by secular means.

It makes good sense, then, for the Church of England to include "The Order for the Visitation of the Sick" in the *Book of Common Prayer* as a special ecclesial action. In our communities, too, this aspect of the Church's activity should be more fully developed, and the exercise of it not left solely to the individual efforts of each pastor. The place of healing through intercessory prayer and the faith of the community would then take on a new importance in our Church, whereas at present it is almost entirely a peripheral matter. Then it would once again be possible to speak of God himself calling the sick person. This call is to be seen as ultimately residing in the fact that, as Jesus explained the sickness of the man born blind, sickness exists "that the works of God might be made manifest" in the sick (Jn 9:3).

Elie MÉLIA

The Sacrament
of the Anointing of the Sick:
Its Historical Development
and Current Practice

INTRODUCTION

The perspective adopted in this study is that of pastoral theology, which has for one of its main tasks to elucidate the meaning of the sacraments in regard to their possible or actual influence (a relationship in which practice and meaning condition each other). At the present time, however, the practice of this sacrament varies not only from one autocephalous Church to another but even within a given Church. The same holds for the theology and current catechesis of the sacrament. Are we dealing in this sacrament with a rite of healing, so that no other use of it is possible? If we accept a connection between physical healing and a spiritual healing through repentance, what is the nature of this connection? Does the rite have to do simply with individual cases (charism), or is it a sign and proclamation with a larger significance and one that is accomplished in the community which is the Church (therefore, a sacrament)?

And if it is a sacrament, can it be administered to the healthy? Under what conditions? Why?

If we look into the euchologia, we will be surprised by the variations in the ritual for this sacrament. We may well have the impression that the oldest manuscripts are independently recording a particular celebration of the sacrament. These celebrations, it seems, could hardly have been regular occurrences once it became the rule that seven priests had to come together for the rite and that the long office of the oil had to be celebrated in a sequence of Vespers, Matins, and Mass. The euchology in manuscript Coislin No. 213 (dating from 1027) prescribed that the service had to be performed on seven successive days, while the Barberini euchology (ninth century) is satisfied with a simultaneous celebration in seven different churches!

In order to answer the questions I have put to myself, I have endeavored above all to explain the structure of the rite in connection with the divine office (mainly the diurnal cycle) and to accept the real risk that in doing so I may be superficial and neglect details which are not unimportant for an understanding of the sacrament. But I had to limit myself to what seems to me not only essential but also adequate, at least for a first probe into basic meaning.

For the early tradition and the subsequent Western tradition, I have based my study on the articles "Huile" and "Extrême-Onction" in the *Dictionnaire d'Archéologie Chrétienne et de Liturgie* and the *Dictionnaire de Théologie Catholique*; in both cases the articles date, unfortunately, from as far back as 1924–1925.[1] For Chavasse's work on the medieval period,[2] I considered myself justified in using the brief presentation of it that is given in Cl. Ortemann, *Le sacrement des malades* (Lyons, 1971).

For the Eastern tradition (which forms the substance of my essay), I have relied on the works produced by Orthodox liturgists before 1917.[3] The year 1917 is now long past, but those scholars had the merit of making a careful and almost exhaustive study of the manuscript tradition of the Eastern euchologies, at least as represented by the rich repertories of Goar, Denzinger, and Dmitrievsky.[4] To the latter must be added the collection of Georgian euchologies preserved in Georgia, made by that erudite and indefatigable scholar, Cornéli Kékélidzé.[5]

Names of the Sacrament

In Greek: *euchēlaion* (a combination of *euchē*, "prayer," and *elaiaon*, "oil"); *to hagion elaion* (holy oil); *heptapapadon* (set of seven priests).

In Russian: *eleosviastcenie; soborovanie.*

In Latin: *oleum orationis* (oil prayed over); *oleum* or *unctio infirmorum* (oil or anointing of the sick). From the twelfth century on: *extrema unctio* (last or "extreme" anointing); *unctio* (anointing); *sacramentum exeuntium* or *egredientium* (sacrament of the dying or departing).

Among the Syrians and Maronites: sacrament of the lamps (because the oil used in the anointing comes from the lamps which stand before the altar or the ikons).

Scriptural Inquiry into the Sacramental Nature of the Euchelaion

Among the ancient peoples who were Israel's neighbors, oil was much used for general therapeutic purposes; this was especially true of the Greeks and Romans. But the Jews also used it in this way (Is 1:6); Philo notes the fact in his *De somniis.*

In ancient paganism, anointing with oil also served as a religious rite of exorcism or consecration. And finally, it served as a burial rite. The Greeks placed vessels containing ointment in tombs and graves; these were the oil-flasks (*lēkuthoi*) now to be seen in the display cases of our museums. Salomon Reinach found a ritual for the anointing of the dead in the Iranian Avesta and regarded this as the origin of the Christian "last anointing." It would be interesting to know by what historical paths the connection was made. St. Irenaeus in the second century A.D. does report that:

". . . in order to redeem the faithful who were ready to leave this life, certain gnostics poured oil mixed with water on their heads and at the same time uttered the invocations mentioned earlier. This they did in order that the dead might not be seized and held by the principalities and higher powers and in order that the interior man might ascend higher by invisible paths."[6]

But it would be centuries before an anointing of the dead made its appearance in the Christian Church.

For Israel I may cite a Jewish apocryphal book, the *Assumption of Moses,* in which we find the dying Adam telling Eve to go with Seth to God and ask him to send an angel to paradise and "the tree which floweth with oil"; Adam will anoint himself with this oil and find peace. But Michael the archangel tells Seth: "Seth, man of God, weary not thyself with prayers and entreaties concerning the tree which floweth with oil to anoint thy father Adam. For it shall not be thine now, but in the end of the times."[7]

Nothing comparable is found in official Judaism. We may even detect there a rejection of any burial anointing that would be of a religious nature. This is all the more remarkable since the Jews did practice the embalming of the dead.

In Israel anointing with oil had a festal character. Even more, the omission of the use of oil was a sign of mourning. Thus in 2 Samuel 14:2, Joab sends a wise woman to David to plead for Absalom when the latter had killed his brother Amnon for violating their sister Tamar. Joab tells the woman to pretend to be in mourning; for this purpose she is to wear mourning garments and *not anoint herself with oil.* Similarly, in Daniel 10:3, before receiving his great vision, the prophet does penance for three weeks during which he takes no meat or wine and *does not anoint himself.* Finally, Isaiah 61:3 contrasts the oil of gladness with the garb of mourning.

Israel also had a rite of consecration through anointing with oil. Thus in Genesis 28:18, after his dream of the ladder joining heaven and earth, Jacob made a pillar out of the stone that had served him as a headrest and poured oil on the top of it. Later on, the tabernacle and various objects used in worship were consecrated by being anointed with oil (Ex 10:26; 40:10; Lv 8:10–11). Aaron and his sons were likewise consecrated for their ministry with an anointing (Ex 40:13–16; Lv 8:12, 30). Some of the prophets received the same kind of consecration; in 1 Kings 19:16, Elijah is told to anoint Jehu as king of Israel and Elisha as the prophet who will succeed Elijah himself. See also Psalm 104:15 (LXX numbering): "Touch not my anointed ones, do my prophets no harm!" Oil was also used for the anointing of kings: Saul, David, Solomon, and others. And finally the Messiah, that is, the Anointed One par excellence, is the eschatological Savior, and his anointing is the sign of his calling and his mission.

There is a noteworthy piece of information in the Talmud, in the Tractate Berakhot. Rabbi Simeon, son of Eleazar, authorizes Rabbi Meyer to anoint the sick with oil and wine on the sabbath. This may be compared with John 9:6 where Jesus on the sabbath uses dirt mixed with his spittle in order to cure the man blind from birth; there is a cry of scandal, but because the healing took place on a sabbath. See also Luke 10:34 for the use of oil as a therapeutic means.

When we turn to the New Testament we must attend first and foremost to the person of the Lord. He is called the Christ, that is, the Anointed One, "Christ" being the Greek translation of the Hebrew word which has come into English as "Messiah."

Although the ancient writers appeal to the parable of the Good Samaritan (Lk 10:30–37), it really sheds no light on our present problem. As for the anointing during supper at Bethany when Mary Magdalene pours ointment on the head of Christ (Mt 26:7; Mk 14:3) or over his feet (Jn 12:3), we must observe that the Lord himself interprets this action as done in anticipation of his burial (all three accounts).

The only instance in the gospels in which an anointing with oil is expressly connected with the charism of healing is found in Mark 6:13, according to which the Twelve on their missionary journey "cast out many demons, and anointed with oil many that were sick, and healed them." Elsewhere, healings are effected by the laying on of hands or by touching, although usually the manner in which the miracle is worked is not stated.

The Acts of the Apostles does not mention an anointing with oil in their accounts of healing. But the laying on of hands for healing appears only in 9:12, 17 (Saul healed by Ananias) and in 28:8 (Paul heals the governor of the island of Malta).

There is a reference to anointing in 1 John 2:20, 27, and 2 Corinthians 1:21–22, though this is usually connected with the sacrament of confirmation. In the second of these two passages the anointing is linked to a "sealing," the nature of which is not further specified. St. Paul speaks elsewhere of a seal impressed on us by the Spirit (Eph 1:13; 4:30); in Ephesians 4:30 the sealing is said to be "for the day of redemption." The same eschatological note is sounded in Revelation 7:3–8 where a seal is said to be placed on the foreheads of the elect; this seal is the name of the Lamb (7;12; cf. 14:1; 22:4). But it is possible that in all these passages "seal" is simply a metaphor.

In a place apart stands James 5:14 to the end of the chapter (and of the letter). Here we have an undeniable apostolic testimony, and tradition has appealed to it for the sacramental nature of the anointing of the sick. But we must define clearly the specific character of this anointing as it is seen in the Church's tradition. Three aspects emerge clearly enough from the passage in James, and all three must be held in balance: (1) the presence and action of the Church as represented by the presbyters whom the sick are urged to summon to their bedside; (2) the anointing with oil, done by the presbyters on the body of the sick person; (3) the prayer of faith and the mutual confession of sins, which, along with the anointing, secures the forgiveness of sins and the healing.

Are we dealing here with a sacrament? We must agree on a definition of this term. It seems to me that three elements are necessary if there is to be a sacrament: apostolic origin, involvement of the catholic Church as a whole, and, finally, the raising of the person to a new and higher state of life, that is, a passage to the eschatological order, to the eternal life which is communicated to believers by the power of the resurrection of Christ and Pentecost.

These three elements are indispensable in order to have, in the full sense, a sensible sign which communicates grace.

All three elements are to be found in the anointing of the sick. (1) Its apostolic origin, together with the quality of divine inspiration that attaches to the entire canon of scripture, ensures the reference to Jesus Christ himself and to his gospel of universal salvation. (2) The call for "the presbyters of the Church" is evidently a call for the Church as immediately accessible in the persons of the presbyters; these men represent the local Church, the latter being a manifestation in turn of the catholic Church. The general confession is made by each Christian to his fellows, but in the presence of the priests, and this collegial penance is sealed by the anointing which the priests confer. At the same time, the sick person is removed from the isolation imposed on him by his failing constitution, and he again takes his place in the full collegiality of the Church of God. (3) Finally, the prayer of faith and his repentance raise the sick person into the realm of eschatological reality, where not only illness but death itself are overcome and trodden underfoot, even while here on earth.

Two Preliminary Questions

Before getting into the historical development of the sacrament, I can make the exposition simpler by settling two preliminary questions that can make more explicit the sacramental value of the euchelaion and its practice.

First, what is the meaning of an anointing with oil that is conferred on the sick person by himself or by his relatives? This practice can be inferred from the oldest prayers for the blessing of oil, and the lives of the saints provide examples of it. To begin with, we must distinguish between the consecration of oil and the anointing done with the oil thus blessed. In all the ancient documents that speak of the sacrament, the oil is blessed either by the bishop (this has always been true in the West) or by the priests (at a very early date this became the practice in the East). Admittedly, we do find in the lives of the saints cases in which miracle workers, without priestly mandate, heal sick persons with oil that is not said to have been previously blessed. But silence regarding any consecration of the oil used should not too quickly lead us to conclude that in fact no liturgical act of blessing had taken place. Moreover, we must not confuse the *charism* of healing and the *sacrament* of the sick in which healing is certainly a much desired effect but not an effect that is an indispensable condition for the existence of the sacrament. The charism wins from God the healing of the sick person, which is accomplished in very diverse ways, often without any action or even without any word being spoken, and sometimes even at a distance. The sacrament, on the other hand, signifies through a rite, that is, a visible, *normative* action of the Church, the unique and comprehensive gift to the Church and through her to the human race of Christ's victory over evil and death. Let me add that this sign-function, far from remaining external to the sick person, really elevates his consciousness as a believer and wins him an increase of spiritual life; it conforms him in some degree to the body of the risen Lord and disposes the whole person—body, soul and spirit—for eternal life.

Only the anointing was practiced by individuals using oil that had been liturgically blessed. The practice only *supplemented,* and did not replace, the sacramental action in cases in which priests were not available (e.g., in times of violent persecution) or in which the sickness was minor and did not necessitate a summoning of the full ecclesiastical apparatus. Even in our own day the faithful take home with them oil that has been blessed at Jerusalem or Bari or some other venerated place, or they may take home wads of cloth that have been dipped in the oil which is blessed at the solemn celebration of the euchelaion during Holy Week; these practices are in no way in competition with the sacrament. Because the Church had reason to fear the mischievous influence of popular superstition in the form of incantations and other uses of anointing, she was soon led to resist anointing as practiced by laypersons, even if they were making use of consecrated oil. But as we well know, customs are long-lived and often survive prohibitions.

A second point that needs to be discussed in order to clear the ground is the number of priests required for the celebration of the anointing of the sick. James 5:14 bids the sick person summon the "priests of the Church." Exegetes see in the term a collective plural or a plural of category. We must remember that at that period the local Church was headed by a college of presbyters (elders). The plural number does not seem in this passage to be a determining factor, but later on the plurality will be required. A very old euchologium, the Barberini (eighth-ninth centuries), already specifies seven priests. John XI Bekkos, the unionist patriarch of Constantinople, wrote to Pope John XXI in 1277: "Along with the other sacraments we also acknowledge the euchelaion which among us is known as the heptapapadon because of the manner in which it is celebrated" (heptapapadon means a group of seven priests). However, the euchologion in manuscript Sinai No. 973 (from the year 1153), while referring to seven celebrants, also adds that "in case of need and if priests are lacking, the rite is celebrated by two or three."[8]

The famous liturgist Simeon, archbishop of Thessalonika (d. 1429), uses biblical allusions to justify both the number three and the number seven; he rejects celebration by a single priest in his Responses to Metropolitan Gabriel of Pentapolis, but this at least shows that the question was being raised in his day. The Ritual of Peter Mogila, Metropolitan of Kiev in the seventeenth century, speaks of seven celebrants, but allows two or three and, in cases when death is imminent, even one. Present-day practice is to celebrate the blessing of the oil during Holy Week in a collegial manner, but there is less formality in the administration of the euchelaion to the sick.

It is to be noted that the use of seven celebrants holds equally in the case of an episcopal celebration. Thus in his condemnation of the practice of administering the euchelaion to the deceased, the Ecumenical Patriarch Nicephorus II (patriarch in 1260) refers to his predecessor Arsenius (1255–1260; 1261–1266), who had decreed that the euchelaion be administered by seven celebrants "even if they be bishops or metropolitans."[9] It seems clear that concelebrating priests could make up the necessary quorum.

HISTORICAL DEVELOPMENT OF THE SACRAMENT

The First Centuries

If we are to get at the specific meaning of the euchelaion and establish a judicious balance among its various elements, we must investigate the ancient tradition. We will see that healing is not the sole purpose of the sacrament and that the concern is rather to integrate the sick person into the catholic Church–Body of Christ, with an emphasis on repentance in view of reconciliation with the Church or, more accurately, with God and in the Church. This action is especially justified in and adapted to the time of sickness, but it retains its meaning even where there is no physical illness.

We find no trace of the euchelaion before the third century. This silence during a period of bloody persecution is really not surprising. It is easy to imagine an interruption in the celebration of the sacrament mentioned in the letter of James, if for no other reason than this may have been a practice peculiar to the Jewish-Christian milieu and would have disappeared at the end of the first century. But Christians never ceased to read the scriptures, and the formal statement in the letter of James could not have remained simply a dead letter.

At the beginning of the third century, in the *Apostolic Tradition* of St. Hippolytus of Rome and in the other documents dependent on it, we find short prayers of blessing which are pronounced by the bishop over the offering of oil and which mention health among the effects asked from God. But is the reference to an anointing of the sick, or is it a vestige of the ancient agapes, such as we have in the ritual presently used on the vigil of great feasts: a blessing of five loaves and of cheese and oil at the end of Vespers, and an anointing with oil at Matins?

The *Apostolic Tradition* puts the prayer over the oil after the prayers of the sacred oblation, the order being: ordination of a bishop, prayers of the oblation, offering of oil, offering of cheese and olives, ordination of priests and other ministers. Here is the Latin text:

"Si quis oleum offert, secundum panis oblationem et uini, et non ad sermonem dicat sed simili uirtute, gratias refert dicens: 'Ut oleum hoc sanctificans dans, d(eu)s, sanitatem utentibus et percipientibus, unde uncxisti reges, sacerdotes et profetas, sic et omnibus gustantib(us) confortationem et sanitatem utentibus illud praebeat.' "[10]

The Latin text is difficult. Dom Botte translates as follows:

"If anyone offers oil, let him [the bishop] give thanks in the same manner as at the oblation of bread and wine; let him say, not in these very words but to the same effect: 'Just as by sanctifying this oil, O God, you grant health to those who are anointed with it and who receive this [oil] with which you anointed kings, priests and prophets, so may it bring consolation to those who taste it and health to those who use it.' "

There is, of course, a similar testimony in Book VIII of the *Apostolic Constitutions* (sixth century), since this Book is a reworking of the *Apostolic Tradition*:

"As for the water and oil I, Matthew, order that the bishop bless the water and oil, or, if he is absent, that a priest bless them in the presence of a deacon; if the bishop is present, the priest and deacon are also to be there. Let him say: 'Lord of hosts . . . sanctify this water and this wine through Christ, in the name of him who has offered them, and grant them the power to produce health, to expel sickness, to put demons to flight, and to ward off every ambush, through Christ who is our hope.' "[11]

While St. Hippolytus may have said nothing about the bishop's obligations to the sick, his Eastern adapters did not do the same. In the *Canons of Hippolytus,* a work later than Hippolytus but closely dependent on him, Canon XXIV, no. 199, prescribes that the deacon is to make known to the bishop who are sick and to accompany him on his visits to them. No. 200 adds: "It is important for the head of the priests to visit the sick; they are lifted out of their sickness when the bishop comes to them, and especially if he prays over them."[12]

Another "Hippolytan" document, the *Testament of Our Lord Jesus Christ* (which has come down to us in Syriac), does not seem to me to be sufficiently clear, and its date is uncertain (third century according to I. E. Rahmani, the editor; fifth century according to others):

"If a priest is to consecrate oil for healing those who suffer, let him set the vessel of oil before the altar and say in a low voice: 'Lord God, you have given to us [priests] the Spirit, the Paraclete, the Lord, the saving Name that is unconquerable and hidden from the foolish but revealed to the wise. Christ, you are our sanctifier and you heal all sickness and suffering. Grant the gift of healing to those whom you have rendered worthy of this favor. Send upon this oil, which is an image of your abundance, the help of your merciful kindness, in order that it may set free those who suffer, heal those who are sick, and *sanctify those who return, having drawn near to you faith.* For you are mighty and worthy of glory through all the ages, Amen.' "

L. Godefroy's French translation of the passage in the *Dictionnaire de Théologie Catholique* suggests that those anointed are dying, but Aguentov translates "sanctify those who return when they come to faith in you" and is of the opinion that the passage is speaking of apostates and serious sinners who are admitted to reconciliation by means of an anointing with blessed oil.[14]

Toward the middle of the third century, Origen is more explicit on the penitential purpose of the anointing. After listing six means of overcoming sin, namely, baptism, martyrdom, almsgiving, forgiveness (of offenses), zeal, and love of God, Origen adds:

"There is a seventh way, but it is hard and painful: I mean the remission of sins through [public] penance. The sinner bathes his bed in tears, and tears become his bread day and night; he does not blush to reveal his sin to the Lord's priest and to ask for a remedy, in accordance with what is written: 'I will admit my unjust act to the Lord, testifying against myself, and you have forgiven the wickedness of my heart.' Thus there is put into practice what the apostle says: 'If anyone is sick, let him call the presbyters of the

Church, and let them impose hands on him, anointing him with oil, in the name of the Lord, and the prayer of faith will save the sick person, and if the person is in sin, his sins will be forgiven him.' ''[15]

Note that Origen introduces mention of a laying on of hands into the text of James, although the canonical text says nothing of it. For Origen, then, penance normally involves personal repentance and confession to a priest, with these actions then being ratified by the laying on of hands and an anointing with oil, both of these being done by priests.

This testimony of the Alexandrine doctor, a man little inclined to sacramental realism, has to be put in the context of the development of public penance, a development which was rapid precisely at this time, the middle of the third century. After Pope Callistus (218–222) had admitted adulterers to (public) penance, to the great scandal of the traditionalist Hippolytus[16] and the rigorist Tertullian,[17] the dispute over penance flared up again, this time with regard to the *lapsi*. The new phase began at Carthage when Cyprian disagreed with certain of the *confessores* and decreed that apostates should be readmitted only through the mediation of priests, and even then only on their deathbeds. This action, insofar as it set death as the limit for ecclesiastical sanctions, was confirmed especially in the thirteenth canon of the First Council of Nicaea (325). The whole business is to be regarded as one factor in the shift from the anointing of the sick to the idea of a "last anointing" of the dying, which subsequently took hold in Western Christianity.

The fourth century provides as yet only infrequent references to the euchelaion. In the Euchologion of Serapion, who was bishop of Thmuis and a faithful supporter of St. Athanasius of Alexandria, there are two prayers for the blessing of oil. The first is included among five prayers of the Mass, coming between the prayer over the faithful after communion and the final blessing of the congregation: "In the name of your only Son we bless . . . these creatures [water and oil]. . . . Bestow healing power on these creatures so that every fever and demon and sickness may be expelled through this drink and this anointing, and so that the use of these creatures may become a healing remedy that restores complete health."[18]

The second prayer occurs in the second part of the Euchologion, which Godefroy describes as an "embryonic ritual." The prayers follow this order: first, baptismal prayers (blessing of water, prayer over the neophytes after the renunciation of Satan; prayer for their entering and leaving the baptismal pool; prayer for baptismal anointing and for chrismation); then a series of ordination prayers, accompanied by the imposition of hands (deacons, priests, bishops); then a prayer over the oil of the sick; and finally a prayer for the dead. The prayer over the oil of the sick focuses on healing and on the forgiveness of sins:

"Prayer over the oil of the sick or over the bread or over the water.—We call upon you who have all authority and power, O Savior of all human beings, Father of our Lord and Savior Jesus Christ, and we ask you to send healing power from the heights of heaven, from the only Son, upon this oil in order that it may remove all sickness and infirmity far from those who are anointed with it or who share in your creatures [the gifts named]; that it may serve them as an antidote against every demon; that it may expel every unclean spirit from them, banish every evil spirit, dispel every fever and chill and sickness; that it may grant them good grace and *forgiveness of sins*; that it may be for them a remedy for life and salvation and bring them health and integrity of soul, body and spirit, a perfect constitution. Lord, let every satanic power, every demon, every plot of the adversary, every blow, torment or pain, every suffering or shock or disturbance or evil shadow fear your holy name which we invoke now, and the name of the only Son, so that glory may be given to the name of him who was crucified for us and was raised and took our sicknesses and infirmities upon himself: Jesus Christ who will come to judge the living and the dead. For through him may glory and power be yours in the Holy Spirit, now and through all the ages. Amen."[19]

Here we seem to have the first appearance of a sacramental euchelaion in two phases: a prayer for the blessing of the oil and a prayer of anointing. These two parts are to be found in all the euchologia.

The close connection between the anointing with holy oil and the forgiveness of sins is again confirmed for Syria by St. Aphraates (ca. 345) in his *Demonstration*. Here he names the various uses of consecrated oil, a "life-giving sacrament that bestows perfection on Christians, priests, kings, and prophets, brings light into darkness, anoints the sick, and brings penitents back."[20]

In Book III of his *De sacerdotio* (ca. 385) St. John Chrysostom refers to James 5 in connection with postbaptismal penance. He compares natural parents with priests: the former give birth from blood and the desire of the flesh, the latter bestow a divine birth. In addition, while parents cannot ward off sickness and death, priests for their part:

". . . have often saved the soul that is sick and ready to die. They have made chastisement sweeter for some; others they have kept from falling at all. And this they have done not only by their teaching and counsel but also by the help of their prayers. Not only at the time when they lead us to rebirth [through baptism] but even subsequently, they also have the power to forgive sins: 'Is anyone among you sick . . . ?' "

St. John Chrysostom's testimony thus complements that of Origen and St. Aphraates.

The fifth century seems set apart in Church history by an evident development of ritual, a fixing of the liturgy, and a concentration on the clergy. The sacrament that interests us here did not escape this development. One witness to it is the anonymous author known as the Areopagite. (I shall discuss his writings a little further on.)

The letter which Pope Innocent I (402–417) wrote in answer to Bishop Decentius of Gubbio (Eugubium) states formally that the anointing of the sick is a sacrament: *genus sacramenti*, and makes this fact the reason for not administering this anointing to penitents. Innocent is here evidently referring to public penitents who were forbidden to receive communion during a specified period of time. Administration to penitents could be taken for granted as long as the anointing was not yet identified as "extreme unction." This oil "has been prepared by the bishop, and . . . not only priests but all Christians may use [it] for anointing, when their own needs or those of their family demand."[21] Innocent I also states the right of bishops to confer anointing; if the bishop is not explicitly mentioned, this is only because his other occupations rarely allow him time to visit the sick and confer the sacrament of anointing.

The priestly role in the administration of the sacrament of the holy oil tended, however, to become an exclusive one, and, as a result, administration in church tended to supplant administration in the home. Thus Isaac, bishop of Antioch (d. second half of fifth century), has occasion to issue the following exhortation:

"Woman, bestow your alms on the recluse, but receive anointing from your priest; feed the monk, but let the oil you use be that of the apostles . . . and receive anointing from your priest. The servants of Christ who are orthodox make it their practice to bring their sick and infirm to the holy altar, but they do not dare administer the oil lest they seem to show contempt for the house of expiation [reference to confession?]; wherever there is a priest in charge of leading the people, the faithful observe the legitimate rules."[22]

The situation is clearly illustrated by an episode in the life of St. Hypatius (fifth century). His disciple, Callinicus, tells us that "if the situation required the patient to be anointed, Hypatius would advise the abbot, who was a priest, and have him anoint the sick person with blessed oil. Often Hypatius would then send the person home cured in a few days' time."[23] St. Cyril of Alexandria[24] and Procopius of Gaza[25] contrast James 5 with the soothsayers and enchanters, whose practices amounted to idolatry and therefore made necessary a formal reconciliation with the Church.

The Nestorian council under Mar Joseph, who was Catholicos in 559, decrees: "When a person who has yielded to this weakness [superstition] is converted, let them offer him, as a means of healing, the oil of prayer (euchelaion) that is blessed by a priest, *just as they would to a person who is sick in body.*"[26]

St. Caesarius of Arles (d. 543) had to combat the same danger, and he recommended the same means:

"Each time a person falls sick, let him receive the body and blood of Christ and then let him anoint his body so that what is written may be proved true in him [there follows the text of James 5]. Consider, my friends, that he who when sick has recourse to the Church will deserve to receive bodily health and the forgiveness of his sins. Since these two blessings can be found in the Church, why go to the enchanters?"[27]

Caesarius returns to the subject in another passage: "How much more holy [than to engage in superstitious practices] and more salutary to have recourse to the Church, to receive the body and blood of Christ, and to anoint oneself and one's family with blessed oil used in a spirit of faith! Then, as St. James says, one will receive not only health of body but the forgiveness of sin as well." The same view reappears in St. Eligious, bishop of Noyan (d. 659), in his *De rectitudine catholicae conversationis.*[28]

In St. Caesarius we see something coming to the fore which, although not new, had not as yet been made so clear and explicit, namely, the formal connection between anointing and eucharistic communion. Note that Caesarius puts the eucharist before the anointing. The oldest Eastern euchologies locate the euchelaion within the Mass. This is the case in the Barberini euchology, which dates from the ninth century but is evidently not introducing a novelty; the same for the euchology in Coislin 213 (from the year 1027) and in Sinai 973 (from 1153). Not until the thirteenth century do we find euchologies in which the euchelaion is separated from Mass.

Western Development of the Anointing of the Sick

In the West the tradition regarding the sacrament of the anointing of the sick was explicitly developed at three levels—the canonical, the juridical, and the theological—during the age of Charlemagne. This age marked an extremely important turning point in the history of the Church and in history generally: an empire that regarded itself as the heir of ancient Rome set itself up as a rival of Byzantium (which made the same claim) under the leadership of the recently acquired power of the Franks and the Pepinid dynasty. The papacy was induced to stand apart from the Byzantine world; it thus acquired great and unshared authority over the western half of an as yet undivided Christendom. The result was a remarkable religious unification that survived the dismemberment of the Carolingian empire and became, at least until the period of the Renaissance, the main axis of civilization in Western Europe.

Various ninth century councils passed legislation regarding the sacrament of the sick: the bishop was to consecrate the oil, and the priests were to anoint the sick with it. Thus the Council of Chalon (*Concilium Caldubiense*) in 813 says in its thirteenth canon: "According to the teaching of St. James, with which the teaching of the Fathers is in accord, the sick should be anointed by a priest using oil blessed by the bishop."[29] Similar testimonies are given by the Councils of Aix-la-Chapelle in 836 and Mainz in 847.

Capitularies of Charlemagne that date from 769[30] and 803[31] connect the anointing of the sick with the forgiveness of sins and with communion, when they list the obligations of which the emperor explicitly reminds priests as being part of their calling. The Capitulary of 803 calls for "priests who are trained to administer the sacrament of penance to the people, to celebrate Mass, to care for the sick and administer the anointing of blessed oil and the sacred prayers that go with it, and, above all, to see to it that no one dies without viaticum." In 789, Theodulf, bishop of Orleans, was already writing: "Priests are to be reminded of their duty regarding the anointing of the sick and the administration to these of penance and viaticum, lest anyone die without viaticum."

Amalarius of Metz is a good representative of the theological thinking current at this stage in the development of the sacrament. He had been a student of Alcuin in the palace school and became bishop of Trier in 811; we see him involved in the eucharistic and predestinationist controversies at Lyons; he died after 850. In his *De officiis ecclesiasticis* (dedicated to Louis the Pious in 823) he establishes the sacramental nature of the anointing with oil: "The visible anointing is a sign, the invisible is the sacrament, and the spiritual takes place within. God has power to give gifts through a spiritual anointing without an accompanying bodily anointing. But because of our animal nature visible actions are done in order that invisible realities may be more easily grasped." He then associates the blessing of the oil, which is done after the Our Father during Holy Thursday Mass, with penance and the eucharist:

"If sickness were not the result of sin, the apostle James would not say: 'If he has committed sins, he will be forgiven.' In the epistle that is read on that same day Paul shows that sins are the cause of sickness [text of 1 Cor 11:28–30]. Paul shows us the wounds and James, his fellow apostle, shows us the remedy [text of Jas 5:14–15]. He shows us here what it is that saves the sick person, namely the prayer of faith, of which the anointing with oil is the sign. If a person falls ill because he has eaten the body of the Lord unworthily, the anointing with oil will bring healing. By the grace of God and through the action of the priest, the consecration of which I am speaking here is united to the consecration of the Lord's body and blood."[32]

The penitential purpose of the sacrament of anointing continued to be maintained for a long time. Thus for the famous canonist Yves of Chartres (d. 1116) the anointing of the sick is a "sacrament of public penance,"[33] and, still later, for Alain of Lille (d. 1202) it is a "sacrament of penance."[34] But well before this time, beginning in the tenth and eleventh centuries, we are told by Chavasse[35] that the anointing with oil was administered only to the dying. The reason for this restriction is to be seen in the idea of "the reconciliation of a penitent just before death"; in other words, it had become customary for people to put off until the end the necessary adjustment of accounts with God and the Church. Only in the ninth and tenth centuries did the rite of private penance, and the frequent use of it, make an appearance. From this point on the law of the division of work and thus of liturgical specialization and systematization come into play. Private and frequent penance absorbed into itself practically the whole mystery of repentance, while the anointing of the sick was increasingly reduced to a preparation for death.

This change in practice was reflected in the new name for the sacrament, which was known henceforth as "extreme unction." In his famous Sentences, which became the basis for all subsequent scholastic theology, Peter Lombard has a chapter entitled "On the Sacrament of Extreme Unction" in Book IV. This was, we might say, a point of no return.

According to St. Thomas Aquinas (1227–1274), this anointing "is to be given to those sick persons who are judged to be close to death." Duns Scotus (1266–1308) even maintained that the priest should wait until the person had become unconscious. The Council of Trent (1545–1563) in its fourteenth session introduced a qualification: "The Council asserts that this anointing is meant for the sick, *especially* for those who are so seriously ill that they seem on the point of expiring; for this reason it is called the sacrament of the dying."

The specifically penitential element of this sacrament had to be redefined in view of the new direction taken by the sacrament. The Thomists and the Scotists were at variance on the subject. In the Thomist view, extreme unction removed not only venial sins but also the *reliquiae peccati* (the remnants left by sin), that is, a kind of spiritual weakness which sin leaves in the soul. The Scotists denied the *reliquiae* and limited the penitential effect of the sacrament to the remission of such venial sins as had not been covered by the sacrament of penance. Pope Benedict XIV (1740–1758) forbade any further discussion of the *reliquiae peccati.*

Anxiety in the face of death and a desire for reassurance about paradise explained to some extent the shift from the anointing of the sick to a last anointing of the dying. But I think it legitimate to look for a positive cause as well, and I interpret the shift as a kind of penitential amnesty that itself was due to pastoral concern for sinners who had been cut off from communion, especially by canonical penalties, and for whom the Church had a special responsibility. We may see a vestige of such an amnesty in the prayer of absolution during the funeral rite; the prayers of the euchelaion likewise suggest the lifting of interdicts or curses pronounced by a priest or by the individual upon others. In its thirteenth canon, the Council of Nicaea (325) had long ago confirmed a practice that was already traditional: "The ancient law of the Church forbids depriving a person near death of the final and necessary viaticum. He must be forgiven and admitted to communion." In his letter to Decentius, Innocent I recalls the practice of the Church of Rome, which granted the forgiveness of sins on Holy Thursday but which would do the same outside of the Easter season if need arose. We may recall here that Holy Thursday was the day for blessing both the oil of catechumens and the oil of the sick.

It is true, of course, that in ancient times as well, once the anointing of the sick came into practice, this anointing was given also, and most of all, to those of the sick who were in danger of imminent death. What is new about "extreme unction" is the explicit shift in the center of gravity, that is, in the main concern of the Church. By the end of the development, healing is hardly even sought as an effect of the sacrament; the effect now sought is a preparation for a good death. This shift may not be visible in the sacramentaries, but it is certainly present in the conscious use to which they were put and in the catechesis that inevitably accompanies every sacrament.

At the same time there appeared the idea that the anointing could be administered only once, either in the course of the person's life, even if he recovered from the sickness, or in the course of the same illness.

Thus the element of penance was still present, but it was greatly reduced, and its meaning had changed. The desire for healing had linked the sacrament with life; henceforth the sacrament is focused on death.

Development of the Euchelaion in the East

In the East, too, the dying were anointed. Thus the disciple and biographer of Theodore of Studios tells us that he died (in 826) "after receiving the Eucharist and having his limbs anointed as was customary."[35a] But such an anointing did not exclude either an anointing of those less seriously ill or an anointing of the healthy or other penitential practices, as we shall see.

The East also saw the rise of a practice even more radical than that of anointing the dying; namely, the practice of anointing with holy oil the bodies of the deceased. This is something that has to be added to the historical record concerning extreme unction. What the two practices have in common is the signing of the believer's body for the kingdom of God and for life after the resurrection.

A first, though not entirely certain, piece of evidence for an anointing of the dead is to be found in the *Carmina Nisibiana* of St. Ephraem; the saint writes in Hymn 73: "Sign your deceased [or your dying, if a different punctuation of the Syriac alphabet is followed] with the cross in order that they may triumph over the second death."

In the fifth century, Pseudo-Dionysius devotes a long section (chaps. 4–7) of his *De hierarchia ecclesiastica* to the subject of "what is done thanks to the holy oils and of the consecrations for which these are used." In chapter 4 he writes:

"1. Such is the greatness of the most holy communion. . . . But there exists another consecration that is of the same [that is, sacramental] order; our teachers call it the sacrament of anointing.

2. . . . After the members of the hierarchy have spread sacred perfumes around the temple and devoutly sung the psalms and remembered the sacred scriptures, the high priest takes the holy oil and puts it on the altar of divine sacrifices under the cover of twelve holy wings. Meanwhile the entire assembly chants the most holy hymn which God gave the prophets through his inspiration [= the

Alleluia; cf. the end of the chapter]. Having consecrated the oil through a holy invocation, he uses it for the holiest liturgical consecrations, on occasion of almost all the hierarchical ceremonies."[36]

After thus describing the consecration of the oil, Pseudo-Dionysius discusses ordinations (chap. 5), monastic tonsure (chap. 6), and finally funeral rites (chap. 7). These rites end with an anointing of the dead with oil.

"The high priest, a man of God, recites over the body a very holy invocation. When this is finished, he kisses the dead person, and all present do the same. When all have given the kiss of peace, the high priest anoints the body with holy oil and prays for all the deceased; then he places the remains in holy ground alongside the remains of other saints of equal dignity [= 'the part of the church reserved for those of his order,' as is specified further on]; there the high priest pours holy oil over the remains of the deceased."

Pseudo-Dionysius ends his discourse with a fine comparison between the anointing of the dead and baptismal anointing: "Formerly, the anointing with holy oil summoned the initiated person to a sacred struggle; now the outpouring of oil signifies that the dead person has won the victory in that sacred struggle." According to Pseudo-Dionysius, then, the spiritual life of the Christian unfolds between two consecrations which form the boundaries of his existence and indicate a complete consecration of his person. In all this, no mention is made of the anointing of the sick. Pseudo-Dionysius was a systematizer and must not have seen sickness either as a sufficiently regular and normative phenomenon or as a boundary situation; consequently it is not liturgically significant and/or capable of forming part of his rigidly hierarchized universe.

In his *Scholia* on Pseudo-Dionysius, St. Maximus the Confessor (seventh century) naturally follows the author on whom he is commenting and whose authenticity he accepted, and this even on a point which he must have thought rather ambiguous. The same was to be true of George Pachimeros (1242–1310) in his commentaries on the *De hierarchia ecclesiastica*. Simeon of Thessalonika, the great fifteenth-century Byzantine liturgist, will also appeal to the man whom he calls "the divine Dionysius."

The Copts, who rejected Chalcedonian orthodoxy in the fifth century, anoint their dead with oil from the lamps that are placed before the holy ikons.[37] The Syriac *Nomocanon* of Bar Hebraeus, a learned Syrian bishop of the thirteenth century and author of a

Chronicle, prescribes that deceased priests be anointed with oil three times on the breast, with the prayer: "For repose from labor, for the dispelling of sadness, and for the blessedness that belongs to the saints: in the name of the Father, of the Son and of the Holy Spirit."[38]

Simeon of Thessalonika appeals to Pseudo-Dionysius for making monks the chief beneficiaries of the anointing of the dead: "We bury no monk except after having poured upon his remains oil from a lamp that has been sanctified by burning before the Lord [before the altar or before an ikon of the Lord]. As for our deceased brothers and sisters in Christ among the laity, (we do not bury them) until we have spread over them ashes from the censer."[39]

The same author writes:

"There are devout people who during their lifetime have recourse to the sacrament of the euchelaion as reparation and for the remission of sins. And if they are close to death, their relatives keep the oil and anoint their worthy remains with it in a holy signing that honors and sanctifies them. For those who have struggled are worthy of being honored with the holy anointing, and those must be marked with the seal of Christ who have lived in the likeness of Christ. Oil is also poured at their burial as the divine mercy is invoked."[40]

We see here how the anointing of the dead originated: holy oil remaining from the anointing of a dying person was poured into the casket; some euchologies explicitly prescribe such a rite.

The Greek ritual now in use prescribes that at the very end of the burial office oil from a lamp be poured into the casket, while a verse from Psalm 50 is recited: "Purge me with hyssop, and I shall be clean; wash me, and I shall be whiter than snow." The present Slavic ritual omits this rite, and prescribes that oil from a lamp or ashes from the censer be poured, or sprinkled, in the grave rather than in the open casket. The Slavic practice I interpret as a deliberate rejection, especially since the old manuscripts and even old editions of the Slavic ritual prescribe the Greek practice.[41]

Further evidence of rejection is to be seen in the office for the burial of priests. The opening rubric says:

"When a priest departs to the Lord, three priests come to remove him in a cloth from the funeral bed and place him in the earth. Since it is not fitting that he be stripped and washed, pure oil is rubbed on him [i.e., on the uncovered parts of the body]. Then his priestly [i.e., liturgical] vestments are put on him, his face is covered with an aer [a silken veil used to cover chalice and paten], and a book of the gospels is laid on his body."

Only after these initial steps, which seem to be rather a preparation of the body, does the burial office begin with the usual opening acclamation: "Blessed be our God. . . ." However, the present Russian ritual still prescribes that oil is to be poured into the coffins of dead monks. However, in the case of mónks, the preparation that precedes the burial office calls for rubbing the unstripped body with warm water and not with oil, as in the case of priests.

Canon 164 in the Nomocanon of the Great Ritual formally forbids the anointing of the dead, but it may be thinking of a complete celebration of the euchelaion for the benefit of the dead: *tas de, eis tous apothanontas, euchelaia mē tolmēsēs hollōs poēsai.* I do not see an anointing of the body of a deceased believer as being inherently impious, as long as there is no danger of superstition. Such an anointing would be a sacramental, but I consider that a sacramental differs from a sacrament only in that it does not have a formally acknowledged apostolic origin. The Church has more than once adapted her liturgies and modified her rites as the conditions of her witness required or to safeguard better the purity of the faith. As I pointed out earlier, the Apocalypse and, in ancient Judaism, the apocryphal *Assumption of Moses* were familiar with an anointing with oil that had an eschatological purpose. The anointing of the dead can signify that the deceased belong to the kingdom of God. It can be a witness against a kind of Platonizing spiritualism, and a sign of that victory over death which the resurrection of Christ has won for us. From this point of view, the idea and practice of an anointing of the dying are likewise justified: on the one hand, it is a preparation for a death in Christ, on the other, it is a sign of the eschatological seal to be set upon the body. But liturgical honesty forces us then to acknowledge that such an anointing is a quite different thing from the anointing of the sick.

Such a confusion of genres was pointed out and denounced at Byzantium in the thirteenth century. Patriarch Nicephorus (1260) expressly forbids using the rite of the euchelaion for the dead; he shows how unsuitable the prayers of the anointing of the sick are when applied to the dead.[42] A century and a half later, Simeon of Thessalonika echoes Nicephorus:

"I have studied this matter [the anointing of the dead], and I find it a praiseworthy practice. But it is not the same as the anointing given by the Lord and the Apostles and of which the gospel speaks: 'They anointed many sick persons with oil and cured them.' The brother of the Lord writes of this anointing in his Catholic Letter. The oil is one; there are not many oils. And the rite in which it is used is one, and is one of the seven sacraments. But in the case of the dead the oil is an offering to the Lord and for his glory, in order to win mercy and forgiveness for the deceased, just as for their sake we offer wax candles and other objects, either in church or at their tombs. By bringing them to the church and offering them, we intercede for the dead, and they obtain God's mercy." [43]

A whole series of fifteenth and sixteenth century euchologies have an office entitled "Euchelaion for the Deceased," which is nothing else than the euchelaion for the sick with little adaptation. Thus, for example, the euchologies in manuscripts Sinai 981 and 995, both from the sixteenth century; Holy Sepulcher of Constantinople 615 (dated 1522); Panteleimon-Athos 305 and Eusigmeni-Atthos 214, from the sixteenth century[44]; the Serbian euchology in the Synodal Library of Moscow, manuscript 374, from the fifteenth century; the Venetian edition of the euchology (1537).

All these euchologies, which were studied by Aguentov, have the same four-part structure as the euchelaion for the sick: Matins, blessing of the oil, seven New Testament readings with prayers, and a conclusion. The only exception is Sinai 981, which after the opening prayers skips Matins and passes directly to the readings. According to two of the euchologies—Holy Sepulcher of Constantinople and Panteleimon—after Matins a celebrant goes to the place where the dead man is and asks forgiveness for the man's sins. All the euchologies mentioned omit, in the third part, the anointing and the prayer specific to it, "Holy Father . . ."; in the fourth part they do not display the open book of the gospels, as they do on a sick person. It is also to be noted that in each of the four parts there are hymns in which the canon and some prayers are taken from the burial office, while others are adaptations of prayers for the sick. The scriptural readings are likewise chosen in view of a burial rite; they are found in the present office on the five days of the week, the number seven being filled out by the addition of Romans 6:11–17 and Ephesians 2:4–10, for the epistles, and John 6:27–33 and 8:12–20, for the gospels.

In the editions printed at Venice and known to Goar, the rite for the euchelaion of the dead is attributed to a Nicholas who was Metropolitan of Athens at an unknown date.

The Church has shown independence and boldness in making her own various pagan religious values, but she has also shown herself reserved toward others such as the anointing of the deceased.

Penitential Euchelaia Unconnected with Physical Sickness

The ancient Christian Churches located East of Byzantium have preserved certain rites of anointing that are exclusively penitential in their purpose. Among the Nestorians, for example, apostates are reconciled by an anointing with oil on the forehead.[45] Among the Monophysite Copts apostates and adulterers are reconciled by an anointing of oil mixed with water.

In Georgia, where Christians belong to the Chalcedonian Orthodox Church, there used to be a rite which is no longer practiced but which is attested by two sixteenth-century manuscripts. It is called the "rite of the elasmon." The word "elasmon" is surely based on the Greek phrase *eis hilasmon,* "for an expiation." This rite is surveyed in detail in Kékélidzë's repertory.[46] The texts are there given in a Russian translation; if the reader wants to see the original he must journey to Tbilisi (Tiflis). Although no Greek original is extant, Kékélidzë is convinced that the Georgian rite was translated from Greek.

In the Georgian euchologies in the Ecclesiastical Museum at Tbilisi, nos. 450 and 72, this rite is set down after the euchelaion. It also follows the same outline as the euchelaion, but has modifications that render it an independent entity. After the opening prayers, which are repeated three times with Psalms 50, 62, and 37, there is the major ektenie which has as one of its specific petitions: "for the forgiveness of sins and for mercy on these servants who have sinned, let us pray to the Lord." Three readings from the Old Testament follow: Isaiah 1:16–21; Micah 7:18–19; Ezekiel 36:25–29; two epistles: James 5:10–16 and I Corinthians 10:1–4; and two gospels: Matthew 3:1–12 and Mark 6:7–13, thus giving seven readings in all. Next come three

". . . prayers of the great archbishop Basil over those who are tempted and have sinned. These are known in Greek by the name of elasmon and they purify from all sin as well as from temptation by the devil, from pollution by day or night, blandishment, illusion, blasphemy, the curse of a priest, a curse against oneself, sickness or weakness, sudden death, murder or hatred of a human being, insatiable hunger and various temptations from evil spirits. The priest reads these prayers [the rubric continues] before the liturgy, while all those present in the church prostrate themselves and, after each prayer, make three metanies [genuflections]. At the place where (the image of) the cross stands, the priest is to make a sign of the cross [= absolution?]."[47]

The first prayer of the elasmon is: "Lord Jesus, Christ, Son of God and Word of the living God. . . ." The priest: "Peace to all!" The people: "And to your spirit." The deacon: "Bow your heads before the Lord." The people: "They are bowed to you, O Lord." Three metanies follow, then the priest reads the second prayer, for the purification of the person who has deliberately and seriously sinned.

The prayer is followed by the same dialogue of priest, deacon, and people, and by three metanies. The priest then reads the third prayer: "Most merciful Lord, our God Jesus Christ, the true God who does not will the death of the sinner . . . ," and the same dialogue is repeated.

Then comes (three) prayers of St. John Chrysostom. (Do the two groups of prayers—by Basil and Chrysostom—correspond to the respective Liturgies of these two Doctors?). The first prayer is over those who allow themselves to be tempted; it is followed by the dialogue, and the penitents make three metanies. The priest says: "Let us pray to the Lord," and reads the prayer over those who are under episcopal interdict or who have bound themselves.[48] The third prayer is over those who have departed from the true faith but have been converted and have repented: "God, our Savior, who through your prophet Nathan . . . ,"[49] and the same dialogue as above forms a conclusion.

After these six prayers the priest reads the prayer over the oil:

"Almighty Lord, God of the powers, Giver of life, benevolent, Providence, Father of the Savior and Redeemer, our Lord Jesus Christ, you sent your only Son who was born of the Virgin and who suffered according to the flesh in order to save us from our passions and from the curse. We pray you, Lord, to send your Holy Spirit on this oil and to bless it with your blessing and with the grace of your Holy Spirit. Let it be for us a weapon for turning back all the attacks of the demons and for crushing all hostile actions and assaults. Let it bring healing of soul and body to these servants, along with knowledge of your divinity, confirmation in faith and hope, and a share in the kingship of your Christ. For you are the healer of our souls and bodies, and to you belong. . . ."

Next comes a prayer over the oil and water:

"Our good God, you have visited us in your mercy and have given us your saving Spirit. Jesus Christ, you hide yourself from the foolish and reveal yourself to the wise. You have purified us and rendered us wise and renewed us with your holy oil. You have sent to us, to us your sinful servants, the Spirit of wisdom and holiness. Now grant blessing and the power of your Spirit to this water and this oil, which are the image of your generosity and the spring that fills your [baptismal] pool, in order that we who are defiled and burdened may be delivered and may be healed of our weaknesses and purified by conversion to faith in you and by the glorification you bestow on us. For you are a God of mercy, and to you belongs kingship. . . ."

After these prayers, an anointing is bestowed on all the members of the person, as is done for a neophyte at baptism. The holy elasmon ends with the acclamation: "Glory to you, our God!"

This ceremony is clearly a rite for the reconciliation of penitents and heretics. It is to be noted that while the Greek euchologies do not have the rite, they have nonetheless retained prayers under the title of *euchai hilastikai*[50] or *euchē eis hilasmon*[51] or *euchai hilasmou.*[52] Perhaps we still need a rite of reconciliation in our day.

Development of the Rite for the Euchelaion in the Manuscript Euchologies

In the manuscript tradition of the euchologies, it is possible to trace the following development of the ritual for the euchelaion. I shall leave aside details which may well be important in themselves and shall concentrate on the essential structure of the euchelaion in relation to the divine office.

The first stage is likely to be represented by the euchology in the Coislin collection, no. 213, in the National Library at Paris.[53] The euchology belonged to Strategios, a priest of the Great Church and steward of the patriarchal chapel. The euchology is dated 1027 but it bears witness to an older tradition and manifests the most archaic structure to be found in the euchologies known to us. The archaizing characteristics are these: (a) The euchelaion is connected only with Mass and not with the other offices of the daily cycle. (b) It is celebrated on feast days and not exclusively during Lent; the rubric says that if it is celebrated on a Saturday of Lent, the Presanctified are to be used, but if it is celebrated outside of Lent, there is to be a proskomide (with seven prosphors). It is also specifically noted that if the euchelaion is celebrated on the day of a great saint, especially St. Theodore "who is commemorated on the first Saturday of Lent, then the ordo of this day is followed and subsequently that of the seven priests." (c) There is still only one epistle and one gospel (in other words, the number seven has not yet taken over at every point).

Here is the order followed by the euchelaion in this euchology (in which the consecration of the oil follows immediately upon the proskomide). After the opening acclamation "Blessed be our God . . . ," a little oil that has already been prepared is poured into a new (i.e., empty) lamp while Psalm 50 is recited, and the consecratory prayer is read; this is done by all seven priests. During the Mass, James 5:10–16 and Mark 6:7–13 are read. After the prayer from the ambo, the broken bread is not distributed; instead the sticheron "Source of healing" is sung, and the priests read the prayer (which is still a single prayer) for the anointing. The priests then anoint all present on the face, breast, and hands, then go in procession to anoint the house by tracing signs of the cross as stichera are sung. After the dismissal of the Mass they return to the chapel of the house (hospice?), read Psalm 33, "I will bless the Lord," break the bread, and distribute it.

The prayer for the consecration of the oil and the prayer for the anointing are found in all known euchologies, with the subsequent addition of other prayers. The following is the prayer of consecration:

"Lord, who through the generous gifts you bestow with a merciful hand heal the weaknesses of our souls and our bodies, sanctify this oil, O Master, that those who anoint themselves with it may experience healing and the disappearance of all suffering, bodily sickness, defilement of flesh and soul and every evil, so that in this too your holy name may be glorified. For to you belong. . . ."

This prayer is already found (though not as part of a rite) in manuscripts Sinai 958 of the ninth century and 959 of the eleventh century.[54]

And here is the prayer for the anointing:

"Holy Father, physician of our souls and our bodies, you sent your only Son, our Lord Jesus Christ, to heal every infirmity and deliver from death. Now heal your servant of the bodily sickness that holds him in its grasp. Do this in accordance with the favor you have shown us in your Christ, and give life, according to your good pleasure, to him who shows his gratitude to you by his good actions. For yours is dominion. . . ."

This prayer is found, again unconnected with a rite, in Sinai 957 of the ninth-tenth centuries and 958 of the tenth century.[55]

The second stage of development is represented by the Barberini euchology of the ninth century.[56] These are its characteristics: (1) the consecration of the oil is at Matins, which are sung in the evening, while the anointing is done at the end of Mass; (2) there is still only one epistle and one gospel (Lk 9:1–6); but (3) there are already seven prayers, which are said at Matins and repeated at Mass.

Here is the order for the euchelaion in the Barberini euchology:

"Rite for performing the holy anointing of the sick when the latter summon seven priests. In the evening. . . . A lamp is washed and a large seven-liter lamp is filled with oil. Each (priest) prepares his own lamp, and the (principal) priest vests and begins the prayers: 'Blessed be the kingly rule. . . . In peace let us pray to the Lord. . . . For heavenly peace. . . . For the health and salvation of the servant of God. . . . For deliverance. . . . Come to our aid. . . . Calling upon our all holy. . . .'

"The priest reads the (first) prayer: 'Lord, who through the generous gifts you bestow with a merciful hand. . . .' During the prayer he lights his lamp and makes a sign of the cross with it. . . . Acclamation: 'For you are a merciful God. . . .' In place of 'God is the Lord,' there is an Alleluia in the sixth mode and troparia: 'Have mercy on us, O God, have mercy. . . .'

"Then the canon is begun. At the third chant the next priest says the next (second) prayer, and each of the seven priests in turn says one of the seven prayers. These are the prayers: Second: 'We pray you, Lord, to make this oil a source of healing for those anointed with it. . . .' After the sixth ode, a third priest says the third prayer, and another says five verses, as indicated. Third prayer: 'Lord, look down from your holy dwelling and sanctify this oil. . . .' When each priest finishes, he makes three signs of the cross with his lamp and lights it. Fourth prayer after the ninth ode: 'Almighty Lord, holy King, you chastise but do not slay. . . .' And after the seven priests have said their seven prayers, the pannychis is concluded. Each has his own prayer: Fifth: 'Lord our God, who alone are good and the friend of men. . . .' Sixth: 'Blessed be you, almighty Lord, Father of our Lord Jesus Christ. . . .' Seventh: 'Holy Father, physician of our souls and our bodies. . . .' "

At the Mass the usual antiphons are sung. At the entrance: "Have mercy on us, O God, have mercy. . . ." The prokimenon is in the fourth mode: "I said . . . ," with the versicle: "Blessed he who bestows his care on the poor and needy." The epistle is a reading from the Catholic letter of James: "Brothers and sisters . . ." (5:10–16). The gospel is from St. Luke (9:1–6). Then another priest says the ectenie, and still another dismisses the catechumens. Everything is done in proper order and the Mass is completed. At this point the sick person comes in, and the singing of the troparia is begun: "Have mercy on me, O God, have mercy. . . ." Each of the priests recites the prayer assigned to him (the seventh is: "Holy Father, physician of our souls and our bodies") and anoints the forehead, ears, and hands of the sick person; then each extinguishes his lamp, as prescribed. After this the house is anointed with signs of the cross, and Psalm 90 is sung. Thus the Mass is concluded.

The euchology Sinai 973, which dates from 1153,[57] has a similar structure, but prescribes that Vespers as well as Matins are to be celebrated in the evening: "Seven priests gather and celebrate Vespers, the Pannychis, and sing the canon which is found at the end of this book; similarly, they sing the corresponding canon at Matins." In addition, great solemnity marks the time of preparation when the oil is poured into the lamps that are subsequently lit, as well as the moment when each celebrant extinguishes his lamp after performing the anointing. These two moments are accompanied by a whole set of ectenies, hymns, and prayers that are repeated seven times, or fourteen [sic] times in all! We can easily understand why no other euchology imitates this practice.

The sevenfold structure of the rite of the euchelaion thus came into existence. Petrovsky offers the following sketch of the subsequent development of the rite.[58]

In the thirteenth century the euchelaion was still integrated with the daily cycle of the divine office: Vespers, Matins, Mass; cf. mss Sinai 973 from the year 1153; Great Laura of Athos 189 from the thirteenth century; Sinai 960, also from the thirteenth century.

Beginning in the fourteenth century, the link with Vespers disappears. At the same time the hymns and prayers of Matins fuse with the office of the euchelaion proper so as to form the first part of this office; cf. Vatopédi 133 (fourteenth century), Sinai 965 (fourteenth century), Kutlumu 491 (fourteenth century), Iviron 780 (dated 1400), Dionysios 450 and Kostamoni 19 (fifteenth century), Holy Sepulcher of Constantinople 8 (fifteenth century) and 615 (dated 1522). The euchology Sinai 965 (fourteenth century) specifies: "If it is evening the dismissal is pronounced; if it is morning the table is set"; the same in Kutlumu 491.[59] From this time on, this first part of the rite is pretty much as it is now: opening acclamation of the priest; trisagion; "Come, let us adore"; Psalm 142; "God is Lord" or "Alleluia"; Psalm 50; canon; stichera (same ones as now); the troparia "Have mercy on us, O God"; trisagion; ectenie; dismissal. As compared with present usage, there were lacking only the exapostilarion after the ninth ode and the usual apolytikon at the end of Matins.

The second part of the euchelaion is a vestige of its earlier association with Mass, which ended in the thirteenth century. These vestiges are to be expected, inasmuch as the Mass itself had been influenced by its ancient connection with the euchelaion, especially at the moment of the little entrance. These vestiges comprise antiphons, troparia, and New Testament readings. The chief innovation in the thirteenth and fourteenth centuries is, here, the multiplication of these readings: henceforth seven epistles, seven gospels, and seven accompanying prayers were read. Compare, for example, Sinai 960 and Great Laura 189 (both of the thirteenth century); Holy Sepulcher of Constantinople 8 and Pantocrator 149 (both of the fourteenth century).[60]

This second or middle part of the euchelaion developed in several phases. First phase: the rite has seven parts, each containing the following elements: trisagion, Our Father, Psalm 50, Alleluia, antiphons, troparia which end with a Gloria and its theotokion, ectenie, a special prayer by each celebrant, and finally a consignation with oil using three signs of the cross.

Second phase: in the fourteenth and fifteenth centuries, instead of seven different prayers, there is a single prayer for the blessing of oil, but it is said by the seven celebrants: "Lord, who through the generous gifts you bestow with a merciful hand. . . ." Consequently there is but a single rite shared in by the assembled priests, instead of (as in the preceding phase) a rite repeated seven times. Henceforth Psalm 90 and the Creed are added. Similarly the seven groups of prayers are united into a single whole by a common Glory with its theotokion. Compare Great Laura 189 (thirteenth century) and the euchologies of the fourteenth century: Vatopédi 133, Sinai 965, and Kutlumu 591.

Third phase: in the euchologies of the fourteenth century, but especially in those of the fifteenth century, the loss of the connection with Vespers and Mass means the loss as well of the opening prayers. As a result the second part of the euchelaion becomes continuous with the first. Compare Sinai 994 (fourteenth century), and a series of fifteenth century euchologies.

Fourth phase: in the fifteenth century, this second part of the euchelaion begins abruptly with the ectenie "In peace let us pray to the Lord," and thus acquires its present-day form. Compare Sinai 996 and 978, and Bibliothèque Patriarcale de Jérusalem 367, all of the sixteenth century.

N.B. At the present time seven epistles and seven gospels are read, and *at the same time* seven anointings are administered. But in the old euchologies, down to the sixteenth century inclusive, the anointings came after the seventh reading. Consequently, the prayer of anointing: "Holy Father, physician of our souls and our bodies," was not repeated seven times as it is today; instead it was said by the seventh celebrant. The seven prayers vary in the euchologies, but Sinai 996 (sixteenth century) has the prayers now in use. The New Testament readings likewise varied, but the present-day readings are already to be found in some of the fourteenth and fifteenth century euchologies: Iviron (dated 1400), Dionysios 450, and Kostamoni 19. Note that the practice of doing the seven anointings during the seven readings has one ancient witness: the Greek euchology in Synodal Library of Moscow ms 279 (probably fourteenth century), in which there is a description of the anointing of an Emperor John, who is probably John VI Cantacuzene, who was emperor from 1347 to 1354 and who then abdicated and died as a monk in 1383.[61] This is probably an isolated witness; in any case it does not reflect what was the dominant practice.

The concluding part of the euchelaion likewise underwent a development. (1) In the euchology in ms Great Laura 189, of the thirteenth century, the conclusion consists of the prayer: "Lord our God, we pray and beseech you to hear the plea of your servant . . . ," which was followed by the insistent ectenie and, finally, an instruction to the sick person. (2) In the fourteenth century, however, the conclusion becomes more complex, as a new element appears: the extension of the open book of the gospels over the head of the sick person, with the prayer: "Merciful Lord, full of pity, who do not wish the death of the sinner"; this is followed by the singing of stichera to the Silverless Saints[62] and the Theotokos. (3) In the fifteenth and sixteenth centuries there was a multiplication both of prayers accompanying the extension of the gospels and of the stichera. Compare Sinai 998 and Holy Sepulcher of Constantinople 8 (both of the fifteenth century). The conclusion presently in use is found in some sixteenth century euchologies: Holy Sepulcher of Constantinople 68 and Sinai 996.

The present-day structure of the euchelaion as a whole is found in Sinai 968 (fifteenth century) and three others: Sinai 977, 798, and 979 (of the sixteenth century).[63]

1. Vespers are omitted. The only thing left is the stichera used with the Psalm: "Lord, I cry unto you" (which is itself omitted).

2. Matins have fused with the office of the euchelaion proper (now become an independent entity), so as to form the first part of it.

3. In the second part of the independent office of the euchelaion there is the prayer of blessing, which is found in the very earliest euchologies, then come troparia to Christ, St. James, the Silverless Saints, St. John the Evangelist, and the Theotokos; then seven New Testament readings, each followed by an ectenie, a special prayer, and the prayer, "Holy Father, physician of our souls and our bodies," during which there is an anointing.

4. The conclusion of the present-day office comprises the extension of the open book of the gospels over the sick person, along with a penitential prayer. The sick person "comes on his own

to the priests, or is carried in by his relatives; if he is helpless, the priests come and gather around his bed." Then there is the insistent ectenie, a troparion to Christ, a theotokion, and finally the dismissal.

The (relatively) definitive fixing of the form of the ritual was greatly aided by the use of printed editions; the first of these appeared at Venice in the sixteenth century.

PRESENT STATUS OF THE EUCHELAION

In the Orthodox Church, despite the lessons and wealth of ecclesiastical tradition that are preserved in the texts of the ritual, the concrete catechetical context created by the preaching of the clergy and by popular belief has reduced the euchelaion to a simple devotional practice, analogous to the *acathistoi* (hymns sung while standing) that are chanted in addition to the regular divine office. These devotional practices are a genre that has tenaciously kept the favor of Church practitioners. As far as the penitential element is concerned, it is given only an intentional value, prominent though it is in these prayers; if absolution for sin is desired, it must be given independently of the euchelaion.

In the Catholic Church, the name and notion of "extreme unction," an anointing reserved to the dying, have been abandoned, and everyone speaks now of the "sacrament of the sick." The penitential element is still limited to the remission of venial sins.

In both parts of Christendom, the canonical form of the sacrament of penance is restricted to private confession with individual absolution.

We may therefore ask: what is the specific liturgical and sacramental meaning of the euchelaion? Is it a rite of healing? But healing, once again, cannot be the object of a rite, even if certain gestures and formulas are used by some wonderworkers.

According to James 5 the effect of the anointing is both healing and repentance, the joint means to this end being the anointing done by the priests and the communal confession in the presence of these same priests. There is thus a single action with a twofold aim: *prayer* for the healing of the sick person and the *effective* remission of sins. Let me recall, in passing, that the rite described by St. James was the only rite of postbaptismal penance in the time of the apostles; compare Hebrews 6:4–6 and 10:26–27 with 1 John 5:16–17.

This interdependence of the physical and the spiritual is already instructive; the same lesson is also clearly taught elsewhere in sacred scripture. In its ritual and its prayers the euchelaion teaches us something about suffering, sickness, and death, namely, that all three must be seen in the perspective of the eternal life that is ours through faith, and must be viewed as integral stages in the process leading to that life.

The concern for healing makes life the focus of the euchelaion, but the life that is the dominant concern here is life in Christ and according to the Holy Spirit. But if we lay the emphasis on the penitential aspect of the euchelaion we do not thereby do away with the concern for healing. We must only not allow this concern to become an obsession that would be fruitless on both the physical and the spiritual levels; the desire for healing must be subordinated to the restoration of interior justice or holiness. Moreover, a moment inevitably comes when the mind must acknowledge that sickness will lead to death; then, in any case, recourse must be had to penance.

The penitential purpose of the euchelaion is clear from the very fact that it can be administered to the healthy as well as the sick; this has been so from early times. The practice of anointing all those present at the rite, including the officiating clergy and the healthy persons among the laity, is attested among the Monophysite Copts, who are naturally opposed to any borrowing from the Chalcedonians from whom they cut themselves off in the fifth century: "When the sacrament of the euchelaion is celebrated, the deacon too is anointed, as is each person present."[64] The Greek euchology in ms Coislin 213 (dated 1027) expressly states that in the home where the sacrament is celebrated all members of the family receive the anointing. The Slavic euchology *Sophienne*, preserved in ms 1054 of the Religious Academy at Petrograd (ms of the fifteenth century), specifies in the very heading of the manuscript that the rite was established for the healthy as well as for the sick.[65] In the modern practice of the Greek Church, the euchelaion is celebrated in families, in their homes, apart from any case of sickness; there is, however, a trend among the bishops to limit this practice.

On the other hand, while in its present form the consecration of the oil is not separated from an anointing given to persons (this is still true in the West), the Orthodox Church has also retained the practice of an especially solemn consecration of the oil, along with a general anointing of those present. This office was initially celebrated on Holy Thursday or Holy Saturday, but it is also celebrated on Wednesday of Holy Week or even earlier, in view of the already lengthy liturgies of the last days of the week before Easter. Some sick people are brought to this solemn celebration, but they are very much in the minority.

N. Krasnoseltzev, liturgist and author of a book entitled *The Orthodox Divine Office: On Certain Ecclesiastical Offices and Rites Not Presently in Use*,[66] thinks that this solemn consecration and anointing is a vestige of the ancient rite for the reconciliation of sinners who had to undergo public penance.

In any case, the rubric calls for a college of seven celebrants, and every effort is made to obey it. Such a rubric shows that this liturgical event took place primarily in the great cathedrals and large monasteries. For the period before 1917 in Russia, we are told by Hieromonk Aguentov that there were four such places of worship; the manuscripts, however, make it clear that in old Russia the practice was much more widespread.[67]

In all cases in which the euchelaion is administered to healthy persons, what purpose can the rite have other than a penitential one? One kind of catechesis, however, proposes the idea of a prevention of illnesses; behind this lies the notion of a universal subjection to sickness, in the sense that we are all sick without realizing it or at least are all on the brink of falling ill. As the reader will recognize, this is a favorite notion of Doctor Knoc.

It seems to me spiritually profitable to give the euchelaion back its penitential scope and to look upon the anointing as an effective act of absolution, once it is linked (as it always is in fact) to an adequate prayer said by the principal celebrant during the extension of the book of the gospel over those present as they bow their heads or prostrate themselves.

The solemn euchelaion during Holy Week could serve as the occasion (canonically the only one) for a general remission of sins. I offer this suggestion to the competent ecclesiastical authorities; this would call for accepting a more widespread practice of general confession, under conditions that would have to be determined. They would have at their disposal an existing rite, upon which, unfortunately, much effort has been expended in an attempt to strip it of its meaning. A further advantage of such a practice is that it would provide a corrective for the ambiguous regulation concerning the Easter minimum in the matter of confession and communion: "at least once a year, at Easter." The Church should not be calling for a minimum of spiritual life. On the other hand, in its compassion and in imitation of the divine economy of salvation, it should announce the messianic amnesty by proclaiming, as part of its essential prophetic and eschatological purpose, a day of forgiveness and liberation of consciences, especially in regard to collective sins such as are committed, for example, in the course of persecutions or wars.

I am not in any sense advocating the establishment of a new

liturgical feast, a kind of Christian Yom Kippur; I am simply giving a more enlightened liturgical meaning to an existing devotional practice.

Whatever be thought of this suggestion, I think it makes good sense to extend the solemn celebration of the euchelaion in Holy Week so as to make it available to those sick persons who are isolated in their rooms, confined either to bed or to an armchair, and physically cut off from the liturgical community. Priests—and why not deacons as well, as part of their "service at table"—would make the rounds of the sick whose names are listed and would anoint them with this oil that was consecrated in the presence of the entire community. Such a practice would strengthen in the sick an expectation of Easter and would announce, on the part of the Church, the lifting of all canonical penalties and a universal reconciliation.

The Church's care for the sick must, of course, be exercised throughout the year. The "individual" celebration of the euchelaion, especially to the benefit of the sick, must be guaranteed at all times and in all circumstances. It should be possible to facilitate these celebrations if we keep in mind that the seven series of prayers-readings-anointings are a maximum, to be used when there are seven celebrants, in accordance with the norm that there should be as many of these series as there are celebrants. The number 7, which was imposed at a certain period of history, is a matter of "literary genre," and should not be considered an unchangeable form for the sacrament of the euchelaion.

Alexandre NÉLIDOW

Rite for the Funeral of Children

My purpose in this study is to analyze and discuss the Orthodox rite for the funeral of children.

The statement of purpose, however, already suggests some preliminary questions. When I say, for example, "rite for the funeral of children," I am evidently implying that this rite differs from that used in other funerals, those of adults, for instance. But then the question may be asked: What is a funeral rite?

Consequently, before tackling the substance of my subject, it seems worthwhile to situate the theme and locate it in relation to our current vocabulary.

Clearly enough, whatever be their race, the color of their skin, their beliefs, their religion, their degree of intellectual or cultural development, and whatever be the times or age in which they live, human beings everywhere are confronted with the problem of death and must face up to it.

And always and everywhere death is an enigma to them. Because no satisfactory answers are forthcoming and there is no unqualified, proven certainty, human beings have always been brought up short in their efforts to explain death. Consequently their attitude to death has been one of fear and respect.

The result has been in all times and places the development of funeral rites, rituals of honor and respect with which human beings surround their dead. As far back as history or science can take us we find signs of such honors and such respect.

I need only mention the tumuli, the necropolises from ages long past that have been discovered in the course of the centuries; the embalming rites and mummies of the Egyptian civilizations with their sarcophagi and pyramids, or the Mayan civilizations with their step-temples; the rites of cremation that are still practiced today in India and that have a special caste of untouchables to carry them out. There are many other practices which I shall not list.

The Bible for its part provides us with information on some details of Hebrew ritual and on the prescriptions regarding the legal uncleanness contracted by those who come in contact with the dead and regarding the rites of purification. The gospels too yield some details on funeral rites.

Recall, for example, the resurrection of Lazarus: "The dead man came out," says St. John, "his hands and feet bound with bandages, and his face wrapped with a cloth" (Jn 11:44). And at the burial of Jesus, Joseph and Nicodemus "came bringing a mixture of myrrh and aloes, about a hundred pounds' weight. They took the body of Jesus, and bound it in linen cloths with the spices, as is the burial custom of the Jews" (Jn 19:39–40). Mark adds the detail that Joseph "wrapped him in a linen shroud" (Mk 15:46). Matthew (27:59) and Luke (23:53) say the same.

Luke tells us, moreover, that the women "returned [from the tomb], and prepared spices and ointments. On the sabbath they rested according to the commandment. But on the first day of the week, at early dawn, they went to the tomb, taking the spices which they had prepared" (Lk 23:56–24:1). After the resurrection when Peter and John went to the empty tomb, they saw "the linen cloths lying, and the napkin, which had been on his head, not lying with the linen cloths but rolled up in a place by itself" (Jn 20:6–7).

There are some other details we ought to bear in mind. As in all the Mediterranean countries so in Palestine funerals were accompanied by ritual lamentations for which professional mourners were often hired.

Recall, for example, the funeral procession of the widow's son (Lk 7:11–17) and of the daughter of Jairus, a synagogue ruler (Mt 9:18–26; Mk 5:21–43; Lk 8:40–56).

The synoptics tell us that when Jesus reached the home of the dead girl he found a noisy crowd of people who were weeping, lamenting, and uttering loud cries. He entered the house and said to them: "Why do you make a tumult and weep? The child is not dead but sleeping" (Mk 5:39). Then, paying no heed to their mockery, he chased them all out and allowed only the child's parents, along with Peter, James, and John, to remain. Our Orthodox ritual has retained the biblical expression "sleeper" as a name for a dead person.

There were, then, funeral practices and rites. In our own times, Jewish tradition still insists that the body of the dead person be washed and purified before being placed on a mortuary bed and then buried. This task is performed by pious and qualified persons.

The Kaddish, or prayer recited at this time and during the whole period of mourning, is not properly speaking a prayer for the dead, in the sense that there is no explicit mention of a petition for the repose of the soul of the deceased person. The Kaddish can be recited only if at least ten males have gathered who have attained the age of Bar-mitzvah (13 years). What, then, is the meaning of the prayer? According to the teaching of Jewish tradition, the supreme homage one can render to those who are no longer of this world is to conform one's own life to God's will here below. By glorifying the reign of God and hallowing it, one links the dead with the homage men together render to God.

Tradition demands that mourning last a year for a father or a mother and a month for a spouse, brother or sister, or child.

Christian tradition, for its part, had no reason to rule out this respect for the dead and these funeral rites, since they do not in any way mean a lessening of faith. The Church did, however, shift the emphasis by accenting the fact that earthly death is really only a birth into a future life, a passage from our brief existence in this world to an eternal life with God, and a time when human beings wait, full of hope, for the day of the final judgment.

Funeral rites, then, are marks of respect rendered to the remains of every being that has been created "in the image of God." The ritual itself speaks of "remains."

In summary, the Church prescribes special rites to accompany the dead from the moment of death to the moment of burial. These rites comprise, in the main, prayers over the body either in the home or in the place of death, the coffining of the body, its transport to the church for prayers in the presence of the Christian community to which the deceased person belonged, and finally the transfer to the place of rest and its placement in the earth, or burial in the strict sense.

The Orthodox Church distinguishes several categories among the faithful and has a special rite for each category.

What are these categories? There are four of them: first, the laity of both sexes; then monks and nuns; then priests and bishops; and finally, children.

Let me add for the sake of completeness, but without dwelling on the point, that these four rites are modified in important ways if the offices fall during Easter week. The solemnity of the feast of Easter prevails over the tone normally proper to a funeral, to the point of excluding it almost entirely.

Such, then, is my answer to the first question: what is meant by a "funeral rite"?

A second question now arises: why a special rite for children? But first a preliminary question: whom does the Church think of as "children"?

The Orthodox Church divides the life of the faithful into four periods or ages. The vast majority of the faithful in the Church are *adults*, that is, those who have reached the age of 21, at which a person can become an active member of a parish and exercise various functions in it. The Church admits an adult of 22 to the deaconate and one of 25 to the priesthood. Adulthood is preceded by *youth*, which embraces the period from the age of 16 (at which the Church admits young men to clerical tonsure as lector-acolyte) to the age of legal majority. The period from 7 to 16 years is the period of *adolescence*. At the age of 7 a human being has reached the age of reason and has received a rudimentary religious education at home or at the church. The person is able to distinguish right and wrong and is now responsible for his actions. For this reason the Church admits the adolescent to the sacrament of penance, and the former "child" now makes his or her first confession. As you can see, this is the equivalent of first communion in the Roman Church; an Orthodox child communicates from the time of his baptism.

Childhood proper is the period from birth to first confession. It is for "children" in this sense of the word that the Church has a special funeral rite.

Let me turn now to my main question: why such a special rite?

Before I answer, let me point out that the other Christian confessions (the Roman Catholic and the Protestant) also have special rites for children. Since the fifteenth century, Rome has had a special funeral rite for children who die after baptism and before the age of reason. The rite was modeled on the rite for adults, but the prayers expressed the conviction that these little children had already entered into eternal life. There was therefore no sacrifice of the Mass offered for them. The Second Vatican Council recently ordered that this funeral rite be revised and that it should have its own proper Mass.

The Book of Common Prayer, for its part, has a special rubric for the funeral of children.

The Orthodox Church has a special rite for children that is based on the principle (which is in turn based on scripture and supported by tradition) that children who have not reached the age of reason are not responsible for their faults and that these faults cannot be called "violations of the divine law" or "sins." It is not possible, therefore, to pray for the "remission of their sins" and the "forgiveness of their faults," as we do for responsible adults; we can only ask the Lord "to grant rest to their souls."

This rite is thus meant for all baptized children, since they are considered to have been made spotless and sinless by the sacrament; being baptized in the name of the Father and of the Son and of the Holy Spirit they have been washed clean of original sin and brought into a new life. Proof of this is the formal and trustworthy promise of the Savior, who says: "Unless you turn and become like children, you will never enter the kingdom of heaven" (Mt 18:1–4; Mk 9:33–40; Lk 9:45–50), and, "Let the children come to me, and do not hinder them; for to such belongs the kingdom of heaven" (Mt 19:13–15; Mk 10:13–16; Lk 18:15–17).

All those, therefore, who have received the complete baptismal rite (exorcisms, anointings, triple immersion, followed by chrismation [confirmation]), have a right to heaven beyond any possible doubt. This is so even if the prayer by which they are brought into the church, and which is in the ritual, has not been read, since this is not obligatory.

By baptism a child becomes a member of the Church with full rights, even if he has not received chrismation (confirmation), and all the more so if he has. It is baptism that gives him a right to all the other sacraments, including the eucharist, which in fact he receives immediately after baptism.

It is to be noted that even if children do nothing after baptism that could win the heavenly kingdom for them, they have been washed and cleansed of original sin by holy baptism. As I said above, they have become spotless and sharers in the merits of Christ; by this very fact, they have become heirs to the kingdom of God.

I mentioned a moment ago the "complete" baptismal rite. But

what is to be done in case of a baptism hastily performed by a layperson or by the midwife when the newborn child is in danger of dying?

Such a baptism is canonically valid, provided it has been done by a Christian (even if it could not be subsequently completed by the missing rites) and provided it has been done "in the name of the Father and of the Son and of the Holy Spirit."

I remind you in this connection of a case mentioned in *Le Messager Ecclésiastique*, no. 28 of 1894. A sickly child was born to a family of Orthodox parents. Because of the infant's frailty, the midwife, a Lutheran, immediately baptized it because she feared death was imminent. And in fact death did occur shortly afterwards. The question was: was the child truly baptized? The Synod's decision was that the baptism was valid, because it was administered by a Christian layperson, and thus the minimum requirement was met. It follows from all this that the funeral of such children is to be celebrated according to the Orthodox rite and that birth, baptism, and death are to be entered in the parish records.

What of unbaptized children? Here a different course is to be followed. No rite of Christian burial is to be celebrated for these children because they have not been cleansed of original sin. The priest may simply bless the grave and carry out the burial to the accompaniment of the Trisagion.

In speaking of the fate of children who die without baptism St. Gregory the Theologian (Gregory of Nazianzus) says that:

". . . they will be neither glorified nor condemned by the just Judge, since they have not been sealed. They are not evil and have suffered more harm than they have caused. For a person's failure to deserve punishment does not mean that he therefore deserves honors, nor does his failure to deserve honors mean that he deserves punishment."[1]

Let me turn now to the differences between the funeral rite for children and the funeral rite for adults.

But first a brief remark is in order. The ritual follows a particular order for certain rites, an order that has been established while taking into account practices current in the Eastern countries. In the West and specifically in France, legal prescriptions make it impossible to follow this order. The prescriptions must be taken into account and the order of the ritual modified. Here is an example. Funerals in Russia, and in the Near East generally, involve the carrying of the mortal remains from home to church in an open casket, with the face of the corpse uncovered. The coffin is closed only in the church after the absolution has been given and the relatives and friends have given a farewell kiss to the dead person. A special prayer of general absolution and the lifting of any interdicts that may have existed at the moment of death is read by the priest at this point, and the printed text of this prayer is then placed in the dead person's hands. A paper crown is also set on the person's brow; it usually carries a representation of the Deisis and the printed text of the Trisagion; it is placed on the head in order to be a reminder of Paul the Apostle's words in his second letter to Timothy: "Henceforth there is laid up for me the crown of righteousness, which the Lord, the righteous judge, will award to me on that Day, and *not only to me but to all who have loved his appearing*" (2 Tm 4:8). In France the law orders the coffin closed when it is put on the bier in the home of the deceased. Therefore the three rites just mentioned are performed at this point.

In this connection I may point out the first difference that marks the rite for children. As I said above, there is no place for absolution or the forgiveness of sins, still less for canonical interdicts, when the deceased person is a child. Therefore the prayer I spoke of a moment ago is not read nor is it placed in the child's hands. On the other hand, the crown of justice is promised "to all who have loved his coming," and therefore belongs to every baptized person; it is therefore placed on the child's brow.

I turn now to the funeral rite proper and will compare it step by step with the rite for adults.

The rite begins with the priest's blessing: "Blessed be our God at all times: now and forever and through all ages." The choir answers: "Amen," and immediately intones Psalm 90: "He who dwells in the shelter of the Most High, who abides in the shadow of the Almighty, will say to the Lord, 'My refuge and my fortress, my God in whom I trust,' " etc.

In the rite for adults three stichologies follow, that is, sets of verses chanted by the choir, with the addition to each verse of an "Alleluia" (in the first and third sets) or "Have mercy on your servant!" (in the second set). The stichologies are separated from one another by a short collect with an ecphonesis: "For you are the resurrection, the life and the repose of your deceased servant, O Christ our God, and we give glory to you and to your eternal Father and your most holy, good and life-giving Spirit, now and always and through all ages."

The third stichology is followed by a series of verses, each with a refrain: "Blessed are you, Lord, teach me your judgment."

In the rite for children, Psalm 90 is followed by an Alleluia with, as a gradual, the verses: "Happy the one you have chosen and received, O Lord," and "And his memory abides from generation to generation."

A reader recites the Trisagion, the Gloria, and the Our Father; these are followed by a conclusion from the priest.

After the recitation of Psalm 50 (generally omitted) there follows the canon, which is usually shortened in both rites, being reduced to odes 1 and 6.

It is to be observed, however, that the refrains differ in the two rites. For children it is: "Lord, give rest to this child," while for adults it is: "Lord, grant rest to the soul of your deceased servant."

Here is the text of the troparia for the sung odes:

"Having crossed the water as though it were solid ground and escaped the Egyptian terror, the Israelite cried out: 'Let us glorify our God and Liberator.'

"Word of God, you abased yourself by taking flesh and you deigned to become a child while abandoning nothing. We pray you: Unite this child, whom you have received, to others in the bosom of Abraham.

"You manifested yourself as a child, though you existed before all the centuries, and because you are good, you promised your kingdom to children. Receive this child.

"Christ our Savior, you took this child to yourself because he underwent testing by the blessings of this world, and you have filled him with eternal blessings, for you are the friend of men.

"You who brought forth the Wisdom and Word of the Father, heal the deep wound of my soul and still the pain of my heart.

"Lord, you created the vault of heaven and established the Church. Strengthen me in love for you, for you are the support of your faithful and calmer of passions, O sole friend of men.

"Perfect Word, you manifested yourself as a perfect child. You called this young child to yourself; grant it rest now amoung the blessed who have been pleasing to you, O sole friend of men.

"Lord, make this innocent child a sharer in the heavenly dwelling, in light-filled rest, and in the blessed choir of the saints, for it is you who have called him, O Savior.

"Abandoned by all others, I take refuge in your protection alone, all-pure sovereign Lady; come to my aid. My sins form a multitudinous heap, and I am naked of any good action."

There follows a short ectenie. In the one for children it is said: "We pray also for the repose of this blessed child N., and that he may be made worthy of the kingdom of heaven, according to your promise." For an adult it is said: "We pray also for the repose of the soul of N., servant of God, who has fallen asleep, and that his sins, deliberate and indeliberate, may be forgiven him." And further on, the petition for a child is not for "the forgiveness of sins" but for "rest among the saints."

In the rite for adults there are also hymns called idiomela, attributed to John the Monk, and a reading of the beatitudes with comments on each. Here are some of these:

"Blessed are the merciful, because they shall obtain mercy. O Christ, you promised that because he was repentant you would bring into paradise the thief who on his cross said to you: 'Remember me!' Render worthy me as well, who am unworthy.

"Blessed are the peacemakers, because they shall be called the children of God. You are the master of souls and bodies, and our breath of life is in your hand. Consolation of the afflicted, grant rest in the place of the just to your servant whom you have called back to yourself.

"Blessed those who are persecuted for justice' sake, because the kingdom of heaven is theirs. Christ will give you rest in the dwelling place of the living; he will open the gates of paradise to you and make you an inhabitant of his kingdom. He will forgive you the sins you committed during your life, because you love him."

In both rites, the prokimena (antiphons) and readings follow, but these differ in the two cases. For adults the prokimenon is: "Blessed is the road which you walk today, O soul, for a place of rest has been prepared for you. To you, my Lord and my God, I lift up my voice." For children, however, the antiphon is: "Blessed is the road which you will travel, O soul. My soul is turned to your rest."

The epistle for adults is from the first letter to the Thessalonians: "We would not have you ignorant, brethren, concerning those who are asleep, that you may not grieve as others do who have no hope . . ." (4:13–17). For children the text is from the first letter to the Corinthians:

"Not all flesh is alike, but there is one kind for men, another for animals, another for birds, and another for fish. There are celestial bodies and there are terrestrial bodies, but the glory of the celestial is one, and the glory of the terrestrial is another. There is one glory of the sun, and another glory of the moon, and another glory of the stars; for star differs from star in glory.

"So is it with the resurrection of the dead. What is sown is perishable, what is raised is imperishable. It is sown in dishonor, it is raised in glory. It is sown in weakness, it is raised in power. It is sown a physical body, it is raised a spiritual body. If there is a physical body, there is also a spiritual body. Thus it is written, 'The first man Adam became a living being'; the last Adam became a life-giving spirit" (1 Cor 15:39–45).

The pericopes for the gospel are also different. The one for adults is from chapter 5 of St. John: "Jesus said to them [the Jews]: 'Truly, truly, I say to you, he who hears my word and believes him who sent me, has eternal life. . . ." (5:24ff.). For children the text is from chapter 6 of St. John:

"Jesus said to them; 'I am the bread of life; he who comes to me shall not hunger, and he who believes in me shall never thirst. But I said to you that you have seen me and yet do not believe. All that the Father gives me will come to me; and him who comes to me I will not cast out. For I have come down from heaven, not to do my own will, but the will of him who sent me; and this is the will of him who sent me, that I should lose nothing of all that he has given me, but raise it up at the last day' " (Jn 6:35–39).

In both rites the gospel is followed by this song:

"Savior, grant rest to the soul of your servant with the souls of the other just who have died, and preserve it for the blessed life that will be ours in your presence, O friend of men.
"In the place of rest which is yours, Lord, and wherein all the saints have their rest, grant rest also to the soul of your servant, for you alone are the friend of men.
"Glory to the Father and the Son and to the Holy Spirit.
"You are the God who descended into the realm of death and broke the chains of those in bondage there. Do you grant rest to the soul of your servant.
"Now and always and through all ages.
"Virgin, alone pure and spotless, who bore God while remaining a virgin, ask him to save our souls."

In the rite for children this hymn is followed by two prayers:

"Lord Jesus Christ, our God, you promised to give the kingdom of heaven to those who are born of water and the Spirit and who come before you after a spotless life. You said too: 'Let the children come to me, and do not hinder them, for to such belongs the kingdom of heaven.' We humbly pray you: In accordance with your trustworthy promise grant the heritage of your kingdom to your servant, this spotless child N., who has departed from us. And make us worthy to live a spotless life, meet a Christian end, and find a place in your heavenly dwelling with all the saints.

NÉLIDOW

"For you are the resurrection and the life and the repose of your servants and of this servant whom you have just called, the child N., O Christ our God, and we give you glory with your eternal Father and your most holy, good and life-giving Spirit, now and always and through all the ages."

And the second prayer:

"Lord, you protect little children in this life, and you have prepared a place, the bosom of Abraham, for them in the world to come. You have prepared dwellings where the purity of the angels sheds its light and where the souls of the just abide.

"Lord Jesus, receive in peace the soul of your servant, the child N., for you yourself said: 'Let the children come to me, and do not hinder them, for to such belongs the kingdom of heaven.' To you belongs all glory, honor and adoration, with your eternal Father and your most holy, good and life-giving Spirit, now and always and through all the ages."

As I said earlier, there is of course no absolution and no lifting of interdicts.

Then comes the leave-taking. Here again the formulas differ somewhat. For adults it is as follows:

"Through the prayers of his all-pure and spotless Mother, of his friend St. Lazarus, the holy and just man who remained four days in the tomb, of our blessed and God-fearing fathers, and of all the saints, may Christ our true God, who has power over the living and the dead, place the soul of his servant N., which he has called back to himself, in the dwelling of the just. May he grant it rest in the bosom of Abraham, number it among the just, and show mercy as well to all of us, for he is good and the friend of men."

For children the prayer reads:

"O Christ, our true God, you rose from the dead and have power over both living and dead. Through the prayers of your most holy Mother and of all the saints, grant rest to your deceased servant N., now departed from us, in the dwellings of the saints, and count him among the just, for you are good and the friend of men."

The choir sings: "Amen."

The ending of the office shows a final variation. In the case of adults the deacon or priest says: "In his blessed sleep grant, Lord, to your dead servant N. everlasting rest, and grant him an eternal remembrance." The choir answers "Eternal remembrance" (three times). In the funeral of a child this formula is omitted from the ritual.

Finally, the priest blesses the coffin three times while saying, in the case of adults, "May you be forever remembered, our brother (sister) who have earned happiness and deserved to leave a blessed memory behind you." In the case of a child he says: "You are eternally remembered, child N., who have earned happiness and deserved to leave a blessed memory behind you."

This prayer should, I think, be understood as follows. The "eternal remembrance" is eternal salvation. In the case of adults we can never be sure they have been saved; for this reason we can only ask the Lord to grant them eternal remembrance, that is, eternal salvation. But in the case of children, we affirm instead of asking or wishing: "You are eternally remembered," that is, you have eternal salvation.

The office ends with the entire congregation coming up to kiss the cross or icon that is placed on the casket, while the choir sings: "Draw near, brethren, and with gratitude to God give the final kiss to him who is no longer here, for he has left all his relatives and is hurrying to the grave, careless now of this world's vanities and of the flesh with its passions. Where now are his relatives and friends? We are already being separated from him, and we ask the Lord to give him rest."

Once the office in the church is finished, the service shifts to the cemetery. Since the cemetery is usually a distance from the church, a priest accompanies the coffin, and when it is being put into the ground he sings a short litia comparable to that sung when the coffin was put on the bier.

Tradition calls for the coffin being so positioned that the dead person faces the East. Here in France this is hardly possible in view of the organization and layout of cemeteries.

First the priest and then the others present throw a spadeful of earth on the coffin, while the officiant says: "The Lord's is the earth and all that fills it, the universe and all who dwell in it."

I have still to discuss some special cases that can arise:

First case: Can one funeral be celebrated for both children and adults (as, for example, after an accident or a catastrophe)? As we have seen, the rites are notably different in their very content: for adults we pray for the forgiveness of sins, for children only that in keeping with his promise the Lord will grant them rest among the just. We cannot speak of sin in connection with children. For this reason it is not fitting to have a single ceremony for both categories.

Second case: Can an Orthodox priest celebrate a funeral rite for a non-Orthodox person? This question has been anticipated: non-Orthodox Christians do not have the right to an Orthodox funeral.

But it there is no minister belonging to the rite of the deceased person, an Orthodox has the duty to don stole and chasuble and accompany the body to the cemetery, to bless the grave, and see that the coffin is put into it while the Trisagion (and nothing else) is sung.

Third case: The same procedure is followed in the case of a child born of Christian parents but not yet baptized at death, and of persons whose baptism is doubtful.

Fourth case: The same procedure is used for a person whose religion is unknown.

Fifth case: This involves a problem often raised and variously answered: should we or should we not pray for the repose of a child's soul after the funeral (in view of the fact that they do not require forgiveness of their sins)? The Church has always judged such prayer necessary and useful, because prayer for them has a twofold meaning: (1) by praying for them we help them ascend to the Majesty on high; (2) we ask in turn that they offer their pure prayers for us.

Adrien NOCENT

Sickness and Death
in the Gelasian Sacramentary

More extensive study has been devoted to the theme of sickness in liturgical texts than to the theme of death. Not surprisingly, the new rite for the anointing of the sick has been the occasion for increasingly serious studies of liturgical theology as it concerns the situation of the sick person and the action of the sacrament of anointing. For this reason I shall lay less emphasis on what the Gelasian Sacramentary has to say to us about sickness and more on its theology of death.

LITURGICAL THEOLOGY OF SICKNESS AND THE SICK

The Formularies

On several occasions the Gelasian Sacramentary expresses its views on sickness and the sick. As the reader will be aware, it is not possible to synthesize the teaching of a sacramentary as one can that of a contemporary missal. If, then, it is legitimate to speak of the liturgical theology of the Gelasian, the supposition is that we have first tried to determine the sources to which its different elements belong. Furthermore, we must realize that any synthesis offered does not necessarily and at every point reflect a literary unit, but is based rather on a composite book which a local Church used for its liturgical celebrations.

The first need, then, is briefly to situate the formularies I shall be using.

These may be divided into five groups, of which two are directly concerned with my subject. The first is the *Blessing of oil* in the chrismal Mass of Holy Thursday. The second comprises three sections which contain various prayers for the sick: *Prayer over a sick person in his home; Prayers at a Mass for a sick person;* and *Prayer for the restoration of health.*

Let me immediately situate these two groups. The *Blessing of oil* is in Book I, section XL, which is entitled *Chrismal Mass on Holy Thursday.*[1] Professor A. Chavasse has studied the structure of the Gelasian Mass for the blessing of oils and the rites accompanying this blessing.[2] He regards the prayers as Roman and shows that while the bishop reserved the blessing of chrism to himself, he often refrained from blessing the other two oils. Moreover, the oil of the sick was blessed at the request of the faithful, as the rubric in the Gelasian still shows (381: "Blessing of the oil. To the people in the following words"). It is not possible to determine at what moment in history priests ceased to bless these two oils, that of catechumens and that of the sick, since the more recent Roman books, which reserve the blessing of the three oils to the bishop, are all derived from the Romano-German Pontifical of the tenth century. At Milan in the eleventh century, a priest still blessed the oil of the sick at the beginning of the administration of the sacrament of the sick.[3]

The second group is made up of three sections of Book III that all contain prayers over the sick.

Sections LXIX, 1535–38: *Prayer over a sick person in his home,* LXX, 1539–42: *Prayers at a Mass for a sick person,* and LXXI, 1543: *Prayer for the restoration of health* are all devoted to the sick. Each of them, however, has its own special characteristics: sections LXIX and LXXI presuppose a visit to the home of an individual sick person, while the Mass of section LXX is celebrated in the church and refers to several sick persons, whose restoration to the Church is desired.[4] Nonetheless, a literary analysis of these three sections leads to the conclusion that one person is author of them all. Moreover, the affinity of certain expressions in these formularies to those found in the *Deprecatio Gelasii* ("Intercession of Gelasius") has also been pointed out.[5]

With these first two groups is connected a Mass for the living:

Prayers at a Mass for the health of the living (CVI, 1696–1700). This section includes, in 1700, a formula bearing the title *Contestatio,* which is a Gallican preface for a dead person.

Finally there are formularies indirectly concerned with sickness. In Book I, section XXXVIII, 364–74 has the title: *Reconciliation of a dying penitent,* but in fact nos. 364–67 are prayers relating purely and simply to the continuation of a ritual of reconciliation; there is no question at all of sinners in danger of death. Moreover 368–74, which have the subtitle *Prayers after reconciliation or after communion,* are really concerned with a sick person who has just been reconciled.[6]

In Book I, section LXVI, no. 592 has the title: *Imposition of hands on a sick catechumen,* and section LXVIII, 595, is a *Prayer over a sick catechumen.* These prayers were introduced into the sacramentary at a later date, as is clear from a rubric at the beginning of these sections, which refers back to the celebration during the Easter Vigil: "On the Saturday of Pentecost you are to celebrate baptism as during the night of the holy Pasch."[7]

The Theology in These Formularies

After having situated these various formularies, I can now turn to the theology they seek to express. It would be an exaggeration to claim that they contain a great wealth of thought. It is of interest, nonetheless, to observe attitudes being taken that are at times different and a bit contradictory.

All of these texts reflect one of two theological outlooks. On the one hand, the prayer offered for a sick person asks for healing of both soul and body. On the other, there are prayers that offer a kind of theology of health and emphasize the healing of the body, while linking this to the importance of the sick person's presence in the community.

The prayer *Send forth* in the *Blessing of oil* (XL, 382), which is considered to be of Roman origin, is clearly bent on asking for a healing of both soul and body. The oil in question is one which the Spirit is to consecrate "for the restoration of mind and body" (382). The emphasis is in fact quite strong: "And may your holy blessing be, for everyone who anoints, tastes or touches this oil, a protection for body, soul and spirit, so that all pains, all weakness, all sickness of mind and body may be dispelled." The text is inspired by the biblical understanding of the unity of the human person: "protection for body, soul and spirit." There is no facile separation of soul and body such as we are tempted to make. The formulary has in view the whole person who is to be anointed with consecrated oil.

An analysis of section LXIX, 1535–38: *Prayer over a sick person in his home,* yields a somewhat different theology. For while 1536 links health of soul and body ("that he may feel your healing not only in body but in soul as well"), the other prayers of this section focus specifically on health of body: "Look with gentleness on your servant who is suffering ill health of body; visit him with your salvation and grant him the medicine of heavenly grace" (1535). The prayer in 1537 is particularly expressive: "God of the heavenly powers, who drive all feebleness and weakness from human bodies by the power of your commanding word, be present in mercy to this servant of yours so that, all weaknesses being removed and his strength restored, he may enjoy renewed health and constantly bless your holy name." Here the desire to have the sick person take part in the praise of the community is connected with the prayer for healing of body. This theme will be developed on several occasions, for example in section LXX, which contains a Mass for the sick, and section LXVI, 592, which is a prayer for a sick catechumen.

In Book III, section CVI, 1696–99, again offers a theology of health. Health is requested for the sick in order that they may seek God ("that they may seek you with their whole heart," 1696), that they may praise him ("that, always rejoicing in devotion to you, they may constantly persevere in the catholic faith and the confession of the holy Trinity," 1698), and that they may persevere in the catholic faith (ibid.).

On the other hand, in this same Book III, in section XXXVIII, 1377–80; *Prayers in time of deadly danger, that it may pass* (a section that is continued in three further sections, XXXVIII–XLI, 1381–92, which have no specific title), death is presented as a result of sin, and conversion is regarded as putting an end to the misfortunes that befall human beings. Prayer 1377 is typical in this respect: "God, you desire not the death but the repentance of sinners. Turn in mercy to your people, we pray, so that because of their devotion to you you may take away the scourges of your wrath."

Sickness is thus connected with sin (1381, 1382, 1385, 1386, 1389); the death in question is the result of God's anger (1378, 1390).

The theology of these prayers is in fact very close to that of the letter of St. James. The "elders of the Church" pray for the sick person. Such prayer is not specifically Christian, and we find it no less in the Old Testament, for example in Ezekiel 34:4, Job 2:11, Tobit 1:19–21, and Sirach 7:34–36. The same must be said of anointing with oil (Enoch 8,3. 5), which in Judaism and in the Egyptian religion had a twofold efficacy, natural and spiritual. The "salvation" of the sick person, that is, his healing, is therefore not to be interpreted in too simplistic a way. The word "save" can mean to rescue from death and Sheol, but it also means to give a new life. That is how the exegetes interpret the word in the Old Testament.

It would be out of place for me to offer here an exegesis of James 5:13–15. Let me simply follow the experts and say that James' use of the word "save" (1:21; 2:14; 4:12; 5:20) is similar to the use of it in the Old Testament. In any case, sin and sickness are closely connected in the New Testament, so much so that Jesus is forced to correct the excessive rigor shown in the judgment passed on a sick person (Jn 9:3; Lk 13:1–2). But, despite this correction, sickness is indeed a consequence and result of sin, and the healings in the gospel are precisely a sign of liberation from sin and of the presence of the kingdom. Thus the New Testament uses the word "healing" with a symbolic reference (Mt 13:15; Jn 12:40; Acts 28:27; 1 Pt 2:24).

While suffering has a supernatural meaning in the eyes of St. James (1:2–12; 4:1–3; 5:7–9, 13), it would be inaccurate to say that "save" is to be given a purely spiritual interpretation. Verses 14 and 15 of chapter 5 show that the subject for whom prayer is offered is sick, not dying, and that the prayer of the priests is effective for the body of the sick person. Verse 15 can be interpreted as referring to a bodily healing, without making this the exclusive meaning. As is well known, *egeirein* means "bring back to life" as well as "rescue from a sickness" or even "alleviate." The context must be allowed to give words a flexible range of meaning. The prayers I am analyzing here seem to reflect the same idea that the letter of James associates with the oil: bodily healing for the sake of spiritual life.

It is possible that some of our prayers which lay a strong emphasis on bodily healing were written in reaction to people having recourse to magical healing rituals. This is, of course, only a hypothesis, and it would doubtless be possible to multiply hypotheses. This much is true, however: Caesarius of Arles was influenced, in his sermons, by the frequent use of magic in his day. In Sermon 13, after citing the passage from James 5, he emphasizes the effectiveness of the oil for the forgiveness of sins and for healing, and asks why, in view of this, people should fall back on magic. The same thought is repeated in Sermon 52. On the other hand, Caesarius sees bodily healing as connected with the forgiveness of sins; such is the theological view expressed in Sermon 184. Caesarius is doing battle with pagan customs from which Christians are finding it difficult to extricate themselves. He therefore tends to compare the effects of the blessed oil with those resulting from the application of magical remedies, which are in fact less effective than anointing with the consecrated oil. Anointing heals both body and soul; magical remedies, on the contrary, make people sinners.[8] Here is a passage from Sermon 13:

"Consider, brothers and sisters, that a sick person who has recourse to the Church, will deserve to receive both bodily health and the forgiveness of his sins. Since, then, we can obtain both of these blessings in the Church, why do wretched individuals seek to do themselves all sorts of harm by turning to enchanters, to fountains and trees and diabolical amulets, to tricksters and soothsayers, diviners and fortune-tellers?"[9]

I shall not cite the other passages lest I overburden this paper. But you are sufficiently familiar with them to have grasped the approach taken by St. Caesarius. It is this approach that resembles the one found in certain groups of prayers in the Gelasian.

In Book III, section LXXI: *Prayer for the restoration of health* (1543), there is a general theology of sickness and healing:

"Lord, holy Father, almighty and eternal God, you pour out your gracious blessing on sick bodies and thereby multiply your creatures and preserve true devotion. Be mercifully present when we call upon you: free this servant of yours from illness and restore him to health; raise him up with your right hand, strengthen him with your power, and protect him with your might; grant him all the prosperity he desires and restore him to your Church and your sacred altars."

This is a balanced theology that avoids all suspicion of recourse to magic. It does not propose bodily healing as the certain and exclusive result of the application of the oil, but rather sees anointing as a remedy that acts upon the entire person of the one who is sick.

LITURGICAL THEOLOGY OF DEATH
IN THE GELASIAN SACRAMENTARY

The Formularies of the Gelasian

The Gelasian Sacramentary contains a rather large number of sections that set forth a theology of death, namely, sections XCI to CV of Book III. This does not mean, of course, that we need pay no attention to other sections in which the prayers are not expressly composed for the *Commendatio animae* or the funeral. As we shall see, it is necessary to examine the entire sacramentary if we are to reconstruct its theology of death.

How are we to evaluate sections XCI to CV? Let me begin by situating section XCI of Book III.

This section has five subdivisions: 1607–14, *Prayers after the death of a person;* 1616–19, *Prayers before the body is carried to the grave;* 1620–22, *Prayers at the grave before burial;* 1623–25, *Prayers after burial;* 1626–27, *Recommendation of the soul* (to God).

If we compare these various items with *Ordo* XLIX,[10] we see that they are far from being all of Roman origin. In fact, the *Ordo* provides only one prayer, and the ancient index to the Gelasian manuscript does not mention all the sections I have listed but gives only the title *Commendatio animae defuncti.* If then we were to limit ourselves to the prayers that are certainly Roman, we would have only 1626 and 1627. Now the antiphons that precede the prayer in the *Ordo* and occur in the course of the celebration seem to show that the prayer intended in the *Ordo* is 1627: *Deus apud quem.* Of the whole series of Gelasian prayers which I listed, only one, then, would be Roman in origin, namely, the prayer *Deus apud quem.* The others, "Gallican" in origin, would have been introduced by the compiler of the Gelasian. It seems that on this point there is no resisting the arguments offered by Professor Chavasse.[11] The process of interpolation explains why the *Commendatio animae* comes in so oddly at the end of the funeral ritual.

What of sections XCII to CV? E. Bishop acknowledged that these formularies had Roman elements and in particular that they showed dependences on the Verona Sacramentary, but he believed that they had not been composed at Rome.[12] But Chavasse has objectively demolished this view.[13] Bishop's fundamental argument had been the presence in the Gelasian of certain expressions which, in his judgment, properly Roman texts would not have used. But Bishop's arguments are weakened and even destroyed by a more careful study. There may, then, have been "Gallican" alterations in these prayers, but in origin they are nonetheless Roman.[14]

The Theology of Death in the Gelasian Sacramentary

In the effort to be objective, nothing is so helpful as to establish a kind of lexikon of the words which the Gelasian uses in connection with death. I offer here a list of words that should certainly be part of a Gelasian vocabulary for death.[15] A simple reading of this list will already give an idea of some of the peculiarities of the Gelasian. At the same time, however, great prudence is needed in drawing conclusions from a comparison with the Verona Sacramentary. The reason for this is that the Verona Sacramentary contains no funeral liturgy and therefore has less reason for using certain terms; the absence of these terms must not lead us to hasty conclusions. Here, then, is an imperfect list of words connected with death in the Gelasian Sacramentary:

Absolutus (freed) 1619
Adsumere (take up) 1607
Advenire (come) 1617
Aeternitas (eternity) 1622
Angelus (angel) 1610, 1621,
    1627, 1665
Arcessire (summon) 1617
Beatitudo (beatitude, blessedness,
    happiness) 1619, 1636, 1637,
    1639, 1644, 1652, 1674, 1681,
    1684, 1692
Benedictus (blessed) 1612
Caelestis (heavenly) 1616, 1626
Caelum (heaven) 1639
Clarificare (glorify) 1610
Claritas (brightness, glory) 1611
    (2x), 1681, 1684, 1692
Clarus (glorified, in glory) 1640
Coetus (assembly, company)
    1608, 1650
Comitatus (service, company)
    1623
Congregatio (assembly,
    congregation) 1637
Consedere (sit with) 1611
Consortium (company) 1623,
    1628, 1642, 1643, 1670, 1691
Corona (crown) 1573
Coronare (to crown) 1611
Decedere (depart, die) 1662
Depositio (burial) 1613, 1614,
    1629, 1631, 1660, 1690 (x),
    1692, 1693, 1694 (2x), 1695
Depositus (buried) 1694
Dies (day) 1627
Dormiens (sleeping) 1674, 1682
Electus (elect) 1614, 1617, 1620,
    1624, 1667, 1691, 1695
Expeditus (freed, released) 1666
Exultare (rejoice, exult) 1633,
    1639
Fidelis (faithful) 1623, 1664
Finis (end) 1649, 1652, 1680

Flamma (flame) 1609
Fructus (fruit) 1639
Gaudere (rejoice) 1577, 1611,
    1649
Gaudium (joy) 1611, 1623, 1625,
    1632, 1647, 1648, 1655, 1656,
    1689
Gehenna (hell) 1609, 1714
Habitaculum (dwelling) 1612,
    1655
Hereditas (heritage, inheritance)
    1647, 1656
Ignis (fire) 1609
Immortalitas (immortality) 1617
Infernus (hell) 1617
Interitus (destruction) 1720
Iudex (judge) 1715
Iudicium (judgment) 1623, 1627,
    1712, 1720
Iustus (just) 1625, 1637
Laetari (rejoice, be gladdened)
    1629, 1679, 1680
Laetitia (joy, gladness) 1626,
    1634
Laqueus (snare) 1620, 1625
Liberare (set free, liberate) 1609,
    1625
Locus (place) 1609, 1617 (2x),
    1621
Lumen (light) 1611, 1625, 1681,
    1684, 1692
Lux (light) 1587, 1617, 1634,
    1644, 1665, 1666, 1670, 1686
Mansio (dwelling place) 1571,
    1607, 1617
Medicina (medicine, remedy)
    1667
Migrans (depart) 1626
Misericordia (mercy) 1666, 1668,
    1676, 1686
Mori (to die) 1627
Mors (death) 1623, 1667, 1678,
    1682, 1694

Mortalitas (mortality) 1658, 1664
Munus (gift) 1536, 1614
Mutare (change) 1627
Paradysus (paradise) 1611
Pax (peace) 1609, 1674, 1686, 1703
Perfrui (enjoy) 1623
Pervenire (reach) 1587
Placens (pleasing) 1631, 1641, 1646
Poena (punishment) 1621
Porta (gate, door) 1611, 1612
Premium (reward) 1630, 1673
Quies (rest, repose) 1617, 1621, 1681, 1684, 1692
Quiescere (to rest) 1670, 1683, 1687
Reddere (give back) 1624, 1694
Redemptio (redemption) 1675, 1687
Redemptus (redeemed) 1679, 1683
Refrigerium (refreshment) 1617, 1621, 1681, 1684, 1692
Refugium (refuge) 1625
Regio (region) 1609, 1625, 1632, 1634, 1686
Remuneratio (reward, recompense) 1617

Requies (rest) 1612, 1613, 1616, 1618, 1639, 1645, 1646, 1664, 1669, 1683, 1687
Requiescere (to rest) 1680
Resurgere (rise) 1612
Resurrectio (resurrection) 1612 (2x), 1613, 1616, 1617, 1618, 1619, 1620, 1700
Resuscitare (raise to life) 1616, 1617, 1623, 1627, 1695
Retributio (recompense, reward) 1663
Reverti (to return) 1608 (2x), 1610, 1611, 1621
Sinus (bosom) 1612, 1618, 1621 (2x), 1627, 1695
Societas (company, fellowship) 1629, 1634, 1667
Tartarus (hell) 1609
Tenebrae (darkness) 1617, 1621
Transire (pass) 1618
Transitus (passage) 1648, 1678
Venire (come) 1559, 1568, 1612, 1695
Vita (life) 1536, 1611, 1612, 1617, 1633, 1663, 1678, 1683, 1694
Vivere (to live) 1602, 1609
Vivus (living, alive) 1625, 1632

This elementary list[16] can be of help in orienting our study, but it must be used with caution. For example, the word *depositio*, which occurs frequently in the Gelasian, is found only once in the Verona Sacramentary (1161), while the words *Gehenna, habitaculum, locus, mansio,* and *Paradysus* (names of places in which the dead person may dwell) do not appear there at all. The word *requies* occurs twice in Verona (1110, 1152), but neither *quies* nor *refrigerium* are to be found. The terms *sinus* and *Tartarus* are absent; and so on. These data may possibly point to the "Gallican" origin of a group of texts in the Gelasian; on the other hand, as I said earlier, the absence of these words from the Verona Sacramentary must not be interpreted too simplistically, since this sacramentary does not have these liturgies for the dead.

The Gelasian sets the faithful before a fact: the fact of the reign of death as connected with sin. Death and sin are two universal phenomena that condition earthly existence: "Mindful, dear brothers and sisters, of the ancient bond to which human life was made subject by the sin and corruption of the first man . . ." (1613). This same idea is already expressed in a preface for the Sunday after the Lord's Ascension: ". . . that [we who had been] formerly lost and laid low by the devil and the sting of death . . ." (589). The same point is made in a preface for the dedication of the baptismal font: ". . . so that we who because of our fleshly origin had come into the world as mortal . . ." (733). Or again, in the *Prayer over a sick catechumen*, the post-Roman origin of which I mentioned earlier: "whatever in him the devil held in subjection to punishment, due to the transgression of original sin . . ." (595). The same fact of sin is recalled again in the Gelasian *Blessing of the [Easter] Candle*: "and that because of the sin of the first man created and his black presumption was condemned to slavery . . ." (426).

In itself, and at first sight, death is regarded as an evil and a punishment. But there is one kind of death that is not subject to this evaluation: the "precious death" of the martyrs. The Gelasian emphasizes less than the Verona this special quality of the martyr's death, but it does not overlook it. It attributes to this death a sacrificial value that is connected with the death of Christ and the qualities of this death: "Lord, on this feast of the precious death of your just ones, we offer that sacrifice which is the source of every martyrdom" (1030).

In the case of the martyrs, death acquires a dignity that wins favor for it in the eyes of God. This idea also finds expression in the preface for the Vigil of St. Lawrence: "for the death of your holy ones is precious in the sight of your divine majesty" (972).

But toward death of whatever kind, Christians should have the attitude which faith calls for and which, without denying that death is the wages of sin, nonetheless assigns it a value which the non-Christian is unable to see. Death must be seen in its biblical context; there must be no imagining that a dead person is in a state of exile and separation from God. Such a view would be utterly opposed to that of the Gelasian Sacramentary, which sees the dead person as the creature and image of which Genesis speaks: "Lord, receive the creature who is your own and was not created by other gods" (1610); "Command that your image be united to your saints and elect in the eternal dwellings" (1624). These two texts are in the Gallican insertion in section XCI: *Prayers after the death of a person*. In addition, death puts us in the presence of a manifestation of the divine omnipotence that creates man and then calls him back to itself, as this same section of the Sacramentary reminds us: ". . . by whose decision we are born and come to the end of our lives" (1618); ". . . who deigned to breathe a soul into the human body for your own sake and at whose command dust returns to dust . . ." (1624). Death is a sign of our fundamental belonging to God, and the dead person is called "servant" (*servus, famulus*) in a large number of prayers.

Death, then, is a passage, a return to God the creator. This theme of passage or return is emphasized in the Sacramentary and is the subject of a development along paschal lines, as we just saw in connection with the death of martyrs. In point of fact, God takes the initiative, for he summons his creature to return to him: "whom the Lord has taken away from the temptations of this world" (1607); "whom the loving Lord has bidden pass from a dwelling in this world . . ." (1618). In his reflections on the gospel of John, St. Augustine writes: "a certain passage from death to life has been consecrated in the passion and resurrection of the Lord."[17]

But this passage forced the "Gallican" liturgists to ask themselves: How does it take place? Three prayers in section XCI are concerned with the matter:

"Send your holy angels to meet him and show him the way of justice. Open the gates of justice to him and ward off from him the princes of darkness" (1610).

"Allow his spirit to pass by the gates of hell and the paths of darkness and to abide in the dwellings of the saints and in the holy light you once promised to Abraham and his posterity. May his soul sustain no wound, but deign to raise him up when the great day of resurrection and reward comes" (1617).

"May Michael, the angel of your covenant, be at his side. Deliver him, Lord, from the princes of darkness and the places of chastisement" (1621).

It would not be correct, however, to attribute such concerns solely to the "Gallicans." For in the *Commendatio animae,* the only prayer accepted as Roman shows the same preoccupation: ". . . that you would command the soul of this your servant to be taken up in the hands of angels to the bosom of your friend, Abraham the patriarch" (1627).

The formularies concentrate on two aspects of the phase between death and resurrection: the dwelling place of the dead and what their lot is.

A review of the vocabulary of the Gelasian turns up a number of "geographical" descriptions of this dwelling place. Here are a few: *aeternum habitaculum* (eternal dwelling, 1612); *regnum* (kingdom,

1612); *Hierusalem caelestem* (heavenly Jerusalem, 1612); *locum lucidum* (place of light, 1617); *locum refrigerii* (place of refreshment, 1617); *in mansionibus sanctorum* (in the dwellings of the saints, 1617).

There is also a localization in relation to the other elect: *in pace sanctorum* (in the peace of the saints, 1607); *in regione viventium* (in the region of the living, 1607); *cum sanctis et electis tuis* (with your saints and elect, 1614).

Along this same line, the Sacramentary locates the dead person in the abode of rest, which is the bosom of Abraham. This theme is to be found in the Gallican prayers. Two formularies are especially noteworthy, because at the same time they emphasize the activity of the angels in effecting the transfer of the dead person to the bosom of Abraham: "Let him be acknowledged by your own and in your merciful goodness let him be carried to the place of refreshment and repose in the bosom of Abraham" (1621); ". . . to order the soul of your servant taken up . . . and brought to the bosom of your friend, Abraham the patriarch" (1627).

The theme recurs frequently (e.g., 1617, 1618), but at times Abraham is joined by Isaac and Jacob: for example in 1618, ". . . and deign to place him in the bosoms of Abraham, Isaac and Jacob," or again in 1695, "in the bosoms of Abraham, Isaac and Jacob."

The angels serve in this transfer to the bosom of the patriarchs, just as they do in the reception of the deceased: "Send your holy angels to meet him" (1610), or ". . . to order the soul of your servant taken up in the hands of the holy angels and brought to the bosom of your friend, Abraham the patriarch" (1627).

Among the angels who minister at this reception, Michael holds a special place: "May Michael, the angel of your covenant, be at his side" (1621).

As is well known, the Bible is the source both of this activity of the angels in the passage of the soul and of the bosom of Abraham. In his parable of the rich man and the beggar, St. Luke is using themes familiar to him: "The poor man died and was carried by the angels to Abraham's bosom" (16:22).

In its dwelling place after death, the departed soul enjoys the company not only of the patriarchs but of the saints and elect as well: "receive him into the peace of your saints" (1609); ". . . with your saints and elect" (1614); ". . . among his saints and elect" (1620).

But the dwelling of the departed may not be with the patriarchs and saints. A departure to places and companions less pleasing is also possible. On the feast of St. Lawrence, inspired in all likelihood by the kind of torment the martyr had undergone, the Sacramentary says in the second prayer: ". . . that by his intercession we may be rescued from the everlasting fires of Gehenna" (975).

There were plenty of scripture passages on which the composers of prayers could draw, thus doing away with any need of having recourse to themes developed in paganism. Psalms 85:13 and 87:4, Job 16:17 and 14:13, Matthew 16:18, and Luke 16:22 all use the same terms. There is an equivalence established among *Gehenna, hell (infernus), place of punishments, fire,* and so on. Here are some examples: "Allow his spirit to pass by the gates of hells and the paths of darkness" (1617); "Deliver him, Lord, from the princes of darkness and the places of chastisement" (1621); ". . . that his soul may avoid the burning of the everlasting fire" (1625). Or there may be a more poetic kind of expression: ". . . that he may escape the place of punishment and the fire of Gehenna and the flames of Tartarus and be in the region of the living" (1609).

The passage, which is at the same time a liberation, a return to the Lord, and a transformation, sets in motion a whole process of purification. The activity of divine mercy is expressed in terms that emphasize purification and the remission of sins. Thus such verbs as *remittat* (remit, 1607), *conpensit* (set in the balance, 1607), *deleas* (wipe out, 1608), *indulgeas* (be indulgent, forgive, 1608), *ablue* (wash away, 1627), *absolve* (absolve, 1658), *exuas* (strip, remove, 1675), and *extergeas* (wipe away, 1690) serve to specify the transformation required by the Lord. This transformation is closely connected with the grace of baptism: "God, you grant entrance into the kingdom of heaven only to those reborn of water and the Holy Spirit . . ." (1648); ". . . that as you granted him your grace in baptism, you would grant him your kingdom as well" (1653); ". . . that having given him a share in adoption, you would make him a sharer in your inheritance" (1656).

The whole Church prays that this grace of purification may be granted to the deceased. The communion of saints comes into play here. References to particular prayers would be superfluous here, since the very existence of the Sacramentary and its prayers is due to faith in the common prayer of the faithful and in its efficacy.

This period occupied by the "passage" of the dead person was intriguing especially to "Gallican" authors of liturgical prayers. One phrase, *prima resurrectio* (first resurrection), occurs with some frequency in the group of texts with which I am dealing here: ". . . and have a share in the first resurrection" (1612); ". . . and raise him up to a share in the first resurrection" (1616); ". . . to give (him) part in the first resurrection of your saints" (1619); ". . . and have a share in the first resurrection" (1620).

The theme is an interesting one and has already been the subject of research, initially by Dom Bernard Botte.[18] In Dom Botte's opinion, "first resurrection" is simply a synonym for the "resurrection of the just." After examining the Spanish Liturgy, he extends the scope of his enquiry and cites 1612 in the Gelasian Sacramentary: ". . . and let him have a share in the first resurrection, and rise with the rising, and receive his body with those who receive their bodies on the day of resurrection, and come with the blessed as they come to the right hand of God, and possess eternal life with those who possess eternal life." The succession of stages is clear: first resurrection, resurrection of the body, possession of eternal life.

Prayer 1620, which is among the *Prayers at the grave*, offers a different but complementary approach: ". . . that the Lord in his mercy will place him among his saints and elect, that is, in the bosom of Abraham and Isaac and Jacob and that he will share in the first resurrection which is granted at the prayer of the saints."

In these passages the resurrection is always that of the saints. St. Zeno clearly distinguishes two resurrections: "There are two manners of rising. The first is that of the saints, as they are summoned by the royal signal of the first trumpet to receive the kingdom of blessedness and enjoy a mighty triumph under Christ the eternal king. The second condemns the wicked to eternal punishment along with sinners and all unbelieving nations."[19]

These words take us into a second theme: the theme of judgment. Prayer 1623 of section XCI presents its various aspects:

". . . that he would raise up in the power and integrity of the saints this body which we have buried in its weakness, and would bid the soul be joined to the saints and faithful, and that he would be merciful to it in judgment and grant the unending joy and fellowship of the saints, in the company of the eternal king, to this soul which has been redeemed from death, released from its debts, reconciled with the Father, and carried on the shoulders of the Good Shepherd.

See also 1627, 1712, 1715, 1720.

Also to be noted are the themes of light (1587, 1617, 1634, 1644, 1665, 1666, 1670, 1686); glory (*claritas:* 1611, 1681, 1684, 1692); joy (1611, 1623, 1625, 1632, 1647, 1648, 1655, 1656, 1689); and immortality (1617, 1626).

Since it is impossible for me to go into all these aspects, important though they are and certainly not overlooked by the Sacramentary when it speaks of death, let me end with a quick summary of their content. A general theology of death, as it

NOCENT

emerges from an analysis of the prayers of the Gelasian, shows first of all that death's reign is connected with sin. But there is more to it than this. In fact, this negative judgment on death is voiced only in order that it may be transcended in an emphasis on a victory. The element of victory stands out with special clarity in the case of the martyrs.

But no matter who the Christian is, we must not be satisfied with a vision of death as linked to sin. A broader perspective carries us further and embraces a paschal interpretation of death. Death is the return of the creature to God its creator. Moreover death is not, as in the Book of Job, something passively accepted: "You give and you take away." It is rather a liberation, and not simply a negative liberation from temptation, the flesh, and so on, but a positive liberation of a paschal kind: passage, return to, transformation, resurrection. The passage includes an encounter with the Lord as judge, so that the person may then travel on joyously to the light and to a glorious immortality. The term of the whole process is rest in the glory of God.

In the Gallican texts of the Sacramentary an effort is made to shed light on the state of separation of soul from body and to mull over the conditions of the passage from earthly life to the next life. The angels exercise a ministry in this passage, which presupposes a forgiveness that is linked to the baptismal conversion of faith. The passage then becomes a journey to the place of repose where the patriarchs and saints dwell, and this with the help of the Church's prayers.

There is nothing very original in this theology, but it is expressed in a concise and, we might say, classical way. Only the problem of the "first resurrection" stands out somewhat. It is to be observed that most of the formularies are faithful to the content and, often, even to the very language of scripture. Also to be noted is the tendency of the "Gallican" formularies to use certain terms derived from paganism or even still close to their pagan meaning, but it is advisable not to draw any radical conclusions from this fact.

Jordi PINELL

The Votive Office
of the Sick
in the Spanish Rite

This essay is divided into two parts: a historico-technical presentation of the formularies of the office *de infirmis* and an analysis of its doctrinal content. For obvious reasons, I devote most of my time to the second part. In an appendix, I add the entire collection of prayer texts.

In the doctrinal analysis I apply a method which consists chiefly of investigating the biblical theology which inspired the authors who composed or adapted the formularies for the office of the sick.

In setting forth the results of my analysis I shall group the texts according to genre, following the classical division of liturgical texts into readings, canticles inspired by the Bible, poetical texts, and prayers. I have thought it worthwhile in this particular case to devote a whole section to the Old Testament canticles. In analyzing the antiphons and responsories I have thought it suitable to inquire above all into their literary and doctrinal dependence on the book of the Psalms.

This method has been suggested by the very material itself with which I shall be working.

The Sources

Five sources have the votive office of the sick: four manuscripts and the Breviary. The manuscripts are: León, Archivo Capitular cod. 8, an antiphonary of the tenth century, fol. 274v–277.[1]; Silos, Archivo de la Abadía cod. 3, *liber ordinum minor* (copied in the year 1039), fol. 50–55[2]; London, British Museum cod. add. 30.851, eleventh century, originating in Silos, part of a *liber misticus*, fol. 188v–192v[3]; Silos, Archivo de la Abadía cod. 7, eleventh century, part of a *liber misticus*, fol. 1–12.[4]

In the Breviary of the Ortiz the identical office appears twice: once in the series of common offices,[5] and again to fill a vacancy in the weekday ferial offices after Epiphany.[6]

The most appropriate place for this office seems to be among the common offices. In fact, in the Breviary, this office of the sick opens the *Commune*. It is followed by the *Officium Mortuorum*, the *In Agenda Mortuorum*, and then the Commons of the Saints. On the other hand, in the León antiphonary and in the London manuscript the offices for the sick and the deceased practically form the close of the *Commune*.

In the London manuscript the offices of the sick follow upon the Commons of the Saints; in the León manuscript the offices for the Commons of the Saints are separated from the offices of the sick by the formularies for various offices that vary greatly in character: *Responsuria de Letania de Clade* (fol. 255v–257v); *Responsuria de Letanias pro plubia postulanda* (fol. 257v–259); *Officium pro gratiarum hactione plubie temporanee* (fol. 259); *Officium de sacratione baselice* (fol. 259v–268); *Officium in anniversario sacrationis baselice* (fol. 268v); *Officium de restauratione baselice* (fol. 268v–270); *Officium de ordinatione episcopi* (fol. 270–271v); *Officium in ordinatione sive natalitio regis* (fol. 271v–273v); and *Officium de nubentum* (fol. 274–274v). The votive offices of the sick—*de infirmis* (fol. 274v–276); *de uno infirmo* (fol. 276–277)—are followed by the *Officium ad commendandum corpus defuncti* (fol. 277) and three offices of the dead: *de uno defuncto* (fol. 277–278v); *de defunctorum episcoporum* (fol. 278v–279); and *de defunctis generalis* (fol. 279–280).

In the *liber ordinum,* the office of the sick is part of an *ordo de infirmis* which includes the Office and the Mass and which is placed in the section which the ritual for the priest devotes to votive Masses. The antiphonary of León also has the Mass for the sick after the office of the sick. We may therefore ask whether this connection between the office and the Mass of the sick existed from the beginning. No very certain answer can be given. But after examining the texts, I have the impression that the office had been conceived autonomously and at a period later than the composition of the Mass. This does not exclude the possibility that the texts, and especially the readings, of the Mass subsequently exercised a certain influence on the composition of new formularies for the office of the sick during the final period of the development of this office.

Let us keep in mind that the office of the sick remained an independent celebration not only in the Breviary but in the London manuscript and in the fragment of ms no. 7 of Silos.

The sources that have preserved the office of the sick for us represent the two traditions within the Spanish rite: the antiphonary of León, the *liber ordinum,* the fragment of the other Silos manuscript, and the London manuscript belong to tradition A; as in many other cases, the Breviary is the sole representative of tradition B.[7]

We shall see, however, that the discrepancy between the traditions is not as important in this case as it might be in other areas of the Spanish rite.

Plurality of Offices

The antiphonary of León provides chants for two offices of the sick, which it distinguishes as "office of the sick [pl.]," and "office of one sick person." The fragment of the London *misticus* has even a triple *ordo:* "office of the sick," "another office of the sick," and "office of one sick person."

On the other hand, both manuscripts of the *liber ordinum* and the Breviary give but a single office, although, as mentioned above, the Breviary repeats the identical office in two different parts of the book.

The fragment of a *misticus* in Silos ms no. 7 seemingly has but a single *ordo* entitled "office of the sick," but in fact it contains formularies for making three distinct offices. At Vespers, after giving all the formularies needed for a first *ordo,* it then introduces—with two distinct subtitles: *alia vespera de infirmis* and *alia vespera*—the chants and prayers for two further offices. The division effected by the subtitles is misleading in that they really distinguish only two sets of chants; the euchological texts of the two offices are all placed together at the end of the second group. At Matins there is no effort at a systematic division of the three groups of formularies. Matins first gives the three groups of chants and prayers that make up the *missa,*[8] I mean formularies for three distinct *missae,* and then gives three groups of formularies for the *completuria* (final prayer of the office) and the *benedictio* (blessing).

The Breviary, in its two versions of the office of the sick, gives us, under the title *alia lauda,* a second formulary for the evening *alleluiaticum.*

We thus have for the office of the sick a repertory of formularies that was amplified at various stages. The compilers of the various sources tried as best they could to codify the material before them, but they applied different criteria. A tendency to compose various offices (for which there was more than enough material) can be seen in the antiphonary of León and the London manuscript. But neither source achieves so complete a codification as to prevent the inclusion of supplementary formularies in the office.

In this sense the most restrained source is the Breviary, which contains only one office and limits itself to one optional formulary, the evening *alleluiaticum,* as I just indicated.

Liturgical Function

As we now find it in the sources, the office of the sick has all the characteristics of a festive office; nonetheless, an analysis of the formularies enables us to detect various signs of an evolution showing a passage from a regular ferial scheme to a festive scheme.[9]

Whatever the place and environment may have been in which the office of the sick originated, it was certainly catalogued as one of the many votive offices in the cathedral *ordo.* Its conception, composition, and development may have been influenced directly or indirectly by monastic spirituality, but this office of the sick was undoubtedly intended for liturgical use in the churches and not reserved to monasteries.[10]

The office was a votive one, not in the sense which the term "votive" was to have later on (a devotional office, added to the regular office of the day), but in the only sense which the term could conceivably have during the Visigothic period, namely, an office whose object did not have a place in the sequence of liturgical feasts and seasons in the calendar or, more generally, among the prayer themes of the period called *de quotidiano* (our "Ordinary Time"). But, as I pointed out above, there was a special office for the day of a bishop's consecration, another for the day of the king's coronation and for the anniversary of the same; there was also an office of thanksgiving for rain, and responsories (to be inserted into the ferial or dominical office) for times of drought or on the occasion of some catastrophe.

In the celebration of the Church's praise of God, there could and had to be room for the voicing of some social need, or a reflection of a local Church feast or a political holiday that was national in character.

As seen against this kind of background, the office of the sick takes as theme for the Church's prayer the concern of the Christian community with regard to the evil that is sickness. As we shall see, the office is not precisely or solely a prayer for the sick; it is primarily a reflection, based especially on scripture, on the mystery of human evil, that is, the weakness or infirmity of the body and the sin of the entire person, body and soul. This, then, is ecclesial praise that is meant to lead to a new awareness of the need of a God who saves. God is the only one who can bestow genuine *salus*, in the twofold sense of health and salvation.

The office of the sick was conceived as a celebration that was to take place in the church and was composed of the two hours of the cathedral ordo: vespers and the morning office. It was thus not a domestic rite to be accomplished in the presence of the sick person. It indicates rather that the ecclesial community—clergy and faithful—accepted the mission of representing before God the human situation of the sick in that community, by living out in prayer the problem of bodily infirmity and seeking a religious explanation of it, again in prayer.

When was this office celebrated? There is no direct information on the point, so I can only conjecture. I do not think that the celebration of this office was always connected with concrete cases of sickness. Such a connection would be easy enough in small parishes and in monasteries (where, let us not forget, the cathedral office was also celebrated, along with the regular monastic office). But it is my guess that, at least in its more developed form, the office of sick would be substituted now and then (not very often) for the regular ferial office; something comparable would be true of the office of the dead.

The great freedom with regard to the regular ferial office—a freedom that lasted throughout the Mozarabic period and, as far as tradition B is concerned, even in the period after the Reconquista—suggests, among other things, the possibility of using one of these votive offices, the object of which would never be out of season. My opinion is based on the following pieces of evidence: the plurality of offices of the sick (a plurality intended to supply a certain variety of formularies rather than a variation in content); the title *de defunctis generalis*, which we find in the antiphonary of León; and, finally, the fact that the Breviary replaces the ferial office for the Friday after Epiphany with the office of the sick may reflect a practice in the Toledan parish of Sts. Justa and Rufina. We should bear in mind that the parish priest of Sts. Justa and Rufina was head of the committee of Mozarabic parish priests of Toledo who helped Canon Ortiz prepare his edition of the Missal and Breviary.

The Votive Office of the Sick in the Spanish Rite

The Reading

The only source that has a reading for the office of the sick is the Breviary.[11] The reading is from Jeremiah 29:10–14 and is identical with the first of the three readings of the Mass for the sick according to the *liber ordinum* as well as according to the two manuscripts of the *liber commicus* (the Lectionary for Mass).[12]

The biblical text has been slightly changed, probably with the pastoral intention of getting the oracle across to the Christian assembly by making it more topical. The principal alteration consists in the omission of the clause which gives the historical circumstances: "when seventy years are completed in Babylon." With these words omitted the word of God becomes directly applicable to all times: "Behold, I will visit you, and I will fulfill my promise to you. . . ."

The essential point of the reading is focused in the word "visit," which may tell us why this pericope was chosen for an office of the sick. In fact, the entire reading emphasizes the divine presence: "You will seek me and you will find me; if you seek me with all your heart, you will find me."

When thus chosen for use in a celebration on behalf of the sick, the biblical text is transformed into a message of consolation, so as to strengthen those afflicted by illness. God is present to them and guiding events in his wisdom. Questions may disturb the soul of the sick person, but he or she has the assurance that the divine mind is controlling everything: "For I know my thoughts with regard to you, says the Lord; they are thoughts of peace and not of affliction, so that you may trust and be patient."

The aim, then, of the reading in the office, which emerges as an assertion of God's visitation and presence, is to rouse confidence and create an atmosphere of serene hope that is based primarily on the fact that the person can turn to God and be sure that he hears: "You will call upon me and reverence me, and I will hear you."

The prophet Jeremiah puts these words in the mouth of God himself, where they take on the character of a blessing—"I will fulfill my promise to you." I use "blessing" here in the basic sense it has in the theology of the Bible: a proclamation of good by God who brings this good to pass among men by the power of this word.

The Canticles from the Old Testament

As in the Roman office, so in the Spanish morning office there was a canticle from the Old Testament.[13] But the Spanish collection of canticles was much more extensive than the Roman,[14] so that the compilers of the office of the sick had a wider choice, especially

PINELL

when they wanted to compose not one but several offices of the sick.

The sources show four different canticles being used, in addition to the *benedictiones* or canticle of Daniel which in the festive scheme was always said in the morning office. The four canticles are: Isaiah 33:2–10; Ecclesiastes 11:9–12:7; Isaiah 12:1–6; Deuteronomy 32:36–39. Let me analyze each in turn.

Isaiah 33. The canticle most often found in the sources is the one from Isaiah 33. It is indicated in the antiphonary of León,[15] in the *liber ordinum*,[16] and in the first of the offices in the London manuscript.[17] It corresponds to no. LXVI of the *liber canticorum* reproduced by Lorenzana in the Breviary.[18]

The choice of this canticle for the office of the sick was surely motivated by the first two verses: "Lord, have mercy on us, for we have been waiting for you. Be our arm in the morning, and our salvation in time of affliction." As we shall see, the noun *salus* and the verb *sana* largely determine the selection of biblical texts used in composing the antiphons and responsories.

The eschatological character of this Isaian canticle suggests that sickness is being viewed as a transition to the next life. The biblical text signs of the victory of the Lord: "You are exalted, Lord. 'Now I shall arise,' says the Lord. 'Now I shall be exalted and now I shall be raised on high.' " His victory will be fully manifested in his majesty at judgment, as he strikes fear by the might of his presence.

I think, then, that in choosing this canticle, the compiler has in mind to bring the praying assembly to see sickness, which is a disturbance of nature, as the effect of the presence of the Lord who is coming: "For we have been waiting for you." That which presents itself as distress and affliction of the flesh must be understood in the light of faith—"and there will be faith in due time"—as a form of submission to genuine *salus*, which is what the Lord is offering to us.

Ecclesiastes 11–12. The canticle from Ecclesiastes, which is signaled only in the London manuscript[19] corresponds to no. LXXV in the *liber canticorum* of tradition A.[20] In content, the biblical text presents itself primarily as an exhortation to live joyously but wisely: "Young man, rejoice while you are young, and may your heart enjoy good things in the days of your youth." The writer of this sapiential book is addressing a young person—that is, someone who apparently has less reason to think about it—and trying to persuade him of the transiency of human life: "Remember your Creator in the days of your youth, before the time of affliction comes."

I think that the selection of this canticle for the office of the sick was motivated primarily by this contrast between the full life lived by the young and the constant threat of collapse that lies over that life. Once again, the idea of death proves to be the explanation of the dramatic element in sickness: "For a man shall go to his eternal home, and the mourners go about in the street . . . and the dust shall return to the earth whence it came, and the spirit shall return to God who gave it." A critical sickness will always point ahead to the mysterious crisis that is death, in which the human being must pass to his eternal dwelling and give back to God the breath of life he had received from him.

Isaiah 12. The third canticle, which again is found only in the London manuscript,[21] corresponds to no. LXV in Lorenzana's book of canticles.[22] Its adaptation to the office of the sick seems rather artificial, at least at first glance. The canticle is essentially a profession of faith in the power of God. It is possible that the canticle was chosen for inclusion in the office of the sick because of its use of the word *salus,* although in its Isaian context the word has nothing to do with bodily health: "For the Lord is my strength and my song, and he has become my salvation (*salus*)."

It is also possible that this canticle was chosen because of expressions which its opening verse has in common with Psalm 6. As we shall see, Psalm 6 plays a very important role in the biblical theology of the office of the sick.

If this be indeed the reason for the choice, then the canticle amounts to a replica of the psalm. The psalm in its entirety is a supplication in which the prophet acknowledges sickness to be the result of God's anger. The canticle begins with the same theme of God's anger, but then it goes on to say that God's wrath has now ceased: "I will praise you, Lord, because you were angry at me, but your wrath was changed and you consoled me. Behold, God is my Savior; I will be trusting and will not fear."

Deuteronomy 32. The canticle from Deuteronomy is found only in the Breviary.[23] These verses from Deuteronomy 32 are not found in the *liber canticorum* of tradition A, which contains only an abbreviated version of the great canticle of Moses (it is reduced to vv. 1–12).[24] But tradition B uses almost the entire canticle (i.e., 32:1–43); on the other hand, it also contains an abbreviated version, and this is the one used by the compiler of the office of the sick.[25] The antiphon: "I shall slay and I shall make alive; I shall strike and I shall heal," which is the one used in the office of the sick, is identically the one for the morning office on Monday of the second week of Lent; this is one of the two occasions on which the Breviary assigns the abbreviated version.[26] In traditions A and B alike, the text of the canticle follows the Vetus Latina instead of the Vulgate.

The choice of this passage is evidently determined by v. 39 in which we hear God saying: "I shall make alive . . . I shall heal." But the content of this short fragment also makes other points that are part of the overall teaching of the office of the sick.

The text of Deuteronomy tells us that when God sees his people prostrated he addresses them and asks them why they have worshipped other gods. The bitter but regenerative and hope-filled lesson taught the Israelites by their experience is that the true God alone abides in time of trial: "See, see that I am the Lord, and that there is no other lord besides me."

If we restate this teaching in terms proper to the office of the sick, we may say that the human situation of sickness highlights one great truth: God is the only transcendent reality. Consequently, if those now sick have lived Christian lives, their physical infirmity becomes a powerful means of intensifying their sense of God's presence to them: a presence that can play a decisive role in their definitive encounter with eternity.

Antiphons and Responsories

As I pointed out earlier, the festive scheme was chosen for the composition of the office of the sick. This means that the psalmody is reduced to the antiphons and *alleluiatica* of Vespers and the morning office. Nonetheless, as we shall see in a moment, a study of the biblical sources for the chants of this office shows the preponderant part indirectly played by the book of Psalms in the doctrinal content of the office as a whole.

I said earlier that the five sources that preserve the office of the sick contain an abundance of formularies. To get an approximate idea of this abundance, we may compare first the number of chants needed for an entire office and the number actually found in all the sources that have come down to us. If we exclude the common antiphons, which all the sources are at one in taking from the book of antiphons for the psalter[27] (these common antiphons are the antiphon for the *vespertinum*, the antiphons for Psalms 3 and 50, and the antiphons for the *Laudate* psalms), the structure of a minor festive office[28] requires ten proper chants which are distributed as follows: three antiphons, two *alleluiatica*, a responsory, two formulas for the *sono*, and two antiphons for the *psallendum*. However, instead of the ten chants needed, the set of offices of the sick provides forty-eight, which are distributed as follows: twenty-three antiphons, eleven *alleluiatica*, eight responsories, four formulas for the *sono*, and two antiphons for the *psallendum*.

Of the twenty-three antiphons in the collection, twenty are based on the text of the psalms, and of the eleven *alleluiatica*, ten are psalmic. In addition, of the four formulas for the *sono*, three are also based on texts from the psalter; on the other hand, of the eight responsories, only three are from the psalms, at least in a verbatim way.

We shall see immediately that the choice of psalms is full of meaning.

Psalm 6. In its original literary genre, Psalm 6 is one of those individual lamentations that have for their vital context a condition of sickness. It is the psalm most used in the Spanish office of the sick. As seen by the Old Testament, sickness can only be the result of sin. God's anger reveals itself in the evil that afflicts a person. For this reason, confident prayer and an acknowledgment of guilt can change the attitude of God, who alone is able to restore health.

Use has been made of almost the entire psalm in composing the chants for this office. Verse 2 goes to the root of the problem when it asks God to lay aside his anger: "Lord, do not accuse me in your anger nor chastise me in your wrath."[29] "Lord, do not accuse us in your anger nor chastise us in your wrath."[30]

Other chants combine parts of v. 2 with vv. 3 and 4: "Lord, do not accuse me in your anger, but have mercy on me; heal me, Lord, for I am feeble.[31] "Lord, do not accuse me in your anger nor chastise me in your wrath, for I am feeble, but have mercy on me. ℣. See my lowliness and my toil, and forgive all my sins, for I am feeble."[32]

This responsory, which uses Psalm 24:18 as a verse, brings out more fully the deeper meaning of the text from Psalm 6.

An *alleluiaticum* is composed from parts of verse 3 which we have just seen used for other chants: "Have mercy on me, O Lord, alleluia, for I am feeble; heal me, Lord, alleluia, alleluia."[33]

Another antiphon uses v. 7 to describe the sick person's state of prostration: "I have grown weary with my moaning; every night I shall wash my bed, I shall drench my couch with tears."[34]

Verse 5 of the psalm asks God to change his attitude: "Turn, O Lord!" This is the heart of the prayer. This part of the psalm is used in various ways in the composition of chants: "Heal me, Lord; my bones are troubled and my soul is deeply troubled; turn, Lord, and rescue my soul."[35] "Heal us, Lord, for we are feeble; our bones are troubled and our soul is deeply troubled. But turn, Lord, for you are merciful, and rescue our souls; save us from your mercy's sake. ℣. Lord, by your name save us, and save us by your power. . . ."[36] "Lord, turn and rescue our souls, and save us for your mercy's sake, for in death no one is mindful of you."[37]

Psalm 102. Another group of chants, based on Psalm 102, displays in part the same themes as the chants based on Psalm 6. The two basic terms in this second group are the verb *sana* (heal) and the plea for the forgiveness of sins: "Forgive our sins." It may be observed that the development of the texts is fuller here than in the first group. All the texts make use of v. 3, and some use part of v. 4 as well. In this psalm the proclamation of God's mercy is part of an anamnesis that motivates the praise of God. The reader should keep in mind that Psalm 102 belongs to the literary genre of blessing and that it begins with the words: "Bless the Lord, my soul, and let all that is in me bless his holy name." As motive for this blessing the psalmist says: "For he forgives all your iniquities; he heals all your infirmities; he redeems your life from destruction."

The authors of the Spanish chants were inspired precisely by this part of the psalm, but they systematically turned the anamnesis (which gives the reasons for the blessing) into a prayer of petition; in the process they changed *iniquitates* to *peccata* and *infirmitates* to *languores.* "Forgive our sins, Lord, and heal all our sicknesses."[38] "Forgive our sins, Lord, and heal all our sicknesses, and rescue our souls from destruction. ℣. Help us, God our Savior, and free us for your name's sake."[39] "Lord, heal all our sicknesses, alleluia, rescue our life from destruction, alleluia, alleluia."[40] "Lord, heal all our sicknesses, alleluia. II. Lord, rescue our life from destruction."[41] "Lord, heal all our sicknesses, alleluia, and rescue our souls from destruction, alleluia, alleluia. II. Lord, set our tears before you, as you promised, alleluia, alleluia."[42]

It is possible that the substitution of *languores* (sicknesses) for the *infirmitates* (infirmities) is intended to remind the one using the office of Matthew 4:23: "And Jesus went about the whole of Galilee, teaching in their synagogues and preaching the gospel of the kingdom and healing every sickness and every infirmity among the people." In this way the prayer, while textually based on the psalm, would take on a New Testament or, more accurately, a Christological dimension. There would be nothing unusual about this way of getting New Testament teaching across; on the contrary, it was quite normal in the Spanish rite. We shall see further on that the hymn and the prayers of the office of the sick systematically complement the Old Testament teaching of the psalms by evoking the miracles which Jesus worked for the sick.

Psalm 105. Another important group of six antiphons is connected with Psalm 105. Two of the antiphons are based on v. 4, where the theme of *salus* is connected with that of the divine visitation.

The compilers of the office of the sick introduced into the collection an antiphon from the book of psalter antiphons; its text is still that of the old African version of the psalms: "Visit us, Lord, with your salvation (*salus*)."[43] The same verse, but in a latter translation, gave rise to an *alleluiaticum* with a more expanded text: "Visit us, Lord, with your salvation (*salutare*), alleluia, so that we may see the names of your elect, alleluia, alleluia."[44]

Three other chants—two *alleluiatica* and a *psallendum*—were based on v. 47, starting with its petition *salva nos* or *salvos fac nos* (save us; make us safe): "Save us, Lord our God, alleluia, alleluia, alleluia."[45] "Make us safe, Lord our God, alleluia, and gather us from among the nations, alleluia, alleluia."[46] "Make us safe, Lord our God, alleluia, that we may praise your holy name, alleluia."[47]

Finally, there is one antiphon that combines verse 6 with the petition "save us" from v. 47: "We have sinned like our fathers, we have acted wrongly, we have committed iniquities; save us, Lord our God."[48] This last antiphon shows forth the composer's intention of linking the themes of sin and health (*salus*). The admission of sinfulness makes it possible to call for the *salus* that comes from God.

Psalm 106. Verse 20 of Psalm 106 inspired two *alleluiatica*. As a matter of fact, the two are really one and the same; it is simply that the London manuscript has two versions, one in the singular and one in the plural. "Send your word and heal us, Lord, alleluia, alleluia."[49] "Send your word and heal me, Lord, alleluia, alleluia."[50] The reader will recall that the psalm has a statement: "He sent his word and healed them." This, then, is another instance in which the composer has turned into a prayer of petition what the psalmist states as an object of anamnesis or remembrance.

This pair of themes—"your word"/"heal us"—brings us to a point made in the overall teaching of the office of the sick. We have already seen it suggested in the readings, and it will reappear in some of the prayer texts. As the praying community reflects on the evil of sickness, discovers that this evil springs from another, namely the evil that is sin, and turns again to contemplate the signs by which God has shown his goodness in the history of salvation, it awaits a new coming of God's word, which has an inherent power to bestow blessing, health, and salvation.

According to the biblical theology that is closest to the meaning of the original text, this waiting upon God's word means a submitting of the self to God's blessing. But the choice of this part of the psalm for use here certainly supposes that the original text is now being read through New Testament eyes and that the Word sent by God is Christ himself. When I come to analyze the hymn and the prayers as well as some further chants that are not so closely based on the text of the psalms, we shall see that the christological dimension is basic to the theological content of the office of the sick, even though from a material point of view it occupies but a very modest place in the thoughts that inspire the formulas.

Other Psalms. We have seen that the chants inspired by Psalm 105 set up a relation between the theme of human sin and the theme of salvation from God. In the final analysis, the idea that humankind needs God's healing power if it is to emerge reborn from the evils afflicting it—inasmuch as its own sins have sunk it into a wretched state—is a conclusion reached by the theology of sickness that has its clearest expression in Psalm 6. According to this theology, sickness is the result of God's anger at man's sin.

There are, however, twelve other chants based on the psalms which emphasize a different thematic couple: sin-salvation. The couple may appear in its complete form within a single chant, as in this *alleluiaticum* based on Psalm 73:2: "We have sinned against you, O God; show your mercy, and let your hand free us before we perish."[51]

But a given chant may also enunciate only one of the two themes, as in the two following antiphons which are taken from Psalms 78:9 and 27:9, respectively: "Forgive our sins, O Lord"[52]; "Lord, save your people."[53] These very simple antiphons were not composed expressly for the office of the sick, but were taken from a book of psalter antiphons for general use. We saw earlier another example of this kind of antiphon. The implication is that in a first stage of the development of the office of the dead, the compilers used primarily these chants for common use, which they would know from memory. The phenomenon also shows that from the beginning the basic theology of the office of the sick was already the theology we see today in the repertories of formularies; these repertories were subsequently enriched with chants composed expressly for this office.

Thus Psalms 78 and 27 yield further themes, but themes, this time, which were taken up and developed expressly for the office of the sick. From Psalm 78:9–10 comes this chant: "Forgive us our sins of your name's sake, O Lord, lest the nations say: 'Where is their God?' "[54] Psalm 27:9 supplies the following: "Save your people, Lord, and bless your inheritance."[55] "Lord, save your people and bless your inheritance, and rule and exalt them for ever."[56] "Lord, bless your inheritance, and rule and exalt them for ever."[57] "Lord, save your people and bless your inheritance, alleluia. II. And rule and exalt them for ever, alleluia."[58]

In the chants from Psalm 27 we find a connection, once again, between the theme of salvation and the theme of God's blessing. Since the connection in the psalm is due to the biblical figure of parallelism, *benedic* (bless) proves to be for practical purposes a synonym of *salva* (save).

Antiphons were also composed from Psalms 59 and 85, the reason for the choice being, once again, the presence in the psalms of the verb "save." The two antiphons from Psalm 59 are taken from v. 7: "Let your right hand save us, and hear us, Lord our God."[59] "Let your right hand save us, alleluia, and hear us, Lord our God, alleluia, alleluia."[60]

The three antiphons from Psalm 85, which form a special *missa* in the León antiphonary, make use, respectively, of v. 22, vv. 2 and 6, and vv. 16 and 5. "Save your servant, Lord my God, for he hopes in you."[61] "Save your servant, Lord, for he hopes in you; let your ears attend to my prayer."[62] "Save the child of your handmaid, Lord, alleluia; for you are good and merciful, and full of forgiveness to those who invoke you, alleluia, alleluia."[63]

Let me conclude this review of the psalmic chants with an antiphon from Psalm 84:8 and an *alleluiaticum* from Psalm 16:6. "Lord, show us your mercy, and grant us your salvation."[64] "Lord, incline your ear and hear my words, alleluia, alleluia."[65] The antiphon states once again the connection between sin and God's saving action; the parallelism of mercy and salvation tells us that the divine act of saving involves the act of forgiving. The *alleluiaticum* is a simple general plea that God would hear the prayer of the Church.

Nonpsalmic Chants. Among the chants not directly derived from the text of the psalms I may call attention first to a *sono* taken from Jeremiah 17:14–16. "Heal me, Lord, and I shall be healed; save me and I shall be saved; for you are my praise, alleluia, alleluia. II. Behold, they say to me: 'Where is the word of the Lord that is coming?' And I was turned from following you as shepherd, for you are my praise, alleluia."[66]

Free centonization, using elements both scriptural and nonscriptural, is especially typical of the five responsories which I shall reproduce here. Observe, however, that the verses which precede the repetition of the last part of the responsory, are always taken verbatim from scripture.

"He who causes suffering also refreshes; he will strike, and his hand bestows health. Remember that no just man has perished, nor will any true worshiper of God be utterly destroyed.

"℣. For he scourges and saves, he·leads down into death and back up again. Remember. . . ."[67]

"Lord, be our protector and physician. In your accustomed fidelity grant medicine for the wounds of our sins. You are a path for the straying, O God, and to those who seek you with love you give a crown.

"℣. You who rule Israel, pay heed, you who lead Joseph like a sheep. You are a path. . . ."[68]

"Lord, grant a perpetual medicine for our souls, alleluia, and let your hand remove all our sickness, for our hope is in you, alleluia, alleluia.

"℣. Lord, by your name save us, and by your power set us free. For our hope. . . ."[69]

"Lord, you are our power. Be a support for the sick, a refuge and a liberator for the oppressed.

"℣. To you who dwell in heaven we lift up our eyes. Be a refuge."[70]

"Lord, I shall be safe if you console me. Though I am unworthy, I believe you will save me.

"℣. Lord, I am not worthy that you should enter under my roof. Only say the word, and you will save me."[71]

One of the antiphons still left for our inspection takes the unusual form of an exhortation: "Holy men and women, pray to the Lord that he would grant his people salvation and that every sickness may be taken from you."[72]

Another antiphon sums up the teaching which we have seen to be emphatically suggested by the formularies of the antiphonary as they repeatedly connect *salus* and purification from sin: "Our Savior, save us in your love, and in your mercy set us free."[73] It is noteworthy that this antiphon is in all the sources for the office of the sick; in this it is unique. This universal occurrence perhaps indicates that it was one of the chants belonging to the first phase of composition of chants peculiar to this office.

Still another antiphon, found only in the Breviary, is a prayer addressed to Christ in which he is called *medicus salutaris* (saving physician): "Lord, Christ, who are a saving physician, grant to the sick the help of heavenly medicine."[74] The description of Christ as a physician is evidently based on Matthew 9:12 (par Lk 5:31) and on Luke 4:23. The first of these two passages (with its parallel) especially accounts for the full phrase "saving physician." Matthew 9:12 says that the healthy do not need a physician; the "healthy," in the context of the gospel, are those who do not feel the need of being saved, since they are already forgiven and purified. As a physician, Christ turns to those who are capable of allowing themselves to be transformed by a profound conversion.

I must call attention, finally, to a *psallendum* which contains an evocative reminiscence of another passage in the gospel: "Here the sick are cured and the feeble are healed; here the dead rise, alleluia."[75] The gospel passage being echoed is Matthew 11:5 (par Lk 7:22). The words "the sick are cured and the feeble are healed" sum up Jesus' own description of his miracles: "The blind see, the lame walk, lepers are cleansed, the deaf hear."

The real stroke of genius in this antiphon is the word "here," which is used twice. Here, in the Church, we see presently exercised the thaumaturgic action of the Christ, who made of his miracles, in behalf of the sick and unfortunate, signs of a transcendent salvation which includes eternal life.

The Hymn

The sources of the office have passed on to us only one hymn: *Christe caelestis medicina Patris* ("Christ, medicine of the heavenly Father"). But this is certainly not the only case in which the same hymn was sung in both Vespers and the morning office.

The manuscript of the *liber ordinum* gives the complete text at Vespers, but Dom Férotin does not transcribe it, referring the reader to column 972 of the Breviary.[76] He does the same in reproducing the office of the sick according to the Silos manuscript.[77] The London manuscript, at Vespers for the first office, cites the first two words of the hymn, *Christe caelestis,* but does not give the full text. The antiphonary of León gives no indication of the hymn. The Breviary reproduces the text in its entirety, both in the ferial office for Fridays after Epiphany[78] and again in the Common[79]; in both cases it gives the entire text at Vespers and then gives only the abbreviated title *Christe caelestis* in the morning office.

The hymn *Christe caelestis medicina Patris* is in the manuscripts of the *liber hymnorum*. It was also in the part of the London manuscript that corresponds to the *liber hymnorum*, but only the last verses of the hymn can now be found there because the manuscript lacks one page at precisely this point.[80] The hymn is also in the *liber hymnorum* of manuscript 10.001 of the Biblioteca Nacional of Madrid; this is the manuscript Lorenzana used when he supplemented his edition of Ortiz' Breviary with a new part containing the psalter, the *liber canticorum* and the *liber hymnorum*.[81] But, since the hymn had already been given in the office of the sick he did not transcribe it in the section devoted to the *liber hymnorum* (he follows the same practice in many other cases) and simply referred the user to folio 105, that is, to the office of the sick, which had been assigned to Friday in the group of ferial offices for the post-Epiphany season.

In his *Hymnodia Gothica,* Clemens Blume has provided us with a critical edition of the hymn.[82] He used for this purpose the two manuscripts of the *liber hymnorum* which I just mentioned, the two editions of the Breviary (Ortiz and Lorenzana), and some non-

Spanish hymnaries. He did not use the *liber ordinum,* which was not known at that time. I have had occasion in the past to find fault with the artificiality of Blume's critical method,[83] but in the present case his edition of the hymn must be acknowledged to be substantially accurate.[84]

I shall first give the text of the hymn and then a summary interpretation of its contents.

1. "Christ, medicine of the heavenly Father, true physician of human health: in your power respond with favor to the prayers of your expectant people."

2. "We pray you on behalf of the sick, whose health a harmful disease has undermined, that in your loving care you would take away the disease with which they are stricken."

3. "With your power you immediately saved Peter's mother-in-law when ill with fever and the official's son and the centurion's servant."

4. "Restore strength to your ailing people, pour out health in generous measure on them, and as is your wont give back to the sick their former vigor."

5. "Heal the sicknesses of body and soul; apply a remedy to the causes of our wounds lest our tortured bodies suffer fruitless pain."

6. "Let every destructive attack be warded off, every tormenting onslaught melt away; let the strength of the health he longs for bring warmth to the sufferer's members."

7. "O God, have pity on our tears that ask your healing power, so that every sick person on his bed may feel your remedy at work."

8. "Then those who are afflicted by the ills that have come upon them will join the splendid ranks of those who have learned through suffering and, entering the kingdom, share its fruits."

The hymn was conceived as a great prayer of intercession for the sick. As often in hymns of the Latin tradition we can detect the same component parts that would have gone to the making of a liturgical prayer (*oratio*) of the classical type.[85]

The hymn begins with an invocation of Christ who is given the two titles of "medicine" and "physician": "Christ, medicine of the heavenly Father, true physician of human health" (1:1–2). As the physician who bestows genuine human health, Christ is the ambassador of the heavenly Father; not only is he a physician, but his very being and activity constitute a medicine, the saving remedy which the human race needs.

The invocation is expanded in the four verses of the third stanza. This stanza represents a typical way of further explaining an invocation since, in the Latin text, it is subordinated to the invocation as a relative clause appended to it. Literally: "Who with your power immediately saved Peter's mother-in-law when ill with fever and the official's son and the centurion's servant." The verses call to mind three cures effected by Jesus: the cure of Peter's mother-in-law (Mt 8:14–17; Mk 1:29–31; Lk 4:38–39), the cure of the royal official's son (Jn 4:46–54), and the cure of the centurion's servant (Mt 8:5–13; Lk 7:1–10).

The last two verses of the first stanza are an obvious introductory petition: "In your power respond with favor to the prayers of your expectant people."

The body of the hymn consists almost entirely of a prolonged plea that the Lord would grant health to the sick; it thus corresponds to the central or specific petition of an *oratio:* "We pray you on behalf of the sick" (2:1); "Restore strength to your ailing people, pour out health in generous measure on them" (4:1–2).

The praying community intercedes for the sick, referring to them in the third person. At times, however, it includes itself among those who are to be the objects of God's healing action: "lest our tortured bodies suffer fruitless pain" (5:3–4); "O God, have pity on our tears that ask your healing power, so that every sick person on his bed may feel your remedy at work" (7:1–4).

This shift from third person to first is the same procedure we earlier saw operative in the composition of the antiphons and responsories: the praying assembly prays for the sick, while also experiencing in itself the human situation of feebleness and illness.

The hymn expressly asks for bodily health: "whose health a harmful disease has undermined, that in your loving care you would take away the disease with which they are stricken" (2:2–4); "give back to the sick their former vigor" (4:3–4); "let the strength of the health he longs for bring warmth to the sufferer's members" (6:3–4).

But in addition to the immediate need, which is bodily health, the hymn goes on to ask for health of soul: "Heal the sicknesses of body and soul" (5:1).

Moreover, in keeping with the biblical theology of the chants, a theology derived especially from the psalms, the hymn asks God to attack sin, which is the root of the evil: "apply a remedy to the causes of our wounds" (5:2).

The final stanza of the hymn corresponds exactly to the *scopus* of the orations. It begins, in the Latin text, with the particle *quo*, which expresses finality and is very common in Spanish orations. Moreover, as is again habitual in Spanish orations, the stanza sets before God the hoped for ultimate effect of what is being requested; it thus projects the whole into the eschatological sphere. In this way the assembly is strengthened in its conviction that its petition is in keeping with the will of God: "Then [literally: so that] those who are afflicted by the ills that have come upon them will join the splendid ranks of those who have learned through suffering and, entering the kingdom, share its fruits" (8:1–4).

In this analysis of the hymn, I have emphasized structural analogies with another genre, the *oratio*. This should make clearer the hymn's literary character and its liturgical function. The hymn thus composed for the office of the sick is in the mainstream of the Latin hymnological tradition. For in the Spanish rite, as in the Roman and the Ambrosian, a hymn may be a song of praise, or it may be a poetical contemplation of God's work or of the Christian community's needs and longings for salvation; but it can also take the form of a prayer of petition, as in the present case.

Euchological Texts

The same abundance of formularies that we saw in discussing the antiphons and responsories also characterizes the euchological repertories. In order that we may have some idea of the proportion between the necessary and the given superabundance, we must realize that for a minor festive office seven euchological texts are needed: two *completurias* (final orations), one for the evening office and one for the morning office; two blessings, for the evening and morning offices respectively; and three antiphonal orations for the *missa* of the little vigil service that is part of the morning office. Since the office of the sick has a special *supplicatio* (an unchanging formula that introduces the *completuria*) and—in one of the sources—a special oration to accompany Psalm 3, the number seven rises to nine.

In point of fact, however, if we gather together all the euchological texts provided by the four relevant sources,[86] the repertory for the office of the sick contains forty-six formularies: one *supplicatio*,[87] twelve *completurias* (divided among Vespers and Matins[88]), nine blessings,[89] one special oration for Psalm 3,[90] and twenty-three antiphonal orations.[91]

A systematic doctrinal study of this extensive euchological repertory would require time and space not available here.[92] In order to make up to some extent for the lack of an exhaustive treatment of all the euchological texts, I shall give the entire collection in an appendix to this study.

Here, in the study proper, I shall first offer some explanations regarding the organization and presentation of the euchological collection. Then, with references to the collection, I shall mention the points which I consider to be of greater historical and doctrinal interest.

Composition and Organization of the Series of Texts. I have put into the collection all the texts found in the four sources for the euchology of the office of the sick, excluding only the common collects that go with Psalms 3 and 50. After each text I indicate the source or sources from which it is taken and the folio or column in which it is found.

I have critically revised all the texts, taking into account the variants in the different sources when a text is found in more than one source. Generally speaking, the corrections are of minor importance. Given the character of the present essay, I have thought it unnecessary to give a critical apparatus explaining the variants and emendations. The four sources are easily accessible, and anyone interested in testing the critical value of my text can do so without any difficulty.

As far as the organization of the collection is concerned, I have tried to follow the system of someone compiling an orational or book of prayers (orations) and attempting to integrate all the texts from the four sources into a single series. In the order demanded by the celebration itself the texts would be as follows:

Ad Vesperum (Vespers)
1. Supplicatio (plea)
2. Completuria (final prayer)
3. Benedictio (blessing)

Ad Matutinum (Matins)
4. De Psalmo III (prayer with Psalm 3)
5. Orationes de antiphonis (prayers after antiphons)
6. Completuria (final prayer)
7. Benedictio (blessing)

Since we find only one *supplicatio* formula, we must suppose that the one in Vespers was repeated again before the *completuria* of Matins.[93]

The title of each function—*completuria, benedictio,* and so on—is here given at the head of all the texts intended for this purpose. I use the heading *Alia* (another)—which is commonly used in the manuscripts of the festive orational as it is in the *psalmographus* orational[94]—before the further texts of the same type, as though they were optional formulas.

I thought it would be a help to the reader if I grouped the antiphonal prayers by threes, with each group of three corresponding to a *missa.* The compilers in the Visigothic period simply put an *alia* before each antiphonal prayer; I have chosen rather to use an *aliae* (others) as a single title for each group of three.

Like the compilers of the orational, I give the *initium* (beginning) of the corresponding antiphon before each antiphonal prayer.

The thing that may seem most artificial about my organization of the series is my division of the *completurias* and *benedictiones* into vespertinal and matutinal. The sources are not always in agreement on the assignment of a given *completuria* or *benedictio* to a particular hour. Except for oration no. 3, which clearly belongs to the evening office, the others could be used in either of the two hours, since the theme of them is proper to the office of the sick, with no clear reference to the particular hour of the day.

In dividing the *completurias* and *benedictiones* between the evening and morning offices, I have followed the norm of providing equal or almost equal blocks of prayers: 6 + 6 *completurias*, 5 + 4 *benedictiones.* The reason why I have five *benedictiones* in the evening office and four in the morning office is simply because one of the sources, the Breviary, has no blessing in the morning office (in this it follows the general pattern of tradition B).

These few observations will, I think, sufficiently explain the set of texts given in the appendix.

Orations Derived from the "Psalmographus." I think it necessary to begin by pointing out the really large part played by the *psalmographus* in the composition of the euchological texts for the office of the sick.

Four of the orations in the collection are psalter collects which have been introduced, without significant alterations, into the office of the sick. Two of these are *completurias* nos. 2 and 38, which correspond to nos. 325 (Ps 6) and 503 (Ps 40) of the *Liber Orationum Psalmographus.* The other two are antiphonal orations nos. 14 and 15, which correspond to collects nos. 65 (Ps 53) and 271 (Ps 102).

But the direct use of the *psalmographus* does not stop here. Another six prayers in the office of the sick are simply abridgments or adaptations of texts in the *psalmographus.* The six include two *completurias,* 39 and 43, which are derived from collects 121 (Ps 105)[95] and 475 (Ps 6),[96] and four antiphonal orations: nos. 17, 18, 19 and 20, derived respectively from collects 257 (Ps 73),[97] 371 (Ps 53),[98] 7 (Ps 6),[99] and 325 (Ps 6).[100] The last-named is a reworking of the same collect which is more faithfully reproduced in *completuria* no. 2 of the series given in the appendix.

Some of these orations were chosen because the content of the collects (which is dependent on the theme of the corresponding psalms) is concerned with sickness as an effect of God's anger or as a moral weakness resulting from sin. Here I must call attention especially to the three *completurias* nos. 2, 38, and 43. It is this thematic that justifies their being made the principal prayer of the office. The other *completuria*, no. 39, speaks of sickness as a stimulus to prayer, but the expressions of this thought were composed for this office and not based on the *psalmographus.*

The theme proper to the office of the sick is also treated in the two collects which provided the basis for antiphonal orations 15 and 19. Two others, those connected with nos. 14 and 18, speaks explicitly of *salus.* Oration no. 17 says nothing directly related to the themes of the office of the sick; it may be have been chosen for us in this office because of its opening words: "Lord, save your people."

It is worth noting that to some extent the psalter collects which have been of service in the office of the sick go with some of the psalms which are also represented in the composition of the antiphons and other chants. I am referring to Psalm 6 (four orations), Psalm 73 (one oration), Psalm 102 (one oration), and Psalm 105 (one oration). But among the collects are also Psalm 40 (one oration) and Psalm 53 (two orations), which did not serve as a basis for antiphons or other chants. From this I infer that, rather than any dependence on a psalm via the antiphon, the main thing which decided the choice of a collect was its objective content.

One characteristic that distinguishes the collects of the *Liber Orationum Psalmographus* from all the other Latin euchological collections of antiquity is precisely the wealth and variety of its doctrinal themes. It is therefore not surprising that the composers and compilers of orations for the festive orational should turn to its inexhaustible riches for prayers which, either as they stood or with slight revisions, could serve for the seasons of Advent or *De traditione Domini* ("Betrayal of the Lord": second half of Lent), the feasts of Christmas or the Blessed Virgin, and even for some feasts of the saints. In adapting psalter collects, therefore, the authors or compilers of the office of the sick were simply following the example of the authors or compilers of the festive orational.

The use of collects from the *psalmographus* is common to the collections in all four sources. The sources which make greatest use of them are the *liber ordinum* (four orations) and the Silos manuscript (four orations). The London manuscript and the Breviary each use one collect. This general agreement among the four sources, at least in the fact of having recourse to the *psalmographus* in establishing a euchological collection for the office of the sick, suggests once again the hypothesis that this office was originally made up of elements from the ordinary ferial office.

Another interesting observation: almost all the psalter collects used

for the office of the sick, in the version of them used in my
reconstruction of the *psalmographus,* are from sources in tradition B.
Only collect no. 505 (Ps 40), which the London manuscript uses as a
completuria in the office of the sick, is based on the psalter in the
same London manuscript. Collects nos. 121 (Ps 105), 257 (Ps 73),
271 (Ps 102), 371 (Ps 53), and 425 (Ps 6) would survive through
their inclusion in the ferial *misticus* for Lent (Biblioteca Nacional of
Madrid, ms 10.110) and in the Breviary. Collect no. 65 (Ps 53) is
preserved as such in the two sources just mentioned, but it also
came to form part of the Carolingian series. Collect no. 7 (Ps 6) was
preserved for us, as a psalter collect, in the Breviary, but it is also
found in one of the appendixes of the festive orational of Verona
and was also used in the collections in the orational of the monastic
office. Finally, collect no. 325 (Ps 6) has been preserved for us solely
in the office of the sick, but the latter gives us two versions of it: the
one in the Breviary, which keeps the original text except for words
of adaptation: "to your servants, all the faithful who are sick,"
which replace what may have been an "us" or "us your servants"
(cf. oration no. 2 in the appendix), and the abridged oration in the
Silos manuscript (oration no. 20 in the appendix).

Doctrinal Contribution of the Psalter Collects. The teaching on
sickness of the psalter collects which have become part of the office
of the sick is substantially the same as that which we derived from
an analysis of the psalmic chants of the same office.

When the psalms speak of sickness, the author of the *psalmographus*
gives the term a chiefly spiritual meaning: "Lord, we pray that you
will not accuse us in your anger nor let your wrath rage against us,
but rather reprove us gently and make us stop sinning, lest if you
chastise us harshly you drive us to destruction" (no. 2). "By your
power free us whom you know to be hindered by our own
sicknesses" (no. 14). ". . . [S]o that hearing our prayer you may
hasten to heal our sicknesses and redeem our lives from destruction"
(no. 15). "And let not the sickness caused by our sins bring us to
death. Heal us, Lord" (no. 19).

This being the case, the remedy sought from God is the gift of his
mercy, his regenerating grace. "Help us, our Redeemer, and may we
who for our sins lie ill on a bed of pain be healed by the medicine
of your forgiveness, and may we who are being brought daily closer
to death by our increasing sins be raised up by your abundant
mercy" (no. 38). "Lord, in your mercy save this man whom you
know to be ill on account of his own wickedness. His soul is
troubled by fear of your just judgments: let your joyous gift of
forgiveness bring him peace" (no. 43). "Have mercy, therefore, on

our weakness and grant healing . . . and if you see any who are troubled by their own sins, forgive them in your mercy and grant them serenity" (no. 2). ". . . [A]nd redeem our life from destruction, so that healed of guilt it may be rendered peaceful by grace. Pour out your healing on the sick and grant forgiveness of their sins" (no. 19).

The literary and doctrinal influence of the *psalmographus* on the office of the sick extends still further. Not a few of the texts composed expressly for the office are full of reminiscences of the psalter collects. Here are but a few examples:

No. 31: "Lord, heal the sicknesses of your people, for you always show mercy to sinners as a father does to his children." And LOPs 566 (Ps 102): "Heal the sicknesses of our bodies, and as a father shows mercy to his children, show mercy to us sinners."

No. 10: "May his loving goodness assist all alike, so that our ill health not grow worse and we may not in our weakness yield to despair." And LOPs 31 (Ps 30): "And may we be so governed by your loving care that we may not despair through anxiety at our ills."

No. 28: "In your goodness grant the aid of most merciful consolation to those whom you afflict with harsh but merited correction." And LOPs 6 (Ps 6): "but with merciful kindness alleviate the harshness of the lash."

No. 7: "We ask that after giving him a realization of his weakness you would now grant him healing." And LOPs 16 (Ps 15): ". . . that as you have deigned to give us understanding . . .," and LOPs 481 (Ps 15): "always grant him healing."

No. 41: "Do you, Lord, cease to scourge us for our sins, increase the cures that come through confession, and open the door by which we may come to you." And LOPs 44 (Ps 38): "remove your scourges"; LOPs 231 (Ps 31): "and because the many scourges of our sins rain blows upon us, we trust in you and feel your mercy surround us"; LOPs 231 (Ps 31): "in order that, wickedness being expelled from our heart, we may not feel the flaming scourges we deserve"; LOPs 57 (Ps 50): "and because we confess to you our wretchedness, we feel your healing mercy at work in us"; LOPs 566 (Ps 102): "redeem our life from destruction, and open the door to you."

No. 46: ". . . [S]o that your soul may not perish under the scourges but rather after enduring reach the rewards of heaven," as well as no. 10: "May he who took our sickness upon himself grant us and them an endless reward for endurance." And LOPs 6 (Ps 6): ". . . [T]hat the discipline you impose may lead not to loss and punishment but to training in virtue"; LOPs 36 (Ps 32): "Our soul waits patiently for you, O Lord, from whom it desires to receive both the virtue of endurance and the reward for its exercise."

Influence of Other Euchological Genres. The authors and compilers of the office of the sick used not only the collects in the *psalmographus* but other euchological repertories for the office.

Oration no. 36 is taken from the festive orational where it serves as one of the antiphonal orations in the ferial series for the period *de Traditione Domini.*[101] It was surely chosen for use in the office of the sick because its implicit citation of Psalm 6: "so that every night we may drench our beds and couches with our tears," fits in so perfectly with the antiphon: "I was oppressed in my groaning, I will every night bathe my bed, I will drench my couch with tears." The first part of this prayer introduces a new theme to the office of the sick: the exemplary patience of Christ in his passion: "We believe, Lord Jesus, that for us sinners you were oppressed in the groans of your passion. Therefore we pray that your outstanding example of patience may be of profit to our souls." But this idea, which could have provided a stimulating addition to the overall teaching of the office of the sick, did not make its way into the other prayers. There are a few mentions of the passion of Christ, but always as cause of salvation, not as an example of patience in suffering.

The introductory part of oration no. 3: "Lord, our protector and physician, hear our evening prayers," is remotely inspired by some of the *completurias* for Sunday.[102]

Less evident but real is the influence of the festive orational or the euchological repertories *de quotidiano* on other prayers in the office of the sick. There is no longer a question of verbal or conceptual reminiscences of the clear kind we have been seeing. I am thinking of a few orations that were composed on the special theme of the office of the sick but that deal with it in what I might call a contemplative way and without formulating an explicit intercessory prayer for the sick.

These prayers treat of sickness in the way of which the author of the *psalmographus* or the authors of the Sunday *completurias* might have treated it. A good example of this kind of prayer is the one (no. 3) which I just cited. It asks for health, but in the moral order, and this after a reflection which emphasizes the need of confessing one's wretched state to the Lord: "The man keeps your mercy from himself who does not show you his wounds. But because you, Lord, summon all the sick back to health and because those whom you heal are sick no longer, heal our wounds, Lord, and grant us your mercy." Further examples might be nos. 16 and 41.

We shall see immediately that the euchological production most characteristic of the office of the sick develops in the form of intercession for the sick, in accordance with some very typical structural patterns. This is the most original part of the orations for the office of the sick.

"Your Servants, All the Faithful Who Are Sick." Before entering upon an analysis of the characteristic elements of the orations which are prayers of intercession, it will be proper to study the emphatic use of this stereotyped formula as well as its source. We will then be better able to explain the passage from a first stage, in which the collects of the *psalmographus* were simply adapted or imitated, to a further stage in which a type of prayer that is completely proper and original to the office of the sick was composed.

When I spoke earlier of the introduction of psalter collect no. 325 (for Ps 6) into the office of the sick, I mentioned that the adaptation of it (oration no. 2) consisted in the substitution of "your servants, all the faithful who are sick" for an "us" or "us your servants." As transmitted to us in the Breviary, which is our only source for it, the adaptation is in fact rather poor. Instead of the genitive case that is used: "famulorum tuorum . . .," a dative would have fitted the context better.

Although the genitive could be justified grammatically (lit.: "grant the healing of your servants," i.e., "grant healing to your servants"), I consider that the Latin text needs to be corrected. I am confirmed in my view by another prayer which presents the same problem: I mean *completuria* no. 4. Both sources—the London manuscript and the Breviary—have *famulorum tuorum omnium christianorum infirmorum* (lit.: of your servants, all sick Christians).[103] Yet clearly these words should be in grammatical agreement with *laborantibus* ("who labor," or, literally, "laboring"). Finally, if further proof is necessary, we may consult the Latin of oration no. 26, which is from the Breviary; here we find *famulis tuis omnibus fidelibus infirmis . . . laborantibus,* or a proper grammatical accord.

The same stereotyped phrase occurs, in the accusative case, in two other orations and a blessing: "In your goodness be present at the invocation of your name, and with your right hand raise up *sick Christians, your servants,* and strengthen them" (no. 22). "Lord, look upon *your servants, all the faithful who are sick* and who rejoice to invoke your name" (no. 40). "May almighty God, who chastises his *most faithful servants, all the sick faithful,* with bodily illness, purify them and us of sicknesses of body and mind" (no. 10).

How are we to explain the odd use of the genitive case in orations 2 and 4? I think it is to be accounted for as a clumsy transfer to these two prayers of the same stereotyped formula which was originally used (in the genitive case) in the *supplicatio* (no. 1): "ask and beseech him in his mercy to heal the wounds of his servants, all the faithful who are sick." The version of the *supplicatio* as given in the Silos manuscript is somewhat different: "that he would deign in his mercy to heal the wounds of his servants, all faithful Christians, and to comfort them."

It is to be observed that in the three texts from the Silos manuscript, the adjective "Christian" appears (*christianorum, christianos*): "of his servants, all faithful Christians" (no. 1); "your servants, all sick Christians" (no. 4); "sick Christians, your servants" (no. 22).

The two versions of the *supplicatio*—the one in the Silos manuscript and the one in the Breviary—are based on a very ancient text of the Spanish liturgy, namely, the embolism for the Our Father: "and hear, O God, the prayers of *your servants, all faithful Christians,* today and at all times."[104] The embolism formula was used daily in the Mass and in the office as a conclusion for the *oratio paterna* ("the prayer to the Father"); it ended with the words I have just quoted. After presenting God with a short intercessory plea for all the needy ("grant joy to the afflicted, ransom to the captive, health to the sick, and rest to the departed") and after asking for peace ("grant peace and safety throughout all our days and break our enemies in their boldness"), the embolism ends with the above-cited expression of union and communion with the prayer of all Christians of all times.

The author of the *supplicatio* proper to the office of the sick simply took the general formula used for a *supplicatio,* scil. "Let us pray. Let us ask and beseech the Redeemer of the world, our Lord Jesus Christ, that in his mercy he would deign . . . ,"[105] and expanded it with the words "[the wounds] of his servants, all the faithful Christians who are sick," which, as we just saw, were inspired by the embolism of the Our Father, and with some other words from the ancient store of prayers: "to heal . . . and comfort." These last are from the dyptych for the Church, which was one of the few fixed formulas of the Mass: "Let us remember all the lapsed, captives, sick and travellers, that the Lord in his mercy would deign to redeem, *heal and comfort* them."[106]

Thus the first version of the *supplicatio* for the office of the sick represented an act of euchological creativity marked by a minimum of effort and originality. This was the version preserved for us in the Silos manuscript.

In the tradition represented by the Breviary, on the other hand, there was a more intelligent assimilation of the elements which had served as inspiration. Let us not forget that the *supplicatio* was much more at home in tradition B (the tradition to which the Breviary belongs) than in the tradition represented by the Silos manuscript. The manuscripts of tradition A systematically ignored the *supplicatio* in the cathedral office. Its presence there was peculiar to tradition B. The *supplicatio* is also known to the monastic office (*liber horarum*) and the ritual (*liber ordinum*), but in both the monastic office and the ritual the structure of the *supplicatio* is less precise and classical. I think there can be no doubt but that the place of origin of the *supplicatio* was the cathedral office in tradition B.

The booklet for the office of the sick that was incorporated into the Silos manuscript and that belonged to tradition A has preserved for us the primitive version of a *supplicatio* proper to this office. Its author, if that be the correct term for him, would have known of the existence of the *supplicatio* either from the monastic office or from the ritual.

But both in the special tradition found in the Silos manuscript and in the tradition represented by the Breviary, the same phenomenon occurred: the stereotyped phrase "of his servants, the sick faithful," with variants, reappeared in the process of composing other texts for the same office. It also happened that in one text of each tradition the original genitive case persisted, despite the fact that the context required a different case (orations 2 and 4).

We can also see traces of the same phrase in other texts which I have not cited. For example: "all your faithful who are in the strong grip of sickness" (no. 29); "that . . . you would drive every sickness and every infirmity from your servants" (no. 40).

It is not accidental that the prayers most proper and original to the office of the sick, prayers characterized precisely by being intercessions for the sick, should develop out of this nuclear phrase and that they should retain, even verbatim, the most venerable intercessory formulas of the Spanish rite.

The Orations Most Specific to the Office of the Sick. I make a distinction between, on the one hand, those prayers which depend more or less directly on the euchological treasury represented by the psalter collects and the other texts of the office and, on the other hand, the prayers to which I now turn and which I regard as being most specific to the office of the sick.

This second group comprises *completurias* 4, 5, 6, 41, and 42, and antiphonal prayers 22, 29, 30, 32, 33, and 34. All these have been preserved for us by the Silos tradition and, more concretely, by manuscript 7 of the Silos archive and by the London manuscript, which had been copied at Silos. On the other hand, none of these prayers became part of the *liber ordinum*, although this too had been copied in the Silos scriptorium.

The eleven prayers are rather homogeneous in style, although there is no need to suppose that all were the work of a single author. They bear some resemblance to the Sunday *completurias*, which I regard as a product of the Toledan school. I would locate them chronologically in the second half (more accurately in the last third) of the seventh century.

Less typical, yet also completely proper to the office of the sick are four other orations: 26, 27, 28, and 40, which are from the Breviary. These are shorter and therefore less rich in motifs. They may be earlier than the eleven orations from the Silos tradition. The structure of the Breviary prayer is more simple and, I would say, more classical. Both groups, however, are in accord on some themes.

I shall analyze both groups of prayers at the same time and shall distinguish, in three sections, the content proper to each of the structural elements of these prayers.

First, I shall deal with the anamnetic element in the orations. Under this heading I shall, to begin with, bring together the phrases which promote a contemplation of God as author of health and life. This listing of divine attributes is appropriate above all to the invocation, but it is to be found at times also in the body of the prayer. I shall then pass on to a set of phrases which attribute an almost thaumaturgic power to the invocation of the name of God. I shall end this first section on the anamnetic element by citing phrases which call to mind miracles of healing and resurrection in the Old and New Testaments.

In a second section, I shall examine the phrases used in formulating an intercession for the sick. I distinguish those which voice an introductory petition (a first, generic, concise plea) and those which are fuller and more detailed, these last being especially characteristic of this euchological repertory.

Finally, I shall bring together in a third section the phrases which correspond to the "finality" or *scopus*. We shall see that the dominant theme in this structural part is the desire to have a reason and opportunity for blessing and thanking God.

"God of Mercy . . . Master of Life and Death." In the classical patterns of Latin euchology (beginning with Roman euchological production from the middle of the fifth century on), the three basic parts of an oration—invocation, petition, and *scopus*—should be closely and securely coordinated with each other. The invocation gives a brief description of God, presenting for the praying community's contemplation the divine attributes most closely associated with the grace that is to be sought. Since it is desired that the prayer make an appeal to the mind and not be merely affective, an effort is made

to show the congregation that there is a logical connection between what is asked and the power and will of him who is being asked.

This full connection between invocation and petition reflected at bottom what we today would call a pastoral sense. By establishing this logic and patiently getting it to take root in the minds of the Christian community, the Church was seeing to it that the prayer of the faithful would be intelligent, serene, and trusting.

Spanish euchology, although it was from a literary standpoint so removed from that of the golden age of Roman euchology, took this same pastoral principle into account. Given the wealth, variety, and freedom of literary schemes that was characteristic of it, Spanish euchology took advantage, with even greater profit if that is possible, of the good aesthetic and pastoral effect that a clear and taut relationship between the anamnetic element in the invocation and the petition proper could produce.

The group of prayers which I am examining affords some good examples of this point. Since the object of the petition was to be, in this case, the healing of the sick, the anamnetic part of the prayer described God as master of the *salus* expected from him. The invocations play with the two grammatical possibilities typical of the tradition: the relative clause and the use of apposition: "God, source of strength and vigor, God, source of eternal salvation and life" (no. 30); "Lord, God of our salvation, for whom no sickness is incurable" (no. 32); "God, who through your only Son exercise the medicinal power of your healing word" (no. 33); "God of mercy, who are master of life and death, and physician of sick souls" (no. 6); "God, who turn away sickness from the ill and cast off the body's weaknesses, and who remove the source of danger by a more perfect salvation" (no. 34); "Lord, holy Father, almighty everlasting God, who have eternal power to slay the living and give life to the dead. You alone can extinguish the fire of fever" (no. 29); "Lord, who show mercy to all, who rule all things and in your goodness hear those who cry to you, and who are the consolation of the burdened, healing for the afflicted of heart, and medicine to the sick; Lord, who are the redeemer of the dying, the resurrection of the dead, the restorer of the sick" (no. 5); "God, inventor of saving medicine, who by infusing your divine gift dispel the manifold sicknesses to which the human body falls prey, and who lead your human creature to the gates of death and then call him back again from the gates of Hell" (no. 42).

No one can deny the wealth and variety of nuances which the author or authors of these orations manage to give a single thematic motif and this in the same part of the prayer (i.e., a motif having the same literary and euchological function), scil. the presentation of

God as the only one possessing the power to give and restore life. All the texts I have just cited belong to the group of prayers from the Silos tradition.

The reader should note the great concern to combine the attributes of power and goodness. The community is right to turn to God and trust that it will win healing for sickness, not only because God has the power to give and restore health and life itself, but also because his power is accompanied by limitless goodness. His will to do good is the source from which we may expect to receive the grace of restoration to life. This thesis, which we infer from the texts, also finds formal expression in one of the prayers: "The ability to do so (*posse*) is in your power alone, and the will to do so (*velle*) is always present in your mercy" (no. 34).

The use of the two verbs *posse* and *velle* was probably suggested by expressions in the sermons of St. Leo the Great as well as in some Roman euchological texts from the same author. St. Leon alters for his own use St. Paul's words: *öperatur in vobis velle et perficere* (Phil 2:13: "God is at work in you, both to will and to work. . . ."), as he exhorts the faithful to bring to completion in themselves the good work which God's word caused them to undertake. The pope reminds them that God will grant them the desire and the power to do: *velle et posse*. It is of interest to observe that this pair of terms— to will and to be able—which had been elaborated in order to give a refined theological formulation to the mystery of grace in man, is in our Spanish text applied to God: With his great power God is able to act, and his desire to act flows, as it were, from his unparalleled goodness, the attribute which scripture calls his "mercy."

Let us turn now to a number of prayers which mention the invocation of the name of God: "Lord, look upon your servants, all the faithful who are sick and who rejoice to invoke your name" (no. 40); "May the invocation of your holy name wash away all their bodily blemishes, all their various sicknesses, all attacks of fever" (no. 5); "In your goodness be present at the invocation of your name, and with your right hand raise up sick Christians, your servants, and strengthen them with your power. Apply medicine, heal sicknesses" (no. 22); "Visit your servants with spiritual grace, so that, as your angel keeps watch, these supplicants may, by invoking your name, receive back the health long kept from them" (no. 42); "so that if any pain is felt in their marrow or vitals, it may depart or be lessened by the invocation of your name" (no. 30); "You are all in all: apply your merciful saving name at the couches of all who are ill" (no. 34).

It is possible that these mentions of the invocation of the divine name were suggested by certain passages in the Bible, for example

Acts 3:6, which tells of the cure which St. Peter works by invoking the name of Jesus. In any case, the references suppose a biblical theology of the divine name that is not foreign to the Christian euchological tradition. This theology sees in the name a sign of God's self-manifestation to human beings, a manifestation which takes the form primarily of the beneficent works he does on behalf of his people. The faithful know the name of the Lord. To invoke this name is not simply to pronounce a word; it is to adhere to the revelation of the Lord and voluntarily submit to his saving activity.

I think, then, that there is a connection between the listing of the attributes of power and mercy in the first part (or "invocation") of an oration and these further phrases which ascribe to the invocation of God's name an instrumental function, namely bringing a restoration of health to the sick.

The section of oration no. 42, which I cited a moment ago, refers to the presence of an angel: "as your angel keeps watch." There is a similar idea expressed in oration no. 29: "that through the presence of your angel you would deign to visit all your faithful who are in the strong grip of sickness."

When we were analyzing the hymn of the office, we saw that mention was made in it of various miraculous healings worked by Jesus. In the orations the same theme occurs in even fuller form: there is mention of healings and raisings from the dead, and the miracles are taken from the Old Testament as well as the New.

The passage most cited is undoubtedly the one telling of the healing of St. Peter's mother-in-law (Mt 8:14–17). But reference is also made to the cure of the centurion's servant (Mt 8:5–13), of the paralytic at the pool near the Sheep Gate (Jn 5:1–16), and of the woman with a flow of blood (Mt 9:20–22). There is also mention made of the cure of Hezekiah in the Old Testament (Is 38:1–8).

Among the miraculous raisings the orations mention those effected by Elijah (1 Kgs 17:17–24) and Elisha (2 Kgs 4:27–37), the two raisings in which Jesus shows his power (the son of the widow of Naim, Lk 7:11–17, and Lazarus, Jn 11:17–44), and also the raising of many bodies that took place at the moment when Jesus has just died on the cross (Mt 27:52–53).

If all five of these orations are the work of a single author, as I think likely, his intention would have been to keep these events before our minds during the orations and to include miraculous raisings along with miraculous cures. The end result of this procedure is that prayer for the sick is not limited to a petition for the restoration of health. Even if the sick for whom intercession is made do not recover their health but their illness brings them to the end of their days on earth, the prayer of the community nonetheless has its value. For the sick then attain to *salus,* "health," in the definitive sense of the word, since God is not limited to restoring health on earth but, being Lord of life, will bring human beings to the final resurrection and eternal life.

Each mention of a scriptural miracle is almost always closely linked to an intercessory prayer for the sick. The words connecting the petition with the anamnetic element are *sicut* or *quemadmodum* ("as") and the relative pronoun *qui* ("who"). "As through Elijah you brought back to life the son of the woman of Sidon and through Elisha the son of the woman of Shunem, so too deign to hear our pleas and grant health of body and salvation of soul to all the sick" (no. 4). "Grant them an extension of life, as you did to your servant Hezekiah; raise them from their beds as you did Peter's mother-in-law and as you raised the widow's son from his bier" (no. 5). "Give aid, Lord, to your servant on his bed of pain, as you did to the paralytic whom on the sabbath you caused to walk away with his pallet, and as with a word of command you healed Simon's mother-in-law when she was confined to bed with a fever" (no. 35).

Completuria no. 6 is the oration that develops the theme most fully. The central part of the prayer consists of four petitions, each of them backed up by a reference to a miracle of healing or raising from the dead:

"Visit them from heaven as you deigned to visit the mother-in-law of Peter and the centurion's servant.—Lord, grant them healing and health, as after your passion you made bodies already corrupted in the tomb come forth to the light again.—Grant them, Lord, the consolation of devotion, as with a word you cleansed of all stains the woman with a flow of blood.—Grant them, Lord, health of mind and body, as you raised Lazarus from the dead after four days in the tomb."

In oration no. 29, the very invocation contains a vague reference to the resurrection miracles worked by the Lord: "Lord . . . who have eternal power to slay the living and give life to the dead. You alone can extinguish the fire of fever, for often it has been your wont to raise the dead to life."

"Look Upon Your People as They Suffer Varied Sicknesses." In the orations of the Silos tradition, which by their extension usually lend themselves to this, it is often possible to distinguish a first general petition for the sick and another, or other, petitions which immediately follow but are always more detailed and concrete. In

other words, there is a first appeal to God's attention, which from a structural viewpoint is an introductory petition. For example: "Visit your servants with spiritual grace" (no. 42); "We pray and beseech you to be present at the bedside of the sick" (no. 34); "Look upon your people as they suffer varied sicknesses" (no. 30); "Look with mercy on your servants who are in bondage to ill health" (no. 6); "We ask that in your tender mercy you would drive every sickness and every infirmity from your servants" (no. 32); "We beg and beseech you to look with mercy on all your servants who are wearied out by violent fever, exhausted by sickness, broken by fatigue, and weakened by chastisement" (no. 5).

In the part of the oration that corresponds to the central petition, the group of orations from the Silos tradition is characterized by an emphasis and detail that sometimes remind us of a litany: "strengthen the weak, support the troubled, make solid what has broken down, renew the ulcerated flesh" (no. 34). "Grant them strength of body, constancy of soul, endurance of suffering, good health" (no. 5). "Let every sickness depart from them, Lord, every anxiety, all sorrow, all the activity of the evil one" (no. 30). "Apply medicine, heal sicknesses. Grant them yourself as their life, and bestow on them, together with good health, all that they look for from you" (no. 22). ". . . [A]nd that any pain, any hurt, any fiery fever, any internal suffering may be expelled from their members and vitals" (no. 42).

Common to both groups of orations—those from the Breviary and those from the Silos tradition—is the practice of joining in a single petition the desire for a spiritual renewal and the desire for a bodily restoration: "Grant forgiveness to your servants, and bestow on their bodies the pure medicine of heavenly grace" (no. 22). "Grant them heavenly medicine, give them protection of mind, and deign to free them from every infirmity and sickness" (no. 40). "From that mercy we ask forgiveness of our sins and from your immense and loving kindness the healing of our fleshly sicknesses" (no. 34). "So too deign to hear our pleas and grant health of body and salvation of soul to all the sick" (no. 4). "Unbind the destructive bonds of sickness so that if illness rages at the body's expense, it may be moderated and if its source be temptation, it may be warded off. And let this servant of yours, who was handed over to sickness for chastisement, know that he has accepted correction, may be restored to health" (no. 33).

Let me point out several petitions which I think deserve separate examination because of their unusual content. Oration 22, when asking health for the sick, asks that God give them himself, who is life: "Grant them yourself as their life, and bestow on them, together with good health, all that they look for from you." Another oration, number 42, mentions the healing effected by natural means: "And may the medicinal poultices which persevering human skill may apply to the infirm body be an aid to health as you, the spiritual physician, watch over them." Finally, oration 32 sees God's healing action as a sign of his power: "They [the sick] look for your heavenly medicine: work in them a sign of your power and your healing, and grant them health of body and spirit."

"Let This Servant . . . Glorify You, the Author of Good Health." The four prayers from the Breviary and a large number of those from the Silos tradition end with the central petition. Only in five orations do we find the structural element to which I have given the name *scopus.*

In classical euchology the function of this part of the oration is to underscore the value of the petition. It expresses what the Christian community hopes will be the fruit of the favor it is asking from God. It serves to show implicitly that there is a supremely desirable ultimate reason or finality which is served through the granting of the petition. It looks beyond the need of the moment and reflects the higher aspirations of Christians. In other words, the *scopus* is meant to strengthen the hope that the object of the petition is fully in harmony with the divine plan of salvation. As such, the *scopus* is a psychological help to the community, for it tells them that what they ask will contribute to the full carrying out of God's will.

In Spanish euchology and, more concretely, in the *psalmographus* (which, as we have seen, was an important source of inspiration for the authors of the prayers in the office of the sick), this concluding part of the oration frequently takes on an eschatological dimension. In this respect the orations we are studying do not resemble very closely the prayers that served as models for them. They do speak on occasion of a thanksgiving and glorification of God which can be supposed to take place both in the present life and in the world to come. Generally, however, the reference is to thanksgiving offered in the present life and within the Church on earth: "Then, restored to health, they may enter your church and bless you, God the Father, in all things" (no. 5); "Then, present once again, healthy and safe, in your holy church, they will thank you, the Lord" (no. 6); "May they feel the dew of your refreshing grace and, having been rescued from the flaming heat, be able to bless you, the Lord, in all things" (no. 29); ". . . [A]nd, restored to health, we may deserve to serve you for ever" (no. 30); "Let this servant of yours likewise receive the health he desires and glorify you, the author of good health" (no. 35).

The Blessings. A very simple style has generally been adopted for the composition of the blessings. The blessings in the office of the sick are closer in kind to the ferial blessings or blessings *de quotidiano* than to those of the festive cycle.

Some of the three members which make up every blessing, and, in one case, the whole blessing could pass as common formulas having no specific application to the office of the sick. For example, in no. 46: "May the Lord give you consolation after sorrow and reward sadness with joy," or in no. 47: "May this best of supporters answer your prayers and in his love bless your desires. May he remove all evils from you, and grant what is good to you and yours," or the whole of no. 44: "May the Lord bless and keep you. May the Lord show his face to you and have mercy on you. May the Lord turn his countenance to you and grant you health and peace."

When the parts of a blessing are expressly related to the office of the sick, they sometimes follow the doctrinal line proper to the *psalmographus.* "May almighty God, who chastises his most faithful servants, all the sick faithful, with bodily illness, purify them and us of sicknesses of body and mind" (no. 10). "May his loving kindness assist all alike, so that our ill health may not grow worse and we may not in our weakness yield to despair" (no. 10). "May the Lord forgive all your iniquities and heal all your sicknesses. May he redeem your life from destruction and satisfy your desire with his gifts" (no. 45). ". . . [T]hat your soul may not perish under the scourges but rather after enduring reach the rewards of heaven" (no. 46).

Other blessings, however, adopt a style like that of the orations in the Silos tradition. "From the heavenly realm may the Lord send you health-giving medicine" (no. 47). "Heal us of our sicknesses, and cleanse the hearts of your servants from the stains of sin" (no. 9). "May he drive off diseases from their bodies and protect their souls from deceptions, so that all troubles being removed you may come to him healed in heart, body and soul" (no. 11). "And may the Lord grant you healing of heart and body, so that you will always be thankful to him" (no. 45).

The point that is perhaps most characteristic of the blessings in comparison with the orations is their slight christological emphasis. We have already seen that with the exception of the text from the festive orational, the orations of the office of the sick, while referring indeed in some instances to the miracles of Jesus, do not engage in theological contemplation of Christ the Savior. Not so with the blessings.

The three parts of blessings which I shall now cite see Christ in terms of the description given in the fourth Servant Song (Is 53). "May Christ the Lord, who is true redemption, heal every disease and every infirmity among his people" (no. 11). "May he heal your sicknesses, for he alone is our Lord and Redeemer. And may he always have care of you, for in him is the fullness of our salvation" (no. 8). "May he who took our infirmity upon himself grant us and them an endless reward for endurance" (no. 10).

The cited part of no. 11 reproduces almost verbatim Matthew 4:23: "healing every disease and every infirmity among the people." We can recognize in no. 10 a citation of Matthew 8:17: "He took our infirmities and bore our diseases," which in turn is based on Isaiah 53:4: "Surely he has borne our sicknesses and carried our pains."

Both numbers 8 and 11 proclaim the saving mission of Christ: "He alone is our Lord and Redeemer. . . . In him is the fullness of our salvation. . . . Christ the Lord, who is true redemption."

Above all, blessing number 10 reminds us that redemption and salvation were accomplished by the sufferings of Christ, and bids us find the secret of "healing every disease" in Christ's own experience as expressed in Isaiah 53:5: "with his stripes we are healed" (a phrase which the New Testament cites in 1 Pt 2:21).

At this point I end my study of the euchological texts. As I warned the reader when I began, I make no claim to exhaustiveness. In fact, while this section is the longest of the entire essay, it is also perhaps the least complete in proportion. I hope, nonetheless, that the points I have made will be an effective help to the reader in his or her own interpretation and fuller study of the texts.

CONCLUSIONS

The office of the sick came into existence in the Spanish rite in response to a pastoral desire: that of giving a place in liturgical prayer to a human situation that is always a reality: the situation of sickness.

It is clear that the formularies which have come down to us represent the cumulative work of various local Churches and successive historical periods. I believe, nonetheless, that the period which contributed most to the formation and development of this office was the second half of the seventh century.

The office probably began its existence as an office composed of elements taken from the ordinary ferial repertory. Psalms and chants would have been chosen which appeared especially suitable for the purpose; the psalms would have been accompanied by the common psalter antiphons and the collects of the *psalmographus.*

The first stage in the formation of the office would have left a profound mark on it, even on the doctrinal line followed by its content. This accounts for the presence of the Old Testament theology that explains sickness almost entirely as a result of sin. The author of the *psalmographus,* whose tendency is to asceticism, took this interpretation of sickness from the psalms and made it his own. By and large, the formularies of the office of the sick, even in its more fully developed form, will not be able to free themselves completely on this interpretation.

In the course of time, the schema proper to a festive office was adopted for the office of the sick: the antiphons struck the dominant note by comparison with the psalms and an effort was made in the prayers and blessings to respond to the theme or proper object of this votive office. It was then that the antiphonal and euchological repertories were enriched to a considerable degree.

The new euchology, both from the tradition represented by the Breviary and from the tradition transmitted by the Silos manuscripts, introduced into the office of the sick, or at least brought out more clearly, the element of intercession for the sick members of the Christian community.

The office of the sick was always an ecclesial celebration; as such it was not a prayer offered in the immediate presence of the sick themselves. Partly for this reason and partly because of its doctrinal bases which had been established in the first phase of the formation of the office, the office of the sick had for its primary function to be a reflection on the evil of sickness and on its causes. In this reflection the entire praying community could not but feel itself to be implicated.

Even when the prayer of intercession for the sick became more consistent and even took predominance (especialy in the euchology), the office of the sick substantially retained its primitive character as an experience which took place primarily in the praying community as such.

The encounter of the assembly with God, the Lord of life and death, was meant to cause this Lord to visit the community and bring with him both health and salvation. Throughout the office of the sick, there prevails a sense of a community that laments certain evils (these may be either physical or moral) and is opening itself to the hope of a heavenly remedy that will restore life in its fullness.

Vespers

Supplicatio.
1. Let us ask and beseech the Redeemer of the world, our Lord
Jesus Christ, that in his mercy he would heal the wounds of his
servants, all the faithful who are sick.
Br 208A (210A), 973B, 976C, S7 (Ord 377–78).

Completuria.
2. Lord, we pray that you will not accuse us in your anger nor let
your wrath rage against us, but rather reprove us gently and make
us stop sinning, lest if you chastise us harshly you drive us to
destruction. Have mercy, therefore, on our weakness and grant
healing to your servants, all the faithful who are sick, and if you see
any who are troubled by their own sins, forgive them in your mercy
and grant them serenity.
Br 208A, 973C: LOPs 325 (Ps 6).

Another.
3. Lord, our protector and physician, hear our evening prayers.
The man keeps your mercy from himself who does not show you
his wounds. But because you, Lord, summon all the sick back to
health and because those whom you heal are sick no longer, heal
our wounds, Lord, and grant us your mercy.
Ord 378–39, S7 (Ord 379).

Another.
4. Hear us, Lord our God, in our various needs, and in your mercy
grant help to your servants, all sick Christians who labor under the
burden of their illnesses. As through Elijah you brought back to life
the son of the woman of Sidon and through Elisha the son of the
woman of Shunem, so too deign to hear our pleas and grant healing
of body and salvation of soul to all the sick.
L 191v, S7 (Ord 379).

Another.
5. Lord, who show mercy to all, who rule all things and in your
goodness hear those who cry to you, and who are the consolation of
the burdened, healing for the afflicted of heart, and medicine to the
sick; Lord, who are the redeemer of the dying, the resurrection of
the dead, the restorer of the sick, we beg and beseech you to look
with mercy on all your servants who are wearied out by violent

The Votive Office of the Sick in the Spanish Rite

fever, exhausted by sickness, broken by fatigue, and weakened by chastisement. Grant them strength of body, constancy of soul, endurance of suffering, good health. May the invocation of your holy name wash away all their bodily blemishes, all their various sicknesses, all attacks of fever. Grant them an extension of life, as you did to your servant Hezekiah; raise them from their beds, as you did Peter's mother-in-law and as you raised the widow's son from his bier. Then, restored to their earlier health, they may enter your church and bless you, God the Father, in all things.
L 189, S7 (Ord 381).

Another.

6. We invoke you, Lord, holy Father, everlasting almighty God, Father of our Lord Jesus Christ, God of mercy, who are master of life and death, and physician of sick souls. From the dwelling you have prepared look with mercy on your servants who are in bondage to ill health. Visit them from heaven as you deigned to visit the mother-in-law of Peter and the centurion's servant. Lord, grant them healing and health, as after your passion you made bodies already corrupted in the tombs come forth to the light again. Grant them, Lord, the consolation of devotion, as with a word you cleansed of all stains the woman with a flow of blood. Grant them, Lord, health of mind and body, as you raised Lazarus from the dead after four days in the tomb. Then, present once again, healthy and safe, in your holy church, they will thank you, the Lord.
L 190v, S7 (Ord 378).

Another: For one sick person.

7. Lord, prove your mercy upon this servant of yours. Call his life back from destruction, show him favor in your pity and mercy. We ask that after giving him a realization of his weakness you would now grant him healing. You are giver of health: be now a saving physician to whom healing bears witness, and let infidelity abandoned and good health restored be evidence of your mercy.
L 192.

Benedictio.

8. May almighty God bless you who deigned to form you from nothing.

May he heal your sicknesses, for he alone is our Lord and Redeemer.

And may he always have care of you, for in him is the fullness of our salvation.
L 189; Ord 380–81, S7 (Ord 379).

Another.

9. Lord, deign to grant your salvation to your servants.

Accept our prayers, grant our petitions, and forgive our sins.

Heal us of our sicknesses, and cleanse the hearts of your servants from the stains of sin.

L 190v–191, Ord 378, S7 (Ord 378).

Another.

10. May almighty God, who chastises his most faithful servants, all the sick faithful, with bodily illness, purify them and us of sicknesses of body and mind.

May he who took our infirmity upon himself grant us and them an endless reward for endurance.

May his loving goodness assist all alike, so that our ill health may not grow worse and we may not in our weakness yield to despair.

Br 208A, 973CD.

Another.

11. May Christ the Lord, who is true redemption, heal every disease and every infirmity among his people.

May he drive off diseases from their bodies and protect their souls from deceptions,

So that all troubles being removed you may come to him healed in heart, body and soul.

L 191v, S7 (Ord 379).

Another: For one sick person.

12. May divine grace enrich him, and God sanctify him with heavenly blessing.

May he ward all sickness from him and protect him always with loving mercy.

May he give a favorable ear to his petitions, and mercifully grant him forgiveness for all his sins.

L 192.

Matins

De Psalmo III.

13. We cry to you, Lord; hear us from your holy mountain. Rise up and save us, Lord our Lord, that the health of your Christ may reign in us and the blessing of your name may abide upon your people.

Ord 382.

The Votive Office of the Sick in the Spanish Rite

Orationes de antiphonis.
Ant.: Lord, save your people and bless.
14. Lord, grant that in your name we may advance in salvation.
And by your power free us whom you know to be hindered by our
own sicknesses, so that all we are may belong to you who brought
us out of nothingness.
S7 (Ord 379): LOPs 65 (Ps 53).

Ant.: May your right hand save us.
15. May our soul bless you, Lord, and all that is in it cry out your
praises, so that hearing our prayer you may hasten to heal our
sicknesses and redeem our lives from destruction. Satisfy our desire
with good things and crown our prayers with fulfillment.
S7 (Ord 379–80): LOPs 271 (Ps 102).

Alleluiaticum: Lord, heal all our sickness.
16. Heal us, Lord, when we cry to you. We are troubled by
discouraging sickness and imminent death: as you use these to wipe
away our sins, lend a merciful ear to us in our wretchedness. Free us
from hell, we pray, and turn our sorrow into joy.
S7 (Ord 380).

Others.
Ant.: Lord, save your people and bless.
17. Lord, save your people and bless your inheritance. Do not forget
your Church which you predestined from eternity in Christ. Mindful
of your mercy, look upon your covenant and constantly endue us
with your promised freedom.
Ord 382: cf. LOPs 257 (Ps 73).

Ant.: Our Savior, save us in your love.
18. Lord, save us by your name and free us by your power. Lead us
out of affliction and fill us with gladness, so that as you freely grant
us your salvation, we may glorify and praise you and our freedom
may lead us to rest.
Ord 383: cf. LOPs 371 (Ps 53).

Allel.: Lord, our strength, be our support.
19. Heal us, Lord our God, and let not the sickness caused by our
sins bring us death. Heal us, Lord, and all the sick, and redeem our
life from destruction, so that healed of guilt it may be rendered
peaceful by grace. Pour out your healing on the sick and grant
forgiveness of their sins.
Ord 383: cf. LOPs 7 (Ps 6), LOF 1187.

Others.

Ant.: Like our fathers we have sinned.

20. Lord God, we ask your mercy. Do not accuse us in your anger nor chastise us in your wrath; but those whom you see troubled by their own sin, forgive in your mercy and grant them serenity.
S7 (Ord 380): cf. LOPs 325 (Ps 6).

Ant.: Forgive our sins because of.

21. Lord, who abide for ever, be a refuge to the poor in their affliction and a timely aid for us; be healing . . . in distress. And as you console the sorrowing, so also give aid to all the sick.
S7 (Ord 380).

Allel.: Send your word and heal us.

22. In your love save us, Lord our God, who always protect your creature with fidelity in many forms. In your goodness be present at the invocation of your name, and with your right hand raise up sick Christians, your servants, and strengthen them with your power. Apply medicine, heal sicknesses. Grant them yourself as their life, and bestow on them, together with good health, all that they look for from you.

Others.

Ant.: Our Savior, save us in your love.

23. Lord, save your people and bless. . . .
S7 (Ord 381): cf. no. 17.

Ant.: Forgive us our sins and heal.

24. Lord, forgive our sins and cancel eternal punishment for us. And since we believe you can always remit sins, may we set aside our guilt and deserve always to have your mercy.
S7 (Ord 381).

Allel.: We have sinned against you, God; show mercy.

25. We have sinned against you, God, we have acted wrongly, for we did not obey your commandments but followed our own wicked thoughts. May we deserve to have these prayers favorably heard, for we have transgressed your commands. We ask, almighty God, that. . . .
S7 (Ord 381).

Others.

Ant.: Our Savior, save us in your love.

26. Almighty, everlasting God, incline your ear to our pleas, and grant the medicine of heavenly grace to your servants, all the sick faithful who are suffering ill health of body.
Br 208D, 974D

Ant.: Lord, show us your mercy.

27. Lord, you purify the hearts of those who make confession to you, and you absolve the accusing conscience from every bond of sin. Grant forgiveness to your servants, and bestow on their bodies the pure medicine of heavenly grace.
Br 209A, 974B.

Ant.: Turn, Lord, and rescue our souls.

28. Lord, be present to your petitioners, we pray. In your goodness grant the aid of most merciful consolation to those whom you afflict with harsh but merited correction.
Br 209B, 974C.

Others.

Ant.: Lord, save your people and bless.

29. We ask for your tender love with all our heart and with deep groans, Lord, holy Father, almighty everlasting God, who have eternal power to slay the living and give life to the dead. You alone can extinguish the fire of fever, for often it has been your wont to raise the dead to life. We therefore humbly pray that through the presence of your angel you would deign to visit all your faithful who are in the strong grip of sickness. May they feel the dew of your refreshing grace and, having been rescued from the flaming heat, be able to bless you, the Lord, in all things.
L 189v.

Ant.: May your right hand save us.

30. God, source of strength and vigor, God, source of eternal salvation and life, look upon your people as they suffer varied sicknesses. Let every sickness depart from them, Lord, every anxiety, all sorrow, all the activity of the wicked one, so that if any pain is felt in their marrow or vitals, it may depart or be lessened by the invocation of your name, and, restored to health, we may deserve to serve you for ever.
L 189v.

Allel.: Lord, heal all our sicknesses.

31. Lord, heal the sicknesses of your people, for you always show mercy to sinners as a father does to his children. Then, rescued from the destruction of eternal death, our souls may bless you and our lives glorify you.
L 189v.

Others.

Ant.: Forgive our sins for your name's sake.

32. Lord, God of our salvation, for whom no sickness is incurable,

we ask that in your tender mercy you would drive every sickness and every infirmity from your servants. They look for your heavenly medicine: work in them a sign of your power and your healing, and grant them health of body and spirit.
L 191.

Ant.: Forgive our sins, Lord.
33. God, who through your only Son you exercise the medicinal power of your healing word, look upon my need, Lord, and do not brush aside my petition, so that what I do not merit by my invocation, I may receive because I expect it from you. Unbind the destructive bonds of sickness so that if the illness rages at the body's expense, it may be moderated and if its source be temptation, it may be warded off. And let this servant of yours, who was handed over to sickness for chastisement, now that he has accepted correction, be restored to health.
L 191.

Ant.: Send your word and heal us.
34. God, who turn away sickness from the ill and cast off the body's weaknesses and who remove the source of imminent danger by a more perfect salvation, we pray and beseech you to be present at the bedside of the sick. You are all in all: apply your merciful saving name at the couches of all who are ill, strengthen the weak, support the troubled, make solid what has broken down, renew the ulcerated flesh. For the ability to do so is in your power alone, and the will to do so is always present in your mercy. From that mercy we ask forgiveness of our sins and from your immense and loving kindness the healing of our fleshly sicknesses.
L 191–191v.

Others: For one sick person.
Ant.: Heal me, Lord, for my bones are troubled.
35. Give aid, Lord, to your servant on his bed of pain, as you did to the paralytic whom on the sabbath you caused to walk away with his pallet, and as with a word of command you healed Simon's mother-in-law when she was confined to bed with a great fever. Let this servant of yours likewise receive the health he desires and glorify you, the author of good health.
L 192–192v.

Ant.: I was oppressed in my groaning, I will every night wash.
36. We believe, Lord Jesus, that for us sinners you were oppressed in the groans of your passion. Therefore we pray that your outstanding example of patience may be of profit to our souls, so

that every night we may drench our beds and couches with our tears and thus receive continual helps to holiness.
L 192v, LOF 560.

Ant.: Send your word and heal me, Lord.
37. Almighty Father, heal the soul of him who has too often sinned against you by his actions. And lest he be any longer bound by sickness, may your blessedness show mercy and free him from his days of darkness.
L 192v.

Completuria.
38. Help us, our Redeemer, and may we who for our sins lie ill on a bed of pain be healed by the medicine of your forgiveness, and may we who are being brought daily closer to death by our increasing sins be raised up by your abundant mercy. And because the persuasions of the world and the deceits of the enemy are destroying us in all kinds of tempests and bringing us to death, we pray you, merciful God, to give us life, rescue us from the hand of the enemy, and always sanctify us with your blessing.
S7 (Ord 382): LOPs 503 (Ps 40).

Another.
39. Lord, heal all our sicknesses and visit us with your salvation. Because like our fathers we have done evil in your sight, we pray and beseech you: rescue our life from destruction, and let us, under the guidance of your grace, be redeemed from the dwelling place of death and from the infection both of the original condemnation and of actual sin.
Ord 384: cf. LOPs 121 (Ps 105).

Another.
40. Lord, look upon your servants, all the faithful who are sick and who rejoice to invoke your name. Grant them heavenly medicine, give them protection of mind, and deign to free them from every infirmity and sickness.
Br 210A, 975B.

Another.
41. Surround our weakness with your strength, Lord our God, and do not, as a mighty judge, angrily accuse those whose consciences are stained with guilt. But because you do not despise any sinner whom you know is returning to you through repentance, do you, Lord, cease to scourge us for our sins, increase the cures that come

through confession, and open the door by which we may come to you. In hell no guilty person is absolved nor is any confession accepted: therefore hear our groans of distress and mercifully redeem those you have created.
S7 (Ord 382).

Another.
42. God, inventor of saving medicine, who by infusing your divine gift dispel the manifold sicknesses to which the weak human body falls prey and who lead your human creature to the gates of death and then call him back again from the gates of hell: visit your servants with spiritual grace, so that, as your angel keeps watch, these suppliants may, by invoking your name, receive back the health long kept from them, and that any pain, any hurt, any fiery fever, any internal suffering may be expelled from their members and vitals. And may the medicinal poultices which persevering human skill may apply to the infirm body be an aid to health as you, the spiritual physician, watch over them.
L 190.

Another: For one sick person.
43. Lord, in your mercy save this man whom you know to be ill on account of his own wickedness. His soul is troubled by fear of your just judgments: let your joyous gift of forgiveness bring him peace. And may he receive the reward of health from him to whom he confesses the wounds caused by his sins.
L 192v: cf. LOPs 475 (Ps 6).

Benedictio.
44. May the Lord bless and keep you.
  May the Lord show his face to you and have mercy on you.
  May the Lord turn his countenance to you and grant you health and peace.
S7 (Ord 382).

Another.
45. May the Lord forgive all your iniquities and heal all your sicknesses.
  May he redeem your life from destruction and satisfy your desire with his gifts.
  And may the Lord grant you healing of heart and body, so that you will always be thankful to him.
L 190v (192v).

Another.

46. May God in his fidelity make you ever praise him, and with
heavenly . . . moderate the vengeful spirit [?].

May the Lord give you consolation after sorrow and reward
sadness with joy,

So that your soul may not perish under the scourges but rather
after enduring reach the rewards of heaven.
S7 (Ord 381–82).

Another.

47. From the heavenly realm may the Lord send you health-giving
medicine.

May this best of supporters answer your prayers and in his love
bless your desires.

May he remove all evils from you, and grant what is good to
you and yours.
S7 (Ord 382).

Damien SICARD

Preparation for Death and Prayer for the Dying

This volume of liturgical studies has taken us to the East and the West, to Byzantium, Georgia, and Russia. We have looked into the Ambrosian and Spanish rites; the Old Testament and the exegesis of James 5; the cultic environment of the dead in early Christianity; the text of the compiler of the Gelasian Sacramentary; the liturgy of the Dormition, the funeral office known as the Pannychis, the funerals of children, priests, and bishops; and the new Roman Rite of 1972. Various papers have dealt either with the anointing with oil and the theology of sickness, or with funerals, the oldest images connected with them, and the theology of the last things, or with both together.

My own purpose here is much more limited and modest. This paper comes from a Catholic priest who had hitherto exercised only the ordinary pastoral ministries of a curate, a youth chaplain, or a pastor.

This short paper will focus on the pre-Carolingian liturgy for the moment when a Christian is dying, and it will deal only with Latin texts. I have not found any Eastern rituals or prayers for last moments of life prior to the ninth century; you may well be able to fill out my data and documentation.

The subject which I have set for myself: "Preparation for Death and Prayer for the Dying" has been dealt with before. In 1935 Dom Gougaud published an *Etude sur les Ordines commendationis animae* that is still cited in more recent work on preparation for death and the rites for the dying. In most instances, the attention of liturgists has focused on the origin of the exhortation *Proficiscere* (Go forth from this world, Christian soul), which is the first of the prayers for the dying in the Roman Ritual.[1] This magnificent prayer, which is found for the first time in two "eighth-century Gelasian sacramentaries," those of Gellone and Rheinau,[2] has been retained to give orientation to the prayer for the dying in the new Roman Ritual for the sick that was published in 1972.[3] It can be said that along with Viaticum and the rites accompanying it, the *Proficiscere* is the oldest and most characteristic part of the prayers for the dying.

I have had occasion elsewhere to discuss the new perspectives shown in the part of the Ritual that has to do with Viaticum,[4] and I shall restrict myself here to a study of the exhortation *Proficiscere*. After noting some peculiarities in the form it takes in the principal witnesses, I shall once again take up the problem of its origin and, at the end, inquire into its pastoral use.

THE MANUSCRIPTS OF THE *PROFICISCERE*

A listing of the manuscript witnesses to the exhortation *Proficiscere* soon shows the importance attached to this prayer and the extent of its diffusion not only in the Gallican circles that produced the eighth-century Gelasian sacramentaries, but also in Roman witnesses of the ninth to the thirteenth centuries,[5] the monastic witnesses of the eleventh and twelfth centuries,[6] and the Ambrosian witnesses of the eleventh to the thirteenth centuries.[7] Generally speaking, the "Gregorian" manuscripts do not have the prayer. But between the sacramentaries of Gellone and Rheinau, which give the first known version of it, and the Roman Pontifical of the twelfth century, I have found twenty-five manuscripts attesting it, while all the intermediaries between the Roman Pontifical of the twelfth century and the Roman Ritual of 1614 have it.

The text of the first part, as found in the Roman Ritual of 1953 (the last before the liturgical reform of Vatican II), showed only minor variations as compared with the text in the sacramentaries of the Gellone and Rheinau—apart, of course, from the phrases concerning the Mother of God and St. Joseph, which were added in 1919 and 1922, respectively.

The reader will be familiar with the text of this first part. I reproduce it here as found in the eighth-century Gelasians.

"Go forth from this world, Christian soul,
    in the name of God the almighty Father who created you,
    in the name of Jesus Christ, the Son of the living God, who
        suffered for you,
    in the name of the Holy Spirit, who has been poured out upon
        you,
    in the name of the angels and archangels,
    in the name of the thrones and dominations,
    in the name of the principalities and powers and all the heavenly
        virtues,
    in the name of the cherubim and seraphim,
    in the name of the patriarchs and prophets,
    in the name of the apostles and martyrs,
    in the name of the confessors and bishops,
    in the name of the priests and deacons and the whole hierarchy
        of the Catholic Church,
    in the name of the monks and hermits,
    in the name of the virgins and the faithful widows.
May his dwelling be established in peace this day and his home be in the heavenly Jerusalem!"

Here an immense retinue is called together for the final journey, when the hour has come to pass from this world to the Father. The atmosphere is the festive one proper to an individual's Passover and a gathering over which the Triune God presides in the midst of the angels and all the saints.

The formulas of introduction and conclusion to the second part, with which we are familiar, are those which the Pontifical of the Roman Curia in the thirteenth century substituted for the ones found in the eighth-century sacramentaries. The introduction in the sacramentaries of Gellone and Rheinau is: "Lord, receive your servant into blessings" ("Suscipe domine servum tuum in bonum"), whereas from the thirteenth-century Pontifical down to the new Ritual of 1972 (inclusive) it is: "Lord, receive your servant into the place of salvation which he hopes for from your mercy" ("Suscipe, Domine, servum tuum in locum sperandae sibi salvationis a misericordia tua"). The conclusion in the eighth century is: "Deign to free the soul of this person and grant him to dwell with you amid the blessings of heaven" ("Sic liberare digneris animam hominis istius et tecum habitare concede in bonis caelestibus"). In the thirteenth-century Pontifical and in the Ritual of 1953 (but altered in the Ritual of 1972), the ending is: "Deign to free the soul of your servant and grant him to rejoice with you amid the blessings of heaven" ("Sic liberare digneris animam hujus servi tui et tecum facias in bonis congaudere caelestibus").

Of the eighteen human individuals or groups who are mentioned in the various manuscripts as symbols and exemplars of servants who have been set free, the sacramentary of Gellone names ten, the Rheinau sacramentary names eleven (three of these peculiar to it), the twelfth century Roman Pontifical and the Ritual of 1614 name thirteen, and the Ritual of 1972 names nine.[8]

Here are the descriptions given of these models of liberation who are invoked at the moment of death (descriptions given at the first appearance of each in the manuscripts):

Abel by his acceptable sacrifice (Hamburg Missal and Collectarium in the Chigi collection—First half of the eleventh cent.).

Noah by the deluge (Gellone sacramentary [G], eighth cent.).

Enoch and *Elijah* from the death common to all in this world (G).

Abraham from Ur in Chaldea (Salzburg book of prayers [Lf1], first quarter of the eleventh cent.) or *Abraham* by his faith and readiness to believe (Sacramentary of Arezzo [Ar], of the tenth–eleventh cent.).

Lot from Sodom and its flames (Rheinau sacramentary [Rh], eighth cent.).

The *Israelites* from the hands of the Egyptians (Lf1).

Moses from the hand of Pharaoh, king of the Egyptians (G).

Isaac from sacrifice at the hand of his father Abraham (Rh).

Jacob by the blessing of your majesty (Ar).

Job from his sufferings (G).

Daniel from the lion pit (G).

The *three young men* from the fiery furnace and the hands of the wicked king (G).

Jonah from the belly of the whale (G).

Susanna from false witness (G).

David from the hand of King Saul, from Goliath, and from all his difficulties (G).

The *human race* by the passion of our Lord Jesus Christ (Ar).

Peter and *Paul* from their imprisonments (G).

Thecla from the three tortures (Rh).

I cannot undertake here a detailed analysis of the variants in the manuscripts of the *Proficiscere,* but such an analysis would show that the literary origin of the prayer is not to be sought in the eighth-century Gelasians themselves but rather in the archetype of the eighth-century Gelasians which liturgical researchers have had to hypothesize.⁹ On the other hand, the various witnesses assert a relative independence of their model.

Among the more remarkable witnesses, the sacramentary of Arezzo, which I have cited for the three models which it is the first to list, shows another peculiarity as well. It is the oldest text containing a prayer "Suscipiat te sanctus michael archangelus" ("May Saint Michael the archangel take you up"), which is an integral element in the first part of the *Proficiscere*. This text from the end of the tenth century contains the essentials of the prayer *Delicta juventutis* ("Do not remember the sins of his youth"), which is known from the Hamburg Missal of the eleventh century and, after being taken into the Roman Pontificals of the twelfth and thirteenth centuries, became the sixth prayer of the *Ordo commendationis animae* in the Roman Ritual of 1614–1953.¹⁰

THE ORIGIN OF THE *PROFICISCERE*

The scholars whom I mentioned at the beginning have concentrated chiefly on the question of the origin of the *Proficiscere*.¹¹ E. Le Blant, followed by H. R. Philippeau, wanted to assign the prayer to the second or third century; this view was based on the Podgoritza cup and the iconography of the catacombs. In his articles Philippeau frequently mentions "the transparent allusions to the Book of Enoch and the Acts of Paul,"¹² and concluded to a date earlier than the date which he still assigned to the decree of Pope Gelasius on the apocrypha (496, according to him).¹³ L. Gougaud also thought the prayer to be very old; for this view he relied on literary similarities.¹⁴ But in his 1949 study of catacomb iconography and catechesis in antiquity, Canon Martimort radically disagreed with the view of Le Blant and completed those of Gougaud.¹⁵ As Martimort shows, the iconography of the catacombs is connected not with funeral rites or the recommendation of the soul to God, but with the catechesis of initiation, the themes of which it repeats (vocation, faith, forgiveness, metanoia, salvation through water, eucharistic meal). I shall not repeat his arguments but simply emphasize, with him, the artificiality of connecting the *Proficiscere* either with the Podgoritza cup (which in any case belongs to the fifth century, not the third¹⁶) or with the paintings in the catacombs.

Furthermore, why should the mention of Enoch suggest an allusion to the apocryphal book rather than to the Bible? Enoch is a biblical figure whose mysterious death had struck the Jewish imagination, as the death of Elijah had.¹⁷ The mention of St. Thecla by almost all the witnesses does undoubtedly depend ultimately on the Acts of Paul, which is a very ancient apocryphal document; on the other hand, the story given there very quickly became part of a multiform tradition which the decree *De recipiendis* in no way discouraged.[18]

I think it important to mention, among other sources of the *Proficiscere*, the *Orationes pseudocyprianae*, which are a Latin translation of a Greek original that probably dates from the fourth century.[19] These exorcisms appeal to the same incidents as the *Proficiscere* does, as symbols of the effectiveness of prayer. Here are some extracts which will help the reader to evaluate the link with the *Proficiscere*:

First prayer: ". . . God of Abraham, God of Isaac, God of Jacob, God of the prophets, God of the apostles, God of virgins, God of those who live good lives . . . for we bend our knees and bow our necks to you to whom the angels, archangels, countless martyrs and choir of apostles and prophets give praise. . . . And as you showed mercy to the three young men in the furnace and to Daniel, do the same for us your servants. . . . Be with us as you were with your apostles in chains, with Thecla in the fire, Paul among his persecutors, Peter amid the waves . . . free us from the destruction of everlasting death."

Second prayer: ". . . I thank and praise you . . . God of the prophets, God of the apostles, God of the martyrs . . . free me from this world, and hear me as you heard Jonah in the belly of the whale. . . . Hear my prayer as you heard Daniel in the lion's den. . . . Hear my prayer as you heard Susanna in the toils of the elders. . . . Free me from this world as you freed Thecla from the midst of the arena. . . ."

When we realize the popularity of these prayers and when we observe how close they are in construction, inspiration and at times even expression, to the *Proficiscere*, we must believe that the author of the latter could not have been unfamiliar with the earlier prayers.

There is no point in my demonstrating that the whole of the Bible and of its major figures are present to the mind of the author of the *Proficiscere*; this is self-evident.[20] I agree with Canon Martimort that we should think also of the same biblical images as used in the old Gelasian Sacramentary in the exorcisms of catechumens.[21]

While it does not seem arguable that the *Proficiscere* itself goes back to the second century or even to the fifth, it does seem that through its various sources it reflects an inspiration which belongs to the very early centuries of Christianity. It also makes clear how in death the dying person brings his baptism to completion. Baptism had buried him with Christ in death.[22] The liturgy of the dying is

244   SICARD

the liturgy of a second and definitive baptism. Thus, as Karl Rahner puts it, "Baptism is the sacramentally visible beginning of that death which is not the culmination of sin but of the sin-suppressing appropriation of salvation."[23]

THE *PROFICISCERE* AND THE DYING

Due to the sources on which it drew, the sap of primitive Christianity flows in the *Proficiscere*. But for several decades now sociocultural changes have altered the habits of our contemporaries: the whole family no longer gathers around the bed of a dying person in order to pray as one of its members departs and to invoke the Holy Trinity and a varied retinue of angels and saints, thus locating each Christian death within the biblical framework of the history of salvation and associating it with the vast company of the redeemed, the liberated, the saved.

The life-style which the people of the twentieth century have adopted or have had forced upon them may have freed them from sexual taboos, but it has tended to defraud them of their deaths. It is clear that in the urban existence which is becoming that of the majority of the human race, most people meet death and will continue to meet it in hospitals or nursing homes or in accidents on the highways; their death will be either collectivized or sudden and unexpected.

This is doubtless the practical reason why, in its liturgical reform after Vatican II (to take one example), the Church concerned itself first of all with a ritual for funerals and a message "after the fact" of death,[24] and only then with a ritual for the sick and preparation for death.

The new "Rite for the Commendation of the Dying," which forms Chapter 6 of the 1972 *Rite of Anointing and Pastoral Care of the Sick* begins with a set of counsels and observations which suggest a pastoral approach for pastors and the entire Christian community (nos. 138–42). As the final instruction in this series makes clear, it is the laity, much more than priests or deacons, who will be called upon to help the dying, and it is for their sake especially that suitable books of prayers are to be published.

In the material offered, readings from the word of God have the most important place, as is to be expected. The *Proficiscere* is suggested for the moment of death, as being "in accord with the Christian disposition for death." The Rite is satisfied here with a quite abbreviated version of the prayer.

If the *Proficiscere* is to be of real help to the person in his final moments of consciousness, it must presuppose some previous acquaintance with the scriptures and a previous experience of concrete Christian community.

In other words, the prayer supposes a more remote preparation for death, something which the sacrament of the sick and the fully conscious reception of viaticum will not be able to provide by themselves.

If human death is to be given its authentic theological dimension as a communion with the Pasch or "pass-over" of Christ, the Church must undertake a vast effort of evangelization. In this task it will doubtless use means which it can adapt with increasing effectiveness. There is no reason for saying that the exhortation known as the *Proficiscere* cannot continue to play the role it has played since at least the eighth century.

Ambroise VERHEUL

The Paschal Character of the Sacrament of the Sick: Exegesis of James 5:14–15 and the New Rite for the Sacrament of the Sick

On November 30, 1972, Pope Paul VI published the Apostolic Constitution *Sacram Unctionem Infirmorum* in which he approved and promulgated the new ritual for the anointing of the sick.[1] On December 7 of the same year, the Congregation for Divine Worship published the new rite.[2] The old rite was to be replaced by the new beginning January 1, 1974, but the Congregation granted a delay to the episcopal conferences because translations into the various languages were not yet ready.[3] Gradually, however, the new rite made its way into the local Churches.

The following are the principal changes which the new ritual makes in the *Rituale Romanum* of 1614:[4]

1. It is clearly stated that the anointing of the sick is not a sacrament of the dying.[5] Rather it is a sacrament for those who are seriously ill; these sick persons need not be in danger of imminent death.[6]

2. The number of anointings is reduced to two: one on the forehead and one on the hands.[7]

3. Where olive oil is not available or is difficult to obtain, it is permitted to use some other vegetable oil.[8]

4. When oil blessed by the bishop is not available, the priest may, in case of necessity, bless the oil himself in the course of the ceremony.[9] In any case, every celebration of the sacrament includes at least a prayer of thanksgiving over the oil.[10]

5. The ritual henceforth comprises:[11]

An introductory prayer (68–70);

A penitential rite (71);

A short liturgy of the word (72);

The sacramental rite proper, which includes:

    a. Prayers of intercession (which may be said after the anointing) (73);

    b. A silent imposition of hands (74);

    c. The blessing of the oil or a prayer of thanksgiving over it (75 and 75b);

    d. The anointing of the sick person while the sacramental formula is pronounced (76);

    e. A prayer (77);

A concluding rite, which includes:

    a. The Lord's Prayer (78);

    b. The final blessing (79).

6. The principal change, however, is in the new sacramental formula.[12] The new formula depends in part on the old: "Through this holy anointing may the Lord in his love and mercy . . . ,"[13] but is also inspired in part by the text of the Council of Trent: ". . . help you with the grace of the Holy Spirit."[14] Finally, in its principal part it is based on the letter of St. James (5:15): "May the Lord who frees you from sin save you and raise you up."[15]

The words which are based on Trent bring out clearly the role of the Holy Spirit in the sacrament. He is invoked at the imposition of hands,[16] in the prayer for the blessing of the oil,[17] and in the prayer that accompanies the anointing.[18]

Nonetheless it is the integration of the text of St. James into the sacramental formula that tells us the deepest meaning and the effects of the anointing of the sick. For this reason, before I study the paschal meaning of the sacrament of anointing, it is important to turn first to a careful exegesis of the passage from the letter of James. My study will therefore have two parts: (1) the exegesis of

James 5:14–16; and (2) the paschal meaning of the anointing
of the sick.

In this passage five points need to be singled out, with the last
three calling for more special attention.

1. The elders (presbyters) pray over the sick person (v. 14a and b);
2. in the name of the Lord (v. 14b);
3. they anoint him with oil (v. 14b);
4. the prayer of faith will save the sick person (v. 15a);
5. the Lord will raise him up (v. 15b).

Let us look at each of these five points.

1. Prayer Over the Sick Person
In his letter, St. James mentions prayer on three occasions. At the
beginning of the letter, in 1:5–8, he speaks of prayer that seeks to
obtain wisdom from God.[20] In 4:2–3 he reproaches Christians who
are covetous and jealous with not praying in the right way.[21]
Finally, in 5:13–18, to which the passage that concerns us belongs,[22]
he exhorts the faithful to pray in all situations: in suffering and in
joy (v. 13), when someone is sick (vv. 14–15), and at the time of
mutual confession of sins (v. 16a); the exhortation is followed by a
brief explanation of the power of the prayer of a just person
(vv. 16b–18).

If someone is sick, let him summon the elders of the Church and
let them pray over him (v. 15). In the next verse this prayer is
described as *euchē tēs pisteōs*, "prayer of faith"; in it we address our
prayer to God with faith and confidence, in the assurance of being
heard.

In several passages of the New Testament, it is said that the
person who prays with faith wins from God what he desires.[23] In
the gospels faith is always a condition required for a miraculous
healing.[24] Prayers offered with faith (cf. 1:6: *aiteitō de en pistei*) are
prayers in which one expresses an unhesitating faith in the divine
generosity.[25] More than once we see Jesus himself and his disciples
praying before raising a dead person to life.[26]

In the passage I am studying here, the prayer in question is
prayer for a sick person. But the text of St. James does not say this
in so many words; he speaks of prayer *over* the sick person
(*proeuxasthōsan epi auton*). They pray over him as they pray over the
offerings of bread and wine in the eucharist. Many exegetes have
seen in the preposition *epi* an allusion to the fact that the prayer *for*
the sick person was accompanied by an imposition of hands *on* him.

In St. Mark we read that in his farewell words, Jesus tells his apostles that those who will believe in him and will lay hands on the sick will heal them.[27] When citing James 5:14, Origen already sees in the *epi* an imposition of hands.[28]

The imposition of hands has been kept in the new ritual, but contrary to the practice in the ritual of 1614, it is no longer accompanied by a formula emphasizing the negative side, namely the forgiveness of sins.[29] In fact, no formula at all is used now. It is also to be noted that the other priests present can likewise lay hands on the sick. This is an impressive action which irresistibly reminds us of the imposition of hands by the bishop and priests at a priestly ordination.[30]

2. Prayer in the Name of the Lord

The letter of James sees the prayer of the elders as the most important element in the rite and subordinates the anointing to it.[31] The text reads: "Let them pray over him [while] anointing him with oil." The main action is the praying; the anointing is secondary.

The prayer is uttered "in the name of the Lord," *en tō onomati tou Kuriou*, that is, it involves an invocation of the Lord's name, an appeal to his power. The meaning is not so much that the prayer is made in the name, that is, on the orders of the Lord,[32] but rather that in the prayer an appeal is made for his help.[33] The "name" of the Lord is the person of the Lord; it is the risen Lord himself, the *Kyrios* who is asked to be present, for in the final analysis it is he who will raise up the sick person.

3. Anointing of the Sick Person with Oil

An anointing with oil was used in the Old Testament and in later Judaism on various occasions:[34]

1. The crowning of a king;[35]
2. The ordination of a priest;[36]
3. The appointment of a prophet;[37] Christian antiquity was already familiar with a postbaptismal anointing by which the baptized person was given a share in the priesthood of Christ;[38]
4. The consecration of objects used in worship;[39]
5. The treatment of wounds;[40]
6. The healing of the sick. This kind of anointing is found in use among the rabbis of later Judaism. A person with a backache may not on the sabbath rub himself with wine or vinegar, but he may do so with oil.[41] In Tractate Berakhot of the Jerusalem Talmud we read: "It is permitted to make for a sick person a compress of stale wine and perfumed oil mixed with water."[42]

VERHEUL

For James and Mark (6:7–13), however, the purpose of the anointing of the sick is not purely medicinal; it is salvific as well. The letter of James speaks of "saving" and "raising up." In Mark, the anointing is connected with the expulsion of demons and the coming of the kingdom of God. It has therefore a symbolic and eschatological purpose, to the extent that the final state of affairs is already being brought to pass in the present world.[43]

7. The embalming of bodies. Postexilic Judaism practiced the embalming of bodies, that is, an anointing with olive oil as a preparation for life in the next world.[44] We find this same symbolic and eschatological meaning of anointing in the gospels, but in direct connection with death as a passage to eternal life. When Jesus allows his feet to be anointed in the house of Simon the Pharisee, he interprets the action as done in preparation for his burial.[45] Subsequently, on the first day of the week, we find the women going to the tomb to anoint the body of Jesus.[46]

In the letter of James, the anointing is connected with numbers 6 and 7 in the list just given. This will not surprise us if we remember that for Jews and Jewish Christians, oil was a reminder of eternal life and of the world to come. The prophets had often described the messianic age as a time when oil, must, and wine would be abundant.[47] B. Reicke[48] refers to Genesis 8:11 where an olive branch, symbol of deliverance, is according to a rabbinic midrash brought by a dove from paradise.[49] Reicke also cites 2 Enoch 8,5 where the rivers of paradise produce oil and wine and where the tree of life is an olive tree. In the *Apocalypse of Moses* (9,3), we read that after being expelled from paradise Adam remembers with sorrow the "oil of mercy" that flows from the tree of life. Seth tries to bring this precious oil to his father from the heights of heaven, but he is told that it will be given only on the last day (13, 1–3). When Adam finally reaches the third heaven, he is anointed by angels.[50]

Like bread and wine, oil, that other important product of the land of Israel, became a symbol of life. Olive oil confers the strength of the life proper to paradise; it already restores in a small way the paradisal state that awaits us in the kingdom of heaven. It will effect, first of all, a spiritual restoration and thereby (the spiritual restoration is thus a condition) the forgiveness of sins. The spiritual restoration is symbolized by bodily healing.

4. The Prayer of Faith Will Save the Sick Person
The first point that strikes us is that it is not so much the anointing that saves as the prayer of faith, or perhaps more accurately, it is both together, the anointing and the prayer. We are

dealing here with a prayer made in the spirit of faith; its effectiveness comes from faith. But the main question that arises here is this: Does the word *sōzein* (save) have in this passage a purely medical and physical meaning, or must we assign it a religious and eschatological meaning as well? I think we can conclude that the religious and eschatological meaning is intended, although not, of course, to the exclusion of the medical and physical.

If we study the use of the verb *sōzein* in the New Testament, we find that twenty-nine times it has the medical sense of healing and being healed,[51] and sixty-eight times a religious and eschatological sense.[52] Moreover, in the letters of the apostles it is not used even once in a physical and medical sense. The word occurs five times in the letter of St. James, and on the other four occasions its meaning is eschatological: the word of God can *save* souls (1:21); faith without works cannot *save* (2:14); there is only one lawgiver and judge who can *save* or condemn (4:12); finally, in close proximity to the verse we are studying, "Let him know that whoever brings back a sinner from the error of his way will *save* his soul" (5:20). This consistent use elsewhere in the letter already makes it unlikely that the verb has an exclusively medical sense in 5:15.

Moreover, when we examine the passages in which the most obvious meaning is medical and physical, we find that an eschatological meaning as well is often to be glimpsed. The verb is regularly used when Jesus or the apostles effect a miraculous healing. But on each occasion, we realize that the gift of messianic salvation is communicated through the gift of bodily healing; the reign of God enters the person who is healed.[53]

This is one reason why the two verbs "believe" and "save" occur together; faith is a condition for being healed by Jesus and his apostles.[54] Except for James 2:14 where eschatological salvation is undoubtedly meant, there is a *connection* between "believing" and "being saved," and this connection is present in our passage.[55] The eschatological meaning can therefore be glimpsed, even if it is not predominant.

The fact that *sōzein* can have this twofold meaning is also clear from the discourse of Jesus in Mark 8:35 (cf. Lk 9:24): "For whoever would save his life will lose it; and whoever loses his life for my sake and the gospel's will save it." In verse 35a the meaning is the usual secular one, while in verse 35b the same verb is used to signify eschatological salvation.

Finally, I must ask whether in the passage that concerns us here there is not an echo of Joel 3:5, which was regularly cited in the preaching of the early Church: "Whoever calls on the name of the

Lord shall be saved."[56] In James there is also question of praying "in the name of the Lord," while St. Peter heals the paralytic "in the name of the Lord" (Acts 3:6). But if Joel 3:5 is implicitly being cited, is this not a reason for seeing an eschatological connotation in our text?

5. And the Lord Will Raise Him Up

It is also surprising that the fact of raising up from sickness should be attributed directly to the Lord, the *Kyrios*, the risen Lord who has been asked to manifest himself. It is not the anointing as such nor the prayer as such that effects the cure or *raising up*, but the risen Lord who in virtue of a prayer inspired by faith and trust is present, sanctifies, and heals. In determining the precise sense of the verb *egeirein* we find ourselves once again, as with *sōzein*, faced with a difficulty. The verb *egeirein* occurs only once in the letter of St. James, namely in the present passage. For this reason we cannot, as we did with *sōzein*, reach a conclusion on the basis of the parallel use in the same author.

In the other New Testament writings *egeirein* occurs 147 times. In 63 instances it has the everyday secular meaning of *arise* (stand up): in 14 cases, from a sitting or lying position,[57] in 16 cases from sleep,[58] in 15 from an illness,[59] in 9 from death;[60] in 7 it refers to the appearance of a prophet,[61] and in three cases it means "to rebel."[62]

It is to be noted that the word has none of these meanings in the New Testament letters; here, rather, it has an eschatological meaning, as it does in a number of gospel passages. We find this eschatological sense as many as seventy-six times in the New Testament. In ten passages it refers to the general resurrection of the dead,[63] in forty-eight to the resurrection of Christ,[64] and in twenty-one to our resurrection with Christ either in baptism[65] or at the end of time.[66] But I must add that in the gospel when Jesus brings a dead person back to life or heals a sick person, the meaning is always also eschatological because the two actions are set in relation to the messianic age when there will be resurrections and healings.

Given that in the New Testament letters *egeirein* always has an eschatological meaning and that in the gospels this meaning appears quite regularly, I ask whether the verb may not have this double meaning in the passage that concerns us here. The *Kyrios* has power not only to raise up someone from sickness but also and even more to bring him back to life, in the sense of giving his suffering a saving dimension by bringing him from a state of bodily suffering to the state of resurrection. Such was precisely the purpose of the Lord's own suffering;[67] it is also the purpose of the Christian's suffering.[68]

An exegetical study has shown that the words *sōzein* and *egeirein* have two meanings in the letter of St. James and that, consequently, a paschal meaning attaches to the anointing of the sick. The question to be answered now is whether or not this paschal character is sufficiently emphasized in the new rite promulgated on November 30, 1972. But I wish also to ask whether this paschal character is clear in the various translations made of the new rite (especially the translations of the sacramental formula) approved by the episcopal conferences[69] and ratified by the Congregations for the Faith and for Divine Worship.[70] I shall therefore inquire successively:

1. Whether in the official documents there is an emphasis on the paschal character of the anointing of the sick;

2. Whether this paschal character is reflected in the texts of the new rite;

3. Whether this paschal character is clear in the Latin sacramental formula and in the translations made of it.

1. The Official Documents

Neither in the definitions of the Decree for the Armenians (Council of Florence)[71] nor in those of the Council of Trent (Session XIV)[72] is this paschal character made explicit. Nor do the passages on this sacrament in the Constitution on the Sacred Liturgy of Vatican II (nos. 73–75) bring out this meaning,[73] although the Constitution does emphasize it for the other sacraments.[74] On the other hand, a passage in the Dogmatic Constitution *Lumen gentium* on the Church is very explicit on the point,[75] and Paul VI cites it in his Apostolic Constitution *Sacram Unctionem Infirmorum*: "By the sacred anointing of the sick and the prayer of her priests, the whole Church commends the sick to the suffering and glorified Lord, asking that he may lighten their suffering and save them [*alleviat et salvet*]" (see Jas 5:14–16).[76] In addition, the Church exhorts the sick to unite themselves freely to the sufferings and death of Christ (cf. Rom 8:17; Col 1:24; 2 Tm 2:11–12; 1 Pt 4:13) and in this way to contribute to the well-being of the Christian people. The text from James is also cited in the Introduction of the *Rite of Anointing* (no. 5).[77]

The anointing is evidently thought of as an encounter with the risen Lord who has the power to save and raise up and who asks the sick to unite their sufferings with his paschal mystery. In numbers 2 and 3 of the Introduction to the *Rite of Anointing*, the suffering of the Christian is again looked upon as a *configuratio* (an assimilation) to the passion of Christ and as disproportionate to the

VERHEUL

glory that will be revealed in us.[78] The suffering of the Christian completes that of Christ himself for the sake of the glorification of the children of God;[79] it is a form of redemption that is effected by the paschal mystery, that is, by the suffering and death of Christ.[80]

This deeper meaning of Christian suffering is underscored during the anointing of the sick. The sacrament links the sick person to the paschal mystery of the Lord. If it be for the person's salvation, the sacrament will bring him a bodily healing that images forth the resurrection of the Lord; but even if he is not healed in body, the eschatological meaning of his suffering will be made clear to him.

It is in number 7 of the Introduction that the paschal character of the anointing of the sick is most clearly brought out. The paragraph is based precisely on our text:

"The anointing of the sick, which includes the prayer of faith (see James 5:15), is a sacrament of faith. This faith is important for the minister and particularly for the one who receives it. The sick man will be saved by his faith and the faith of the Church which looks back to the death and resurrection of Christ, the source of the sacrament's power (see James 5:15), and looks ahead to the future kingdom which is pledged in the sacraments."[81]

In this passage the paschal character and the eschatological character are linked. This is not surprising, if we reflect that the resurrection of Christ marks the beginning of the eschatological age. In the risen Christ, Pasch and eschatology fuse; in him the end time has already begun. But it is through the sacraments that he gives us a share in his life. Therefore the eschatological nature of the anointing of the sick does not of its nature require that the sick person be in danger of imminent death or that he be dying, in order for him to be able to receive the sacrament.[82] Every sickness, of whatever kind and degree, is a slow destruction of our earthly dwelling and, at the same time, reminds us that God is preparing for us a dwelling in heaven.[83]

A footnote to this same seventh article of the *Rite of Anointing* refers us to a very enlightening passage of St. Thomas' commentary on the *Book of the Sentences.*[84]

2. The Paschal Character of the Texts for the Anointing of the Sick

Let me turn now to the rite of anointing and the prayers that accompany it, in order that I may call attention to the elements that have any relation to the paschal mystery of Christ. In this analysis I shall leave aside the sacramental formula itself and return to it in the final section of my study.

In the introductory rite our attention is caught by the words that accompany the sprinkling of holy water: "Let this water call to mind your baptismal sharing in Christ's redeeming passion and resurrection."[85] Moreover, in the short address of welcome that is offered as a model, there is a reminder that Christ is present in the midst of the assembled brethren as the one who has suffered for us.[86]

In the penitential rite offered in no. 71, there is no reference to the paschal mystery of Christ,[87] but in the alternative given in Chapter 7 it appears very clearly: "You brought us to salvation by your paschal mystery: Lord, have mercy. You renew us by the wonders of your passion: Christ, have mercy. You make us sharers in your paschal sacrifice by our partaking of your body: Lord, have mercy."[88]

In place of Matthew 8:5–10,13, which is suggested in the rite, one of the readings listed in Chapter 7 may be chosen (nos. 152–223). Several of the latter speak of Christian suffering as a sharing in the paschal mystery.

The alternate prayer to be said after the anointing proper asks God to "help him (her) find hope in suffering, for you have given him (her) a share in your passion."[89]

All of this indicates that it is possible, by using the options made available in the ritual, to compose an entire rite that has the paschal mystery as its leit-motiv.

I cannot end this section of my study without pointing out the new emphasis placed on the role of the Spirit in the anointing of the sick.[90] To begin with, there is the imposition of hands[91] which has long been the symbol par excellence of the communication of the Holy Spirit. The fact that the imposition is no longer accompanied by an exorcistic formula but is done in silence[92] is a clear indication that we can regard the imposition as having value in and of itself.

In the sacramental formula the grace of the Holy Spirit is expressly petitioned in words containing a brief citation from the teaching of the Council of Trent on the anointing of the sick: "May the Lord . . . help you with the grace of the Holy Spirit."[93]

The prayer accompanying the blessing of the oil is clearly an epicletic prayer in which God is asked to send the Holy Spirit: "Send the Holy Spirit, man's Helper and Friend, upon this oil."[94] And the first of the two alternative prayers to be said after the anointing likewise refers to the Holy Spirit: "Lord Jesus Christ, our Redeemer, by the power of the Holy Spirit, ease the sufferings of our sick brother (sister)."[95]

Let us not forget that the Holy Spirit is the supreme gift of the risen Christ to his Church. We are therefore justified in thinking that the repeated mentions of the Spirit's role in the anointing of the sick indirectly gives the latter a paschal character.

3. The Latin Sacramental Formula and Its Translations

Whenever the Council of Trent,[96] the Constitution on the Sacred Liturgy, and the Dogmatic Constitution on the Church[97] cite 5:15 of the letter of St. James, they use the verb *alleviabit.* This is the reading in the Vulgate, which was used for these citations. The verb *alleviare* is based on *levis* (light, not difficult) and thus means "to lighten; to ease; to comfort *or* console." But many manuscripts of the *Itala*[98] as well as a number of codexes of St. Jerome's Latin translation[99] have the reading *allevabit,* a verb derived from the verb *levare* which can mean "to raise up; to rise; to restore to life."

There are four other passages in the Vulgate in which *allevare* has this meaning.[100] Moreover, in the new critical edition of the Vulgate that was published in 1970, the verb *alleviare* has been replaced by *allevare* in James 5:15.[101] This reading is much closer to the original Greek text which speaks not of consoling the sick person or rendering his physical or moral suffering lighter and more tolerable, but rather of raising him from his bed or restoring him to full life. As a result of this recent change in the Latin translation of the Greek text, the paschal meaning of the passage from James is once again asserted. This observation holds for the text accompanying the anointing of the sick even though all the documents of Vatican II still read *alleviare.*

The commissions established in the various countries for the translation of liturgical texts cannot overlook the difference between *alleviare* and *allevare.* For this reason, the Congregations for the Faith and for Divine Worship will have to examine carefully the translations submitted to them by the episcopal conferences.

In the March 1974 issue, *Notitiae* published five translations which Rome had accepted of the sacramental formula for the anointing of the sick.[102] Only the English version can be regarded as completely satisfactory: "May the Lord who frees you from sin save you and raise you up." The Spanish (*y te conforte*), Italian (*nella sua bontà ti sollevi*), Portuguese (*alivie os teus sofrimentos*) and Dutch (*moge u verlichten*) translations do not capture the full content of *allevare* because they translate it as though it were *alleviare.* The provisional French (*et vous relève*) and German (*richte dich auf und rette dich*) are already closer to the original text. It is to be hoped that the two responsible Roman Congregations and the various translation commissions will pay careful attention to this small word that ought to make clear the paschal meaning of the sacrament.[103]

Cyrille VOGEL

The Cultic Environment
of the Deceased
in the Early Christian Period

Apart from its progressive ritualization, the cultic environment of
the deceased has, in its essentials, remained remarkably unchanged
through the centuries. There is only one exception to this statement:
the funeral banquet which fell into disuse at the end of the early
Christian period and survived only in the form of the *convivia*, or
banquets, that were celebrated on the anniversaries of the martyrs
and saints.

My inquiry is limited to the early Christian period and therefore
to the period prior to the appearance of the earliest *Ordo
defunctorum* that is known to us.[1] The two cutoff points which I
suggest and which determine the chronological limits of the subject
matter are different in kind but seem beyond challenge.

The *terminus ante quem non*, or earliest possible starting point, is
forced upon me here by the state of the documentation and must be
located about 200–250 A.D. No trace remains from the earlier period
of any Christian burial (this includes even the tombs of the apostles

and the martyrs) or any catacomb, private or communal.[2] Nor is there any trace of any liturgical activity whatsoever with regard to the deceased, any funeral inscription, any painting in a cemetery, any Christian sarcophagus.[3] Hippolytus of Rome speaks of places of burial but says nothing of any liturgical rite in connection with them.[4] Tertullian, to whom we owe most of our knowledge about the early Christian conception of the next world, nowhere refers to specifically Christian funeral practices; he is satisfied to put Christians on guard against pagan customs and to recommend that they pray for the dead and offer the eucharist for them.[5] Aristides (ca. 138–147), writing a half century before Tertullian and Hippolytus, seems not even to know of any intercession for the dead.[6]

The second cutoff—the *terminus post quem non* or latest date to be considered—is provided by the work of Gregory I (d. 604). At this period, the vision of the next world that is common throughout our period and must necessarily provide the basis for any interpretation of the funeral rites makes way for an entirely different representation.[7] As the reader will recall, according to the eschatology that prevailed before the beginning of the seventh century, the "soul" of the deceased, or, more accurately, his "double," his likeness, dwelt after death in a place of waiting and in a shadowy state in which he looked forward to the one, final judgment that would take place at the end of time. The *refrigerium interim* ("interim refreshment"), in the broad sense of a provisional, intermediate state, included two "places": the *refrigerium* in the proper sense, which was a place of relative liberation and rest, and the *tormentum*, where the most unfortunate and sinners found themselves in complete deprivation. Neither the *tormentum* nor the *refrigerium* were definitive dwelling places; only in the judgment at the end of time would a definitive determination be made of the fate of both groups. But current ideas of martyrdom meant that the Christian who died from his or her sufferings had already been taken possession of by Christ (Tertullian, *De pudicitia* 22,6: "Christ is in the martyr") and therefore bypassed the *refrigerium* and immediately after his or her sufferings reached eternal blessedness.[8]

Within the chronological period thus defined I shall endeavor to gather together all the gestures, actions, and attitudes with which Christians surrounded their dead. Many elements in this "cultic" environment will already be familiar to everyone. These I shall simply recall here and then concentrate my attention on the sequence of commemorations after a death and on the relations between the *refrigerium* or funeral banquet and the eucharist that was celebrated at the grave.

There were no Christian funeral practices or cult of the dead (or cult even of the martyrs) that were not directly connected with a topographically localized grave. Nor were there any funeral practices not directly connected with an individual deceased person or persons. (The only exception to this second statement seems to have been the Petrine celebration on February 22: The *Natale Petri de cathedra,* which was connected with the *Cara cognatio.*[9]) In some sense or other, the soul of the deceased person dwelt near the grave, at least for a time, or prowled about the immediate area.[10]

Everything suggests that Christians, like their pagan contemporaries, were extremely careful to envelop the dead person with many precisely determined rituals. Above all, by their own efforts, if they had the financial means, or through the agency of a burial club the Christians saw to it that they had a burial place (mausoleum, *cubiculum* [chamber containing graves], *arcosolium* [wall-niche], *loculus* [shelf-tomb], *forma* [floor-tomb, trough-tomb]) or at least a place in the *sepulchra familiaria* or *haereditaria,* and this, if possible, in their native place, close to friends and acquaintances who would provide the care they needed in their existence beyond the grave. All this was done in accordance with civil laws that were very explicit but also very liberal toward all.[11] The thought of remaining unburied was as intolerable to Christians as it was to pagans, and Augustine's remark that burial (or the lack of it) was irrelevant to a peaceful existence in the provisional postdeath world does not seem to have reflected the general outlook of his age.[12]

These practices had their immediate origin in Greco-Roman and Jewish burial rites as practiced in the various countries or regions in which Christians were living, although these Greco-Roman and Jewish rites were pruned of any mythological or erotic elements they might contain.[13] Adaptation to local custom in the matter of funerals was expressly recommended.[14] Here, then, is a quick summary.[15]

The immediate family and friends took care themselves of preparing the body of the deceased for burial, displaying it on a funerary couch, and conveying it to the grave. As a general rule, however, this final step was done by a specialized body of men— *funerarii* (undertakers), *pollinctores* (buriers), *vespillones* (corpse-carriers)—who provided the necessary means and acted as bearers. The *fossores* or *fossarii* or *copiatae* (gravediggers) opened the grave, or cut out the floor-tombs or wall-tombs, or obtained the sarcophaguses, or arranged for the grave chamber or a mausoleum of whatever kind. If the private resources of the deceased or his family were inadequate, a funeral club would acquire ownership of the grave, unless a friendly family would accept the corpse in their own mausoleum. The club also saw to it that the basic laws regarding burials were observed, and in particular that the grave was a *locus purus*, i.e., *locus neque sacer, neque sanctus, neque religiosus* (a place uncontaminated, that is, not consecrated or inviolable or of evil omen), and that it was outside the wall or circumference of the town.

Preparations in the Home of the Deceased

As a general rule the *dies obitus* (day of death) of a Christian was also the *dies depositionis* (day of burial). The documents we have are in agreement (apart from minor variations) in suggesting that the deceased was buried during the twenty-four hours following his or her death.[16] The manner of the *depositio* was interment; there is no evidence (funerary inscription, funerary urn, Christian *columbarium* ["dovecote," i.e., a large chamber with many niches for ash-urns]) to justify the notion that Christians had adopted cremation. Cremation was excluded not for philosophical or dogmatic reasons but, it seems, due to the persistence of Jewish usage.[17]

Family or friends devoutly closed the eyes of the deceased person. Then cries and laments broke out, the purpose being to soothe the dead person by showing him the regret and sorrow of his friends. Those present tore their garments, the women unbound their hair, people struck their heads against the ground. These manifestations were not to be too noisy, lest the rest of the dead person be disturbed or he be incited to return. They called him by name (*conclamatio*) and sang psalms. During this time the body of the dead person was made ready: it was washed and perfumed, chiefly with myrrh, but embalmment was rare.[18] The dead person was then dressed, either very simply in a linen cloth secured by narrow strips, or more richly in a white tunic or official robes, if the person had been someone of importance.

The placing of a crown on the dead person's head was initially disapproved (Tertullian, *De corona* 10,13; Clement of Alexandria, *Paedagogis* II, 73,1; Minucius Felix, *Octavius* 38,3) but soon became a Christian practice (Eusebius, *Historia ecclesiastica* VI, 5,6; Gregory I, *Dialogorum libri* IV, 47, where a white crown descends upon Merulus as a sign of his approaching death).[19]

Exposition of the Dead Person on a Display-bed (Prothesis)

In shape the funerary bed (*feretrum, klinē*) was the bed of antiquity: legs artistically shaped, pillows in a vertical position, and red or violet cushions. The display-bed was used several times over; it was more or less ornate depending on the wealth of the family.

The exposition or lying-in-state took place *in the home* of the deceased person; only later on did the *prothesis* take place in a church or oratory, in imitation (it seems) of monastic custom. Lamps were lit by the display-bed, and incense was burned in them.

Most often, the body was displayed on the *feretrum* for only one day, since the day of death was also the day of interment, as I said above. If death occurred in the evening, burial was postponed to the following day; in this case, a wake was held for the deceased during the night. At times, however, the display of a corpse lasted for three or four days, probably in order to allow relatives to take part in the funeral.[20]

The Funeral Cortege or Procession (Pompa or Exsequiae)

The funeral procession set out for the place of interment during *the day*, probably before sunrise; night interment seems to have been reserved, among Christians, for the poor and the executed.[21] Emperor Julian had tried, unsuccessfully it seems, to make nighttime funerals the general practice. "And so, because sorrow felt at funerals loves privacy and because it is of no concern to the dead whether they are buried by night or by day, it is fitting to free the people as a whole from the sight, so that funerals may be marked by sorrow rather than by pomp and ostentation."[22]

The deceased was carried by hand (rarely placed on a vehicle) on his funerary couch, often covered with a more or less expensive cloth but with the head uncovered. We learn that in the sixth century, liturgical palls were used for this purpose.[23] When the bodies of martyrs were transferred, the palls was torn into strips afterwards in order to provide phylacteries. The deceased might be carried in a wooden coffin, but attestations of this are much less numerous than of transferral on the *feretrum*.[24] The use of coffins became widespread only later on, toward the tenth century.[25]

The procession followed behind the display-bed. The participants, more or less numerous, wore dark-colored clothing; the color white was felt to be offensive on such an occasion.[26]

Despite constant reproof from ecclesiastical writers, the friends of the deceased tore their garments, wrung their hands, and scratched their faces. The women walked with hair unbound, the men with heads veiled. Psalms were sung by all the faithful or by choirs of women who replaced the hired mourners of antiquity. Not infrequently, torches or candles were carried.[27]

The Interment (Depositio)

The mode of burial of the faithful during the early Christian period was always interment and not cremation, as I stated earlier.[28]

At the grave or close by[29] the *feretrum* was laid on the ground. As they had done previously when placing the body on the display-bed, relatives and friends kissed the deceased person on the forehead or the lips. In the case of important persons, a speaker delivered a *laudatio funebris* (eulogy). The body was anointed, and those present addressed him with a final farewell and acclamations.[30] He was placed in the grave on a bed of laurels or aromatic herbs; quicklime was then spread over him, especially when interment took place in a catacomb. The grave hollowed out in the earth was then closed, or the lid of the sarcophagus was sealed, or the *loculus* was closed up with tiles carefully joined and sealed. Some evidence suggests that in the grave the dead person was placed facing east; this funerary orientation, or eastward position, has no direct connection with the eastward position adopted in prayer.

The grave was then covered with flowers or garlands, with roses and violets. A medallion, a piece of gilded glass, or an oil lamp would mark and identify the graves of the most humble; the more well-to-do were careful to have affixed to the grave a funerary inscription which would mention, along with the person's name and the acclamations, the day and month of the *depositio* (rarely the year), with the celebration of anniversaries in mind.

Before departing, the participants gathered near the tomb (if the layout of the cemetery allowed) or close by, sometimes in an appropriate covered place, to share the funeral meal (*refrigerium*). The presence of a bishop or priest, which is mentioned from the beginning of the third century, *remained optional* throughout the entire early Christian period, except when the eucharist was celebrated at the place of the *depositio,* either by itself or independently of the *refrigerium.*[31]

The complex funeral ceremonial which I have briefly sketched did not end on the day of the *depositio;* the part directly connected with the grave (i.e., the funeral banquet and/or the eucharist) was renewed on the third, seventh (or ninth), and thirtieth (or fortieth) day. It was also renewed on the anniversary of the *depositio* as well as on the *Rosalia* (Feast of Roses) or *dies violarum* or *violationis* (days of violets or violet-strewing) and at the time of the funerary *charistia* (family repast).

In the light of what has been said, there are three questions to be answered. What is the meaning of the deeds and gestures which surround the dead person, not only up to the interment but after the *dies depositionis,* and this, theoretically, until the end of time or, in practice, until the dead person has vanished from the memory of the living? More particularly, what is the explanation of the

VOGEL

commemorations at the third, seventh, and thirtieth (or fortieth) day after death? And finally, what is the meaning of the eucharist and the funeral banquet that are celebrated for the deceased?

MEANING OF THE CULTIC ENVIRONMENT OF THE DECEASED
(APART FROM EUCHARIST AND *REFRIGERIUM*)

For lack of a better and more practical word, I have been speaking of the *cultic* environment as a collective term for all the actions, gestures and attitudes thus far described. As a matter of fact, however, apart from the eucharist and the funeral banquet, we are dealing less with a cult and a ritual than with customs and practices with which the survivors surround the remains of one dear to them. The terms "liturgy" and "cult" are used only in an improper sense. For, while two of the three criteria for regarding an action as cultic are verified here (stereotypy and an attitude of prayer in dealing with the divinity), the third is missing, or may be missing. This third element is the participation of the *hierarchy* or of representatives of the religious community as such, and it is missing, or may be missing, unless there is a eucharistic celebration—which *need not be celebrated*—at the funeral or on anniversary days.

Only in a very broad sense, then, can early Christian funeral practices be regarded as "liturgical." The first trace we have of a *funerary cult in the strict sense*—if we limit ourselves to the manuscript tradition—comes in an *ordo defunctorum* of the seventh–eighth century.[32]

What meaning, then, did the "cultic environment" have for the Christians of the day (I leave aside for the moment the eucharistic celebration and the *refrigerium* banquet, if these occurred)? The practices involved were surely meant as expressions of respect for the remains of a human being who had been redeemed and would rise from the dead. Doubtless too, they served to console the living, for whom the care bestowed on the deceased by friends and neighbors was proof of sympathy and regard. Augustine says as much to his friend Paulinus of Nola, though he writes as one somewhat disenchanted with the whole business.[33]

It is also likely that all these practices were a ceremonial intended, though unconsciously or instinctively, to make the living more "secure," to lessen their sense of guilt toward the deceased, and to diminish their own anxiety in the face of death by means of a certain ostentation, even if this were somewhat ridiculous in nature.

But there seems to have been something more. The funeral rites had an apotropaic function, and a somewhat ambiguous one at that: to pacify the deceased and reconcile him or her with the survivors, but also to protect the survivors against the deceased and prevent a return. This defensive function was valued and desired especially when the deceased was an *ahoros* (prematurely dead) or a *biothanatos* (dead at the moment of life)—more accurately a *baiothanatos* (short-lived)—that is, a child who died at the moment of birth. The extraordinary superstitions to which each of the many funerary practices (from the preparation of the body to the procession to the place of burial) gave rise after the early Christian period would be enough by themselves to support this explanation.[34]

One explanatory hypothesis that might quite naturally suggest itself must in fact be eliminated. I mean the hypothesis that the funeral rites would be helps in the struggle between the "soul" of the deceased person and the demons of the air after death.

Now it is quite true that at the moment of passing, that is, *during the final agony* of the believer, just as during the passion of a martyr, the demons unleashed their fury against the Christian.[35] But help for the dying person came from the *Commendatio animae* and not from any funeral rite or rites. On the contrary—and all the available information is unanimous on this point—*after death,* as after the passion of a martyr, a great silence falls.[36] In point of fact, the sources at our disposal with regard to the activity of demons after the death of a Christian are sparse and deal primarily with the martyrs, whose situation is a special one by reason of the eschatological privilege which is theirs. But these texts, such as they are, confirm what I have been saying. Justin, for example, admits, in connection with Psalm 22(21) (which begins, "My God, my God, why have you forsaken me"), vv. 21–22: "Deliver my soul from the sword, my only one from the paw of the dog," etc., that *before* the saving death of Christ the souls of the dead could fall into the hands of the demons; *after* the Savior's death, however, this is no longer true, because the power of the demons has been broken.[37] Tertullian knows nothing of any diabolic activity, whether during the final agony or after death; he speaks only of "the angel who calls the soul" and whose face, either kindly or full of rage, enables the dying person to foretell whether it is *refrigerium* or *tormentum* that he will find in Hades after he has died.[38]

Finally, there is one further detail in the Christian vision of the next world that confirms what I have been saying. It is this, that the Christian Hades, into which "souls" *descend,* is not the dwelling place of demons but is inhabited only by the shades of the dead and by the angels who guard the place.[39] If there are demons in the air they are located in a region *above* the earth's surface, whereas, as everyone knows, the early Christian Hades was located within the cosmos.[40]

VOGEL

From these rare texts (which, in fact, exhaust all that the sources have to tell us), it follows that the cultic environment of the deceased, apart from the *refrigerium* meal and the eucharist, reflects *pietas* in the broad sense and an ambiguous apotropaic activity rather than an effort to facilitate the journey of the soul in the next world.

THE FUNERARY COMMEMORATIONS

As I said earlier, the ceremonial with which Christians surrounded their deceased did not end on the day of interment. Apart from certain periods of the years which the ancient world set aside for funerary commemorations and which were the same for all of the deceased, certain other days directly connected with the *dies depositionis* were devoted to celebrating the memory of the departed, and this always at the tomb or in the immediate vicinity.[41] With regional variations these days were the third, seventh (or ninth), and thirtieth (or fortieth) after the day of interment. This rhythm of three, seven (or nine) and thirty (or forty) is exactly the same as that found in the ancient world and in Judaism.[42]

The question arises of where this sequence originated. Its symbolism is obvious, and it occurs in other places besides the funeral calendars of Christians and pagans. The historicist or mythological explanations offered were created a posteriori, as were the exclusions of one or other date.[43] It seems more in conformity with the truth of the matter to look for the origin of the scheme in certain notions of human physiology. At the end of the last century K. Krumbacher called attention, in a different context, to a number of anonymous documents in Greek that are of the highest interest.[44] In these documents the days for commemorating the deceased are connected both with the formation of the human embryo and with the decomposition of the corpse. Here are the documents which, as far as I know, have never been translated.

1. Common version of the physiological explanation for the commemorations of the dead (ed. K. Krumbacher, pp. 345–47, according to eighteen manuscripts).

"On the origin of a human being and on the reason for the commemorations on the third, ninth and fortieth days.

"On the *third* day the seed that has been introduced into the womb changes into blood and the heart begins to take shape. On the *ninth* day the sperm solidifies into flesh and thickens into marrow. On the *fortieth* day the definitive appearance of a human being takes shape. As with the days, so with the months. In the *third* month the embryo moves in the mother's womb; in the *ninth* month the child is complete and seeks to be born.

"The embryo turns female or male depending on the intensity of the heat of the sperm. If the thickening takes place rapidly, the embryo becomes a male; if the spermatic flow thickens more slowly, the embryo becomes a female. The more slowly the sperm thickens, the more slowly it develops. This is why in cases of abortion a male embryo, even if less than forty days old, is expelled fully formed, whereas a female embryo, even after forty days, resembles a mass of shapeless flesh. [There is an herb that leads to the begetting of boys or girls; a boy or a girl will be born if one drinks an extract of it (before sexual relations).]

"Let us turn now to the decomposition of a human being. When a person dies, on the *third* day he deteriorates and his external appearance is destroyed. On the *ninth* day the entire body decomposes, except for the heart. On the *fortieth* day the heart comes undone, along with the rest. *This is why we celebrate the third, ninth and fortieth days for the deceased.*"

2. *Text giving a physiological and eschatological explanation* (ed. K. Krumbacher, pp. 345–47, reproducing *Parsinus graec. 1140 A,* f. 82r–v).

"On the conception, formation and birth of a human being, and on his death and appearance before the throne of God.

"When a man and a woman have sexual relations, the woman's womb opens and receives the flow of sperm. As soon as the sperm enters the womb, the womb closes and carefully preserves the sperm until the *third* day. On the third day the blood flowing in the woman mixes with the man's sperm, and a kind of mass of flesh is formed which remains in this state until the ninth. On the *ninth* day (this embryo) becomes covered with a skin and remains thus until the fortieth day. On the *fortieth* day a form of fetus is established, and this fetus receives the soul.

"So too in the *third* month the child moves in the mother's womb; in the *ninth* month it is born; and on the fortieth day after its birth it is carried to the temple and sanctified.

"In like manner after death, on the *third* day after death the viscera of the human being—stomach and intestines—liquefy; this is what we call dissolution. On the *ninth* day the flesh decomposes like yeast that has turned rotten; this is what we call corruption. On the *fortieth* day the body falls apart, joint after joint; this is decomposition. There are thus three stages after death: dissolution, corruption and decomposition."

"So too the soul after death remains on earth until the third day. On the third day the angels carry it on high. On the ninth day the soul is separated from the spirits in the air [lit.: the controllers of the air] and the angels. On the fortieth day after death the soul is led before the throne of God where it receives its sentence, which is to dwell in a place apart until the resurrection of the dead. Note, then, that the stages of the human journey take place on the third, ninth and fortieth days.

"*This is why we assign our commemorations of the dead to the same days and months, in accordance with the successive phases of human development.*

"There is this further point to be noted: if the man shows a great deal of ardor in carnal relations and if the woman conceives, the child born will be a boy. If he is less ardent and more cold, the child conceived will be a girl, by reason precisely of this coldness of the man during embraces. On the other hand, if the seed of the man is more abundant than the blood supplied by the woman, the child will follow the paternal line; in the contrary case, the mother's line. This is so in everything."

3. *Text without direct reference to commemorations of the dead* (ed. K. Krumbacher, pp. 352–53, according to *Parsinus graec. 2610,* with variants from three other manuscripts).

"On the birth and death. . . . [*beginning of ms is unintelligible*]

"It is said that the sperm entering the womb is changed on the *third* day into blood and that then the heart is formed; the latter, the first thing to be formed, is also said to be the last to decompose. The principle of numbers is the number "three"; this is very extraordinary, and man in his original formation depends on it.

"On the *ninth* day the flesh is formed and the marrow thickens. On the *fortieth* day the definitive shape is acquired and the embryo can be described as a complete human entity.

"In the *third* month the embryo in the mother's womb receives a soul. In the *ninth* month the fetus is completely constituted and endeavors to leave the maternal womb.

"If the child is of the female sex it is better that it be born at the beginning of the tenth month [i.e., after nine complete months], because nine is the number of woman and of the moon, whereas the tenth month is undoubtedly that of the male.

"Let us put aside for a moment what has been said, and let us ask the physicians why the child to be born will turn out boy or girl. It will be born a boy or a girl depending on the degree of heat; if the heat of the sperm is high, it thickens quickly, and what is formed quickly is a boy. If there is less heat at the moment of the flow of sperm, the child will be a girl, because when the sperm thickens less quickly, the embryo forms more slowly. So true is this that when there is an abortion, and boys not yet forty days old come into the world they are already perfectly formed, whereas under the same conditions girls are still a mass of shapeless flesh.

"(Antigonos says that there are herbs which favor the birth of either girls or boys if the person consumes them, before intimate relations, in three obol's worth of wine.)

"All this has to do with conception and pregnancy. After birth, the swaddling-clothes are removed from the nursling on the third day. On the ninth, the child, acquires strength and stamina. On the fortieth, he learns to smile and recognize his mother."

None of the manuscripts containing these texts predates the eleventh-twelfth centuries. It seems certain, however, that they are closely connected with a passage in Joannes Lydus, *De mensibus* IV, 26 (ed. R. Wünsch, p. 84), which in turn seems to echo physiological teachings that to a great extent predate Christianity.[45] In all cases, the number patterns which the texts seek to explain are much older than the documents themselves.

The physiological and eschatological explanation given in these texts is evidently valid only for the sequence of commemorations as practiced in the East (third, ninth, and fortieth days). It does not fit so neatly with the Western tradition, which is practically unanimous except for the Church of Milan.[46] In the West, the seventh day, with an aposteriori scriptural justification, was systematically opposed to the ninth day as a day of commemoration, and this despite the *novemdiale* or ninth-day funeral offering practiced in ancient Rome.[47] The same holds for the thirtieth day, the justification for which, instead of the fortieth day, was even more labored.[48] The old Gelasian Sacramentary (*Vat. Reg. 316*), which in its present form dates from the middle of the eighth century helped greatly to spread the three, seven, and thirty pattern throughout the whole western part of the Church.[49]

THE EUCHARIST AT THE GRAVE AND THE FUNERAL BANQUET

It can be accepted as probable, though not absolutely certain, that from the middle of the third century on the full eucharist was celebrated near the grave on the third day after burial as well as on the anniversary of burial, *rather than on the day of burial itself.*[50] Explicit testimonies to a funeral eucharist will become numerous and detailed only from the fourth century on.[51]

In all the early Christian texts the third day is presented as more important than the day of interment.[52] The explanations for this peculiarity is to be sought, it seems, in the idea that during the three days following death the soul, which always "prowls" near the grave, is bound in a very special way to the place of burial. Death becomes effective only when the third day is over (resurrection of Lazarus, resurrection of Christ). Recall here the physiological data given in the texts edited by Krumbacher as well as remarks made by secular authors and the ecclesiastical writers.[53]

Tertullian tells us that a commemoration of the dead (very probably with a celebration of the eucharist) took place *also* on the anniversary day which, contrary to pagan usage, was the anniversary day of the person's death (and *depositio*), not of his birth.[54]

In its manner of celebration a funeral eucharist was like a Sunday eucharist, except that the name of the deceased was mentioned.[55] The celebration was therefore a funeral eucharist only *by reason of the place* where it was celebrated, and everyone is aware of the lasting consequences of the connection between grave and eucharist when the grave was that of a martyr.[56] Like every eucharist, a eucharist at a grave was conducted by an ordinated celebrant (bishop or presbyter), even if the participants might be few in number. But, contrary to what was the case when the Eucharistic prayer was celebrated at the tomb of a martyr, the celebrant in other cases did not represent the community as such. Finally, it must be noted that a funeral rite did *not* necessarily *require* the celebration of the eucharist; the latter was always optional.

What meaning did Christians give to a "funeral" eucharist in the period before representations of the next world changed into their modern form? It was certainly a comfort for the deceased person, analogous to that which he derived from the funeral banquet. But in addition the Eucharist tended to express the "communion" of all the faithful, living and dead, in a recall of the last things that was inherent in every eucharist but was felt with particular keenness in these circumstances.[57] If the eucharist included any intercession for the dead, it took the form, in the period with which we are dealing, of a prayer that the person might enjoy greater well-being *within* the provisional Hades.[58]

The funeral banquet (*refrigerium* meal) probably followed upon the eucharist, if the latter was celebrated.[59] This *refrigerium*, which had an almost identical counterpart in the pagan world (apart from the mythological and erotic acclamations), came into use quite early (at Rome around 250; in Africa during the third century, *after* Tertullian) as part of a total funeral rite. Unlike the eucharist, the *refrigerium* did not require that a member of the hierarchy be present.[60]

The literary dossier on the Christian funeral banquet is rather narrow in scope; the documents have to do with Africa, the area of Milan, Verona, and Syria, while there is nothing for the city of Rome.[61]

In this manner the archeological, iconographic, and epigraphic documentation is more important than the literary. From the middle of the third century on, *refrigeria* were celebrated in Rome at the memorial to the apostles Peter and Paul on the Via Appia.[62] Other inscriptions or graffiti leave no doubt about the popularity of *refrigeria* among Christians and about the extent of these geographically.[63]

According to the most recent studies, which are in agreement on this point, all the sacred meals depicted in cemetery frescoes are to be interpreted as representations of funeral banquets; some of these paintings go back to the second half of the third century, while most belong to the fourth century. All of them are irreplaceable sources for our knowledge of the concrete celebration of these banquets.[64]

Being so narrow, the galleries or *cubicula* of the catacombs would hardly lend themselves to a commemorative gathering in the immediate vicinity of the tomb. Above-ground places of cult, but within the cemetery area, were used for gatherings of the relatives and friends of the deceased person. Some of these places have survived from the pre-Constantinian period: the *triclia* (funeral banquet hall) on the Via Appia near the Memoria Apostolorum (present catacomb of St. Sebastian) where visitors had a covered place near the apostles' tombs, a stone bench to sit on, and a cistern of water; these visitors left graffiti recalling the *refrigerium* they had celebrated there.[65] Structures with a similar function were provided at the *Coemeterium Maius* on the Via Nomentana (cubiculum 33), at Domitilla on the Via Ardeatina (in the atrium), and in the catacomb of Priscilla on the Via Salaria (the place called *Capella Graeca*).[66]

If we put together the data provided by the literary texts and the archeological documents, we can reconstruct closely enough the manner in which the Christian funeral banquet was celebrated.

The meal was always set up as close as possible to the grave. It was repeated at regular and fixed intervals (on the commemorative days discussed earlier), or according to the devotion of friends and relatives, starting on the day of interment or, more probably, on the third day after interment. Most often it was celebrated in the evening or at nightfall.[67]

The number of participants varied according to the fame, wealth, and piety of the deceased person's family. More important *refrigeria*

VOGEL

occurred on the *anniversaries of the martyrs,* at which the hierarchy were present.[68]

Since the *refrigerium* was a sacred meal, pagans were excluded from it or at least were supposed to be excluded.[69] The foods and beverages, which were brought from home, together with the cups, were very simple, but also, it seems, of a particular kind: bread, wine, water, porridge of meal or grain, and—judging by indications in the cemeterial frescoes—fish. Meats, vegetables, and fruits were excluded.[70] On the other hand, we cannot say that, given the properly funerary libations, the meals always retained a frugal and austere character.[71] Relatives and friends ate close to the grave when this was on the surface (and not underground) and easily accessible or, more often, in places constructed for the purpose in the cemetery precincts when the graves were underground. The smallness of the catacomb *cubicula* would hardly allow more than five persons to assemble at the same time, and even then only very briefly. The *refrigerium* might be reduced to a draught of wine or a mouthful of bread consumed while standing.[72] But the habitual practice was for the diners to sit on chairs that were either fixed (cut into the rock) or movable, or to stretch out on benches which had the shape of an uncial sigma (whence the name "sigmatic" meals for the funeral banquets) and were covered with padding and cushions.[73]

The deceased person was regarded as taking part in the *refrigerium* in his honor.[74] As the frescoes and the bas-reliefs on the sarcophaguses show, a place was assigned to him at the end of the sigmatic table. Often, when the character of the spot allowed it, a votive funeral *cathedra* (chair) gave his presence a material dimension; about twenty of these chairs have survived because they were cut out of the volcanic rock in the underground cemeteries, but all the movable chairs have disappeared.[75]

The deceased person was explicitly invited to the banquet; the formulas of invitation have been preserved in many variants on the funerary slabs (over the graves), on the gilt glasses or on the cemeterial frescoes. For example, before the *compotatio* (drinking together): *"pie, zeses* ("drink and you will live" = "to your health"), "ave, vale, bene refrigera," ("hail, farewell, enjoy the banquet"), "refrigeret tibi Deus; in refrigerio; esto in refrigerio; refrigera cum spirita sancta" ("May God refresh you; in refreshment; be refreshed; enjoy refreshment with the Holy Spirit").[76]

Some of these acclamations containing the terms *refrigerium* and *refrigerare* can be interpreted as wishes for well-being in the next world, but in most instances they have a very realistic meaning, especially when accompanied by expressions that refer to the pouring of wine: *Agape da calda! Irene misce mihi!* ("Agape, give me some warm wine! Irene, mix some for me!").[77] To be compared with such appeals are other acclamations—"Pax tecum; in pace; in bono" ("Peace be with you; In peace; In blessing")—which refer both to *refrigerium*-as-rest and *refrigerium*-as-meal.[78]

Toward the end of the early Christian period, Jacob of Sarug (d. 521) offers us his reflections on the *conclamatio mortuorum* (joint invocation of the dead). He speaks of a banquet but seems to be thinking more of the eucharist than of a *refrigerium*:

"Organize a banquet and invite your dead to it, in order that they may come to the oblation which is a source of strength and support for all souls. . . . Do not call upon the dead person near his grave, for he will not hear you; for the time being he is in effect absent. Seek him rather in the house of mercy [i.e., the place of worship] where the souls of all the dead are gathered, for it is here that they draw life in order to console themselves."[79]

The portion of the dead person is set on the table in the *triclia* or on the grave (in the case of solid food) or, in the case of the wine, it is poured over the grave or into the sarcophagus through a libation tube.[80]

Despite the symbolic libations to the deceased, the funeral banquets were genuine meals to satisfy hunger, or could serve as such; they were joyful and relaxed, and excesses were not infrequent.[81] They habitually ended with a distribution of food or coins to the poor.[82]

It is easier to determine the purpose of the banquet for the deceased than it is to determine the purpose of the eucharist that was celebrated at the tomb. The atmosphere of joy and peace in which the banquet was eaten (in arbors or in *triclia* that were like taverns), the hidden but real presence of the deceased person, the acclamations with which he was greeted, and the wishes addressed to him: these leave no doubt that the banquet was regarded as procuring for the "pale double" or shade or "soul" of the dead person a consolation and refreshment, understood very realistically as a true restoration, and, if God willed, a transfer of the person from *tormentum* to the provisional place of peace and rest in the Christian Hades.

There is a wonderful episode in the *Passio Perpetuae et Felicitatis* that gives us a concrete insight into the precarious situation of the shades in the Christian Hades and into the possible effects on them of the commemorations organized in their behalf:

"*Episode of Dinocrates* [*narrative of Vibia Perpetua.*] Some days later when we were all at prayer, suddenly while praying I spoke out and uttered the name Dinocrates. I was surprised; for the name had never entered my mind until that moment. And I was pained when I recalled what had happened to him. At once I realized that I was privileged to pray for him. I began to pray for him and to sigh deeply for him before the Lord. That very night I had the following vision.

"[*The tormentum.*] I saw Dinocrates coming out of a dark hole, where there were many others with him, very hot and thirsty, pale and dirty. On his face was the wound he had when he died. Now Dinocrates had been my brother according to the flesh; but he had died horribly of cancer of the face when he was seven years old, and his death was a source of loathing to everyone. [*Dinocrates was an ahoros.*]

"Thus it was that for him I made my prayer. There was a great abyss between us: neither could approach the other. Where Dinocrates stood there was a pool full of water; and its rim was higher than the child's height, so that Dinocrates had to stretch himself up to drink. I was sorry that, though the pool had water in it, Dinocrates could not drink because of the height of the rim. Then I woke up, realizing that my brother was suffering. But I was confident that I could help him in his trouble; and I prayed for him every day until we were transferred to the military prison. . . .

"[*The refrigerium.*] On the day we were kept in chains, I had this vision shown to me. I saw the same spot that I had seen before, but there was Dinocrates all clean, well dressed, and refreshed (*refrigerans*). I saw a scar where the wound had been; and the pool that I had seen before now had its rim lowered to the level of the child's waist. And Dinocrates kept drinking water from it [*Greek version:* the water flowed without ceasing], and there above the rim was a golden bowl full of water. And Dinocrates drew close and began to drink from it, and yet the bowl remained full. And when he had drunk enough of the water, he began to play as children do. Then I awoke, and I realized that he had been delivered from his suffering."[83]

The story told here by Vibia Perpetua is a perfect illustration of this sentence from Tertullian: "For she prays for his soul, and asks for him refreshment during the interim and a share in the first resurrection [= the resurrection of the dead at the end of time], and she offers the sacrifice each year on the anniversary of his falling asleep" (*De monogamia* 10).

Only a short conclusion is needed. On the whole, the funeral practices and customs of Christians were the same as those of pagans, including the funeral banquet; but mythological and erotic elements were eliminated, as was the disillusioned skepticism that appears in some ancient funerary inscriptions. For reasons given earlier, I would hesitate to describe these practices as "liturgical" in the strict sense during the early Christian period. The things that were specifically Christian were, first, prayer of the living for the dead, which is attested from at least the year 200 on but for which no formularies have survived; second, the celebration of the eucharist, which was always optional and was conducted in more or less close topographical connection with the grave of the simple believer. This topographical link between grave and eucharist is found in the cult of the martyrs, once this developed (ca. 250). This cult, as we know, was simply a more solemn cult of the dead and was liturgical in the proper sense, by reason of the presence of the community as such and therefore of the bishop and clergy. However, the eschatological privilege which the martyr was recognized as having radically modified the meaning of this particular cult and differentiated it from the general cult of the dead.

In all other cases besides that of the martyrs, the prayer and the eucharist or *refrigerium* meal had for their purpose, during the period I have been considering, simply to comfort the deceased person during his or her perilous and provisional existence in the next world and to win a more pleasant place of rest as he or she awaited the one judgment at the end of time.

Georges WAGNER

The Death and Funeral of a Martyr According to a Liturgical Document of the Nineteenth Century

The purpose of this paper is to draw attention to two liturgical offices composed at the end of the eighteenth or beginning of the nineteenth century. One is an office of ecclesial intercession for a new martyr during the time of his suffering; the other is an office for the funeral of a new martyr.

The two offices were published at Venice in 1819 in a volume entitled *Neon Leimōnarion* and republished at Athens in 1873 with the blessing of the Holy Synod of the Church of Greece. In our own day, in 1971, Professor John Foundoulis, liturgist of Thessalonika, has published a special edition of these two offices with a valuable detailed introduction.[1]

The two offices were from the pen of a priest and monk, Nicephorus, of the island of Chios, who died in 1821 and is venerated by the Orthodox Church as one of its saints. Nicephorus proves himself in these offices to be one of the more remarkable hymn writers of the Orthodox Church in recent centuries. These two akolouthias are an important document of the spiritual renewal of the Greek Church at the end of the eighteenth and beginning of the nineteenth century, a renewal associated with the names of St. Nicodemus the Hagiorite, St. Macarius of Corinth, Athanasius of Paros, and the author of these offices, St. Nicephorus of Chios.

Those active in this spiritual movement were not satisfied with gathering up the treasures of the past. One characteristic of the movement was the fostering of a fuller and more lively eucharistic life; another was its awareness of the importance of the new martyrs whom the Orthodox Church had had throughout the period since the fall of Byzantine Empire. The two liturgical offices which I shall be studying bear witness to a deeper insight into the mystery of the death of martyrs, but at the same time the formularies satisfied real needs in the ecclesial life of the age.

I

The prayers for a martyr during his sufferings remind us of the prayers which the primitive Church at Jerusalem offered for Peter the Apostle while he was in prison, as we read in Acts 12:5: "So Peter was kept in prison; but earnest prayer for him was made to God by the Church."

In its external form the office is a liturgical service constructed on the model of the well-known hymnographic canon: *Pollois sunechomenos peirasmois* ("Surrounded by many dangers"). The faithful on earth come together and pray in union with the heavenly powers and all the saints for a Christian who is imprisoned and suffering. The canon which St. Nicephorus composed is addressed "to the holy, consubstantial and indivisible Trinity." For it is the Holy Trinity whose name is being confessed and glorified by the new martyr. Each ode of the canon has four troparia: the first addressed to God the Father, the second to God the Son, the third to God the Holy Spirit, and the fourth to all three hypostases of the Holy Trinity. Before the troparia of the opening odes of the canon, the refrain is repeated: "God, Holy Trinity, have mercy on your servant." From the fourth ode on, the refrain changes to: "God, Holy Trinity, help your servant." Finally, from the seventh ode on, it is "God, Holy Trinity, grant strength to your servant."

Here, to serve as an example, is the text of the first, fourth, and seventh odes:

First Ode
  "God, Holy Trinity, have mercy on your servant.
  "Lord, friend of men, God the almighty, all-powerful and

sovereign Father, through the intercession of all the saints grant strength to your suffering servant.

"God, Holy Trinity, have mercy on your servant.

"Christ our God, who bore the first witness under Pontius Pilate, through the intercession of the angels and the prayers of the prophets and martyrs, grant strength to your suffering servant.

"Glory to the Father and to the Son and to the Holy Spirit.

"God, heavenly King, divine Spirit of Truth, through the holy intercession of the martyrs and ascetics, grant strength to your suffering servant.

"Now and for ever. . . .

"Trinity in Unity, Father, Son and divine Spirit, one Strength and one Power, through the supplications of the holy Mother of God grant strength to your suffering servant."

Fourth Ode

"God, Holy Trinity, help your servant.

"Almighty Father, grant strength to the mortal weakness of this man who in his sufferings sings to you: 'O Thou who art almighty, glory to your power!'

"God, Holy Trinity, help your servant.

"Christ, friend of man, render invincible this man who desires to give himself to you as a spotless sacrifice and who sings: 'Glory to your power!'

"Glory to the Father. . . .

"Spirit-Consoler, grant the consolation of your grace to this man who is greatly tested because of his devotion and who sings: 'Glory to your power!'

"Now and for ever. . . .

"Almighty Lord, Father, Word and Spirit, grant strength to this man who is suffering for the faith and who sings: 'Glory to your power!' "

Seventh Ode

"God, Holy Trinity, grant strength to your servant.

"O Father without beginning, utter Unity and hidden Foundation, strengthen in the faith your suffering servant who sings to you from the heart: 'Blessed are you, God of our fathers!'

"God, Holy Trinity, grant strength to your servant.

"Heedless of torture and caring nothing for his life, your servant, O Christ, has determined to suffer and die with joy, while singing: 'Blessed are you, Creator, God of our Fathers!'

"Glory to the Father. . . .

The Death and Funeral of a Martyr

"All-holy Spirit, who strengthens the souls of the martyrs, by your presence give strength to your suffering servant who sings: 'Blessed are you, God of our fathers!'

"Now and for ever. . . .

"Indivisible Trinity, through the prayers of the martyrs, prophets and apostles, give power to this man who is closely imprisoned because of his limitless love for you and who sings: 'Blessed are you, God of our Fathers!' "

Before the seventh ode, a reading from the gospel of St. Luke is inserted:

"The Lord said: . . . Do not fear those who kill the body, and after that have no more that they can do . . . Every one who acknowledges me before men, the Son of man also will acknowledge before the angels of God. . . . And when they bring you before the synagogues and the rulers and the authorities, do not be anxious how or what you are to answer or what you are to say; for the Holy Spirit will teach you in that very hour what you ought to say" (Lk 12:2–12).

After the gospel there is a special prayer "for one who is suffering for the holy faith." Athanasius of Paros composed the text of this prayer.

The choice of the gospel pericope and the content of the prayer just mentioned are connected with the personal tragedy of the life of the new martyrs: many of them were Christians who had formerly denied Christ and for one reason or another accepted the faith of Islam, but who later repented and made up for their lapse by confessing Christ officially before the civil authorities. After such a confession they had to suffer death as apostates from Islam. This is why the prayer refers to the repentance of St. Peter and that of the great and holy martyr James the Persian (commemorated on November 27); both of these saints are considered models of repentance after a denial of faith in Christ.

II

Sometimes, while prayers were being offered for someone suffering in prison, news of his death would arrive. Anguish then changed into a sense of triumph as the name of the new martyr was for the first time included among the names of the other saints.[2] Ecclesial veneration of the new martyr began immediately after his death and prior to any official approval of such veneration by higher ecclesiastical authorities. And like the Christians of second-century Smyrna after the martyrdom of St. Polycarp, so the Greek Christians of the eighteenth and early nineteenth centuries did everything they could to obtain the martyr's remains and give them suitable burial.

None of the funeral offices in the liturgical books could worthily serve for the burial of a martyr. It was for this reason that St. Nicephorus of Chios composed a special service for the funeral of a new martyr, taking as his model Matins for the great and holy Saturday before Easter, or in other words, taking the burial of Christ himself as a model. The new office is thus a copy, an imitation, but it is a felicitous and well-justified one, because the death of a martyr is of its nature an imitation of the death of Christ and a special form of union with him. How could the Church more clearly proclaim the victory which Christ himself had won in the human weakness of the martyr, and the Paschal radiance that bursts forth after the death of the saints who have died with Christ?

Like other funeral rites, the office for the funeral of a martyr begins with Psalm 90: "He who shelters under the protection of the Most High." There follows the singing of the Alleluia in the fourth mode, with the psalm verses commonly used in the offices of martyrs: "God is wonderful in his saints. . . . The saints who are in his land. . . ." (Ps 67:36; 15:3), and the troparion which is also commonly used for martyrs: "In his combat, O Lord, your martyr . . . received an incorruptible crown from your hand, our God."

After this introduction the singing of Psalm 118 is begun: "Blessed those whose way is blameless." As in Matins for the Great Saturday, the verses of the psalm alternate with troparia (*enkōmia*). In the office for a new martyr, the psalm is notably abbreviated: only three sets of twelve verses of it are sung. The author has chosen those verses in which the divine law is called "testimonies" and in which the psalmist speaks of a fearless confession before the powers of this world. "I have spoken of your testimonies (*ta marturia*) before kings, and I have not been ashamed." In our daily offices Psalm 118 serves to express an unshakable devotion to our faith; here it has become an expression of the martyr's love as manifested in a fearless confession and the sacrifice of his or her life.

As in the Great Saturday office, the singing of Psalm 118 begins with a troparion in honor of the Savior's burial: "O Christ, you who are Life were placed in the tomb, and the armies of angels were astonished as they praised your condescension."

There follows a series of troparia in honor of the new martyr; they were composed by St. Nicephorus and all follow the same rhythm and melody. As I said above, these troparia, which I shall reproduce here, are sung alternately with verses of the psalm.

"We, the faithful, are gathered to give glory and praise to Christ, who filled his martyr with strength.

"We exalt you, O Christ, Giver of life, for you glorified your servant in his struggle with enemies visible and invisible.

"In the past the deaths of the saints were greeted with tears, affliction and sadness, but now we rejoice with a great joy.

"The death of the martyrs who suffered for you, O Christ, is truly a falling asleep and a joyful departure to you.

"We sing hymns for your departure, O martyr, with joyful souls and hearts, and with faith we glorify your sufferings.

"You came fearlessly, O martyr, before the tribunal of the wicked, and fortified by the Savior's cross you confessed Christ.

"Now your desire is fulfilled, for you have shared the sufferings of Christ. Rejoice, therefore, and be triumphant with him.

"Today you enter the rich dwellings of the heavenly kingdom; rejoice, O blessed one, with the choirs of saints.

"The choirs of martyrs and the assembly of the saints have won a new member in you, O martyr, and those who dwell on earth have acquired an intercessor before Christ.

"You reached the end of this temporal life, but you won an endless life and now you live in Christ for ever.

"By your prayers before God, O martyr, protect those who have been present at your funeral service, and preserve them from all temptations.

"Earth covers your body, O martyr, but endless light has welcomed your spirit into the dwellings of the just.

"Glory to the Father and to the Son and to the Holy Spirit . . .

"Father, Word, and Spirit, Trinity in Unity, show your servants mercy through the prayers of the new martyr.

"Now and for ever. . . .

"We call you blessed, Theotokos most pure. In his sufferings the martyr proclaimed you true Mother of God."

After this a hymn from the Great Saturday is sung: "It is right that we should glorify you, Giver of life, who stretched out your hands on the cross and broke the power of the enemy."

At this point a second series of psalm verses and troparia begins. Of this I shall give but two examples: "It is right to exalt you with songs and hymns, glorious new martyr, for you died with Christ and now live with him. . . ." "You have fallen sleep, for the death of the saints is a sleep; but let your eye, which does not sleep, look upon those who sing your praises. . . ."

Finally, the choirs sing a third hymn from the Great Saturday: "All generations sing a hymn to your burial, O my Christ."

At this point the final series of psalm verses and troparia is begun. In this series St. Nicephorus, the hymnographer, has been inspired by what St. Paul says of his own coming martyrdom: "I have fought the good fight . . ." (2 Tm 4:7–8).

"All generations call you blessed, martyr of the Lord.

"You fought fearlessly and were worthy to receive a crown from the hand of the Lord.

"You fought in accordance with the law and finished the course of witness to God.

"You kept the faith and glorified your creator, O martyr wise in the ways of God.

"The crown of justice is already prepared for you, O martyr.

"The choirs of angels and the assemblies of men sing the praises of your struggle.

"Today heaven opens in glory; come, then, O martyr, and enter in!

"The divine choirs of the martyrs come to meet you, because you too died for Christ.

"Rejoice throughout eternity with the choirs of the martyrs, O martyr and soldier of Christ.

"Be the delegate before God of all of us, an intercessor for those who venerate you.

"Deliver from all dangers this city that offers you its veneration.

"Forget not those who have been accounted worthy to serve you on earth."

In the office for the Great Saturday, the singing of Psalm 118 is followed by troparia for the resurrection, beginning with the words: "The choir of angels was astonished." St. Nicephorus composed similar troparia for the funeral of a martyr. Here is the text in slightly abbreviated form:

"Now the choirs of angels and the assembly of all the saints surround your soul at the altar, O martyr, and rejoice together as they glorify Christ who sent you strength and gave you a crown.

"In place of perfumes, we on earth offer you our hymns and our love, and now with devotion we bury your body. . . .

"Very openly you confessed Christ as Son of God and as God the Word before wicked judges, O blessed one, and by your sacrifice you received the life that does not grow old but remains through eternity. . . .

"We adore the Father and his Son and the Holy Spirit, the Holy Trinity for which you did fearless battle, O martyr, and from which you have received the crown of incorruptibility.

"O Virgin, the glorious martyr whose death has led to immortality has confessed you as Mother of the Savior for the salvation of the human race, as Mother of him who gives life, as truly Mother of God."

Then comes the singing of the prokimenon that is common to the feasts of the martyrs and is taken from Psalm 91: "The just man will grow like a palm tree" (91:13). The gospel for the feasts of martyrs is read (Lk 21:12–19). Our office ends with stichera that are sung during the veneration of the martyr's relics. From among these hymns I shall cite two which are especially noteworthy from the theological standpoint:

"When Christ comes from heaven with his holy angels in order to judge the world, and when your body too is raised up in incorruptibility, as it is written, and in glory—this same body which we now bury in the earth as a mortal thing—then, blessed one, remember your servants, we pray you, and make the Judge be merciful to all of us.

"The earth takes your holy body into depths, and heaven on high has welcomed your spirit into the light, O martyred one, and into the holy dwellings where it rejoices with the choirs of the saints. But both will be united again in the resurrection of the dead and glorified together throughout eternity."

The beauty of these texts is doubtless obscured in translation. But with the original Greek before us it is difficult not to feel profound respect for the spiritual vigor to which the hymns bear witness. Christian history and especially the history of the Christian East has of course never ceased to be, in one way or another, a history of martyrs. But contemporaries have not always shown such a profound awareness of the martyrs' deaths as St. Nicephorus shows in these two liturgical offices.

Douglas WEBB

The Funeral Services
of the Nestorian Church

The Nestorian Church possesses a comprehensive collection of funeral services, ranging from the burial of a patriarch to the burial of an unbaptized child. In common with the other Eastern Churches, the Nestorians make a distinction between those whom they designate "the sons of the Church" (*bnay 'edtha*), that is, the clergy, and those whom they call "the sons of the world" (*bnay 'alma*), that is, the laity. It is this distinction, as we shall see later, that accounts for one important difference between the structures of the services for the clergy and those for the laity.

The manuscripts which contain the Offices for the Burial of the Clergy can be divided into four classes. The first class consists of those most comprehensive manuscripts containing the Office for the Burial of a Patriarch, with ten kathismata (Syr. *mawtbe*).[1] The oldest manuscript in this category would seem to be British Museum ADD. 17260, which may be dated from the twelfth to the thirteenth centuries. Slightly later is the British Museum ADD. 14706, which is of the thirteenth century. It has only seven of the kathismata.[2] The second category consists of those manuscripts which contain the rites for all the degrees of the clergy, including bishops, but with only five kathismata. The oldest of these is Mardin Diarbekir 35.11.[3] The third category is that of manuscripts containing the rites for all the ranks of the clergy, exclusive of bishops, in which the services for each rank are not separated. These, again, contain five kathismata. The oldest of this type of manuscript is Cambridge University Library ADD. 2044, which is dated 1541.[4] Finally, there are those manuscripts which contain the rites for the burial of priests and deacons, each written separately, and which contain five kathismata. The earliest manuscript of this class is Mardin-Diarbekir 35.14, which is dated 1696. Another example is the Cambridge University Library manuscript ADD. 1986, dated 1759.[5] In addition to these manuscripts containing the Offices for the Burial of the Clergy, there are others which contain the funeral services for the laity.[6]

The history of the development of the rites is not easy to trace, although some of the hymns which occur in them are also to be found in a Jacobite funeral collection of 823, and are there attributed to St. Ephraem.[7] One Syriac author has much to say upon the subject, the Pseudo-George of Arbel (ninth–tenth centuries), whose *Interpretatio Officiorum Ecclesiae* contains a section on the burial offices.[8] From what he says, it may be deduced that some changes occurred as a result of the reforms of Isho'yabh III (647–659). Apart from that, however, there is little reason to suppose that the offices have changed much over the years, and certainly the printed books show very little variation from the manuscripts in their texts. Like the other services of the Nestorian Church, the funeral rites are distinguished by the number of archaic features which they contain, and this applies not only to their structure, but also to the theology which finds expression in them.

Broadly speaking, the Nestorian funeral services may be divided into four parts in the case of the laity, and five in the case of the clergy. First, there is the ritual washing of the body. During the washing, a kind of vigil office is recited in the house. The third part of the office consists of the procession from the house to the cemetery, and finally there are the prayers and ceremonies at the grave site. In the case of the clergy, however, the procession does not proceed directly to the cemetery, but to the church, where there are prayers and ceremonies, including a celebration of the eucharist.[9] It is unusual for the bodies of laity to be taken into church, although masses are celebrated on their behalf on the most suitable day following the death, usually the next Sunday or an adjacent saint's day. This is the most important difference between the rites for the

WEBB

clergy and the rites for the laity. The reason for the difference is to be found in the distinction made in the titles of the services already mentioned, the distinction between the "sons of the Church" and the "sons of the world". The funeral services are conceived as a kind of leave taking of this world, and a setting forth upon the journey to the real life of the world to come. The layperson has, as it were, lived life in the world, and it is therefore thought appropriate that on the way to the cemetery he or she should take leave of the world on coming out of the village in which his or her life was spent. The clergy, on the other hand, "the sons of the Church" have lived all their lives in the service of the Church and therefore their bodies are brought to the church in which they ministered, and there they take their leave.

One of the most interesting features of the funeral rites is the wealth of scriptural allusion which they contain, a feature which they share with all the Nestorian services. This is true, not only of the actual psalmody in which the rites abound, and of the use of appropriate verses from the psalms as introductions to the various anthems, but also, as we shall see, to the content of the anthems themselves. As might be expected, there are constant references to the resurrection of Christ, the hope and ground of our own resurrection. The fall of Adam, the raising of Lazarus, and the parable of the ten virgins also figure in the hymns and anthems. Here is an example from one of the hymns towards the close of the service:

"The voice which summoned Lazarus and the daughter of Jairus will call thee also, and will raise thee, and make thee to stand upon the right hand."

The whole outlook in the funeral rites is one of hope, the sure and certain hope of the resurrection to eternal life through Jesus Christ. This is emphasized by the constant use, at the conclusion of the prayers, of the formula, "Ruler of the two worlds which thou hast made, Lord of our death and of our life." It is a reminder of the fact that God rules, both here and hereafter, and "our life" in this context surely means "the life of the world to come." Death is regarded as the consequence of the fall of Adam, whose sin infected the whole human race that came after him, but through the passion, death and resurrection of Jesus Christ humankind is redeemed and brought to new life in the heavenly kingdom. An example of this line of thought is seen in the following quotation:

"And when we had been corrupted through the transgression of the commandment by Adam, the head of the human race, who transgressed the commandment, thou didst humble thyself in thy love, and didst exalt our dust by thy holy manifestation."

There is a complete recognition of our sinfulness and reiterated pleas for mercy and forgiveness. The hope of the future life is seen to rest upon God's merciful forgiveness and on what Christ has done for the human race, rather than upon any human merits. The future life is described in terms of biblical imagery—"Christ's kingdom," "the kingdom of heaven," "the kingdom above," "the heavenly bridal chamber," and "the bridal chamber of light."

We will turn now to a detailed examination of the Office for the Burial of a Priest, relying for the text upon the manuscript Cambridge University Library ADD. 1986.[10] The manuscripts open with detailed instructions for the washing of the body. This is a reflection of the reverence, inherited from the Jews, which the Christians have always shown toward the bodies of their dead. According to the modern rituals, the deceased shall be dressed "in white garments as on the day of his wedding."[11] In the case of the clergy, it is laid down that "in that Order in which he approached the altar in his life, in the same Order shall they carry him to the grave," which seems to imply that the clergy are buried in the vestments appropriate to their rank. These directions reflect the note of hope which pervades the service. For a Christian, death means a removal from this world of suffering and sin into the life of the resurrection, and therefore, as the Pseudo-George of Arbel remarks, "we attend the dead with hymns, as though conducting them to a banquet."[12]

While the body is being washed, a kind of vigil office is recited. This consists of a number of kathismata (*mawt'bha* is the Syriac term), the number varying according to whether the deceased was a layperson or a cleric. The Pseudo-George of Arbel says that two kathismata were recited over a layman, and in the case of the clergy the number was increased by one each time according to the rank of the deceased. Thus one kathisma was added for a monk, two for a deacon, and three for a priest. Furthermore, it may be inferred from what he says that these additional kathismata were recited in church in his time. The later manuscripts, however, state quite clearly that all the kathismata were recited in the house.[13] As we have already noted, some manuscripts prescribe ten kathismata for a patriarch, and the Pseudo-George of Arbel confirms this.[14] Other manuscripts prescribe five kathismata for a bishop, while Cambridge ADD. 1986 prescribes five for a priest (and despite what the Pseudo-George says) five also for a deacon. It is highly probable that these differences are the result of developments after the time of the

Pseudo-George of Arbal, for the manuscripts are much later. It may also be pointed out that at least some of the kathismata are the same whatever the rank of the deceased. According to the manuscripts, and also to the printed Urmi edition, three kathismata are recited for a man or a woman, and also for a baptized child. In the case of an unbaptized child, however, it is laid down that if he is not more than ten days old he shall be buried by the women. The rubrics add, however, that if "a child shall live to be six months old without receiving baptism, and his mother shall have partaken of the life-giving Body and Blood, which shall have mingled with the milk which he has sucked, one kathisma shall be said over him, and, in consideration of his parents, one priest shall attend his funeral."

The structure of the kathismata for clergy and laity alike is the same. They consist of a prayer, the shurraya (the word means literally, "beginning" or "exordium," and in this case, a portion of a psalm), a prayer, a further shurraya which introduces the anthems, another prayer, the subbaḥa (a few verses of a psalm; the word itself means "praise"), a prayer, and finally two or three hymns. In the case of the laity, however, there appears to be no shubbaḥa. According to the Pseudo-George of Arbel, whose commentary on the rites of the Nestorian Church is characterized by the number of symbolic, if somewhat fanciful, interpretations it contains, the shurraye of the first kathisma symbolize the twofold nature of man, "that he consists of soul and body," while the anthems declare his unity. The theme of the prayers in all the kathismata is almost entirely the glorification of God, as the following example shows:

"We confess thy grace which created us, and we praise thy compassion which cares for us, and we worship thy greatness which makes our race glad in the two worlds which thou hast created, Lord of our death and of our life."

The hymns and anthems are of two kinds, one setting forth the theology of death and resurrection; the other consisting of a few stanzas sung by a cantor, with a refrain for the chorus. Dr. W. F. Macomber suggests that this latter type of hymn is a kind of liturgical substitute for professional female mourners.[15]

In the first kathisma for a priest, the shurraye are Psalms 20:1–5 and 43:3-end.[16] The general progression of thought in the anthems seems to be from the declaration of the sinful nature of man to a proclamation of the resurrection of Christ. The former is exemplified in the following:

"Have mercy upon me, O God. Have mercy upon me, O Lord my God because I have sinned against thee and have not done the things that I wished to do: but the evil I hate I have committed. And I love repentance, but lusts war against me; and I rejoice in thy commandments, but I am vanquished by sin. Have pity upon my soul, thou lover of men, and rescue me from the sea of sins that are troubling me."

The proclamation of the resurrection of Christ is exemplified in the following:

"Come and hearken. Mary saw the Lord when he had risen in glory from the tomb, and she spake with him and said, 'Show me where is my Lord and my God, for my soul hath gone forth in desire of him, that I may delight in seeing him again.' "

Finally, in the Gloria comes a hint of our own resurrection:

"O King Christ, our Savior, raise me up in the day of thy appearing, and make me to stand at thy right hand with the righteous who are well pleasing before thee, and who believe and trust in thy cross, that with them I may inherit everlasting life."

The final psalm of praise, the shubbaḥa, is Psalm 116:1–5, and this is followed by a prayer and three hymns.

The shurraye of the second kathisma are Psalms 88:1–9 and 88:10–end,[17] with the following prayer between them:

"May thy grace, O my Lord, shine upon us when thy merciful justice judges us, and forgive our offenses and our sins, O Lord of our death and of our life."

The theme of the anthems is the fall of Adam, and the subsequent redemption of the human race by Christ. The following quotation will serve to illustrate the point:

"Incline, O Lord. O Son, the Christ, who didst come for our salvation that thou mightest renew the image of Adam that had been corrupted, and didst put on our body, and didst give encouragement for the resurrection of the dead: pardon thy servants by thy grace in the day of thine appearing."

There are continual pleas for our pardon, for example,

"The High Priest of our praise, Jesus our great King, pardon our offenses through thy Body and Blood."

In this kathisma also there is particular reference to the priestly office. The subbaḥa which is used for both priest and deacon is

Psalm 123:1–3a, and it is followed by three hymns which bring the kathisma to a close. The first of these hymns reads as follows:

"*Antiphon.* Go forth, O noble Priest, earthly messenger. Go, hold fast the befitting blessing in Abraham's bosom.
Verses. The everlasting Kingdom and the spiritual blessings are kept for thee in the becoming dwelling place with the appointed and chosen priests. The hosts of the house of Hananiah, and Aaron the priest, and Zachariah receive thee immediately in the habitations not made with hands."

The tone of the third kathisma is somewhat different from those which preceded it. The shurraye are Psalms 139:1–14 and 34:18–end.[18] The anthems are best described as "apocalyptic" in outlook, and their subject is the Last Judgment, and the joys in store for the righteous and the punishment reserved for the wicked. It is in the final two anthems, the "*Gloria patri*" and the "Everlasting" that this aspect is most marked, and these two sections can best be described as a lengthy apocalypse in the tradition of Jewish and early Christian apocalypses. The *Gloria patri* sets out a vision of God surrounded by his spiritual hosts as the judgment proceeds. The "everlasting" gives a picture of the dissolution of the world. The subbaha is Psalm 130:1–7, and the concluding prayer reads:

"Raise up the dead, O Lord, in thy compassion, and make them to stand at thy right hand, and clothe them with befitting glory in thy kingdom with the just and with the righteous who are pleasing to thee, O merciful One, who forgives the offenses and sins, Lord of our death."

The fourth and fifth kathismata, the additional kathismata for priests and deacons, are similar to the preceding ones. The shurraye for the fourth kathisma, for both priests and deacons, are Psalms 102:1–12 and 102:16–22. The anthems deal with the themes of sin and its forgiveness, and emphasize the blessings which follow the observance of God's commandments. The last two anthems contain between them twenty-six verses arranged alphabetically. The shubbaha is Psalm 123:1–3, and the kathisma is brought to a close by three hymns. Here is a verse from one of the hymns:

"Stand up, O Priest, and look upon thy disciples who are gathered together to attend upon thy body. May the Lord whom thou has served all the years of thy life bless thee in the bridal chamber of light."

The fifth kathisma is somewhat longer than the others and contains a number of alternative anthems. Its contents, however, are similar to those of the preceding kathismata. The shurraye are Psalms 146:1–6 and 34:16–end. In this kathisma, some of the introductory verses to the anthems are taken from scriptural sources other than the Psalter, as the following example shows:

"Let the priests, the ministers of the Lord, weep between the porch and the altar, and let them say, Spare thy people O Lord. Who does not grieve that our sins are many, and our crimes multiplied, and that all men are sunk, as in a sea, in the sleep of lusts. Truth is darkened, and iniquity shines in the thorny tangles of our hateful crimes; and righteousness is moved to indignation so that it works retribution upon us in ruin and famine and earthquake. In our days all the signs which our Lord indicated are fulfilled that the end of the world has arrived by reason of our sins. Let us abundantly shed doleful tears as we say, Lord who hast created us by thy grace, spare our souls and have mercy upon us."

This kathisma differs slightly from the others in its construction in that there is no final psalmody, prayer, or hymn. The reason for this would seem to be that this kathisma is followed by a procession to the church during which hymns are chanted. There is a discrepancy between what is said in the Psuedo-George of Arbel and the rubrics of the manuscripts. According to the former, the procession to the church took place after the first two kathismata, and the others, in the case of the clergy, were said in church. The rubrics of the manuscripts, however, are quite clear. In Cambridge ADD. 1986, after the fifth kathisma, we read, "Until now they remain in the house where the deceased is until the kathismata of the washing are completed. And after, then they take up the bier and come to the church. And when they set out from the house they begin this hymn as they come to the church."

Much more important to note, however, is the difference at this point between the construction of the service for the clergy and the service for the laity. In the case of the laity, it would appear that the lessons are read in the house after the kathismata have been recited, and before the procession leaves the house for the grave. In the case of the clergy, however, the lessons are read in the church after the body has been taken there.

There is a difference between the number of lessons read for a layperson and the number for the clergy. In the case of a layman, the lessons prescribed are Isaiah 38:10–20, Hezekiah's prayer to God after recovery from sickness: and Ezekiel 37:1–14, Ezekiel's vision of the valley of dry bones. For a woman the lessons are Genesis 28:1–19, the account of the death and burial of Sarah: and Acts of the Apostles 9:36–42, the story of Peter's raising of Dorcas.[19] The

Pseudo-George of Arbel informs us that just as the number of kathismata recited increased according to the rank of the deceased, so too the number of lessons is increased. He tells us that for a deacon, a third lesson taken from the epistles is added, and from the time of Isho'yabh III, there was also a lesson drawn from the gospels.[20] The lessons for the burial of a priest are Numbers 20:22–end, the death of Aaron and the investiture of Eleazar; Acts of the Apostles 20:17–38, St. Paul's farewell to the elders of the Church at Ephesus; for the epistle, 1 Corinthians 15:34–38, St. Paul's declaration of the resurrection; and, for the gospel, St. John 5:19–30, which includes the passage, "Marvel not at this, for the hour is coming in which all that are in the graves shall hear his voice and shall come forth: they that have done good into the resurrection of life, and they that have done evil unto the resurrection of damnation."[21] Macomber suggests that, in the case of the laity, the lessons are drawn only from the Old Testament or the Acts of the Apostles because they are read in the house and not in the church.[22] In the case of the clergy, however, it is reasonable to suppose that the lessons are regarded as an integral part of the eucharist which is celebrated when the body has been carried into church, and this has influenced both their source and their number. This supposition is strengthened by the fact that, as in the eucharist, a shurraya is recited before the reading of the epistle, and also the following prayer:

"O wise Ruler, who wonderfully carest for thy household, O great Treasury, who pourest forth in thy pitifulness all aids and blessings, we beseech thee, turn, O my Lord, pity and have mercy on us as thou art wont at every season, O Lord of all, Father and Son and Holy Spirit for ever."

This prayer is used at this point in the eucharist on fasts and memorials. Also supporting the supposition is that after the epistle, a zummara (literally "the song," again a few verses of a psalm, like the shurraya) is chanted.

The litany which follows the lessons is quite short, and includes the petition:

"And let us also pray for our brother, the associate of our ministry and companion of our faith, and our intimate acquaintance, the priest N. who is dead, and is gone forth from this world; that God who approved his will and took him in the true faith may lead him to the assembly of all the righteous."

The litany is followed by a prayer which is worth quoting if only for its interesting, though somewhat artificial, construction.

"When this one world shall be dissolved, and the two lights extinguished, and the three trumpets shall sound, and the four winds shall be still, and the five senses shall cease, and the six days coalesce into one day, and the seven thousand years shall come to an end, and the eight tones of music shall sound, and the nine ranks of angels shall be disquieted, and the Ten Commandments shall be discussed, and the eleven apostles with him who received the lot of the ministry shall sit upon the thrones, and the twelve tribes of Israel shall be judged, and the righteous shall shine, but the wicked shall be sad; in that awful and bitter day, O my Lord, make thy servant worthy to hear that gladdening pronouncement, Well done, good and faithful servant, enter thou into the joy of thy Lord: O Lord of all, Father and Son."

Following this prayer, the celebration of the eucharist continues. On the eucharist the Pseudo-George remarks, "After we have fulfilled the ministry which he performed, we commit him to his Lord, and just as he distributed the Body and Blood for his own and his congregation's propitiation, so in his death, the sacred mysteries are distributed, through which propitiation is made, both for him, and for those who are burying him."[23] As we have already mentioned, the Pseudo-George implies a Mass of the Presanctified: "The priest does not, however, consecrate the mysteries because he cannot signify the resurrection through them. The deceased goes up as far as the sheqaqone,[24] that he may partake of the already consecrated mysteries [*ut sumat iam consecrata mysteria*]. And they partake of the mysteries while he remains in the sheqaqone, so that he may communicate in the mysteries, not bodily but spiritually."[25]

The actual rubrics of the manuscript at this point read, "Anthem of the Bema, while the people communicate." Here is one of the verses of the anthem:

"O God, in thy mercy, make a good hope for thy worshipper and grant him, O my Lord, that he may rejoice at thy right hand in thy kingdom."

Then comes the rubric, "They receive the Holy Thing, and they conclude." Then follows a hymn which is chanted while the deceased is carried round the church. This hymn, "Abide in peace, O Church," according to the Pseudo-George of Arbel, was said by some only over bishops, whose bodies were carried into the apse (sanctuary) of the church. Others, however, recited it over all the ranks of the clergy, "*quia omnes ecclesiae addicti sunt.*"[26] Again, according to the Pseudo-George, it was Isho'yabh III who ordered that the hymn should be said over all the ranks of the clergy. If the deceased were a priest, he was carried round the church by priests, and if a deacon, by deacons. The first verse of the hymn is to be said at the step of the bema,[27] the second at the entrance of the sanctuary, where ordination is received, the third at "the lower step of the nave," and the fourth at the door of the church. The hymn begins thus:

"Rest in peace, O Church, for I am going away: may those who remain in righteousness pray for me. O my brethren and companions and beloved, keep my memory in remembrance, for I am now separated from you for ever, and pray for me. I am going away, yet I am not afraid, for my Lord is calling me, and will place a crown of praise upon my head, and will refresh me."

When this hymn is ended they all go out into the courtyard of the church, where further hymns are chanted. There are ten of these, and they are very similar in content to the anthems and hymns in other parts of the service, as can be seen from the following examples.

"The joy of the whole earth is Mount Zion. In the great day of thy appearing, Jesus our King, the Lord of praise, thy blessed will shall save: and the horn and the trumpet shall sound, and the dead shall rise and offer praise to thy greatness.
"There shall be thine abode and thy rest. With the hosts of spiritual beings thy soul shall sing praise to the Creator in the place which is full of blessing, and life, and good things without end, which Christ has prepared for his saints and who desire his love and believe in him.
"The Lord fulfill all thy petitions. Be not sad, O holy priest, that thou hast departed from this Church which is upon earth, for behold, thy Lord shall give thee the reward which shall recompense thy labors, as he promised."

At the conclusion of these hymns, the body of the deceased is carried from the church to the grave to the accompaniment of further hymnody. The funeral procession from the church to the grave in the case of the clergy, and from the house or village in the case of the laity, is really the central feature of the whole rite, and that which gives it its whole meaning. It represents symbolically the journey of the Christian from this world to paradise, and in this connection the first and last of the hymns are of supreme significance. The first is changed as the funeral procession sets out, and expresses the deceased's farewell to the world or to the environment in which he has lived. The opening stanza for both clergy and laity alike is the same:

"Abide in peace, O temporal dwelling which cannot redeem those who possess thee: for I am going to the place of light in which dwell the righteous who have labored."

For the clergy it continues:

"Rest in peace, my brethren and companions: may our Lord grant you the reward of your love, and when you stand in the midst of the sanctuary remember me in your prayers. Rest in peace, O my companions. May our Lord comfort your hearts, and in that hope which shall not deceive, banish from you adversity and distress."

These chants are sung by two choirs formed from the mourners, which precede the deceased in the procession. This custom is mentioned by the Pseudo-George of Arbel, who says that the two choirs represent symbolically the Old and the New Testaments. His description of the proceedings at this point in his day exactly tallies with the rubrics of the Urmi Printed Edition of the rite. The singing is begun by the choir nearest the bier, and while they are singing they stand still while the other choir moves on. Then the second choir sings, standing still in the meantime, as the other choir moves forward. This, says the author, signifies that the way forward is through death, and the silence of the choirs signifies the silence of death.[28]

The Pseudo-George clearly sets out the Christian attitude to death which finds expression in these services. He says:

"They go forth praising and honoring the deceased as though accompanying him to the kingdom; and they doubt not that he is an heir to the heavenly mansions. Because he has lived in the faith which is written in the holy books and which was signified by the Old and the New Testaments, and was signed in baptism, and sanctified by the Body and Blood of Christ, and has obtained the forgiveness of sins, he is worthy of the heavenly kingdom. And because he is worthy, they attend him with honors: neither do they lament, because he is freed from sorrow and has attained the joys which he desired. For our Christian home is in heaven."[29]

On arrival at the cemetery the last hymn is sung, in which is expressed the immanence of the resurrection. The hymn is referred to by the Pseudo-George of Arbel, who quotes the opening words. In his comments he declares that hitherto the proceedings have been a symbolic representation of death, but henceforth they will symbolize the resurrection. They begin, he says, "with a word which declares the coming of the Lord." This beginning is:

"I was glad when they said unto me. Our Lord shall come and shall raise the dead, and give hope to the departed."

The second stanza of the hymn is worth quoting, if only for the sentiments which it expresses,

"His name endureth for ever. Blessed is he who hath made death incapable of being bribed: for it carries off the good and the bad alike."

At the conclusion of this hymn the bier is placed at the side of the grave, and there follows a series of prayers and hymns and ceremonies, all of which are dominated by the thought of the resurrection. First the deacon proclaims a litany in which the prayers of the mourners are requested on behalf of the deceased:

"Pray for our brother, the priest N., the companion of our faith who has gone forth from this world; that God, to whom he was pleasing, and who took him away in the true faith, may lead him to the assembly of the righteous; that when he shall awaken and raise all those who sleep in the dust, and when the righteous shall attain a just end, he may call him and set him at his right hand. Amen.
"And write his name in the Book of Life. Amen.
"And number him with the number of his elect. Amen.
"And mingle him with the assembly of those who praise him, with all the just and righteous who are pleasing before him, through the grace of his Christ for ever. Amen."

Two further prayers follow, the second of which prepares for the lowering of the body into the grave. It is identical for all ranks.

"Blessed be the powerful commandment of thy greatness, which killeth and maketh alive, and which bringeth down to Sheol."

At this point there is a difference in the structure of the forms for the burial of the clergy and for the burial of the laity. We will deal with the office for the laity first. After the prayer mentioned above, there follows a "Farewell," a chanted homily, in the course of which the body is lowered into the grave. According to Macomber, this "Farewell" is usually drawn from one of the Homilies of Narsai. It expresses the hope of the resurrection and describes the separation of the wicked from the righteous at the parousia.[30] According to the rubric in Mingana 570, after the opening words, the people reply, "May Christ bless the reader and the hearers by the grace of his compassion for ever." The rubrics further order that the body shall be lowered into the grave after three sections of the "Farewell" have been read, and that the "Farewell" shall be pronounced from the east side of the grave, facing the deceased.

The rites for the clergy are rather fuller. It would seem from the

rubrics of Cambridge ADD. 1986 that three sections of the
"Farewell" are said, and then a hymn is sung, during which a
"Procession of Peace" is formed, and they give the "Peace" to the
deceased, as it is given in the eucharist.[31] The hymn (*madhrasha*) is
in the form of a dialogue between the deceased and the
congregation. Here is a verse of the hymn:

"Rest in peace, my brethren and companions. The Lord in his grace
take away your distress.
"Go in peace, O happy brother, the Lord give you everlasting life."

After this hymn, according to the rubrics, the body of the deceased
is lowered into the grave, and another hymn is chanted. This hymn
is the most somber of the whole service, emphasizing the apparent
triumph of death.

"Come, enter in, and see how many heroes sleep here, and are
made dust for the moth and the worms in the abyss of Sheol.
Come, enter in, and see how the great spoils which death hath
captured are made worthless dust in the pit of Sheol."

It ends, however, on a note of hope:

"May our Lord, in his mercy, grant resurrection to all the dead, and
give them bliss, O Lord, at thy right hand in the kingdom above.
"And thou, brother, who art separated from among us this day: may
our Lord gather thee into the companies of the assemblies on high."

This chant is followed by another which is described in the rubrics
as a "Farewell," and it is specified that it is said "in the Second
Person." It makes request, in the name of the deceased, for the
prayers of the congregation.

"O my brethren and companions and associates, abide in peace.
Death has separated me from your company. Pray for me.
"O ye sons of the Church, with whom I ministered, abide in peace,
for I am separated from you for ever. Pray for me.
"O ye children of the town from which I have gone out, abide in
peace. May the tranquillity of the Lord be with you. Pray for me."

At the conclusion of this hymn, and at the conclusion of the
"Farewell" in the case of the laity, the priest takes earth in his right
hand and pronounces a blessing over the deceased. The terms of
this prayer are almost identical for both clergy and laity. Here is the
prayer for the clergy:

"God, the maker of all, who hast decreed unto our mortal nature,
that dust thou art, and unto dust shalt thou return: may he raise
thee up therefrom, rejoicing in the glory of the resurrection: and

may the holy mysteries which thou hast received plead for thee, and be to thee for pardon in the fearful judgment of righteousness, when the righteous shall receive the recompense of their labors, and the just their reward. Then mayest thou meet Christ with open face, and lift up praise and render glory to the Father, Son, and Holy Spirit, Amen."

After this prayer, according to the rubrics of Cambridge ADD. 1986, the priest scatters the earth into the grave in the form of a cross, and all present say three times, "Give rest, O Lord, to the spirit of thy servant in the place where the righteous dwell." In Mingana 570, the service for the burial of the laity, the rubric states quite explicitly that the earth is *not* to be scattered into the grave in the form of a cross (*w-lâw çlîb'âîth*). The short prayer mentioned above is not found in Mingana 570. A final chant of considerable length is then sung. It echoes the hope and prayer for a glorious resurrection.

"To thee, O Lord, I lift up my soul. King Christ, our redeemer, in the day of thy coming raise me up and set me at thy right hand in the day when thy greatness shall appear.
"The heavens are thine. The two worlds, O Lord, are thine, now and hereafter equally. Keep the living by thy grace, and give resurrection to the dead."

Many of the stanzas of this hymn are to be found also in the hymn in the service for the burial of the laity. The final stanza is the lakhumara, a hymn found in many of the Nestorian services:

"We confess thee, Lord of all, and we praise thee Jesus Christ, for thou art the reviver of our bodies, and thou art the savior of our souls."

Following the hymn, Psalm 90 is recited, with the refrain, "Thou art a dwelling place unto us for ever and until everlasting," between each verse. The Gloria is not said at the end, but, in the case of the clergy, a hymn is sung, and then two final prayers are said which stress the forthcoming resurrection. They are followed by the huttama ("seal" or "conclusion") in which further supplication is made for the deceased. Here we will bring our study of the Nestorian burial offices to a close with the second of the two prayers mentioned above.

"In thy compassion raise up those who have fallen asleep, and in thy overflowing mercy guard the living, and give a good resurrection to the dead who have fallen asleep in the hope of thy resurrection, for thou art the ruler of the two worlds which thou hast created, Lord of our death and of our life, Father, Son, and Holy Spirit. Amen."

Abbreviations

AAA	*Acta Apostolorum Apocrypha*
AAS	*Acta Apostolicae Sedis*
ALw	*Archiv für Liturgiewissenschaft*
Amb	*Ambrosius*
AST	*Analecta Sacra Tarraconensia*
Bib	*Biblica*
BuL	*Bibel und Leben*
BZ	*Biblische Zeitschrift*
BZAW	Beihefte zur Zeitschrift für die alttestamentliche Wissenschaft
CBQ	*Catholic Biblical Quarterly*
CCL	Corpus Christianorum, Series Latina
CR	*Clergy Review*
CSEL	Corpus Scriptorum Ecclesiasticorum Latinorum
DACL	*Dictionnaire d'archéologie chrétienne et de liturgie*
DBS	*Dictionnaire de la Bible: Supplément*
DC	*Documentation catholique*
DTC	*Dictionnaire de théologie catholique*
ETL	*Ephemerides Theologicae Lovanienses*
GCS	Die griechischen christlichen Schriftsteller der ersten drei Jahrhunderten
Gd	*Gottesdienst*

HBS	Henry Bradshaw Society
HS	*Hispania Sacra*
LJ	*Liturgisches Jahrbuch*
LQF	Liturgiegeschichtliche Quellen und Forschungen
LumVie	*Lumiére et vie*
LXX	Septuagint
MD	*La Maison-Dieu*
MEL	Monumenta Ecclesiae Liturgica
MHS	Monumenta Hispaniae Sacra
NRT	*Nouvelle revue théologique*
PG	Patrologia Graeca
PL	Patrologia Latina
PO	Patrologia Orientalis
QLP	*Quaestions liturgiques et paroissiales*
RAC	*Reallexikon für Antike und Christentum*
RB	*Revue biblique*
RE	*Realencyklopädie der klassischen Altertumswissenschaft*
REJ	*Revue des études juives*
RevSR	*Revue des sciences religieuses*
RivAC	*Rivista di archeologia cristiana*
RQ	*Römische Quartalschrift*
RSPT	*Revue des sciences philosophiques et théologiques*
RTAM	*Recherches de théologie ancienne et médiévale*
ScEccle	*Sciences ecclésiastiques*
SSL	Spicilegium Sacrum Lovaniense
ST	Studi e Testi
TDNT	*Theological Dictionary of the New Testament*
ThGl	*Theologie und Glaube*
TOB	Traduction oecuménique de la Bible
TPQ	*Theologish-Praktische Quartalschaift*
TU	Texte und Untersuchungen
TvL	*Tijdschrift voor liturgie*
ZKT	*Zeitschrift für katholische Theologie*

Notes

Preface (pp. vii–ix)

1. [Because of their highly technical character, two papers published in the original of this book have been omitted in the English translation: M. Arranz, "Les prières presbyterales de la 'Pannuchis' de l'ancient Euchologe byzantin et la 'Pannikhida' des défunts" ("The Priestly Prayers of the Pannychis of the Ancient Byzantine Euchologion, and the Pannikhida for the Deceased"), and A. M. Triacca, "Le rite de l' impositio manuum super infirmum dans l'ancienne liturgie ambrosienne" ("The Rite of the 'Imposition of Hands' in the Old Ambrosian Liturgy").—Tr.]

Andronikof, Constantin (pp. 1–16)

1. I have developed this idea in greater detail in the chapter on the Dormition in my book *Le sens des fêtes* (Paris, 1970).
2. Nor, for that matter, the Ascension of Christ or any other aspect of Christianity, since we must never tire of repeating, especially in our unhappy age, that Christianity is realistic, and in no sense idealistic or spiritualistic, since it is the religion of the Word made flesh.
3. Andronikof, op. cit., p. 293.
4. I am therefore completely unable to agree with the attitude of J. Bellamy in his article "Assomption" in the DTC, when he says: "Earthly paradise, burning bush, ark of the covenant—these are comparisons and symbols . . . which supposedly express the idea of incorruptibility. . . . They are oratorical accommodations, not dogmatic

proofs" (1:2132). But what is a dogmatic *proof?* There is no such thing to be had when it is sought in the realm of logical reasoning. Is not dogma simply an approximative formulation of a datum of revelation, the justification of which is in fact to be found solely in the faith received by the Church, which is "the pillar and foundation of truth" and which sings at all times of naught else but its dogmas?

5. Cf. the very interesting and impressive reflections of Paul Florensky, *La Colonne et le Fondement de la Vérité* (Russian original: Moscow, 1914; French tr.: Lausanne, 1975), in the chapter entitled "La Géhenne."

6. Cf. Chapter 7: "La mort et la condition outre-tombe" in *L'Epouse et l'Agneau* (in Russian; Paris, 1945), pp. 378–406.

7. Ibid., p. 406.

Botte, Bernard (pp. 17–32)

1. For a good survey cf. P. M. Gy, "La mort du chrétien," in A.-G. Martimort (ed.), *L'Eglise en prière*, 1st ed. (Paris, 1961), pp. 618–30; 3rd ed. (1965), pp. 636–48.

2. P. Van Sull, *"In Paradisum!"* NRT 49 (1922), 141–48.

3. B. Capelle, *"L'antienne In paradisum,"* QLP 8 (1923), 161–76.

3a.[The author is following the text of the Vulgate for the psalms and other Old Testament texts, as well as for the numbering both of the psalms and of verses in the psalms and elsewhere.—Tr.]

4. "Await your shepherd, *he will give you the repose of eternity,* for he is very near—he who is to come at the end of the world. Be ready for the rewards of the kingdom, because *the unending light will shine for you* in the eternity of time."

5. F. Cumont, *Lux perpetua* (Paris, 1949).

6. Cf. C. Mohrmann, *"Locus refrigerii,"* in B. Botte and C. Mohrmann, *L'Ordinaire de la messe* (Paris-Louvain, 1953), pp. 123–32.

7. Mohrmann, op. cit., p. 131.

8. Edited by M. Férotin (MEL 5; Paris, 1904), p. 104.

9. LXX: *eis topon chloēs . . . epi hudatos anapauseōs.* Vg.: *in loco pascuae . . . super aquam refectionis.* The old Mozarabic psalter translates *chloēs* as *viridi.*

10. Edited by Jr. C. J. Kraemer, *Excavations at Nissana* III (Princeton, 1958), p. 310.

11. V. Bruni, *I funerali di un sacerdote nel rito bizantino* (Jerusalem, 1952), pp. 146–58 (text: pp. 152–55; Italian tr.: p. 200).

12. F. Brightman, *Liturgies Eastern and Western* 1. *Eastern Liturgies* (Oxford, 1896), p. 170; J. A. Assemani, *Codex liturgicus ecclesiae universae* IV, 4: *Missale Alexandrinum* (Rome, 1754; photographic reprint by H. Welter, VII, Paris and Leipzig, 1902), p. 62. The complete prayer takes up in succession the themes of rest, Abraham's bosom, refreshment, paradise, the heavenly Jerusalem, and light: "Deign, Lord, to give all these souls repose in the bosom of our holy fathers Abraham, Isaac and Jacob; lead them into a verdant place beside the refreshing waters, into the paradise of pleasure, the place whence grief of heart, sadness and sighs take flight, and where the light of your saints shines."

13. B. Botte, "Abraham dans la liturgie," *Cahiers sioniens* 5 (1951), 180–87 (especially pp. 184–85).

14. F. X. Funk, *Didascalia et Constitutiones Apostolorum* (Paderborn, 1905), 1:550.

15. Ibid., 2:192.

16. Cf. note 12.

17. Cf. Pseudo-Dionysius, *De ecclesiastica hierarchia* 7, 3, 4 (PG 3:560B).

18. Bruni, op. cit., p. 152.

19. Ibid., pp. 158–61 and 202; 161–63 and 203; 164 and 201.

20. B. Botte, *"Prima resurrectio.* Un vestige de millénarisme dans les liturgies occidentales," RTAM 15 (1948), 5–17.

21. Ambrose of Milan, *In psalmum I,* 53 (PL 14:994–95).

1. MD, no. 15 (1948), 105.

2. *Sacrosanctum Concilium: Constitution on the Sacred Liturgy*, no. 73, tr. in A. Flannery (ed.), *Vatican Council II: The Conciliar and Postconciliar Documents* (Collegeville, Minn., 1975), p. 22.

3. Bibliography in MD, no. 113 (1973), 81–85. Add: R. Béraudy, "Le sacrement des malades," NRT 96 (1974), 600–34. Here are the recent commentaries I have found most useful: B. Reicke, *The Epistles of James, Peter and Jude* (Anchor Bible 37; New York, 1964); F. Mussner, *Der Jakobusbrief* (Herders theologischer Kommentar zum Neuen Testament 13/1; Freiburg-Basel-Vienna, 1967²); J. Cantinat, *Les Epîtres de S. Jacques et de S. Jude* (Sources Bibliques; Paris, 1973).

4. J. Hempel, "Heilung als Symbol und Wirklichkeit im biblischen Schriftum," *Nachrichten der Akademie der Wissenschaften in Göttingen* I. Philologisch-historische Klasse (Göttingen, 1958), pp. 290f.; A. Oepke, "Nosos," TDNT 4:1091–98.

5. J. A. Fitzmyer, *The Genesis Apocryphon of Qumran Cave I. A Commentary* (Rome, 1966), p. 59.

6. *Antiquitates Judaicae* 8, §§46–47.

7. G. Crespy, *La guérison par la foi* (Cahiers Théologiques 30; Neuchâtel-Paris, 1952); X. Léon-Dufour, "La guérison de la belle-mère de Simon-Pierre," in his *Etudes d'Evangile*, (Paris, 1965), pp. 125–48; *Evangile*, no. 8 (1974): *Les miracles de Jésus*, which contains an essay of mine, "Le sens des miracles dans l'Evangile" (pp. 49–55).

8. E. Cothenet, "Sainteté de l'Eglise et péchés des chrétiens," NRT 96 (1974), 449–70, especially pp. 452–54, and also in *Liturgie et rémission des péchés* (Actes de la XXᵉ Semaine d'Etudes Liturgiques de Saint-Serge, Paris, July 2–5, 1973; Rome, 1975), pp. 69–96.

9. Léon-Dufour, op. cit., pp. 128–29.

10. The basic study is that of H. J. Held, "Matthew as Interpreter of the Miracle Stories," in G. Bornkamm, G. Barth, and H. J. Held, *Tradition and Interpretation in Matthew*, tr. by P. Scott (Philadelphia, 1963), pp. 165–299. There is a good summary of Held's study by L. L'Eplatenier, in *Evangile*, no. 8, pp. 21–26.

11. Léon-Dufour, op. cit., p. 129.

12. Oepke, "Nosos," TDNT 4:1097; R. H. Gundry, *The Use of the Old Testament in St. Matthew's Gospel* (Supplements to Novum Testamentum 18; Leiden, 1967), pp. 109–10, 230.

13. The emphasis on the almost visceral pity of Jesus (*splanchnizesthai*: Mt 9:36; 14:14; 15:32; 20:34; Mk 1:41; 6:34; 8:2; 9:22; Lk 7:13) runs counter to the Greek ideal of the impassibility of the wise man.

14. J. Dupont, "L'ambassade de Jean-Baptiste (Matthieu XI, 2–6; Luc VII, 18–23)," NRT 83 (1961), 805–21, 943–59.

15. Cramer, *Catenae graecorum Patrum in Novum Testamentum* (Oxford, 1844), 1:324.

16. C. Ruch, "Extrême-Onction," DTC 5:1927.

17. D. M. Stanley, "Liturgical Influences on the Formation of the Gospels," CBQ 21 (1959), 24–38; reprinted in his *The Apostolic Church in the New Testament* (Westminster, Md., 1966), p. 119–39.

18. Cf. most recently the introduction in Cantinat, op. cit., pp. 14–15.

19. B. Reicke groups vv. 12–20 under the heading "Manual of Discipline," and subdivides thus: 12–13 (swear not, but pray and sing); 14–18 (healing of the sick person); 19–20 (salvation of apostates). This subdivision has the serious drawback of breaking the connection between v. 13 and what follows.

20. The verb *proseuchesthai* occurs five times in 5:13–18 and not elsewhere; *euchē* and *proseuchē* occur once each.

21. Cf. most recently L. Dussaut, *L'Eucharistie, Pâque de toute la vie* (Lectio divina 74; Paris, 1972), pp. 15–54.

22. Luther, on the contrary, declares: "No apostle has the right on his own authority to institute a sacrament": *The Babylonian Captivity of the Church*, tr. by A. T.

W. Steinhäuser, F. C. Ahrens, and A. R. Wentz (Luther's Works 36; Philadelphia, 1959), p. 118.

23. "Promulgation" can be taken in two senses: publication of a new law (a sense which I reject for this passage) or publication of a text which ratifies a custom. It is in this second and weaker sense that one may say, with the Council of Trent, that James 5 promulgates Extreme Unction. I need not discuss here the exegesis of the conciliar text; cf. A. Duval, "L'extrême-onction au concile de Trente," MD, no. 101 (1970), 127–72.

24. On the origin of the presbyterate cf. A. Lemaire, Les ministères aux origines de l'Eglise (Lectio divina 68; Paris, 1971), and the collection of essays edited by J. Delorme, Le ministère et les ministères dans le Nouveau Testament (Parole de Dieu; Paris, 1974), to which I contributed a chapter entitled "La première épître de Pierre. L'épître de Jacques" (pp. 138–54).

25. Note y in TOB is ambiguous: from the viewpoint of textual criticism the location of ep'auton after proseuxasthōsan is certain; on the other hand, the manuscripts are divided over the presence of a second auton after aleipsantes. The editions of Von Soden and Vogels follow the textus receptus and keep this second auton. Other editors (Tischendorff, Westcott-Hort, Nestle, the United Bible Society's Greek New Testament) remove it on the authority of B, P, 88, 453, 915, etc., and on the principle of lectio brevior potior. The suppression of the auton after aleipsantes does not however mean that ep'auton relates to the participle rather than the main verb: "let them pray" (proseuxasthōsan). The Vetus Latina follows the short text: orent super ipsum unguentes oleo in nomine Domini (text F of the Beuron edition), with the addition of oleo which specifies the matter used in the anointing; super ipsum is understood as connected with orent. In his well-known letter to Decentius of Gubbio, Innocent I writes orent pro eo (according to the Beuron edition).

26. The verb aleiphein always takes an accusative in the New Testament (seven times); in Lk 7:38 the verb is coordinated with katephilei so that the complement of the latter also goes with ēleiphen.

27. Examples with peri: Col 1:3; 4:3; 1 Thes 5:25; with hyper: Col 1:9; Jas 5:16. The meaning is the same.

28. Béraudy, art. cit., pp. 602–3.

29. In Leviticum homiliae 16 (translation of Rufinus): si quis infirmatur vocet presbyteros ecclesiae et imponant ei manus unguentes eum oleo in nomine Domini (cited from the Beuron edition), "If anyone is sick let him call the presbyters of the Church and let them impose hands on him, anointing him with oil in the name of the Lord."

30. Cf. the paper of A. M. Triacca, "The Rite of the 'Imposition of Hands' in the Old Ambrosian Liturgy" (in French), in La maladie et la mort du chrétien dans la liturgie, pp. 339–60 [not included in the present translation]. Compare with Mt 9:18; Mk 16:18.

31. Berakhot 1, 3ᵃ, 9 Bar.

32. W. Heitmüller, Im Namen Jesu (Göttingen, 1903).

33. J. Dupont, "Nom de Jésus," DBS 6:514–41, especially cols. 524–25.

34. As in Acts 5:41; 3 Jn 7. The short reading in B: en to onomati, "[anointing] in the name," can be explained in this way.

35. B. Sesboüé, L'onction des malades (Profac; Lyons, 1972), p. 73.

36. The second of these verbs is used, however, in v. 16 in connection with the mutual confession of sins.

37. W. Foerster, "Sōzō, Sōtēr," TDNT 7:968–69, 1004–5, 1009–12; A. Duprez, Jésus et les Dieux guérisseurs (Cahiers de la Revue Biblique 12; Paris, 1970).

38. W. C. van Unnik, "La notion de SOZEIN 'sauver' et ses dérivés dans les évangiles synoptiques," in La formation des Evangiles (Recherches Bibliques 2; Bruges, 1957), pp. 178–94.

39. A full bibliography on the subject will be found in the recent book of B. Rigaux, Dieu l'a ressuscité (Gembloux, 1973).

40. Léon-Dufour, op. cit. (n. 7), p. 129. The TOB note a on Jas 5:15 is excellent.

41. J.-C. Didier, "L'onction des malades dans la théologie contemporaine," MD, no. 113 (1973), 64: "The solution given by St. Thomas and concretized in the forgiveness

of the *reliquiae peccati* does not completely satisfy the requirements of the inspired texts and falls short of the possibilities offered by the sacrament."

42. Cf. my article, "Sainteté de l'Eglise et péchés des chrétiens," NRT 96 (1974), 459–62, and in *Liturgie et rémission des péchés* (n. 8), pp. 81–85.

43. W. Rordorf, "La rémission des péchés selon la Didaché," *Irénikon* 46 (1973), 283–97, and in *Liturgie et rémission des péchés* (n. 8), pp. 225–38.

44. *Sabbat* 32ᵃ Bar, cited in H. Strack and P. Billerbeck, *Kommentar zum Neuen Testament aus Talmud und Midrasch* 4:576.

45. J. Jeremias, *New Testament Theology* 1. *The Proclamation of Jesus*, tr. by J. Bowden (New York, 1971), p. 287.

46. The Greek Church has kept the collegial rite for the anointing of the sick.

47. E. Testa, *L'Huile de la Foi. L'Onction des malades sur une lamelle du Iᵉʳ siècle*, tr. and adapted from the Italian by O. Englebert (Jerusalem, 1967).

48. B. Bagatti, *L'Eglise de la Circoncision* (Jerusalem, 1965), pp. 212–16.

49. Bib 47 (1967), 450–51. E. Testa's reply: Bib 48 (1968), 249–53.

50. RB 75 (1968), 278–80.

51. Jerusalem Talmud, *Aboda Zaran* 2, 40d, 35.

52. Bagatti, op. cit., pp. 78–80.

53. Béraudy, art cit. (n. 3), pp. 603, 634.

54. B. Reicke, "L'onction des malades d'après Saint Jacques," MD, no. 113 (1973), 50–56.—The citation from Reicke's Anchor Bible commentary is from p. 59.

55. Cf. my article, "Paradis," DBS 6:1177–1220, esp. cols. 1207–13.

56. A. Stolz, *Théologie de la mystique* (Chevetogne, 1947²), pp. 18–38.

57. E. Cothenet, "Onction," DBS 6:701–32, esp. cols. 725–32.

58. *Apocalypse of Moses* 13, 1–3, in R. H. Charles (ed.), *The Apocrypha and Pseudepigrapha of the Old Testament in English* (Oxford, 1913), 2:144, col. 2.

59. We may recall here the importance which St. Irenaeus attaches to the salvation of Adam (*Adversus haereses* III, 23).

60. Cf. my article "Marie dans les Apocryphes," in H. du Manoir (ed.), *Maria* 6 (Paris, 1961), pp. 71–156 (especially p. 125 on the Syriac fragments). My thesis on the antiquity of the *Transitus* genre has been confirmed by the studies of B. Bagatti on the tomb of Mary at Gethsemane; on this subject cf. R. Laurentin, "Bulletin sur la Vierge Marie," RSPT 58 (1974), 78–81.

61. *De ecclesiastica hierarchia*, cf. 7 (PG 3:565A), cited by Sesboüé, op. cit., p. 21. Compare this with Simeon of Thessalonika (PG 155:675–76, 685–86). On the funeral rites cf. Bagatti, op. cit., pp. 217–54.

62. Irenaeus, *Adversus haereses* I, 21, 5 (PG 7:666).

63. An anointing of the sick according to C. Ruch in DTC 5:1931; a baptismal initiation according to J. Daniélou, *The Theology of Jewish Christianity*, tr. by J. A. Baker (Chicago, 1964), p. 325, and Sesboüé, op. cit., p. 19.

64. Bagatti, op. cit., p. 230.

65. G. W. Lampe, *The Seal of the Spirit* (London, 1951), and J. Daniélou's review in RSR 40 (1952), 286–89.

66. There is a list in Cantinat's commentary, pp. 27–28.

67. Apart from the gospels, the New Testament has no occasion to mention the miracles of Jesus (exceptions: Acts 2:22; 10:38).

68. Cf. my article, "Sainteté de l'Eglise et rémission des péchés," NRT 96 (1974), 463 and in *Liturgie et rémission des péchés* (n. 8), p. 86.

69. Sesboüé, op. cit., pp. 53–54.

Dubarle, André-Marie (pp. 53–64)

1. On the practice of medicine in Israel cf., in addition to the encyclopedia articles, J. Hempel, "Heilung als Symbol und Wirklichkeit im biblischen Scriftum," *Nachrichten der Akademie der Wissenschaften in Göttingen* I. Philologisch-historische Klasse (Göttingen, 1958), pp. 237–314 (cf. the first section, pp. 237–60).

2. On these traces of magical ideas cf. A. Lods, "Les idées des Israélites sur la

maladie, ses causes et ses remèdes," in *Vom Alten Testament. Karl Marti zum siebzigsten Geburtstag gewidment* (BZAW 41; Giessen, 1925), pp. 181–93.

3. Cf. R. Martin-Achard, "La prière des malades dans le psautier d'Israël," LumVie, no. 86 (1968), 25–44.

4. For the application to 2 Peter of the literary genre of pseudonymous testament cf. C. Spicq, *Les épîtres de saint Pierre* (Paris, 1966), pp. 191–94.

5. Cf. N. Lohfink, *The Christian Meaning of the Old Testament*, tr. by R. A. Wilson (Milwaukee, 1968). The final chapter describes "Man Face to Face with Death" (pp. 138–69).

6. A more detailed description of mourning practices is given in R. de Vaux, *Ancient Israel: Its Life and Institutions*, tr. by J. McHugh (New York, 1961), pp. 56–61.

7. French translation by G. Contenau, *L'épopée de Gilgamesh* (Paris, 1939). The passage cited comes from the very end of the epic, the final lines of tablet XII.

8. In addition to the commentaries there is a Catholic study of the passage by E. O'Brien, "The Scriptural Proof for the Existence of Purgatory from 2 Mac. 12:43–45," ScEccl 1 (1949), 80–108.

9. I. Lévi, "La commémoration des âmes dans le judaïsme," REJ 29 (1894), 43–60; S. Reinach, "De l'origine des prières pour les morts," ibid., 41 (1900), 161–73.

Kniazeff, Alexis (pp. 65–94)

1. Manuscript of the Dionysate Library of Mount Athos no. 450 and the Euchologion of the Saint Sabbas Monastery, in Dmitrievsky, *Repertory of Liturgical Manuscripts* (in Russian) 2: *Euchologia* (Kiev, 1901), pp. 331, 41. Cf. also Kékélidzé, *Georgian Liturgical Manuscripts* (in Russian; Tiflis, 1908), pp. 456–59.

2. Odintzoff, *The Order of Communal and Private Worship in Old Russia before the 16th Century* (in Russian), p. 294; cf. also Mansvetov, *Metropolitan Cyprian and His Liturgical Activity* (in Russian; Moscow, 1882), pp. 194–202; Kékélidzé, op. cit., p. 456.

3. Kékélidzé, op. cit., p. 456.

4. V. Bruni, *I funerali di un sacerdote nel rito bizantino* (Jerusalem, 1972).

5. PG 151 and 154. Cf. also A Lebedev, *Essays on the History of the Eastern Byzantine Church from the 11th Century to the Middle of the 15th Century* (in Russian) in an appendix to the Russian translation of the works of the Fathers of the Church (Moscow, 1891).

6. Mansvetov, op. cit.

7. The Hexapsalm comprises Pss 3, 37, 62, 87, 102, 142, which are grouped at the beginning of the present-day orthros.

8. All of this information is taken from the course on the Trebnik that was given by the late Archimandrite Cyprien Kern; the course has thus far not been published.

9. Decree of the Holy Synod, November 20, 1773. Cf. also *Church News (Tserkovnia Viedomosty)*, 1895, pp. 29, 39.

10. If this office is used for a deacon, the stichera of Lauds are omitted as are all the other hymns of the office that expressly mention the priestly dignity of the deceased.

11. V. S. B. Boulgakov, *Manuel pratique pour le clergé* (Nastolnaya kniga dlia sviastchennosloujitieliej), 3rd ed. (Kiev, 1913), p. 1222.

12. Cf. M. Arranz's study, "The Priestly Prayers of the Pannychis of the Ancient Byzantine Euchologion, and the Pannikhida for the Deceased," delivered (in French) at this 21st Week of Liturgical Studies at the Saint-Serge Institute [not translated in the present volume].

13. In the case of laypersons and monks this vigil consists of an uninterrupted reading of the psalter, with troparia and prayers for the deceased at the end of each kathism.

14. *New Writing-table (Novaya Scrijal)*, Part IV, Chap. 22, §2.

15. Cf. Bruni, op. cit., pp. 146–58. The text is in Goar, *Euchologion sive rituale Graecorum complectens ritus et ordines* (Venice, 1730), p. 424.

16. C. Nikolsky, *Manual* (in Russian), p. 768.

17. The verses used are taken from the Septuagint. I therefore cite the psalms according to the numbering there.

18. The psalm texts are thus being used in a free way. Another example of this kind of use is the prokimenon for the office of crowning.

19. In the present-day Byzantine-Slavic funeral liturgy, the verses of Ps 50 are no longer separated and sung with hymic compositions. Not so in the past. In the fourteenth century office that was used for all categories of deceased, Ps 50 was sometimes sung before the closing of the casket, but each of its verses was followed by a troparion (cf. Kékélidzé, op. cit., pp. 457ff., 70ff.).

20. Carnival, lit., farewell to meat (*Apokreōs*).

21. Kékélidzé, op. cit., pp. 456–59.

22. "The Lord's is the earth and its fullness"—the opening words of this psalm— are taken from their context and sung for every deceased person at the moment when the first shovelsful of earth are thrown on the casket which has already been lowered into the grave.

23. Cf. n. 22.

24. These psalms are used on other occasions and in other offices. Thus Ps 87 is found in the orthros as the fourth psalm in the Hexapsalm. Some of its verses are sung as prokimena on Good Friday.

25. Rom 14:6–9 is the pericope which some manuscripts give as read with Jn 5:24– 30 in the pre-fourteenth-century funeral office common to all the deceased. Nowadays it is the epistle for the funeral of monks.

26. Except in the funeral office for small children. This office has a special prayer of its own.

27. Cf. n. 15.

28. Before being inserted into the funeral office for priests, these prayers existed for a long time as isolated entities having no specific liturgical context. Russian liturgical manuscripts of the sixteenth and seventeenth centuries show them (with their variants) in very diverse liturgical contexts.

29. Kékélidzé, op. cit., p. 71; Goar, op. cit., p. 452.

30. Ibid.

31. There is a fourth special prayer for the funeral of a priest. It too was once read in the common office of the fourteenth century when this was sung for a deceased priest, but it has not been retained in our present office. Here is a translation of it: "Lord our God, we prostrate ourselves before you and pray: cleanse us of our sins. And since you willed that this servant of yours should serve at your altar, let him also be counted worthy of the heritage of those who please you. Through the generous gifts . . ." (Kékélidzé, op. cit., p. 71).

32. Kékélidzé, ibid.; Goar, op. cit., p. 427.

33. The antiphonal part of the funeral office for a priest contains only three groups of antiphons. The office for deceased monks has eight, that is, one group for each of the eight modes.

Kovalevsky, Pierre (pp. 95–106)

1. Michel Testuz, *Papyrus Bodmer XII: Méliton de Sardes, Homélie sur la Pâque* (Cologne-Geneva, 1960); Joseph Blank, *Meliton von Sardes. Vom Passa* (Freiburg, 1963); Odo Casel, "Art und Sinn der ältesten christlichen Osterfeier," JLw 14 (1934), 1–78 (French tr. by J.-C. Didier, *La fête des Pâques dans l'Eglise des Pères* [Les orandi 37; Paris, 1963]); Alphonse Raes, *La resurrezione di Gesù Cristo nella liturgia Bizantina* (Rome, 1939); Kilian Kirchhoff, *Osterjubel der Ostkirche* (2 vols.; Münster, 1940 and 1961).

2. This matter has recently been studied by H. J. Schulz, "Die Hollenfahrt als Anastasis. Eine Untersuchung über Eigenart und dogmengeschichtliche Voraussetzungen byzantinischer Osterfrömmigkeit," ZKT 81 (1959), 1–66.

1. The citation is from the essay "Die Frage der Glaubensheilungen in der Gegenwart," in op. cit., p. 129.

2. Nor is the question usually raised in expositions of Luther's theology.—Without any intention of offering a complete bibliography, I refer the reader to the following works: H. Greeven, *Krankheit und Heilung nach dem Neuen Testament* (Stuttgart, 1949); D. Hoch, *Heil und Heilung. Eine Untersuchung zur Frage der Heilungswunder in der Gegenwart* (Basel, 1955); J. Leipoldt, *Von Epidauros bis Lourdes. Bilder aus der Geschichte volkstümlicher Frömmigkeit* (Hamburg-Bergstedt, 1957); E. Frost, *Christian Healing. A Consideration of the Place of Spiritual Healing in the Church of Today in the Light of the Doctrine and Practice of the Ante-Nicene Church* (London, 1954³); O. Witt, *Krankenheilung im Licht der Bibel* (Marburg, 1957); idem, *Krankenheilung. Eine Frage an Kirche, Gemeinschaft und Heilungsbewegung* (Marburg, 1959); R. Brown, *Ein Handbuch über die Fragen der Krankenheilung* (Wetzhausen, 1968); S. Grossmann, *Das Charisma der Krankenheilung* (Wetzhausen, 1968); R. Brown, *Beten und Heilen* (Wetzhausen, 1969).

3. *Weimar-Ausgabe* [WA] 1:267–73, delivered as a Lenten sermon on the Wednesday after Laetare Sunday, 1578; it is published along with a sermon on the raising of Lazarus according to Jn 11:1–45 (ibid., pp. 273–77). The sermon is translated by J. W. Doberstein in H. T. Lehmann (general editor), *Luther's Works 31: Sermons I* (Philadelphia, 1959), pp. 35–43.

4. WA 1:267, lines 16–21 (*Sermons I*, p. 36).

5. Ibid., lines 21–26.

6. Ibid., lines 27–33 (*Sermons I*, p. 36).

7. Ibid., p. 268, lines 3–9 (*Sermons I*, ibid.).

8. Ibid., lines 19–27 (*Sermons I*, p. 37).

9. Ibid., lines 28–29 (*Sermons I*, ibid.).

10. Ibid., p. 269, lines 18–27 (*Sermons I*, p. 38).

11. Ibid., lines 31–39 (*Sermons I*, pp. 38–39).

12. Ibid., p. 270, lines 1–12 (*Sermons I*, p. 39).

13. Ibid., lines 13–24 (*Sermons I*, pp. 39–40).

14. Ibid., p. 271, lines 11–15; p. 272, lines 7–9 (*Sermons I*, p. 41).

15. Ibid., p. 271, lines 4–8 (*Sermons I*, p. 41).

16. WA, *Tischreden* 5:318, lines 2–3. Cf. on this subject WA 48:241, lines 1–7 and the accompanying text-critical remarks on what Luther says.

17. WA 6:484–573. Tr. by A. T. W. Steinhäuser, F. C. Ahrens, and A. R. Wentz in *Luther's Works 36: Word and Sacrament II* (Philadelphia, 1959), pp. 3–126.

18. Cf., e.g., B. Poschmann, *Penance and Last Anointing*, tr. and rev. by F. Courtney, S. J. (Herder History of Dogma; New York, 1964), pp. 234–42, especially pp. 234–36.

19. WA 6:568, lines 9–14.

20. Ibid., lines 30–34 and p. 569, lines 16–21.

21. Ibid., p. 569, lines 9–11.

22. Ibid., lines 16–21 (*Word and Sacrament II*, p. 120).

23. Ibid., lines 26–36.

24. Ibid., line 37; p. 570, line 5.

25. Ibid., p. 570, lines 7–10.

26. Ibid., lines 11–12.

27. Ibid., lines 18–21 (*Word and Sacrament II*, p. 121).

28. Ibid., lines 22–28.

29. Ibid., line 36; p. 571, line 2 (*Word and Sacrament II*, p. 122).

30. WA 26:508, lines 17–20. The "personal confession" is Part 3 of *Confession Concerning Christ's Supper*, tr. by R. H. Fischer in *Luther's Writings 37: Word and Sacrament III*, p. 370.

31. WA, *Briefe* 8:623, line 53.

32. Ibid., lines 53ff.

33. Ibid., p. 512, lines 20–29: a letter of June 1 (?), 1545 to Pastor Severin Schilze in Belgern on the healing, through prayer and laying on of hands, of a man suffering from melancholia.

34. WA 10/III: 386, lines 16–22.
35. Ibid., p. 390, lines 30–36.
36. WA 38:347, line 35, to p. 348, line 5.
37. WA 10/III: 269, lines 1–10.
38. WA 38:491, lines 11–16.
39. Ibid., lines 17–20.
40. Ibid., lines 23–25.
41. WA 53:206, lines 13–18, tr. by J. Raun in *Luther's Works* 43: *Devotional Writings II* (Philadelphia, 1968), p. 248.
42. Ibid., p. 207, line 32; p. 208, line 10 (*Devotional Writings II*, p. 250).
43. WA 43:381, lines 15ff., and p. 382, lines 35ff., especially p. 381, lines 19ff.: "Whence we learn that all needs, even bodily, but primarily those that are spiritual, are to be brought to God."
44. *Bekenntnisschriften,* p. 65 (*Marburger Artikel* 15).
45. Cf. P. Meinhold, *Luther heute* (Berlin, 1967), pp. 134–35.
46. WA 23:243.
47. WA 26:353.
48. WA 23:205 and 25:352.
49. WA 23:205.

Mélia, Elie (pp. 127–160)

1. H. Leclercq, "Extrême-Onction," DACL 5:1029–37; F. Cabrol, "Huile," DACL 6:2777–91; L. Godefroy, "Extrême-Onction," DTC 5:1897–2022.
2. A. Chavasse, *Etude sur l'onction des infirmes dans l'Eglise latine du IIIe siècle au XIe siècle* 1. *Du IIIe siècle à la Réforme Carolingienne* (Lyons, 1942).
3. Hieromonk Benedict Aguentov, *Ritual of the Sacrament of the Consecration of Oil. A Historico-Liturgical Essay (=Tcin taïnstva eleosviascenia. . . .)* (Serguiev Posad, 1917); A. Petrovsky, "On the History of the Ritual for the Sacrament of the Consecration of oil" (=K istorii posledovania . . .*"), Hristianskoe Tsčenie,* July, 1903, pp. 4–59; idem, "The Consecration of Oil in Its Ritual Aspect," in the article "Oleosviastčenie," in *Pravoslavnaya Bogoslovskaya Enciklopedia de Lopuhin* (Petrograd, 1904).
4. Repertories of liturgical manuscripts: J. Goar, *Euchologion sive rituale Graecorum complectens ritus et ordines* (Venice, 1730); H. Denzinger, *Ritus Orientalium, coptorum, syrorum et armenorum* (Würzburg, 1863); A. Dmitrievsky, *Repertory of Liturgical Manuscripts in the Libraries of the Orthodox East (=Opisanie liturguitceskih rukopisei. . . .),* 1. *Typika* (Kiev, 1895); 2. *Euchologia* (Kiev, 1901).
5. C. Kékélidzé, *Georgian Liturgical Documents Stored in the National Libraries, and Their Scientific Importance (=Liturguitceskie gruzinskie pamiatniki. . . .)* (Tiflis, 1908).
6. Irenaeus, *Adversus haereses* I, 21, 51 (PG 7:666).
7. Cited in Aguentov, op. cit., p. 2.—The passage from the *Assumption of Moses (=Apocalypse of Moses)* is translated in R. H. Charles (ed.), *The Apocrypha and Pseudepigrapha of the Old Testament in English* (2 vols.; Oxford, 1913), 2:144, col. 2.
8. Dmitrievsky, op. cit., 2:104.
9. PG 140:805–8.
10. B. Botte, *La Tradition Apostolique de saint Hippolyte. Essai de reconstitution* (Münster, 1963), p. 18.
11. *Constitutiones Apostolicae* VIII, 29 (PG 1:1125).
12. D. B. de Haneberg (ed.), *Canones S. Hippolyti Arabice e condicibus Romanis* (Münster, 1970). There is a Latin translation in Appendix 6 of L. Duchesne, *Christian Worship: Its Origin and Evolution,* tr. by M. L. McClure (London, 1903).
13. I. E. Rahmani (ed.), *Testamentum Domini Nostri Jesu Christi* (Mainz, 1899), Book I, chap. 25.
14. Aguentov, op. cit., p. 64.
15. Origen, *In Leviticum homiliae* 2, 4 (PG 12:418).
16. Cf. Hippolytus, *Philosophoumena* IX.
17. Cf. Tertullian, *De pudicitia* I, 6.
18. Serapion, *Euchologion,* chap. 27 (ed. G. Wobbermin; TU, Neue Folge 2/3b; Leipzig-Berlin, 1898).

19. Ibid., chap. 33 (Wobbermin, pp. 13–14).
20. *Demonstratio* 23,3 (*Patrologia Syriaca*, ed. R. Graffin [3 vols.; Paris, 1894–1926], 2:10).
21. Innocent I, *Epistula* 25 *ad Decentium* (PL 20:560), tr. by P. Palmer, *Sacraments and Forgiveness: History of Penance, Extreme Unction and Indulgences* (Sources of Christian Theology 2; Westminster, Md., 1959), p. 283.
22. G. Bickell, *Conspectus rei Syrorum litterarius* (Munich, 1871), pp. 77–78.
23. *Acta Sanctorum,* Junii, p. 213.
24. Cyril, *De adoratione in spiritu et veritate* (PG 58:472).
25. Procopius, *In Leviticum* 19:31 (PG 87:762).
26. Hefele-Leclercq, *Histoire des conciles* 3 (Paris, 1910), Appendix II, p. 1204.
27. Caesarius, *Sermo* 265,3 (PL 39:2258–59; in the appendix to the sermons of St. Augustine) or, now, *Sermo* 13,3 (CCL 103:66).
28. PL 40:1172 (among the works of St. Augustine).
29. *Collectio conciliorum* 4:1040.
30. PL 97:124.
31. E. Baluze, *Capitularia Regum Francorum* 1:409.
32. PL 105:1012–13.
33. PL 162:260.
34. *Theologiae regulae,* Regula 103 (PL 210:681).
35. Chavasse, op. cit., pp. 212–16.
35a. *Vita* (PG 99:326).
36. The French translation of this and the other citations of Pseudo-Dionysius is by M. de Gandillac, *Oeuvres complètes du pseudo-Denys l'Aréopagite* (Paris, 1943).
37. Denzinger, *Ritus Orientalium* 1:189.
38. Ibid.
39. *Ecrits* 2:366–67.
40. PG 155:520–21.
41. Aguentov, op. cit., p. 286.
42. PG 140:805–8.
43. PL 155:521.
44. Dmitrievsky, op. cit., 2:336–38, 447–49; 722–25; 827, 843–44.
45. Renaudot, *Ordo poenitentiae Iesujabi,* in Denzinger, op. cit., 1:468. Cf. also the council held by Catholicos Mar Joseph in the middle of the sixth century (n. 26, above).
46. Kékélidzé, op. cit., (n. 5), pp. 108–13.
47. Goar, op. cit., p. 536.
48. Ibid.
49. Ibid., p. 537. This is a formula of absolution that is in use today.
50. Dmitrievsky, op. cit., 2:775.
51. Ibid., 2:292.
52. Goar, op. cit., p. 963.
53. Dmitrievsky, op. cit., 2:1017–19.
54. Ibid., 2:35, 49.
55. Ibid., 2:5, 35.
56. Goar, op. cit., pp. 346–48.
57. Dmitrievsky, op. cit., 2:101–9.
58. Petrovsky, art. cit. (n. 3).
59. Dmitrievsky, op. cit., 2:320, 353.
60. Ibid., 2:197–202, 184–87, 490.
61. Dmitrievsky, *L'office divin dans l'Eglise russe au XVIᵉ siècle,* Appendix, pp. 107–18.
62. [The "Silverless (*Anargyroi*) Saints" are Cosmas and Damian and other holy physicians who would accept no money for their services.—Tr.]
63. Dmitrievsky, *Repertory of Liturgical Manuscripts . . . ,* 2:405–10, 710, 869.
64. Denzinger, op. cit., 1:189.
65. The complete text of this euchelaion is in Aguentov, op. cit., Appendix 1.
66. In Russian; Kazan, 1888.
67. Aguentov, op. cit., p. 39.

Nélidow, Alexandre (pp. 161–174)

1. St. Gregory of Nazianzus, *In baptismum homilia* 40.

Nocent, Adrien (pp. 175–190)

1. L. C. Mohlberg (ed.), *Liber sacramentorum romanae Aeclesiae Ordinis anni circuli: Sacramentarium Gelasianum* (Rerum Ecclesiasticarum Documenta, Series major: Fontes 4; Rome, 1968), pp. 381–82.
2. A. Chavasse, *Le sacramentaire gélasien* (Paris, 1957), pp. 135–39.
3. Ibid., p. 138, n. 94.
4. Ibid., p. 460.
5. Ibid., p. 461.
6. Ibid., p. 151.
7. Ibid., p. 174.
8. *Sermones* 13, 52, and 184 are cited by A. Chavasse in his *Etude sur l'onction des infirmes dans l'Eglise latine du IIIe au XIe siècle* (mimeographed dissertation; Lyons, 1938), pp. 43ff. (Vol. 1 of this dissertation was later published: Lyons, 1942.) The text is from G. Morin (ed.), *Sancti Caesarii Arelatensis Sermones* (Maredsous, 1937), now reprinted in CCL: *Sermo* 13 in 103:64–68; *Sermo* 52 in 103:230–33; *Sermo* 184 in 104:749–52.
9. *Sermo* 13, 3 (CCL 103:66–67).
10. M. Andrieu, *Les Ordines Romani du Haut Moyen Age* 4 (SSL 28; Louvain, 1956), pp. 529–30.
11. Chavasse, *Le sacramentaire gélasien*, pp. 59–60.
12. E. Bishop, "Liturgical Note," in A. B. Kuypers, *The Book of Cerne* (Cambridge, 1902), pp. 252, 253, 269.
13. Chavasse, *Le sacramentaire gélasien*, pp. 61ff.
14. Ibid., pp. 66–71.
15. In the following reflections and observations I am extensively indebted to a doctrinal dissertation in liturgical theology by Dom Germán Martínez, a student of mine at the Pontifical Liturgical Institute of San Anselmo, Rome. I directed this excellent work which has now been published as *La escatología en la Liturgia Romana Antigua* (Estudios des Instituto Superior de Pastoral 10; Salamanca-Madrid, 1976); it draws upon the Verona and Gelasian sacramentaries.
16. Let me remind the reader that I owe this list in large measure to the work of Dom Germán Martínez. His book focuses primarily on the parousia and the final things but includes a study of death.
17. St. Augustine, *Epistula* 55, 1, 2 (PL 33:205).
18. B. Botte, "*Prima resurrectio*—un vestige du millénarisme dans les liturgies occidentales," RTAM 15 (1948), 5–17; J. Ntedika, *L'évocation de l'au-delà dans la prière pour les morts. Etude de patristique et de liturgie latine (IVe–VIIIe s.)* (Louvain-Paris, 1971). On the Spanish liturgy alone: J. Llopis, "La Sagrada Escritura fuente de inspiración de la liturgia de difuntos del antiguo Rito Hispánico," HS 37 (1964), 349–91.
19. Zeno of Verona, *Tractatus* I, 2 (CCL 22:20).

Pinell, Jordi (pp. 191–238)

1. *Antifonario Visigótico Mozárabe de la Catedral de León. Edición facsímile* (MHS, ser. litúrg., 5/2; Madrid-Barcelona-León, 1953), fol. 274v–277. L. Brou and J. Vives (eds.), *Antifonario Visigótico Mozárabe de la Catedral de León*, text, notes, and indexes (MHS, ser. litúrg. 5/1; Barcelona-Madrid, 1959), pp. 455–59.
2. M. Férotin, *Le Liber Ordinum en usage dans l'Eglise wisigothique et mozarabe d'Espagne du Ve au XIe siècle* (Mel 5; Paris, 1904), cols. 377–84. [A *liber ordinum* was a book corresponding to our Ritual and Pontifical combined.—Tr.]

3. J. P. Gilson (ed.), *The Mozarabic Psalter* (ms. British Museum add. 30.851) (HBS 30; London, 1905), pp. 197–229. [A *liber misticus* (*misticus* probably from *mixtus*) was a book containing the songs, prayers, and readings for the Mass and the cathedral office.—Tr.]

4. Reproduced by Dom Férotin in a note to his edition of the *Liber Ordinum*, cols. 377–82. Cf. J. Pinell, "Las horas vigiliares del oficio monacal hispánico," *Liturgica* 3 (Montserrat, 1966), 197–229.

5. I cite the edition of F. A. Lorenzana, *Breviarium Gothicum secundum regulam beatissimi Isidori* (Madrid, 1776), reprinted in PL 86:974–76.

6. Br. 207–10.—I shall henceforth use the following abbreviations for the liturgical sources: AL, Antifonario de Léon (cf. n. 1); I cite the folios of the ms. Br, *Breviarium Gothicum* . . . (cf. n. 5); I cite the columns in PL 86. L, London, British Museum ms. add. 20.851 (cf. n. 3); I cite the folios of the ms. LOF, *Liber Orationum Festivus*. I use the numbering in the edition by J. Vives and J. Claveras, *Oracional Visigótico* (MHS, ser. litúrg. 1; Barcelona, 1946). LOPs, *Liber Orationum Psalmographus*. I cite the numbers in my own edition: *Liber Orationum Psalmographus. Colectas de salmos del antiguo rito hispánico* (MHS, ser. litúrg. 9; Barcelona-Madrid, 1972). Ord, *Liber Ordinum*. I refer always to ms. n. 3 of the Archivo de Silos, but I cite the column in Dom Férotin's edition (cf. n. 2). S7, Silos, Archivo cod. 7. In parentheses I cite the column in the edition of the *Liber Ordinum*, i.e., the note in which Dom Férotin reproduces the office of the sick according to this manuscript (cf. n. 4).

7. On the question of the two Spanish traditions cf. my historical hypothesis in the article "Liturgia Hispánica" in the *Diccionario de Historia Eclesiástica de España* 2 (Madrid, 1972), 1303–20. The liturgy of tradition B is represented by four manuscripts from the parish of Sts. Justa and Rufina in Toledo and by the Missal and Breviary of Canon Ortiz. This would have been the liturgy of the see of Seville and therefore of the entire metropolitan province of Bética; it would have been transferred to the parish of Sts. Justa and Rufina in Toledo in the tenth century when the Christian community in Sevilla had to emigrate because of civil strife among the Muslims.

8. A *missa* is a set of chants, consisting in this case of three antiphons and a responsory. The votive celebration of the office of the sick followed the pattern for a minor festive office and therefore had but a single *missa*. Cf. J. Pinell, "Las 'missae,' grupos de cantos y oraciones en el oficio de la antigua liturgia hispana," HS 8 (1955), 85–107.

9. On the differences between the three schemes followed in the Spanish cathedral office—festive, dominical and ferial in ordinary time—cf. my studies: "El oficio hispánico-visigótico," HS 10 (1957), 385–427; LOPs, pp. [83–102]; "El Ordo Catedral," in my article "Liturgia Hispánica" (n. 7), pp. 1310–13.

10. On the traits distinguishing the cathedral *ordo* from the monastic *ordo* cf. the introduction to my edition of the *liber horarum*: "Las horas vigiliares del oficio monacal hispánico" (n. 4).

11. Br 209–10, 975.—Although we can be quite certain that a reading from scripture was likewise a regular part of the morning office in tradition A, the manuscripts of the *misticus* do not include it or mention it. On the other hand, not only the Breviary but the manuscripts of the *misticus* in tradition B either give the entire text of the reading or at least give its incipit. The real difference between the two traditions, then, is in the manner of compiling a full *liber misticus*. Consequently, the fact that only the Breviary has the reading for the office of the sick should not be taken as indicating anything unusual.

12. Férotin, *Le Liber Ordinum* . . . , col. 384; J. Pérez de Urbel and A. González, *Liber Commicus* (MHS, serie litúrg. 3; Madrid, 1955), 2:548. In a note on page 549, the editors cite a fragment of a *commicus* that is joined to cod 35,4 of the Biblioteca Capitular of Toledo and that corresponds to the Mass *de infirmis* but has a reading from 2 Kgs 1:2–5 instead of Jer 29:10–14. [The *liber commicus* was the Lectionary of the Mozarabic rite, usually containing just the readings for Mass (prophecy, epistle, gospel); the name is probably from *comma*, "section, part."—Tr.]

13. As the reader will know, the Byzantine office gathers the nine odes or canticles into a single collection intended for the daily celebration of the orthros. The Ambrosian office distributes its collection of canticles in a special way, but in any case

supposes a plurality of canticles for each day. It was the Roman basilical office that began the practice of distributing a set of seven Old Testament canticles over the seven days of the week. The Rule of St. Benedict adopted the Roman system but added three canticles from the prophets for the vigils of Sundays. The Spanish monastic office also included three prophetic canticles every day in the *ordo ad nocturnos*. On the other hand, the cathedral *ordo ad matutinum* of the same Spanish rite called for only one Old Testament canticle, thus following the Roman example in a distant manner.

14. The *liber canticorum* (book of canticles) of tradition A has seventy-seven different canticles; the Breviary, sole representative of tradition B, has forty-seven. The collection for tradition B is thus much more limited, but it is characterized by the fact that a greater number of its canticles are in the Vetus Latina version.

15. Fol. 275v.

16. Col. 383.

17. Fol. 190; ed. Gilson, p. 342.

18. Br 881.

19. Fol. 191v; ed. Gilson, p. 344.

20. Br 885.

21. Fol. 192v; ed. Gilson, p. 346.

22. Br 881.

23. Br 209, 974.

24. Br 879. This is no. LVIII in the manuscript reproduced by Lorenzana.

25. The Breviary transcribes it in its entirety on the first Sunday of Advent; thereafter it uses it on various occasions, with a reference back to fol. 4 of Lorenzana's edition (cols. 52–55 in Migne).

26. Br 331. In this part the Breviary follows the distribution of forumularies that is found in the manuscript of the Biblioteca Nacional of Madrid (formerly Toledo 35,2), fol. 21. Ms Toledo 35,5, fols. 62v–63, also gives the abbreviated version of the canticle; it corresponds to Br 442.

27. There must undoubtedly have been collections of psalter antiphons, canticles, and other chants for the daily office, but no book grouping them separately has come down to us. The contents of this hypothetical book are included in some psalters and books of canticles and, in part, in the *liber misticus*, which contains all the parts needed for the office and Mass. Cf. J. Pinell, *Los textos de la antigua liturgía hispánica: Fuentes para su estudio. Estudios sobre la Liturgis Mozárabe* (Toledo, 1965), pp. 127–28.

28. The most important difference between a minor festive office and the office of the major feasts or solemnities was the number of *missae* in the morning office (cf. n. 7). The greatest number of *missae*, eight, is on the feast of the Epiphany. The chants which increase in number on such occasions are therefore the antiphons, *alleluiatica*, and responsories.

29. Antiphon: AL 276v, L 192.

30. Antiphon: AL 275.

31. Antiphon: AL 276.

32. Responsory: AL 276v, L 192v.

33. AL 276v, L 192. [An *alleluiaticum* was an antiphon with one or more alleluias in its text.—Tr.]

34. L 192v. The antiphonary of León gives only the incipit of the antiphon, in fol. 276v.

35. Antiphon: L 192.

36. Responsory: AL 275v, L 190.

37. Antiphon: Br 209, 974.

38. Antiphon: S7 (Ord 381).

39. Responsory: L 191v, S7 (Ord 380).

40. *Alleluiaticum*: AL 275v, L 189v, S7 (Ord 380), Ord 383.

41. *Sono*: AL 274v, L 188v, S7 (Ord 377), Br 207, 971. [A *sono* was an antiphon sung in an ornate style at Vespers.—Tr.]

42. *Sono*: AL 275. The versicle is from Ps 55:9.

43. AL 275, S7 (Ord 378).

44. AL 275, S7 (Ord 378–79).

45. AL 275, 275v; L 189.

46. AL 275, L 190v, S7 (Ord 377), Ord 378, Br 207, 972.

47. Br 208, 973. [A *psallendum* in the office was a processional song sung at the end of Vespers and Matins.—Tr.]

48. S7 (Ord 380).

49. L 191, S7 (Ord 377), Ord 380.

50. L 192v.

51. S7 (Ord 381).

52. L 191.

53. AL 275v.

54. L 191, S7 (Ord 380).

55. Antiphon: AL 275, L 190v, S7 (Ord 381), Ord 378.

56. Antiphon: AL 275v, L 188v–189, S7 (Ord 377, 379), Ord 382.

57. Antiphon: AL 275v.

58. *Sono:* AL 275v–276.

59. Antiphon: AL 275, L 189, S7 (Ord 379).

60. *Alleluiaticum:* L 188v–189, Br 207, 971.

61. Antiphon: AL 276v.

62. Antiphon: AL 276v.

63. *Alleluiaticum:* AL 276v.

64. Br 208, 974.

65. AL 276v.

66. AL 276, L 191v–192.

67. S7 (Ord 380–81).

68. L 190.

69. AL 275v.

70. AL 275, L 190, S7 (Ord 380), Ord 383, Br 209, 974.

71. AL 276v.

72. L 188v.

73. AL 275, L 189, S7 (Ord 381), Ord 383, Br 208, 974.

74. Br 207, 971.

75. S7 (Ord 382).

76. Ord 378.

77. Ord 377.

78. Br 207.

79. Br 972–73. In the first edition of the Breviary, prepared by Canon Ortiz in 1502, the hymn was already in the two offices of the sick.

80. L 160. The part still remaining of the hymn begins with the second verse of the seventh stanza: ". . . that ask your healing power."

81. In Lorenzana's edition (1775), after p. 450 and at the beginning of the psalter, a new numbering starts, using Roman numerals. The content of manuscript 10.001 of the Biblioteca Nacional of Madrid corresponds to pp. I–CXXIII of Lorenzana's edition. In Migne (PL 86), this part corresponds to columns 739–940.

82. C. Blume, *Hymnodia Gothica. Die mozarabischen Hymnen des alt-spanischen Ritus* (=Analecta Hymnica Medii Aevi 17; Leipzig, 1897), pp. 284–85.

83. J. Pinell, "Vestigis del lucernari a Occident," *Liturgica* 1 (Montserrat, 1956), p. 133, n. 118.

84. Only at two points do I not accept Blume's corrections but prefer the unanimous reading of the manuscripts: in the third verse of the third stanza, *salvans* (manuscripts) instead of *salvas* (Blume); and in the second verse of the seventh stanza, *mederi* (manuscripts) instead of *medere* (Blume). In any case, the variants are unimportant.

85. In my interpretation of euchological texts, I distinguish the following main elements in the structure of an oration: invocation, introductory petition, main petition, and *scopus* (the ultimate purpose of what is being requested). Cf. J. Pinell, LOPs (n. 6), pp. [59–65], [72–76].

86. The León antiphonary does not contain the euchological texts, so that there are only four sources for these.

87. As a matter of fact, the *supplicatio* in S7, as we shall see further on, is somewhat different from that in the Breviary. They might be regarded as two distinct formularies.

88. The distinction between Vespers and Matins is not always very clear. More than once, what is placed in the evening office in one source appears in the morning office in another source. For example, *completuria* no. 4 is in Vespers in the Silos manuscript and in Matins in the London manuscript; no. 5, on the other hand, is in Matins in the Silos manuscript and in Vespers in the London manuscript.

89. In keeping with the practice of tradition B, the Breviary has a blessing only in Vespers.

90. I have already said that this special prayer is from the *liber ordinum*. The other sources use common collects from the *psalmographus* as accompaniments to Ps 3. They do the same for the collect for Ps 50. This was the usual procedure. It was very rare for festive offices to have a collect of their own for Ps 3; they never had one for Ps 50. If the book of festive orations sometimes gives a collect for Ps 50 as proper to the liturgical season or to a particular feast, what it is in fact doing is choosing one of the psalter collects as being most appropriate.

91. These were distributed in eight *missae*. This means that the antiphonal orations number twenty four, but one of them is repeated (the one numbered as 17 and 23 in the collection given in the appendix).

92. It may be worth reminding the reader that the present study was originally a conference paper at the Saint-Serge Week of Liturgical Studies. In the oral presentation I was forced to abridge my study to a great extent.

93. Both the Silos manuscript and the Breviary give the *supplicatio* in the evening office. The Breviary also gives it in an office for Terce which it appends to the morning office and which was otherwise made up exclusively of common formularies: psalter antiphons and psalter collects.

94. In the only fragment left us of the *psalmographus*, the number of the psalm and its incipit are given before the collect. Other collects for the same psalm have only the generic title *alia* ("another"). Cf. J. Pinell, "Fragmentos de códices del antiguo rito hispánico. III–IV–V: Reliquias del Psalmographus," HS 25 (1972), 185–208.

95. LOPs (Ps 105): "Lord, be mindful of us in your good will toward your people and visit us with your salvation. Because like our fathers we have done evil in your sight, may we be redeemed from the infection both of the original condemnation and of actual sin."

96. LOPs 475 (Ps 6): "Lord, in your mercy save us whom you know to be ill on account of our own wickedness. Our soul is troubled by fear by your just judgments: let your joyous gift of forgiveness bring it peace. And may it receive the reward of health from him to whom it confesses the wounds caused by its sins, so that cleansed by grace it may receive forgiveness and come to you without being confounded."

97. LOPs 257 (Ps 73): "Be mindful of your congregation, Lord, which you created from the beginning, and do not forget your Church which you predestined from eternity in Christ. Mindful of your mercy, take heed of your covenant and constantly endue us with your promised freedom."

98. LOPs 371 (Ps 53): "Lord, save us by your name and free us by your power. Lead us out of affliction and fill us with gladness. Do not cease to defend our salvation nor to exercise your power for our liberation, so that as you freely grant us your salvation, we may glorify and praise you, and our freedom may lead us to rest."

99. LOPs 7 (Ps 6): "Have mercy on us, Lord, have mercy on us, and let not the sickness caused by our sins bring us everlasting death. Heal us, Lord, so that the soul troubled by guilt may be rendered peaceful by grace. Pour out your healing on the sick and grant forgiveness of their sins."

100. LOPs 325 (Ps 6): "Lord, we pray that you will not accuse us in your anger nor let your wrath rage against us, but rather reprove us gently and make us stop sinning, lest if you chastise us harshly, you drive us to destruction. Have mercy, therefore, on our weakness and grant us your healing, and if you see any who are troubled by their own sins, forgive them in your mercy and grant them serenity."

101. LOF, no. 560.

102. I have prepared a critical edition of the evening and morning *completurias* for Sunday. The two examples I cite are nos. 15 and 30, respectively, in this edition: "In our evening prayers we ask you, almighty everlasting God, that in your mercy you would help us in our needs" (Toledo manuscript 35,4, fol. 122); "In our evening prayer we ask you, everlasting Lord . . ." (Silos manuscript 6, fol. 61–61v, Br 228).

103. The London manuscript adds *illorum* after *tuorum* (". . . *these* your servants"); it thus supposes that the names of the sick are listed at this point.

104. *Missale Mixtum* (PL 85:119): "Being freed from evil and confirmed permanently in good, may we deserve to serve you, our God and Lord. Lord, put an end to our sinning. Grant joy to the afflicted, ransom to the captive, health to the sick, and rest to the departed. Grant peace and safety throughout all our days and break our enemies in their boldness. And hear, O God, the prayers of your servants, all faithful Christians, today and at all times."

105. J. Pinell, "Una exhortación diaconal en el antiguo rito hispánico," AST 36 (1964), 3–25.

106. *Missale Mixtum* (PL 85:114): "Let us remember the holy catholic Church in our prayers, that God would mercifully deign to deepen its faith, hope and charity. Let us remember all the lapsed, captives, sick and travellers, that the Lord in his mercy would deign to redeem, heal and comfort them."

107. [Some of these prayers are translated so as to reflect the Latin text more closely and thus to illustrate points being made by the author (who cites only the Latin text), for example, with regard to the use of relative clauses in the invocation of the orations. Others of the prayers have been translated in a manner more adapted to English usage.—Tr.]

Sicard, Damien (pp. 239–246)

1. The following studies, among others, may be cited: E. Le Blant, *Etude sur les sarcophages chrétiens de la ville d'Arles* (Paris, 1878), pp. 27–33; Idem, "Les bas-reliefs des sarcophages chrétiens et les liturgies funéraires," *Revue archéologique* (1879), pp. 229–31; 276–79; L. Gougaud, "Etude sur les *ordines commendationis animae*," EL 49 (1935), 12–13; 24–26. At this time the writer had probably not yet become acquainted with the eighth-century Gellone sacramentary; A.-G. Martimort, "L'*Ordo commendationis animae*," MD, no. 15 (1948), 150; Idem, "L'iconographie des catacombes et la catéchèse antique," RivAC 25 (1949), 105–8; Idem, "Comment meurt un chrétien," MD, no. 44 (1955), 20–24; J. Ntedika, *L'évocation de l'au-delà dans la prière pour les morts* (Louvain, 1971), pp. 72–83; J. Th. Maertens, "La liturgie de la mort et son langage," *Le Supplément*, no. 108 (1974), 46–92.

2. Sacramentary of Gellone, Paris B. N. lat. 12.048; Sacramentary of Rheinau, Zürich, Zentralbibliothek cod Rh 30.

3. *Rite of Anointing and Pastoral Care of the Sick*, nos. 146 and 148 (published 1972; tr. in *The Rites of the Catholic Church* 1 [New York, 1976], pp. 625–26).

4. D. Sicard, "Le Viatique: perspectives nouvelles?" MD, no. 113 (1973). 103–14.

5. E.g., Rome, Archiv. San Pietro H 58, F 11, etc.

6. E.g., Collectary of La Grasse, Paris B.N. lat. 933; Ritual of Jumièges, Orleans B.M. Y 127; Consuetudinaries of the Abbey of Bec and other abbeys.

7. E.g., Milan, Bibl. Ambros. T 27 sup., Bibl. Capt. M, m.

8. I shall here draw up a table showing the order in which these figures and groups appear in the most typical manuscripts. The ones I have chosen are: eighth-century Sacramentary of Gellone (G), Paris, B.N. lat. 12.048; eighth-century Sacramentary of Rheinau (Rh), Zürich, Zentralbibliothek cod Rh 30; Libellus floriacensis (Lf1) from the first quarter of the ninth century, Orleans, B.M. 184 (161); Sacramentary of Arezzo (Ar) from the tenth-eleventh century, Rome, Vat. lat. 4772; "Martyrology of Bede" (Pt) from the eleventh century, Rome, Archiv. San Pietro H 58; Liber monachorum Mediolani (Mal) from the eleventh century, Milan, Bibl. Ambros. T 96 Sup; Collectary and Ritual in the Chigi collection (Ch) from the first half of the eleventh century, Rome, Vat. Chigi CV 134; Hambrug Missal (Val) from

G	Rh	Lfl	Ar	Pt	Ch/Val	Mal	Ord	Pru	Gra	Rip	Rem	Ro	Lug Pc Sr Sa RR	RR 72
					Abel 1									
Noah 1		1	1	1	2	1	1		1	1		1	2	1
Enoch, Elijah 2	1	7	2	2	3	2	2	1	2	2	1	2	1	
		Abraham 2	3	3	4	3							3	2
	Lot 2	3	4	6	5	4	3	2	3	3	2	3	6	
		Israel 4												
Moses 3	3	5	7	7	8	7	4	3	4	4	3	5	7	4
	Isaac 4	5	4	6	5	5	5	4	5	5	4	4	5	
			Jacob 6	5	7	6								
Job 4	5	8	8	8	9	8	6	5	6	6	5	6	4	3
Daniel 5	6	9	11	10	12	11		6	7	7	6	8	8	5
Three youths 6	7		12	11	13	12	7	7	8	8	7	9	9	6
Jonah 7	8	10	9		11	9			10	9		10		
Susanna 8		8	13	12	14	13		8	9	10	8	11	10	7
David 9	9	6	10	9	10	10	8	9	11	11	9	7	11	8
			Race 14	13	15	14								
Peter, Paul 10	10		15	14	16	15	9	10	12	12	10	12	12	9
	Thecla 11		16	15	17	16	10	11	13	13			13	

the eleventh century, Rome, Vallicelliana B 141; "Ordines de Haute-Italie due XIe siècle" (Ord), Milan, Bibl. Ambros. T 27 Sup; Pseudo-Pontifical of Prudentius of Troyes (Pru) from the eleventh century, Paris, B.N. 818; Collectary-Ritual of La Grasse (Gra) from the end of the eleventh century, Paris, B.N. lat. 933; Sacramentary of Rippoll (Rip) from the eleventh century, Vich, Episcop. Mus. cod 67; Missal of St. Pierre de Remiremont (Rem) from the twelfth century, Paris, B.N. lat. 823; Orational of St. Peter of Rome (Ro) from the twelfth century, Rome, Archiv. San Pietro F 11; Roman Pontifical of the twelfth century LIB (Lug), Lyons, B.M. 570; Pontifical of the Roman Curia in the thirteenth century LI (Pc), ed. Andrieu; Roman Sacerdotale of 1523 (Sr); Ritual of J. A. Sanctorius, cardinal of St. Severin, 1584–1602 (Sa), Rome, Vat. lat. 6116; Roman Ritual of Paul V (RR), 1614, 1953; Roman Ritual of Paul VI (RR 72), 1972.

9. Cf. A. Chavasse, "Le Sacramentaire Gélasien du VIIIe siècle," EL 73 (1959), 249–98.

10. It is unfortunate that in his article "La liturgie de la mort et son langage" (n. 1, above), p. 62, J. Th. Maertens assigns the prayer Delicta juventutis to the sixteenth and seventeenth centuries when in fact it was being used back in the tenth century. His deductions on the development of language are therefore in need of some qualification. If, as he desires, we are to "turn away from the beaten tracks followed by the liturgists" and to "renew our analysis on the basis of findings of the psychological and social sciences" (p. 62, n. 7), we will need a more solid historical basis than the one he provides. This is all the more regrettable inasmuch as his observations do have a certain interest.

11. Cf. above, n. 1. For one particular point in the Proficiscere I may add: J. Hennig, "Quelques notes sur la mention de sainte Thècle dans la Commendatio animae," Nuevo Didaskaleion 14 (1964), 21–27.

12. Cf., e.g., "Textes et rubriques des agenda mortuorum," ALw 4/1 (1955), 62.

13. He will say the same of the Requiem aeternam which is taken from the fourth Book of Esdras.

14. In his article "Etudes sur les ordines commendatonis animae" (n. 1, above), Gougaud cites a prayer of a priest Severus who suffered martyrdom ca. 304; the prayer is given in the Passio S. Philippi, ed. by Ruinard in his Acta primorum martyrum sincera et selecta (Paris, 1689), p. 452. Gougaud also cites the Oratio II pseudocypriana, ed. by G. Hartel, Sancti Cypriani opera omnia CSEL 3; Vienna, 1871), pp. 144–51; I shall come back to this prayer later on. But here is how Gougaud concludes his study:

"There is no evidence enabling us to determine the precise relations between these three texts or to say which is the model for the others" (p. 27).

15. Martimort, "L'iconographie des catacombes et la catéchèse antique," RivAC 25 (1949), 1–5–14. Martimort's views perhaps require modification in the light of Cyrille Vogel's analyses, but the essential points made by Martimort are still valid.

16. Ibid., p. 105, n. 1.

17. Cf. Gn 5:21–24; Sir 44:16; Heb 11:5; Jude 14–15. Cf. also 2 Kgs 2:11.

18. Are we, moreover, really so certain of the authenticity and date of this decree? The most recent critics (Turner, Caspar, Schwartz) are in agreement that chapters 4 and 5 (it is chapter 5 that deals with the apocrypha) are the private work of a sixth-century compiler living in northern Italy or southern Gaul. Cf. *Clavis Patrum Latinorum* (2nd ed.; Steenbrugge, 1961), no. 1676, p. 370, and the good bibliographical survey of A. Van Hove, *Prolegomena ad codicem iuris canonici* (2nd ed.; Malines-Rome, 1945), p. 140, n. 5. Cf. also J. Festugière, "Les énigmes de saint Thècle," *Comptes-rendus de l'Académie des Inscriptions et Belles Lettres*, 1968, pp. 52–63.

19. H. Leclercq, "Défunts," DACL 4 (1916), 430–32, a handy edition of these prayers. There is a slightly different edition in the article "Oratio Cypriani," DACL 12 (1936), 2330–34. It is odd, moreover, that in his 1936 article, Leclercq makes no reference to the 1916 article. Let me, in passing, express my regret that no more recent and more substantial study of the *Orationen cyprianae* has appeared. For according to Leclercq this Greek document, the importance of which is indicated by the existence of Latin, Arabic, Ethiopic, Slavonic, and Syriac versions, has ties with Jewish texts in the Mishnah and with the rituals of the Diaspora. A more precise dating of these apocryphal texts and their sources would certainly be a help in ascertaining with greater assurance the origin of the *Proficiscere*.

20. The reader can easily compare the references to the angelic hierarchy in the first part of the *Proficiscere* with the lists given by St. Paul: Col 1:16; 2:15; Eph 1:21; etc.

21. Cf. nos. 291, 293, 295 in the Mohlberg edition of the *Sacramentarium Gelasianum*. The litany genre used in the *Proficiscere* may be compared with that in the *Deprecatio Aurelii* (Pl 68:395), in books of private prayers (Lfl, or the Book of Cerne), or in the *Oratio ad poscenda sanctorum suffragia* which was published by J. Condamin and J. B. Vanel, in *Martyrologie de la sainte Eglise de Lyon* (Lyons, 1902), pp. 137–40.

22. Cf. Rom 6:3–4.

23. K. Rahner, *On the Theology of Death*, tr. by C. H. Henkey (Quaestiones Disputatae 2; New York, 1961), pp. 82–83. Like the liturgy of baptism, the liturgy of death is a liturgy of initiation. Consider, e.g., the alternation, in the Gelasian, between exorcism and entrance into the communion of heaven, the reminder of the triple signation, the *redditio symboli*, etc.

24. Cf. Maertens, art. cit.

Verheul, Ambroise (pp. 247–258)

1. AAS 61 (1973), 5–9.

2. *Ordo Unctionis Infirmorum eorumque Pastoralis Curae* (Vatican City, 1972). The Apostolic Constitution and the *Rite of Anointing and Pastoral Care of the Sick* are in English in *The Rites of the Catholic Church* 1 (New York, 1976), 577–642. Some commentaries on the new rite: Z. Alszeghy, S. J., "L'unzione degli infermi," *Civiltà Cattolica* 124 (1973), 319–28; J. Baumgartner, " 'Ist jemand krank unter euch . . .': Zur neuen Ordnung der Krankenliturgie," *Schweitzerische Kirchenzeitung* 35 (1973), 525–29; 36 (1973), 544–47; G. Berti, "L'unzione degli infermi," Amb 49 (1973), 106–14; idem, "La Costituzione Apostolica sull'Unzione degli Infermi," ibid., 49 (1973), 159–62; P. De Clerck, "Orientations du nouveau ritual des malades," *La foi et le temps*, nos. 3–5 (1973), 536–48; P. Farnés, "Los textos eucológicos del nuevo ritual de la Unción de los enfermos," *Phase* 13 (1973), 143–56; A. Gots, "Die erneuerte Liturgie für die Kranken und Leidenden," *Heiliger Dienst* 27 (1973), 58–62; P. Gy, "Le

nouveau rituel des malades," *Notitiae,* no. 81 (1973), 108–11; idem, "Le nouveau rituel romain des malades," MD, no. 113 (1973), 29–49; R. Kaczynski, "Neubesinnung auf ein vergessenes Sakrament," TPQ 121 (1973), 346–59; A. Knauber, "Sakrament der Kranken: Terminologische Beobachtungen zur Ordo Unctionis infirmorum," LJ 4 (1973), 217–37; idem, "Neuordung der kirchlichen Krankensalbung," Gd 7, no. 3 (1973), 17–18; J. L. Larrabe, "El nuevo ritual de la Unción de los Enfermos," *Lumen* 22 (1973), 97–112; A. G. Martimort, "Le nouveau rituel des malades," *Notitiae,* No. 80 (1973), 66–69; idem, "Constitution Apostolique sur l'onction des malades. Texte et commentaire," DC 55 (1973), 101–4; idem, "El nuevo ritual para enfermos," *Phase* 13 (1973), 137–43; idem, "Commento pastorale alla Costituzione Apostolica sull'unzione degli infermi," Amb 49 (1973), 115–20; B. Newns, "The Ordo Unctionis Infirmorum," CR 58 (1973), 451–58; G. Oury, "L'onction des malades. Constitution Apostolique: Traduction, Présentation et Commentaire," *Esprit et Vie* 83 (1973), 145–48; idem, "Le nouveau Ritual des Malades," idid., 83 (1973), 375–79; H. Plock, *Liturgie mit Kranken. Vorschläge und Übertragungen* (Essen, 1973); J. Rabau, "Le nouveau rituel de l'onction des malades," *Feu nouveau,* 16, no. 15 (1973), 6–34; K. Richter, "Heilssorge der Kirche für die Kranken," BuL 46 (1973), 178–89; A. Verheul, "De nieuwe romeinse orde van dienst voor de ziekensalving," TvL 57 (1973), 228–29; idem, "Rituale dell'unzione e della pastorale degli infermi," *Liturgia* 7 (1973), 70–130.

3. Decree of January 10, 1974, in *Notitiae,* no. 89 (1974), 36.

4. *Rituale Romanum Pauli V Pontificis Maximi iussu editum die XVII iunii 1614* (editio typica; Vatican City, 1952).

5. *Constitution Sacrosanctum Concilium on the Sacred Liturgy,* no. 74; *Rite of Anointing,* Introduction, nos. 8–15.

6. *Rite of Anointing,* Introduction, no. 16.

7. *Constitution on the Sacred Liturgy,* no. 75; Apostolic Constitution *Sacram Unctionem (The Rites,* p. 581); *Rite of Anointing,* Introduction, no. 23.

8. Apostolic Constitution *Sacram Unctionem, (The Rites,* pp. 580–81); *Rite of Anointing,* Introduction, no. 20; cf. *Rite of the Blessing of Oils; Rite of Consecrating the Chrism* (in *The Rites,* pp. 517–27), Introduction, no. 3.

9. *Rite of Anointing,* Introduction, nos. 21–22; ch. II, no. 75.

10. Ibid., ch. II, no. 75b.

11. Ibid., ch. II, nos. 68–79.

12. Apostolic Constitution *Sacram Unctionem (The Rites,* pp. 580–81).

13. Latin of old and new formulas: "Per istam sanctam unctionem et suam piissimam misericordiam"; cf. *Rituale Romanum* (n. 4), pp. 186–87 = *Ordo ministrandi Extremam Unctionem;* nos. 8–9.

14. Latin of formula: "adjuvet te Dominus gratia Spiritus Sancti." Council of Trent, Sess. XIV: *De Extrema Unctione,* cap. 2: "Res etenim haec gratia est Spiritus Sancti. . . ."

15. Latin of formula: "ut a peccatis liberatum, te salvet atque propitius levet."

16. *Rite of Anointing,* ch. II, no. 74.

17. Ibid., no. 75.

18. Ibid., no. 77.

19. I have consulted the following commentaries: W. Beyschlag, *Der Brief des Jakobus* (Göttingen, 1897); J. Cantinat, *Les épîtres de S. Jacques et de S. Jude* (Paris, 1973); M. Dibelius, *A Commentary on the Epistle of James,* rev. by H. Greeven, tr. by M. A. Williams (Philadelphia, 1976); L. Gaugusch, *Der Lehrgehalt des Jakobus-Epistel* (Freiburg, 1914); W. Grosheide, *De brief van Jakobus* (Kampen, 1961); A. Hamman, "Prière et culte dans la lettre de Saint-Jacques," ETL 34 (1958), 35–47; M. Meinertz, "Die Krankensabung Jak. 5, 14f.," BZ 20 (1932), 23–26; F. Mussner, *Der Jakobusbrief* (Herders Theologischer Kommentar zum Neuen Testament 13/1; Freiburg, 1964); J. Michl, *Die Katholischen Briefe* (Regensburg, 1968), pp. 62–68; B. Reicke, *The Epistles of James, Peter and Jude* (Anchor Bible 37; New York, 1964); E. Thurneysen, *La foi et les oeuvres. Commentaire de l'épître de Jacques* (Neuchâtel, 1959); H. von Soden, *Die Briefe an die Kolosser . . . Die Briefe des Jakobus. . . .* (Freiburg-Leipzig, 1893); A. Wikenhauser, *De Katholieke Brieven* (Antwerp, 1969); R. Williams, *The Letters of John and James* (Cambridge, 1965).

20. "If any of you lacks wisdom, let him ask God, who gives to all generously and without reproaching, and it will be given him. But let him ask in faith, with no doubting, for he who doubts is like a wave of the sea that is driven and tossed by the wind. For that person must not suppose that a double-minded man, unstable in all his ways, will receive anything from the Lord" (Jas 1:5–8).

21. "You desire and do not have; so you kill. And you covet and cannot obtain; so you fight and wage war. You do not have, because you do not ask. You ask and do not receive, because you ask wrongly, to spend it on your passions" (Jas 4:2–3).

22. Here is the text that concerns us. I shall give it first in Greek, then in the Latin of the Vulgate, and finally in English:

asthenei tis en humin; proskalesasthō tous presbuterous tēs ekklēsias kai proseuxasthōsan ep'auton aleipsantes auton elaiō en tō onomati tou Kuriou. kai hē euchē tēs pisteōs sōsei ton kamnonta, kai egerei auton ho Kurios kan hamartias ē pepoiēkōs, aphethesetai auto.

Infirmatur quis in vobis? inducat presbyteros Ecclesiae, et orent super eum, ungentes eum in nomine Domini; ea oratio fidei salvabit infirmum, et allevabit eum Dominus; et si in peccatis sit, remittentur ei.

Is any among you sick? Let him call for the elders of the church, and let them pray over him, anointing him in the name of the Lord; and the prayer of faith will save the sick man, and the Lord will raise him up; and if he has committed sins, he will be forgiven
(Jas 5:14–15).

23. Jas 1:6; Mt 7:7–8; Lk 11:9–10; Jn 16:24; 1 Jn 6:3, 32.

24. Mk 5:34; 16:18; Mt 9:22; Lk 8:48; etc.

25. Mk 5:34; Lk 17:19.

26. Jn 11:41–43; Acts 9:40.

27. Mk 16:18.

28. *In Leviticum homiliae* 2, 4.

29. *Rituale Romanum: Ordo ministrandi Extremam Unctionem*, no. 7: ". . . exstinguatur in te omnis virtus diaboli per impositionem manuum nostrarum" ("May any power of the devil over you be destroyed by the laying on of my hands").

30. Cf. *Ordination of Deacons, Priests and Bishops* (in *The Rites* 2 [New York, 1980], pp. 31–108).

31. Cf. Cantinat, op. cit. (n. 19), pp. 250–51.

32. Mk 6:13.

33. Mk 9:38; 16:17; Lk 10:17; Jn 14:13; 15:16; 16:24, 26; Acts 3:6, 16; 4:7, 10; 10:43; 16:18; 2 Cor 5:20; 1 Jn 5:20; 2:12.

34. In what follows I rely especially on B. Reicke, "L'onction des malades d'après Saint-Jacques," MD, no. 113 (1973), 50–56.

35. Jgs 9:8; 1 Sm 9:16; 10:1; 15:1, 17; 16:3, 12; 2 Sm 2:4; 3:19, etc.; 2 Kgs 9:3, 6; Pss 23:5; 45:8; 89:21.

36. Ex 28:41; 29:7, 29; 30:30–33; 40:13, 16; Lv 4:3; 6:13; 7:36; 8:12; Nm 3:3; Dn 9:25; Sir 45:15.

37. 1 Kgs 19:16; Is 61:1; Lk 4:18.

38. 1 Jn 2:20, 27; Tertullian, *De baptismo* 7; Hippolytus, *Traditio Apostolica* 21, 6–22.

39. Gn 28:18; 31:13; Ex 29:36; 30:23–29; 37:29; 40:9; Nm 7:1, 10, 88; Dn 9:24.

40. Is 1:6; Lk 10:34; Lv 14:15–18; 26:29.

41. Mishnah, *Sabbath* 14, 4.

42. Talmud, *Berakhot* 1, 2.

43. Mt 3:2; 11:12; Mk 12:34; Lk 17:21.

44. Mishnah, *Sabbath* 28, 5.

45. Mt 26:12; Mk 12:34; Lk 17:21.

46. Mk 16:1; Lk 24:1.

47. Hos 2:4, 7; Am 6:6; Is 25:6; Jl 3:18; Zech 10:7.

48. Reicke, art. cit. (n. 34), pp. 54–55.

49. *Genesis Rabbah* 33, 206. 30.

50. *Apocalypse of Moses* 9, 3; 13, 1; 40, 2.

51. Mt 8:25; 9:21–22; 14:30; 16:25; 27:40, 42, 49; Mk 3:4; 5:23, 28, 34; 6:56; 8:15;

10:52; 15:31, 32; Lk 6:9; 8:36, 48, 50; 9:24; 17:19, 33; 18:42; 23:35, 39; Jn 11:12; 12:27; Acts 4:9; 14:9; 27:20; Heb 5:7.

52. Mt 1:21; 10:22; 18:11; 19:25; 24:13; Mk 8;35; 10:26; 13:13, 20; 16:16; Lk 7:50; 8:12; 9:24; 13:23; 18:26; 19:10; Jn 3:17; 5:34; 10:9, 12, 47; Acts 2:21, 40, 47; 4:12; 11:14; 15:1–11; 16:30, 31; Rom 5:9, 10; 8:24; 9:27; 10:9, 13; 11:14, 26; 1 Cor 1:18, 21; 3:15; 5:5; 7:16; 9:22; 10:33; 15:2; 2 Cor 2:15; Eph 2:5, 8; 1 Thes 1:10; 2:10; 1 Tm 1:15; 2:4, 15; 4:16; 2 Tm 1:9; 4:18; Ti 3:5; Heb 7:25; Jas 1:21; 2:14; 4:12; 5:15, 20; 1 Pt 3:21; 4:18; Jude 5 and 23.

53. Mt 3:2; 11:12; Mk 12:34; Lk 17:21.

54. Mt 9:21–22; Mk 10:52; Lk 8:48, 50; 17:19; 18:42; Acts 14:9.

55. Lk 7:50; Acts 16:31; Rom 10:9; 1 Cor 1:21.

56. Acts 2:21; 4:12; Rom 10:13.

57. Mt 9:19; 17:7; 26:46; Mk 3:3; 10:49; 14:42; Lk 6:8; 13:25; Jn 11:29; 13:4; 14:31; Acts 9:8; 10:26; Rv 11:1.

58. Mt 1:24; 2:13, 14, 20, 21; 8:25, 26; 25:7; Mk 4:27; Lk 8:24; 11:8; Acts 12:7.

59. Mt 8:15; 9:5, 6, 7; Mk 1:31; 2:9, 11, 12; 9:27; Lk 5:23, 24; 6:8; Jn 5:8; Acts 3:6, 7.

60. Mt 9:25; 10:8; 11:5; 14:2; Mk 5:41; 6:14, 16; Lk 7:14; 8:54; 9:7.

61. Mt 11:11; 24:11, 24; Mk 13:22; Lk 1:69; 7:16; Jn 7:52; Acts 13:22, 23.

62. Mt 24:7; Mk 13:18; Lk 21:40.

63. Mt 3:9; 27:52; Mk 12:26; Lk 3:8; 7:22; 20:37; Jn 5:21; Acts 26:8; 2 Cor 1:9; Heb 11:19.

64. Mt 16:22; 17:9, 23; 26:32; 27:63, 64; 28:6, 7; Mk 14:28; 16:6; Lk 9:22; 24:6, 34; Jn 2:19, 20, 22; 21:14; Acts 3:15; 4:10; 5:30; 10:40; 13:30–37; Rom 4:24, 25; 6:4, 9; 7:4; 8:11, 12, 34; 10:9; 1 Cor 6:14; 15:4–52 (9 times); 2 Cor 4:14; Gal 1:1; Eph 1:20; Col 2:12; 1 Thes 1:10; 2 Tm 2:8; 1 Pt 1:21.

65. Rom 8:11; 13:11; 1 Cor 6:14; Eph 5:14; Col 2:12.

66. Mt 12:42; Lk 11:31; 1 Cor 15:4–52 (9 times); 2 Cor 1:9; 4:14.

67. Mt 16:21; Mk 8:31; Lk 9:22; 17:25; 24:26; Acts 3:18; 17:3.

68. Rom 8:17; 1 Pt 4:13.

69. *Constitution on the Sacred Liturgy,* no. 36, §§3, 4.

70. According to the *Constitution on the Sacred Liturgy* (no. 36.3), translations of liturgical texts must, as a general rule, be approved by the episcopal conferences and this approval must in turn be confirmed by the Congregation for Sacred Worship. However, a letter of October 25, 1973, which Jean Cardinal Villot, Secretary of State, and Msgr. A. Bugnini, Secretary of the Congregation for Sacred Worship, sent in the pope's name to the presidents of the episcopal conferences, prescribes that a special approval of the pope is needed for the translations of sacramental formulas. Cf. *Notitiae,* no. 89 (1974), 37–38.

71. *Decretum pro Armenis,* in G. Hofmann (ed.), *Concilium Florentinum* I–II, p. 130.

72. Council of Trent, Sess. XIV: *De Extrema Unctione,* cap. 2 et 3.

73. *Constitution on the Sacred Liturgy,* nos. 73–75: AAS 56 (1964), 118–19.

74. For the sacraments in general, cf. ibid., no. 61; for the Eucharist, no. 47; for burial, no. 81.

75. *Dogmatic Constitution on the Church,* no. 11: AAS 57 (1965), 15.

76. *The Rites,* p. 580.

77. *Rite of Anointing,* Introduction, no. 5.

78. Ibid., no. 2: "Christ himself was sinless, yet he fulfilled what was written in Isaiah: he bore all the sufferings of his passion and understood human sorrow (see Isaiah 53:4–5). Christ still suffers and is tormented in his followers whenever we suffer. If we realize that our sufferings are preparing us for eternal life in glory, then they will seem short and even easy to bear (see 2 Corinthians 4:17)" (*The Rites,* p. 582).

79. Ibid., no. 3a: "It is part of the plan laid down by God's providence that we should struggle against all sickness and carefully seek the blessings of good health. . . . Yet we should always be prepared to fill up what is lacking in Christ's sufferings for the salvation of the world as we look forward to all creation being set free in the glory of the sons of God (see Colossians 1:24; Romans 8:19–21)" (*The Rites,* p. 582).

80. Ibid., no. 3b: "Moreover, the role of the sick in the Church is to remind others

not to lose sight of the essential or higher things and so to show that our mortal life is restored through the mystery of Christ's death and resurrection" (*The Rites*, p. 582).

81. *The Rites*, p. 584.

82. The eschatological character of the anointing of the sick, therefore, by no means implies that this anointing is a sacrament for the dying, despite what some Dutch writers have recently been saying. Cf. J. van den Bosch, "De zalving der zieken. Verantwoording en toelichting van een vorstel," TvL 52 (1968), 377–87; H. Wegman, "Liturgie met zieken en stervenden," TvL 53 (1969), 179–96. Similar ideas have been defended in Germany, especially by K. Rahner, in his *Sur le sacrement des malades* (Paris, 1966) and his *On the Theology of Death*, tr. by C. H. Henkey (Quaestiones Disputatae 2; New York, 1961), pp. 85–86, and by A. Grillmeier, "Le Sacrement de la résurrection," *Evangéliser* 16 (1962), 455–71. These writers see the anointing of the sick as a sacramental consecration of death, and they appeal for support to St. Thomas, *Summa contra Gentiles* 4:73.

83. Cf. 2 Cor 5:1.

84. St. Thomas, *In IV Sententiarum*, d. 1, q. 1, a. 4, qc. 3.

85. *Rite of Anointing*, ch. 2, no. 69 (*The Rites*, p. 600).

86. Ibid., no. 70.

87. Ibid. no. 71.

88. Ibid., no. 233 (*The Rites*, p. 635).

89. Ibid., no. 77 (*The Rites*, p. 604).

90. Is 52:13–53:12; Acts 13:32–39; Rom 8:14–17; 8:18–27; 1 Cor 15:12–20; Col 1:22–29; Heb 4:14–16; 5:7–9; Jas 5:13–16; 1 Pt 1:3–9; Rv 22:17, 20–22; Mt 8:5–17; Jn 6:54–59; 10:11–18; Mt 26:36–46; Mk 15:33–39; 16:1–6; Lk 23:44–49; 24:1–6a, 13–35; Jn 20:1–10.

91. *Rite of Anointing*, no. 76.

92. Ibid., no. 74.

93. Ibid., no. 76 (*The Rites*, p. 603).

94. Ibid., no. 75 (*The Rites*, p. 602).

95. Ibid., no. 77 (*The Rites*, p. 603).

96. Council of Trent, Sess. XIV: *De Extrema Unctione*.

97. *Dogmatic Constitution on the Church*, no. 11. [The Latin text has *alleviabit*; some English translations of the document translate as though the Latin were *allevabit*, "will raise up."—Tr.]

98. *Vetus Latina. Die Reste der altlateinischen Bibel*. Nach Petrus Sabatier, neu gesammelt und herausgegeben von der Erzabtei Beuron, vol. 26: *Epistolae Catholicae. Apocalypsis* (1956), p. 61. Many manuscripts read *allevabit* or *elevabit* or, even more explicitly, *suscitabit*.

99. *Novum Testamentum Domini nostri Jesu Christi Latine secundum editionem Sancti Hieronymi*. Editio critica a J. Wordsworth et H. J. White, 3: *Actus Apostolorum. Epistolae Canonicae. Apocalypsis Johannis* (Oxford, 1954), p. 263; cf. the critical apparatus for v. 15.

100. Ps 72:18: "You cast them down, as they were attempting to rise"; Ps 114:14: "May the Lord raise up all who are falling"; Sir 36:3: "Lift up your hand against foreign peoples"; Acts 3:7: "Taking him by the hand . . . he raised him up."

101. Pontificia Commissio pro Nova Vulgata Bibliorum Editione. *Epistolae S. Pauli Apostoli et Catholicae* (Vatican City, 1970), p. 201.

102. It seems to me that in his article "Le nouveau rituel romain des malades," MD, no. 113 (1973), 29–49, Father Gy does not take enough account of this essential difference when he writes: "Whatever be the difference in meaning between the two words in patristic Latin (a difference which is perhaps not all that clear), the new ritual prefers *allevare* with complements designating a person (e.g., *infirmum*) and *alleviare* with those designating a suffering (e.g., *dolorem*)" (p. 42, n. 28).

103. *Notitiae*, no. 91 (1974), 89–106. In agreement with the author of that article, I cite here J. Rabau, who was a member of the postconciliar commission for the ritual. In his article, "Le nouveau rituel de l'onction des malades," *Feu nouveau*, nos. 16–17 (1973), 6–24, 33–34, he says: "The risen Lord will save and raise up: *allevat*, which means "raise up," is the biblical word so often used in the gospels to designate the

resurrection. The meaning, then, is that the risen Lord gives the sick person a share in the power of his resurrection. This shows the full scope of the sacrament; by reason of Christ's resurrection, the ordinary life of a sick person who is a believer takes on a new dimension. The point, then, is quite different from consoling or applying a little balm!"

Vogel, Cyrille (pp. 259–276)

1. *Ordo XLIX: Ordo qualiter agatur in obsequium defunctorum* (first redaction 700–750), in M. Andrieu, *Les Ordines Romani du Haut Moyen Age* 4. *Ordines XXXV–XLIX* (SSL 28; Louvain, 1956), 529–30, which reproduces *Vat. Ottobon. 312.*—Another *Ordo defunctorum*, slightly older than *Ordo XLIX,* has been discovered by D. Sicard in a copy of the "8th century Gelasian sacramentary," namely, *Berol. Phillips 1667,* f. 173v–174, under the title *Incipit de migratione animae.* Cf. A. Chavasse, *Le Sacramentaire Gélasien (Vat. Reg. 316)* (Paris, 1958), pp. 57–71 (on the country of origin of the *Ordo defunctorum*); H. Frank, "Der älteste erhaltene *Ordo defunctorum* der römischen Liturgie und sein Fortleben in Totenagenden des frühen Mittelalters," ALw 7/2 (1963) (the archetype is of the sixth–seventh century); D. Sicard, "Le Viatique: perspectives nouvelles?" MD, no. 113 (1973), 105.

2. P. Styger, *Die römischen Katakomben* (Berlin, 1933); idem, *Die römischen Märtyrergrüfte* (Berlin, 1935); A. M. Schneider, "Die ältesten Denkmäler der römischen Kirche," in *Festschrift der Akademie der Wissenschaften in Göttingen. II. Phil.-Hist. Klasse,* 1951, pp. 166–98; P. Testini, *Le catacombe e gli antichi cimiteri in Roma* (Roma cristiana II) (Bologna, 1966).—For proof of what is said in the text about the tombs of the apostles cf., from a vast bibliography, Th. Klauser, *Die römische Petrustradition im Lichte der neuen Ausgrabungen unter der Peterskirche* (Cologne-Opladen, 1956); D. W. O'Connor, *Peter in Rome. The Literary, Liturgical and Archeological Evidence* (New York-London, 1969); J. Toynbee and J. W. Perkins, *The Shrine of St. Peter and the Vatican Excavations* (London-New York-Toronto, 1956). It does not seem that Christian graves prior to about 200 are to be looked for in possible but as yet undiscovered underground cemeteries inside the wall of Aurelian. Christian communities were quite small before the third century, and their members were buried, like their pagan contemporaries, in accordance with the provisions of Roman law, which was quite liberal in its prescriptions for burials, and there would have been no external distinguishing signs.

3. "We collect the bones [of the martyrs] as though they were gold and precious stones and see to their burial. As the Lord commanded, we gather joyfully on the birthday of martyrdom": this passage from the *Martyrium Polycarpi* (156), 18,3, often cited as evidence of a cult of the martyrs as early as the middle of the second century, is not pertinent. It is practically certain that the text has been interpolated or rewritten; cf. H. v. Campenhausen, "Bearbeitungen und Interpolationen des Polycarpsmartyriums," *Sitzungsberichte Heidelberg. Phil.-Hist. Klasse,* 1957, fasc. 3, pp. 29–33. The starting point proposed by H. Delehaye (no cult of the martyrs before about 250) must be maintained; H. Delehaye, *Origines du culte des martyrs* (2nd ed.; Brussels, 1933), p. 263; cf. Th. Klauser, *Christlicher Märtyrerkult, heidnischer Heroenkult, und spauatjüdische Heiligenverehrung* (Arbeitsgemeinschaft für Forschung des Landes Nordrhein-Westfalen: Geisteswissenschaften 91; Cologne-Opladen, 1960), p. 30.

4. In his *Apostolic Tradition* 40 (ed. B. Botte, *La Tradition Apostolique de saint Hippolyte. Essai de reconstitution* [LQF 39; Münster, 1963], p. 87), a passage which has survived only in the Sahidic version: "The people are not to be heavily charged for burying their dead in the cemeteries, for these belong to all the poor. However, the salary of the grave-digger and the price of the bricks are to be regulated. The bishop is to provide those who live and work there with food out of the gifts made to the Church so that these people will not become a burden on the families of the dead" (in L. Deiss, *Springtime of the Liturgy,* tr. by M. J. O'Connell [Collegeville, 1979], p. 150). To the extent that this text suggests the existence of cemeteries administered by

the Christian communities, it is to a large extent posterior to the beginning of the third century; we must bear in mind that for this passage the Latin text (Hauler fragments), the oldest text known to us, is lacking.

5. Ca. 197–220, Tertullian (in *De resurrectione carnis* 1 and *De testimonio animae* 4) seems not to be acquainted with the existence in Africa of Christian funeral meals, if we may judge by the way he speaks of such meals among the pagans. He recommends prayers and probably the eucharist for the deceased; cf. *De corona* 3: "We make offerings for the deceased on the anniversary of their death instead of on the anniversary of their birth"; *De monogamia* 10: "For she prays for his soul and asks for him refreshment in the interim and a share in the first resurrection, and she offers the sacrifice each year on the anniversary of his falling asleep." On these texts of Tertullian cf. n. 54, below. On all the problems raised here cf. F. Wieland, *Mensa und Confessio* (Veröffentlichungen aus dem Kirchenhistorischen Seminar München II/11; Munich, 1906) (though I have reservations about the chronology and the exegesis of some texts).

6. Aristides (ca. 138–47), *Apologia* 15 (Goodspeed, p. 21; Geffcken, p. 2): "And if a just person in their community has died, they rejoice and thank God; in procession they follow his corpse as though he were a traveller passing from one place to another. If a child dies, they praise God; and if he dies very young they praise God all the more, because he has passed through this world without sinning. And if one of them dies as a wicked man and a sinner they weep and mourn over him as over one who will be punished." Cf. also Clement of Alexandria, *Stromata* VII, 12 (PG 9:508B).

7. For those who are not impressed by this change in representations, there is a different cutoff of a literary kind that argues in favor of the *terminus post quem non* which I have proposed. The works of M. Andrieu, A. Chavasse, D. Sicard and H. Frank, which I listed above in n. 1, give 700–750 as the date of the oldest *ordines defunctorum* that are accessible to us by paleographical means. The models used by the editors of long ago, which have not come down to us and seem to have originated in southern Gaul, cannot, in any hypothesis, be earlier than about the beginning of the seventh century (cf. Frank, art. cit., p. 379).

8. On the representations of the next world that were current in the early Christian period cf. especially A. Stuiber, *Refrigerium interim. Die Vorstellungen vom Zwischenzustand* (Theophaneia 11; Bonn 1957), a basic work with a bibliography of earlier writings that is practically exhaustive; A. M. Schneider, *Refrigerium* I. *Nach literarischen Quellen und Inschriften* (Freiburg i. B., 1928); H. Fine, *Die Terminologie der Jenseitsvorstellungen* (Theophaneia 12; Bonn, 1958); J. Ntedika, *L'évocation de l'Au-delà dans la prière pour les morts* (Recherches africaines de théologie 2; Paris-Louvain, 1971). On the different situations of the ordinary dead person and the martyr in the next world cf., among other texts in the dossier drawn up by Stuiber, *Refrigerium interim*, Tertullian in his *De anima* 55: "See, then, the difference between a pagan and a believer in death, provided you die for God as the Paraclete exhorts, not in a gentle fever and in bed but in the witness of suffering; if you take up your cross and follow the Lord, as he commanded. The only *key to paradise is your blood. . . .* How then was it that the region of paradise, which was revealed to John in the Spirit as being under the altar, contained *no souls but those of the martyrs?*" Parallel texts: Tertullian, *Scorpiace* 10,12; *De resurrectione mortuorum* 43. On *gnostic* representations of the next world, which in the early Christian period differed radically from those of the official Church (but were not dissimilar from the Christian representations prevalent *after* the end of the early period), cf. Stuiber, op. cit., pp. 88–89: "Die gnostischen Ansichten über den Zustand nach dem Tode." On relations between the Christian Hades and the pagan Hades cf. F. Cumont, *Lux perpetua* (Paris, 1949), with the valuable *Notes complémentaires* added by L. Canet, pp. 387–461.

9. On this last point cf Th. Klauser, "Der Ursprung des Festes Petri Stuhlfeier am 22. Februar," in his *Die Cathedra im Totenkult der heidnischen und christlichen Antike* (LQF 21; Münster, 1927), pp. 152–83.

10. Cf. as late as the Council of Elvira (ca. 306), canon 34 (in F. Lauchert, *Die Kanones der wichtigsten altkirchlichen Concilien* [Freiburg-Tübingen, 1896], p. 19): "We

have decided that candles are not to be lit in cemeteries during the day, *because the spirits of the saints are not to be disturbed."*

11. For a summary of Roman funerary law cf. E. Ferrini, *De iure sepulcrorum apud Romanos* (Bologna, 1883); J. Favout, *Du ius sepulchri en droit romain* (Paris, 1884); G. Ponzataro, *Il diritto di sepoclro nella sua evoluzione storica* (Turin, 1895).

12. Augustine, *De cura pro mortuis* 2,4 (PL 40:594): "There are many Christians whose bodies the earth has not covered, but nothing has kept any of them from heaven or earth, for all things are filled with the presence of him who knows how to restore life to what he has created." The care shown by many Christians, who had the wherewithal, to prepare during life the grave in which they would rest; their concern to have their burial place marked by funerary inscriptions or distinctive signs; in fact, the entire complex set of funerary practices: these all ran counter to the detachment expressed by Augustine.

13. Christian funerary expressions, though often expressing tenderness, love, and admiration for a husband or wife, never contain either mythological allusions or erotic outcries (of the type: "Mix the wine and drink on, brows wreathed in flowers/and do not deny yourself intercourse with lovely girls") or disillusioned remarks (of the type: "I was not, I was, I am not, I care not").—On Christian inscriptions cf. C. M. Kaufmann, *Handbuch der altchristlichen Epigraphik* (Freiburg i. B., 1917), and the examples in E. Diehl, *Inscriptiones latinae christianae veteres* (3 vols.; Berlin, 1925–1931).

14. Augustine, *In Johannis evangelium tractatus* 120,4 (CCL 36:662): "Unless I am mistaken, he [John the Evangelist] bade us, in showing respect for the dead, *to follow the customs of each nation"; Confessiones* IX, 12,32: "When the time came to carry out the corpse . . . when the sacrifice of our redemption was being offered to you for her, as the corpse lay beside the grave before burial, as was customary there [i.e., at Ostia]."—Ancient practices, both Jewish and Greco-Roman, are described by L. Koep, E. Stommel, and J. Kollwitz in RAC 2 (1954), 194–207.

15. Cf. Th. Klauser, *Die Cathedra im Totenkult* (n. 9), pp. 126–41, and idem, "Bestattung, christlich," RAC 2 (1954), 208–19. The reader will there find the references to the sources.

16. On this point cf. F. J. Dölger, "Die Totenmesse," in his *Ichthys* 2 (1922), 556–58, and, above all, E. Freistedt, *Altchristliche Totengedächtnisstage und ihre Beziehung zum Jenseitsglauben und Totenkultus der Antike* (LQF 24; Münster, 1928), pp. 36–46.

17. The fact that Christians practiced only interment as a form of burial and excluded cremation is all the more surprising since the legend of the phoenix, the bird that is reborn from its own ashes, was known to them and since the phoenix even appears often in frescoes in the catacombs. True enough, the legend of the phoenix as voluntarily allowing itself to be burned, was transformed into the legend of the phoenix as decomposing in a nest-tomb. The usual story of the phoenix according to the *Physiologus* (in F. Lauchert, *Geschichte des Physiologus* [Strassburg, 1889], p. 237): "The bird named phoenix comes from India. It lives 500 years and when it has reached this term it betakes itself to the Forest of Lebanon; from there, wings coated with perfumes, it flies to Heliopolis in Egypt and *burns itself* on the altar of sacrifice. The next day, the priest finds *in the ashes a worm that sprouts wings, and on the third day* the risen bird regains its native land." The "Christianized" legend is given in Clement of Rome, *Letter to the Corinthians* 25–26: "Let us consider the strange wonder that takes place in Eastern countries, that is, in Arabia. There we find a bird called the phoenix. It is the only one of its species and lives for 500 years. As its end draws near, it builds itself a nest of incense, myrrh and other perfumes, and enters into it, when the time comes, in order to die there. *From its decomposing flesh a worm is born* that feeds on the corrupting flesh of the dead bird and sprouts feathers; then, when it has become strong enough, it lifts up *the nest in which the bones of its ancestor are resting* and, carrying this burden, goes from Arabia to Egypt and the city of Heliopolis. There, in broad daylight and in the sight of all, it comes flying and places its burden on the altar; it then begins its return flight. Then the priests consult their chronicles and determine that the bird has returned after 500 years. Shall we, then, find it strange and surprising that the Creator of the universe should restore to life

those who have served him in holiness and with the trust born of perfect faith, when he allows us to see from the example of this bird how magnificent his promise is?"

18. On Christian mummies cf. A. de Waal, "Totenbestattung," RAC 2:878.

19. The crown is connected with the victory of the martyr; the *pompa*, or funeral procession, especially when it was the procession for a martyr, turned into a triumphal procession. As such, the crown also figures on the so-called "Passion" sarcophaguses of the Constantinian period.

20. Thus Jerome, Epist. 108,29.—Cf. also n. 16 (*dies obitus* and *dies depositionis*).

21. *Acta Proconsularia Cypriani* 5, 6: "Thus did blessed Cyprian suffer. . . . [His body] was taken thence *at night* with wax-tapers and torches, amid prayers and in great triumph."

22. *Codex Theodosianus* IX, 17, 5 (February, 363).—This text was not taken over into the *Code* of Justianian.—In the early Christian period there seems to be no distinction between *funus* and *exsequiae;* in classical Latin *funus* designates the funeral rites generally, while *exsequiae* in the proper sense is the funeral cortege or procession. *Funera,* in the plural, occurs frequently, because the funeral rite contained a number of elements.

23. Council of Clermont (535), canon 3: "The bodies of the deceased are not to be covered with palls or other effects used in divine services"; canon 7: "The body of a priest being carried to its grave is never to be covered with the cloth used to cover the Lord's body."

24. Constantine was carried in a gilt casket (Eusebius, *De vita Constantini* IV, 66, 1). Cf. also Gregory of Tours, *De gloria confessorum* 104. In any case, the casket was used only for transporting the body, not for interment.

25. Cf. the Menologion (or, better, the Synaxarion) of Basil II Bulgaroktonos (d. 1025).

26. Except for the emperor; in his case, white was the color of mourning.

27. The *pompa* or funeral procession of antiquity lived on in the procession for the translation of relics in the dedication of a new church; cf., e.g., Ordines XLI, XLII, and XLIII (Andrieu, Ordines 4:309–413).

28. Cf. n. 17.—It is necessary here to remind the reader that interment (or inhumation, as opposed to cremation) was not something peculiarly Christian. This manner of burial was always practiced by pagans (and was even traditional in some families); at the beginning of the third century inhumation was far more common throughout the ancient world than cremation; evidence of this is that from the end of the second century on sarcophaguses, still rare in the first century, became increasingly numerous.—The coexistence of cremation and inhumation can be seen in the necropolis of Porto (Isola Sacra) and in the Vatican necropolis under the basilica of St. Peter.

29. We must keep in mind that during the early Christian period, Christian cemeteries, whether on the surface or underground, were never anything more than places of burial; the only cultic acts performed there were those connected with burial. This fact has been fully established; cf. Klauser, *Die Cathedra im Totenkult,* pp. 123–36.

30. On these funeral acclamations, preserved for us in funerary inscriptions, cf. Kaufmann, *Handbuch der altchristlichen Epigraphik* (n. 13) and P. Testini, *Archeologia cristiana* (Rome, 1958), pp. 349–542 (with references to the great collections and anthologies of *tituli*).—On the anointing of the dead cf. Pseudo-Dionysius the Areopagite, *De ecclesiastica hierarchia* VII, 2. This anointing is still practiced in the Armenian Church in the case of a deceased priest; cf. F. Heiler, *Urkirche und Ostkirche* (Munich, 1937), p. 522.

31. The presence of a presbyter is attested from the beginning of the third century, but it is optional, unless the Eucharist is to be celebrated. Cf. Tertullian, *De anima* 51 (CSEL 29:383): "I know a woman who . . . when she had died in peace and was waiting for burial, was meanwhile given composure by the prayer of a priest."

32. Cf. above, n. 1.

33. Augustine, *De cura pro mortuis* 3, 2–3 (CSEL 41:627): "The care of funeral

arrangements, the provision of a burial site, and the pomp of the funeral procession are more a consolation to the living than a help to the dead."

34. On the *ahoroi* and the *biothanatoi (baiothanatoi)* as well as on the unburied cf. F. J. Dölger, "Antike Parallelen zum leidenden Dinokrates," in *Antike und Christentum* 2 (1930), 1–40; F. Cumont, *Lux perpetua* (Paris, 1949), pp. 303–40; J. H. Waszink, "Biothanati," RAC 2 (1954), 391–94. For medieval superstitions cf. the bibliographical references in A. Dörrer, "Totenbräuche. IV. Religiöse Volkskunde," LTK 10 (1955), 266–69, and especially the information in H. Bächtold-Stäubli, *Handwörterbuch des deutschen Aberglaubens* 8 (1936–1937) (for practical purposes, the entire volume).

35. Thus in the *Passio Perpetuae et Felicitatis* 4, 10 (vision of the ladder); 10, 4–14 (the combat in the arena is a combat against the demon): "And I understood that my fight would not be against the beasts but *against the devil.*" Cf. F. J. Dölger, "Der Kampf mit dem Ägypter," in *Antike und Christentum* 3 (1932), 177–88; Stuiber, *Refrigerium interim,* pp. 81–88 ("Die Wirksamkeit von Dämonen beim Sterben").

36. What is said here is true of the ordinary deceased person as well as of the martyr, although it must be acknowledged that the texts, rare to begin with, relate primarily to the believer who suffers torment for the faith. The lack of interest shown by early Christian antiquity in a supposed struggle between the souls of the dead and the demons after death is in sharp contrast with the great importance assigned to demonic plots during the Christian's lifetime; cf. Stuiber, op. cit., pp. 82–83, against J. Quasten, "Der Gute Hirt," in *Miscellanea G. Mercati* 1 (ST 121; Vatican City, 1946), pp. 1–273. There is a basic text in the *Passio Perpetuae et Felicitatis* 11 (vision of Saturus): "And four angels began to carry us eastward" (no reference to any struggles with the spirits of the air). A postmortem struggle between the soul and demons, which is nonexistent in the early Christian vision of death, must be distinguished from the popular idea of a struggle between angels and demons (and not between dead humans and demons) with the corpse of the deceased as the stakes (e.g., the struggle between St. Michael and the demons for the body of Moses); cf. F. Endres, *Die Engellehre der griechischen Apologeten des 2. Jh.* (Paderborn, 1914), and the relevant articles in Bächtold-Stäubli (n. 34).

37. Justin *Dialogus* 105,3–5 (Goodspeed, pp. 221–22): "And when [the psalmist] asks that his soul be saved from the sword, from the jaws of the lion, from the paw of the dog, he is praying that no one may take possession of our souls. When we reach the end of our life, we ask the same of God who has power to repulse every shameless evil angel and keep him from taking possession of our soul. . . . It is God who teaches us . . . to ask, at the end of life, that our souls not fall into the power of any spirit like this one [scil., the one that manifested itself in connection with Samuel; cf. 1 Sm 28]."—Cf. the dossier in Stuiber, op. cit., pp.81–88.

38. Tertullian, *De anima* 53, 5–8 (CCL 2:860–61): "Then he [the dying person] says what he sees, then he rejoices or trembles as he realizes the dwelling that has been prepared for him and as soon as he sees the face of the angel who calls souls forth, the Mercury of the poets." In his commentary on the *De anima* (Q. S. F. Tertulliani, *De anima* [Amsterdam, 1947], pp. 546–47), J. H. Waszink also asserts that before the fourth century, there are no traces in Christian literature of the idea of any demoniacal activity whatsoever at the moment of death.

39. This follows from a fragment *Contra gentes* or *De universo* attributed to St. Hippolytus of Rome; cf. B. Botte, "Note sur l-auteur de 'De universo' attribué à saint Hippolyte," RTAM 18 (1951), 5–18 (against the attribution to Josippus, a priest of Rome, as proposed by P. Nautin in his *Hippolyte et Josippe* [Paris, 1947], pp. 98–99).—The text has been edited by K. Holl., *Fragmente vornicänischer Kirchenväter aus den Sacra Parallela, Fragm. 353 "de Universo"* 137–143 (TU, N.F. 5/2; Leipzig, 1899). The *Sacra Parallela* (in which the Fragment has been preserved) is an ascetical work attributed to John Damascene.

40. Cf. Pauly-Wissowa, RE Suppl. 3:267–322 (s. v. Daimon), and W. Foerster, "daimōn," TDNT :2:6–8, with n. 59.

41. I must repeat that in the early Christian period, cemeteries, whether on the surface or underground, were places solely for burial (and not places of communal worship); the only liturgical actions performed there had to do solely with funerals.

Notes: Vogel   329

Cf. F. Wieland, *Mensa und Confessio* (n. 5); Klauser, *Die Cathedra im Totenkult*, pp. 123–26.

42. Cf. Freistedt, *Altchristliche Totengedächtnisstage* . . . (n. 16).

43. This is true of the explanation given by Photius, *Bibliotheca, cod. CLXXI* (ed. Bekker, p. 118; PG 103:499; ed. R. Henry: Photius, *Bibliothèque* 2 [Paris, 1960], p. 166), which he attributes to a priest named Eustratius. In this explanation, the third day was chosen because of the resurrection of the Lord, the ninth because on that day Christ appeared to his disciples for the first time, and the fortieth because on the day of the Ascension, the Lord manifested himself for the second time. Goar's explanation is of the same kind (*Euchologion* [Venice, 1730], p. 434, n. 3): the third day is that of Christ's resurrection, the ninth recalls the nine choirs of angels, and the fortieth the period of Israel's mourning over the death of Moses.

44. K. Krumbacher, "Studien zu den Legenden des hl. Theodosios," Nachtrag zur Sitzung der philos.-phil. Classe vom 7. Mai 1892, in *Sitzungsberichte der königl. bayr. Akademie der Wissenschaften* (Munich, 1892), pp. 341–55.

45. The reader will have observed that in the second of the three documents, an eschatological explanation is added to the physiological explanation of the commemorations; this eschatological explanation was not that of the official Church in the early Christian period, but was widespread in circles close to gnosticism. Cf. e.g., the *Acta Philippi* (second half of second century), no. 137 (ed. Bonnet, AAA II/2, p. 69): "You shall die in a holy manner and, led by my holy angels, shall reach paradise with them. . . . But you will be excluded from paradise for forty days and will be terrorized by the flaming sword and will lament, because you did evil to your enemies. After those forty days I shall send Michael the archangel who will overcome the sword at the gate of paradise, and you will then contemplate the just who have lived in innocence, and then you will fall on your knees before the magnificence of my Father in heaven."—Starting in the high Middle Ages the idea of a particular judgment after death spread in the East as in the West; for example, in the *Nomocanon* of Manuel Malaxos (compiled in 1561 but making use of older documents): "On the fortieth day the soul departs to adore [God] and receives a place in accordance with the life it has led on earth, until the second parousia of our Lord Jesus Christ" (text communicated to me by Sp. Troïanos and A. Sifoniou-Karapa, of the Academy of Athens, who are preparing a critical edition of the *Nomocanon*).

46. Ambrose, *De obitu Theodosii oratio* (PL 16:1386).—The following was the situation in the Churches of the West: Roman, "Gallican" and Anglo-Saxon Churches: third, seventh, and thirtieth days; Church of Milan: seventh, ?, and fortieth days; Visigothic Church: ?, ?, and fiftieth days; Church of Africa, third, seventh, and ? days.

47. Augustine, *Quaestiones in Heptateuchum* I, 172 (CSEL 28/3:91, lines 3–15) with a reference to Gn 50:10 and Sir 22:12.—But recall here the Roman custom of celebrating the office of the dead for *nine* consecutive days after the death of a pope (Pope Pius X, Constitution *Vacante Sede Appostolica*, December 25, 1904).

48. Gregory of Tours, *Dialogi* IV, 54–55 (PL 77:418); *Vitae Patrum* XV, 5 (MGH, *Script. Rerum Meroving.* I, 724), and the Latin recension (which is older than the Greek) of the *Passio Bartholomaei* 9 (ed. Bonnet, AAA II/1: 149).—On the whole question cf. Du Cange, *Glossarium*, s.v. "Septenarium" and "Trigenarium," as well as A. Franz, *Die Messe im deutschen Mittelalter* (Freiburg i. B., 1902), p. 243.

49. L. C. Mohlberg (ed.), *Liber sacramentorum romanae aeclesiae ordinis anni circuli (Sacramentarium Gelasianum)* (Rerum Ecclesiasticarum Documenta, Series maior: Fontes 4; Rome, 1960), III, 105 (p. 246): "Missa in depositione defuncti tercii septimi XXXmi dierum vel annualem."—Cf. Chavasse, *Le Sacramentaire Gélasien* (n. 1), pp. 69ff., who does not give an opinion on the Roman or Frankish origin of this section.

50. The oldest testimonies are these: (1) Tertullian, *De exhortatione castitatis* 11: "You pray for her and offer *annual sacrifice* for her. Will you then stand before the Lord with as many wives as you remember in prayer, and will you offer the sacrifice for two wives and recommend them to the Lord through a priest?" Tertullian mentions only the *dies annualis* (the anniversary) and says nothing of the *dies depositionis* or the *dies tertius,* the day of burial or the third day after it.—(2) *Acta Johannis* (ca. 150–180; ed. Bonnet, AAA II/1:186): "The next day, John, Andronicus

and the brethren came to the sepulcher at dawn—it was the *third day* after the burial of Drusiana—for the breaking of bread."—(3) There is an indirect testimony in a letter of Cyprian in which the bishop forbids the celebration of the eucharist for those of the faithful who have appointed a cleric as a guardian; *Epist.* I,1 (CSEL III/2:466): "No dying brother should name a cleric as guardian or trustee, and if he does no prayers are to be offered for him nor is the sacrifice to be celebrated for his repose. For no one deserves to be mentioned at the altar in the prayer of the bishop if he has tried to draw bishops and ministers away from the altar." Cyprian thus testifies to the celebration of the eucharist for the deceased, but without reference to a particular day.—(4) *Martyrium Polycarpi* 18: "We collect the bones [of the martyrs] as though they were gold and precious stones and see to their burial. As the Lord commanded, we gather joyfully on the birthday of martyrdom." This passage is interpolated and therefore cannot serve as testimony to a eucharist (?) celebrated for the deceased as early as the middle of the second century; cf. n. 3, above.—On all these testimonies, cf. Dölger, "Die Totenmesse," in *Ichthys* 2 (Münster, 1922), pp. 555–69, where evidence is given of the favor which the *Acta Johannis* enjoyed in communities of the official Church (ibid., p. 567, n. 3).

51. Thus Augustine, *Confessiones* IX, 12, 32: "Not even during the prayers we said to you when the sacrifice of our redemption was being offered to you for her [Monica], as the corpse lay beside the grave before burial [inhumation], as was customary there [Ostia]—not even during those prayers did I weep." Cf. Dölger, art. cit., p. 567,n. 4.

52. The "third day" is a cultic designation that has many parallels in antiquity; e.g., Aristophanes, *Lysistrata*, 614: "Will you accuse us of not having properly 'displayed' you [as was done for the dead]? At least, the day after tomorrow, early in the morning, you will receive from us well-prepared offerings for the *third day.—* Palladius, *Historia Lausiaca* 21 (ed. Butler, p. 68): "The third day of the deceased."— *Constitutiones Apostolicae* XIII, 42 (ed. Funk, 1:552): "The third day of the departed."—On the "third day of the resurrection of Christ" and the correspondences with the third day of the deceased cf. F. J. Dölger, "Das Todesgedächtniss Jesu und die antike Memoria mortuorum," in *Ichthys* 2 (1922), 549–55.

53. See, above, the translation of the texts edited by K. Krumbacher.

54. Tertullian, *De corona* 3: "Oblationes pro defunctis, pro nataliciis, annua die facimus," which should be translated as "We make offerings for the deceased on the anniversary of their death instead of on the anniversary of their birth," and not as "We make offerings for the deceased (the martyrs), we celebrate the anniversary day (of their martyrdom)." The point is that the *natalicia* are not the anniversary days solely of the martyrs as distinct from ordinary Christians.—In Tertullian the *dies annua* is certainly the anniversary of the day of death; cf. *De monogamia* 10: "For she prays for his soul and asks for him refreshment in the interim and a share in the first resurrection, and she offers the sacrifice each year *on the anniversary of his falling asleep.*" There is a parallel text in Ambrose, *De excessu fratris Satyri* II, 5 (PL 16:1316C): "We too forget the birthdays of the dead and recall the day of their death in a solemn celebration."—The rejection of the birthday is deliberate.

55. Cyprian, Epist. 1, 2: "For no one deserves to be mentioned at the altar in the prayer of the bishop. . . ."—It was certainly on the occasion of the eucharistic celebration at the grave, while the deceased person still remained on the *feretrum*, that communion was given to him (despite the prohibition of this practice by the hierarchy). Council of Hippo (393), can. 4: "Some dare to celebrate the sacrifice in the presence of the corpse and to give part of the sacred Body to the lifeless corpse. This must be prohibited" (ed. Munier, CCL 149:21). This canon seems to forbid both the giving of communion to the dead and the celebration of the Eucharist in the presence of the corpse.—Council of Auxerre (578/590), can. 12: "It is not permitted to give either the Eucharist or the kiss of peace to the dead, or to wrap the bodies of the dead in a veil or pall" (Bruns, *Canones* II:238).

56. On the connection between the *mensa* (table) of the eucharist and the tomb of the martyr cf. Th. Klauser, "Altar III (christlich)," RAC 1 (1950), 334–54; J. Braun, *Der christliche Altar in seiner geschichtlichen Entwicklung* (2 vols.; Munich, 1924); A. M.

Schneider, "Mensae oleorum oder Totenspeisetische," RQ 35 (1927), 287–301.—The connection is still maintained through the inclusion of relics in the altar table.

57. As far as I know, the only works of a nonexhortatory kind that deal with the eschatological finality of the eucharist offered for the dead are F. J. Dölger's essays, "Das Todesgedachtniss Jesu und die antike Memoria morturoum" and "Die Totenmesse," in *Ichthys* 2 (Münster, 1922), pp. 549–69.

58. The eucharistic celebration on the anniversaries of the martyrs (from 250 on) was radically different in meaning from the eucharistic celebration for the ordinary deceased person. The martyr enjoyed immediate beatitude after his suffering and, because of this eschatological privilege, avoided the provisional Christian Hades. The Eucharist celebrated in his memory could only be an expression of joy and not a supplication procuring for him a change from *tormentum* to *refrigerium*.

59. *Canons of Hippolytus* (336–340, ed. Coquin, PO 31:137–38); can. 33: "If there is a [liturgical] assembly for the deceased, let those present receive the mysteries before being seated. Let it not take place on a Sunday. After the [eucharistic] offering, give those present the bread of exorcism before being seated. . . . Let them eat and drink sufficiently, not to the point of drunkenness but peacefully as a homage to God."— On the funerary *refrigerium*-meal, as distinct from *refrigerium*-repose, cf. A. M. Schneider, *Refrigerium* I (n. 8); A. Stuiber, *Refrigerium interim* (n. 8), pp. 105–20 ("Der Zwischenzustand im Lichte der Grabinschriften"); H. Fine, *Die Terminologie der Jenseitsvorstellungen* (n. 8), pp. 150–96.—On the conduct of a funerary meal and the problems connected with it cf. Klauser, *Die Cathedra im Totenkult* (n. 9), and his "Das altchristliche Totenmahl nach dem heutigen Stande Forschung," ThGl 20 (1928), 599– 608. These two works are of fundamental importance; they have been supplemented and updated by Stuiber, op. cit., pp. 120ff. ("Bildliche Darstellung als Niederschlag des Totenkultes"); A. Parrot, *Le refrigerium dans l'Au-delà* (Paris, 1937); J. Doignon, "Refrigerium et catéchèse à Vérone au IVe siècle," in *Hommages à Marcel Renard* 2 (Latomus 102; Brussels, 1969), pp. 220–39.

60. The Christian *refrigerium* was identical in its conduct to the *refrigerium* practiced by the pagans of the same era, except for the elimination of mythological and erotic elements and for the choice or rejection of certain foods (e.g. *sinciput*, boar's head). The Christian continuation of the pagan practice was facilitated by a possible reference to Tb 4:18: "Place your bread and wine on the tomb of the just, and do not eat and drink of it with sinners" (Vg.), and an erroneous reading of Rom 12:13: "Be attentive to the memorials (*mneiais*) of the saints," instead of "Be attentive to the needs (*chreiais*) of the saints."—cf. n. 70.

61. These literary documents are distributed as follows: (a) Africa: Tertullian is still without knowledge of any Christian *refrigeria*, as is clear from *De testimonio animae* 4 and *De resurrectione carnis* 1. Augustine, *Confessiones* VI, 2, 2: "When she [Monica] brought porridge and bread and unmixed wine to the memorials of the martyrs, as she was used to doing in Africa, . . . she would bring a bread basket with the festal foods to be eaten and distributed [foods to be eaten at the tomb and wine for pouring a libation to the dead], but she poured only one small cup, diluted for her sober palate."—(b) Northern Italy: Ambrose, *De Helia et ieiunio* 17: "They bring cups to the graves of the martyrs and drink there at evening. . . . O stupid people who regard drunkenness as a sacrifice." Zeno of Verona, *Tract.* I, xv, 6, 16–17: "They sacrifice foods to the stinking corpses of the dead."—(c) Campania: Paulinus of Nola, *De Felicis nativitate carmen* IX, 556: "In their simple devotion they wrongly think the saints rejoice to have their tombs drenched in smelly wine."—(d) East (Syria? Constantinople?): *Constitutiones Apostolorum* VIII, 44, 1: "When you [presbyters and deacons] are invited to the commemorations of the dead, drink with moderation and in fear of God, so that you may be able to offer your prayers for the departed."—The city of Rome and Gaul are missing from the literary dossier.

62. Memoria Apostolorum (present catacomb of St. Sebastian), on the Via Appia, graffiti in the *triclia* (a funeral-banquet hall): "Petro et Paulo / Tomius Coelius / Refrigerium Feci; At Paulo / et Pet(ro) Refri(geravi); cf. P. Styger, "Il monumento apostolico della via Appia," in *Dissertazioni Poct. Acad. archeol.* II, 13 (Rome, 1918), pp. 59 and 61, Pl. II. The date of the *triclia* is now established thanks to R. Marichal's proposed reading of a graffito: "Celeri(nus) / V Idus Aug(ustas) Saecul(ari) II/ et

Donatio II cos" (= 260); cf. R. Marichal, "La date des graffiti de la triclia de Saint-Sébastien," in *Archéologie paléochrétienne et culte chrétien* (=RevSR 36 [1962]. 111–54).

63. Graffito in the catacomb of Priscilla (G. B. de Rossi, *Bullettino,* 1890, tav. 6): "In pace / I Idus Febr. / conss. Gratiani III et Equiti [=374–75] Florentius Fortunatus et / (Fe)lix ad calice benimus [=ad calicem venimus]."—Terni, Cemetery (Diehl 1565 B): "Mallius Tigrinus / ob refrigerium c(aris suis) / domum aeternalem / vivus fundavit."—Rome, Cemetery of St. Pamphilus (Schneider p. 32): "Fecit . . . merentibus in refrigerium."—Gilded glass in the Vatican (Diehl 2304): "Hilaris vivas cum tuis feliciter. Semper refrigeris / in pace Dei."—Satafis (Mauretania), Inscription from the year 299 [A(nno) pr(ovinciae CCLX)] (Diehl 1570): "Memoriae Aeliae Secundlae / Funeri mu(l)ta quid(e)m condigna iam misimus omnes / Isuper ae(a)equ(e) deposit(a)e Secundulae matri / Lapideam placuit nobis atponere mensam / in qua magna eius memorantes plurima facta / Deum cibi ponuntur calicesq(ue) e(t) copoertae / . . . ."—Other inscriptions in Diehl (s.v. *refrigerium, refrigerare*); Schneider, *Refrigerium* I, pp. 19–23, 27–33; Parrot, *Le refrigerium* . . . , pp. 131–71.—On the connections between the terms *refrigerium* and *refrigerare* in inscriptions and in the liturgy cf. Schneider, *Refrigerium* I, pp. 25–27.—Little study has been done of the Greek equivalents of *refrigerium*-repose and *refrigerium*-meal; there is some information in Schneider, *Refrigerium* I, pp. 23–25, and Stuiber, *Refrigerium interim,* pp. 105–20.—Relevant here are all the appeals asking the dead to drink with the participants in the funeral banquet; e.g., "pie, zeses" (= drink and you will live = To your health!); cf. Diehl, s.v., "pi(n)e," "refrigera," etc.

64. Essential iconographic documentation: Callistus (Via Appia): J. Wilpert, *Die Malereien der Katakomben* (Rome-Freiburg, 1903) (=W.), XX, 2; XXVII, 2; XLI, 1, 3, and 4; Priscilla (Via Salaria): W. XX, 1; Domitilla (Via Ardeatina): W. VII, 4; Peter and Marcellinus (Via Labicana): W. LXII, 2; LXV, 3; CXXXIII, 2; CLVII, 1 and 2; CLXVII; CLXXXIV.—For a commentary on these depictions of the *refrigerium,* cf. Stuiber, *Refrigerium interim,* pp. 120–36 ("Bildliche Darstellungen als Niederschlag des Totenkults").

65. Basic documentation on the *triclia* of the Memoria Apostolorum (Via Appia) in P. Styger, "Il monumento apostolico nella via Appia," (n. 62), pp. 48–89, pl. I–XXV; A. v. Gerkan, "Die christlichen Anlagen unter San Sebastiano," in H. Lietzmann, *Petrus und Paulus in Rom* (2nd ed.; Berlin-Leipzig, 1927), pp. 248–301. On the date of the graffiti cf. R. Marichal, "La date des graffiti de la Triclia de Saint-Sébastien" (n. 62).

66. Documentation on the places for the *refrigerium* that are mentioned here is in Klauser, *Die Cathedra im Totenkult* (s.v. "Coemeterium Maius," "Domitillae," "Priscillae") and in P. Testini, *Le catacombe e gli antichi cimiteri cristiani in Roma* (Roma cristiana II; Bologna, 1966).

67. Ambrose, *De Helia et ieiunio* 17: "They bring cups to the graves of the martyrs and *drink there at evening.*"—Funerary inscription for Aelia Secundula (299; Satafis in Mauretania): ". . . as we return at *a late hour*" (Diehl 1570). This practice was in conformity with the custom of antiquity; cf. Dölger, *Ichthys* 2:13.

68. The celebration of the anniversaries of the martyrs had a radically different meaning than the celebrations for the ordinary faithful. Nonetheless the cultic practice both of the eucharist and of the *refrigerium* was the same in both cases. The cult of the martyrs was an offshoot of the "cult" of the dead generally.

69. Cyprian accepts the complaints of the bishops of Spain, gathered at León, Astorga, and Merida, with regard to a Martialis, and answers them in 254. Cyprian, *Epist.* 67, 6: "In addition to attending for a long period the shameful and elegant banquets of the pagans at the college, and interring his children in the same college in profane graves according to the custom of foreign pagans and burying them with foreigners, Martialis. . . ." Cyprian is here finding fault with a Christian for burying his children with pagans through the mediation of a funerary college or club. A fortiori funerary banquets with pagans were prohibited.

70. The fish does not figure as a sacred food at the *refrigeria* according to the literary texts or according to inscriptions that refer directly to funeral banquets; but it is found in all the pictorial representations of this meal (frescoes and bas-reliefs on the sarcophaguses) as well as in many funerary inscriptions (the epitaphs of Licinia

Amias, of Abercius, and of Pectorius, in particular); cf. C. Vogel, "Le repas sacré au poisson chez les chrétiens," in *Eucharisties d'Orient et d'Occident* I (Lex orandi 46; Paris, 1970), pp. 83–116, reprinted from RevSR 40 (1966), 1–26. Against the interpretation given in that article: J. Engemann, "Fisch," RAC 7 (1969), 1021–97. A rather strange graffito in cursive writing, from the *triclia* near the Memoria Apostolorum on the Via Appia, shows that the banqueters gathered there ate "apricots, honey, berries [or: bilberries?], artichokes, fish, chicken, a suckling-pig, cakes, and sardines" (Styger, op. cit., pl. XXIV).—R. Marichal had subjected this odd menu to a paleographical examination and dates the graffito from the years 235–260 (from the same period, therefore, as the rest of the graffiti from the same *triclia*). The writing is more careful than in the other inscriptions; the writing is incised on the edge of the parapet around the *triclia*. Marichal deduces from this that it is probably the menu offered by the keeper of the *triclia* which would also have served as a country restaurant (as already maintained by A. v. Gerkan, op. cit.); cf. Marichal, "La 'carte' de la triclia de Saint-Sébastien," RevSR 36 (1962), 150–54.

71. The expressions used in the documents—drunkenness, feasts, reeking with wine, sumptuous meals, immoderate drinking—seem to indicate the contrary. Cf. n. 80.

72. This was the case with Monica (Augustine, *Confessiones* VI, 2, 2): "a small cup, diluted for her sober palate." Cf. the illustrations in Klauser, *Die Cathedra im Totenkult*, pl. XIX, 1 and 2, in connection with individuals named Cristor and Eutropos.

73. Standing and reclining may have been ritual gestures; cf. Klauser, *Die Cathedra im Totenkult*, pp. 2–13, and Th. Ohm, *Die Gebetsgebärden der Völker und das Christentum* (Leiden, 1948).

74. In connection with funeral banquets, of which he disapproves, Tertullian, *De testimonio animae* (CSEL 20:139), writes: "[the deceased are] as it were present and reclining at the banquet held for them."—The deceased person appears in many Christian cemetery frescoes, or is considered to be present by reason of his depicted act of *compotatio* (holding out a cup to the participant in the banquet).

75. Cf. Klauser, *Die Cathedra im Totenkult*. The narrowness of these chairs makes it clear they did not serve a practical purpose and were not used in liturgical functions (as a chair for the bishop!).

76. Documentation in Diehl, *Inscriptiones latinae christianae veteres* (3 vols.; Berlin, 1925–1931). Cf. also P. Paolucci, *Refrigerium* (Camerino, 1923), p. 12, and Schneider, *Refrigerium I*. The Christian acclamations to which I refer corresponded to the pagan sommonings of the dead; e.g. "N., rise up, eat and drink and refresh yourself" (Epiphanius, *Ancoratus* 86, 5 [GCS 1:106]).

77. On these frescoes and the inscriptions they contain cf. Stuiber, *Refrigerium interim*, pp. 134–36.

78. In addition to the already cited works of E. Diehl and C. M. Kaufmann cf. F. Cabrol, "Acclamations," DACL 1 (1924), 239–65; L. Jalabert and R. Mouterde, "Inscriptions grecques chrétiennes. III. Le formulaire," DACL 7 (1926), 670–92; and H. Leclercq, "Inscriptions latines chrétiennes. IX. Formulaire épigraphique, 1: La mort," DACL 7 (1926), 773–78. The two articles on Christian epigraphy are still among the best.

79. Jacob of Sarug, *Poema in Missam defunctorum*, vv. 80ff. Parallel texts: Origen, *De oratione* 31, 5 (GCS, *Origenes* 2:399): "Souls come more rapidly than living persons to the places of worship." Gregory I, *Dialogi* II (*De vita sancti Benedicti*) 23, speaks of an opposite movement, when at the summons of the deacon, "If any are not to communicate, let them depart," the souls of the religious women buried in the church depart from it: "The nurse who had been accustomed to make the offering for them to the Lord saw them come forth from their tombs and leave the church." Cf. Dölger, *Ichthys* 2:562, n. 2.

80. Augustine, *De moribus ecclesiae* 34 (PL 32:1342): "to drink immoderately at the graves of the dead and offer banquets to corpses"; *De civitate Dei* VIII, 27: "to bring their feasts to him [the dead person]; *Contra Faustum* XX, 21 (PL 42:384): "to placate the shades of the dead with wine and feasts"; *Confessiones* VI, 2: "When she [Monica] brought porridge and bread and unmixed wine to the memorials of the saints, as she

was used to doing in Africa"; *Sermo* 13, 4 (PL 46:857): "to hasten to the memorials of the martyrs, bless cups at the memorials of the martyrs, and return sated." Paulinus of Nola, *De Felicis nativitate carmen IX*, 566 (PL 61:661): "[they wrongly think] the saints rejoice to have their tombs drenched in smelly wine." Zeno of Verona, *Tract.* I, xv, 6, 15–18: (PL 11:366): "dashing about among the tombs, they sacrifice foods to the stinking corpses of the dead; for love of revelling and drinking in disreputable places and for the sake of their flasks and bottles they suddenly devise martyrs for themselves."

81. Cf. the preceding note. The *refrigeria* survived throughout the Middle Ages in the form of banquets and dances organized on the feasts of the patron saints of the churches or corporations, despite the often repeated prohibitions issued by councils; cf. on this point the conciliar canons from Gaul and Africa that are singled out by Ch. Munier in the indexes of his editions, s.v. "Convivia."—The *refrigerium* also survived in the *Natale Petri de cathedra* (February 22); cf. Klauser, *Die Cathedra im Totenkult*, pp. 152–84.

82. Augustine, *De civitate Dei* VIII, 27; *Confessiones* VI, 2; Pseudo-Origen, *In Iob* 3 (PG 15:517A). Illustration in Wilpert, op. cit., pl. LXII, 2 (the poor extend their hands and come to the *refrigerium* with bags of provisions).

83. *Passio Perpetuae et Felicitatis* 7–8; tr. by H. Musurillo, *The Acts of the Christian Martyrs* (Oxford, 1972), pp. 115, 117. On the Dinocrates episode cf. F. J. Dölger, "Antike Parallelen zum leidenden Dinocrates in der Passio Perpetuae," in *Antike und Christentum* 2 (1930), 1–40.

Wagner, Georges (pp. 277–284)

1. In *Mnēmē 1821*, a special issue of *Epistēmonikē Ephēmeris Theologikēs Scholēs*, 1971 (University of Thessalonika).
2. Cf. St. George the Chiopolite, martyred in 1807 (Foundoulis, ibid., p. 69).

Webb, Douglas (pp. 285–300)

1. Kathisma (Syriac, *mawtba*). This is the name given to the anthems of the burial services. They are sung while sitting, hence the name. Greek, χάθισμα.
2. Other manuscripts in this class are, B.M. Or. 4067 (fifteenth century): and B.M. Or 6719 (dated 1598). The fullest text, however, is contained in Séert 58 (dated 1618).
3. All the known examples of this type of manuscript are at Mardin.
4. The first thirty-two leaves of this manuscript are a supply of a later date. It also contains services, in summary form, for the burial of laymen and laywomen, and also the service used when a body is transferred from one grave to another. Another manuscript of this class is Cambridge University Library, ADD. 1985, which dates from the eighteenth century.
5. Other manuscripts in this class are, Notre Dame des Semences, ciii, (1714); civ, (1724); cviii, (1882); Berlin 55, (1614).
6. The following manuscripts contain the Order for the Burial of the Laity, British Museum Or. 4420, (eighteenth century); Or. 4421 (seventeenth century); Or. 4416, (1720); Notre Dame des Semences, cv, (1731); cvi, (1808); cvii, (1873); Berlin State Library 54, (1871); 49, (seventeenth century); Vatican Library, Siriaco lxi; Selly Oak Colleges Library (Birmingham University Library), Mingana 570 (1883). I do not claim that this is a complete list of the manuscripts of the burial services. There may well be others in other libraries.
7. There is a collection of the texts of these funeral hymns, together with a Latin translation, in S. E. Assimanus, *Sancti Patris Nostri Ephraemi Syri Opera Omnia*, Vol. III, pp. 225–359.
8. *Interpretatio Officiorum Ecclesiae*, Ed. R. H. Connolly, Series III, Vols. 91 and 92, Section vii.

9. There is reason for believing that it is the part of the eucharist from the karozutha onwards that is used in these circumstances, but the rubrics are obscure. The Pseudo-George of Arbel implies that it was a Mass of the Presanctified that was celebrated in his time.

10. Where reference is made to the Offices for the Burial of the Laity, the text is taken either from the Selly Oak Colleges Library, Mingana 570, or from the printed Urmi Edition of the rite.

11. *Ktaba d-kurrasta d-'annide bnay 'alma.* (Trichur, 1954).

12. Connolly, op. cit. p. 124, *"iure"* nos defunctos cum hymnis (tesbᵉ ḥatha) comitamur, *quasi* ad cenam aliquam ducendos."

13. At the end of the fifth kathisma, "Until now they remain in the house where the deceased is until the kathismata of the washing was completed. And after, then they take up the bier and come to the Church. And when they set out they begin this hymn as they come to the Church." Cambridge ADD. 1986, f. 28a.

14. Connolly, op. cit. p. 129. "Ita et catholico, eodem consilio, et patriarchae quoque, honorem addunt aliorum cathismatum, tribuentes ei (sc. patriarchae) novem cathismata, vel etiam quandoque decem: cum tamen novem debeant esse."

15. In a private letter to the author. The Pseudo-George of Arbel seems to suggest that female singers took their part in the service. "Quare in singulis cathismatibus mulieres canunt; hoc est autem, hymni (madhrashe) dicuntur, quorum cantor typice vices gerit mulierum canentiᵘⁿm?" "Mulieres vero canunt, quia mortem significant quae in naturam nostram debilem intravit." Connolly, op. cit. pp. 125, 126.

16. The shurraye of the first kathisma for other ranks are as follows: For a deacon, the same as for a priest; for a layman or laywoman, Ps 88:1–9, and Ps 88:10–end. For a child, Psalm 3:1–8, and Psalm 88:15–end.

17. The shurraye for other ranks in the second kathisma are as follows: for a deacon, the same as for a priest; for a layman or a laywoman, Ps 6:1–5, and Ps 13:1–end; for a child, Ps 47:3–end, and Ps 71:5–8.

18. The shurraye for other ranks in the third kathisma are as follows: for a deacon, the same as for a priest; for a layman, Ps 103:15–19; for a laywoman, Ps, 103:1–6, and for both men and women, Ps 39:1–7. For a child, Ps 129:1–7, and Ps 131:1–end.

19. The lessons for the burial of a child are as follows: 2 Sm 12:10–14, David's prayer for his son in mortal sickness; and 1 Kgs 17:17–end, Elijah raises the widow's son.

20. Connolly, op. cit. pp. 130–31.

21. For the burial of a deacon, the first lesson is a catena of passages from the book of Daniel: Dn 10:5; 12:2–4 (with some variations from the Peshitta text); 12:8–10, 13. The second lesson is Acts 6:1–8 (the appointment of the seven deacons). The epistle is 1 Thes 4:13–end (on the resurrection). The gospel is John 12:23–36a (death and glory).

22. W. F. Macomber, *The Funeral Liturgy of the Chaldean Church,* in Consilium, 1968, p. 20.

23. Connolly, op. cit. p. 131.

24. According to the Pseudo-George of Arbel's description of the church, the sheqaqone (literally, "a narrow passage") was the passage between the qeṣtroma and the bema.

25. Connolly, op. cit. p. 132.

26. Connolly, op. cit. p. 132.

27. The bema was the large raised platform in the center of the nave of the church. It contained an altar and seats for the clergy, and part of the eucharist was conducted from it.

28. Connolly, op. cit. p. 133. "quo ostendunt, quod ii, qui ministrant, sive in vetere sive in nove testamento sint, in hoc mundo sunt, et quando proficiscuntur, per mortem proficiscuntur. Et tacentes procedunt hoc est mors silentium est.

29. Connolly, op. cit. p. 134.

30. Macomber, op. cit. p. 21.

31. Each member of the congregation touches the hands of the deceased with his hands, and then raises his joined hands to his lips.